Rugged Justice

Rugged Justice

The Ninth Circuit Court of Appeals and the American West, 1891–1941

David C. Frederick

With a Foreword by
Justice Sandra Day O'Connor

UNIVERSITY OF CALIFORNIA PRESS
Berkeley · Los Angeles · London

University of California Press
Berkeley and Los Angeles, California

University of California Press
London, England

Copyright © 1994 by The Regents of the University of California

Library of Congress Cataloging-in-Publication Data

Frederick, David C.

   Rugged justice : the Ninth Circuit Court of Appeals and the
American West, 1891–1941 / David C. Frederick ; foreword by Sandra
Day O'Connor.
     p. cm.
   Includes bibliographical references and index.
   ISBN 0-520-08381-4 (alk. paper)
   1. United States. Court of Appeals (9th Circuit)—History.
2. Law—West (U.S.)—History.   I. Title.
KF8752 9th.F74 1994
374.78′03—dc20
[347.8073]   93-1309
                                         CIP

Printed in the United States of America
9 8 7 6 5 4 3 2 1

The paper used in this publication meets the minimum requirements of American
National Standard for Information Sciences—Permanence of Paper for Printed Library
Materials, ANSI Z39.48-1984. ∞

In large measure the work of a just and able judge is taken for granted. He works in seclusion. His opinions do not attract wide attention, and, if for some unusual circumstance the public notes the decision, the interest is but temporary. He can expect no monuments of stone, no heroic statue in the market place or at the crossroads. These are reserved for the soldier, the sailor, and the executive, the results of whose work is [*sic*] more obvious. Kingdoms rise and fall, wars are won or lost, and all can see the dramatic result and crown the victor. But the results of judicial work are not spectacular. Their effect is not as a rule obvious, nor can such an effect be readily anticipated or traced. Nevertheless, silently and constantly judges are engaged in building the Temple of Justice in which future generations are to dwell. Justice is essential to happiness. Injustice produces unhappiness and provokes disorder and war. The judge, if he is worthy and successful, wins the battles and the wars that are never fought, that is, his good work prevents wars, and renders unnecessary the struggle of the soldier.

Judge Curtis D. Wilbur, 1931

Contents

Foreword

It has been just over one hundred years since Congress passed the Evarts Act establishing the circuit court of appeals on March 3, 1891. The first session of the Ninth Circuit Court of Appeals was convened in San Francisco on June 16, 1891, by Circuit Justice Stephen J. Field. The story of that circuit now spans more than a century, a period of western expansion and development that is reflected in the cases and opinions of the circuit court. This remarkable history through the first fifty years is here recounted by David Frederick.

The Evarts Act signaled a significant change for the Supreme Court of the United States and its justices. The establishment of a court of appeals and the expansion of the discretionary power of the Supreme Court to grant or deny review in many cases meant that from 1891 on the great majority of federal court appellate decision making would be made at the level of the circuit court of appeals. That effect is still felt today as the Supreme Court on which I sit accepts for review each term less than 2 percent of the petitions filed. The great bulk of federal case law is developed and made in the courts of appeals. It is there that we must look for a broad understanding of federal law.

Mr. Frederick has wisely chosen to analyze how the Ninth Circuit helped shape the development of the West from 1891 to 1941. This work chronicles the story of how a federal case helped save my alma mater, Stanford University. It relates how the court dealt with the exclusion of Chinese in the late nineteenth and early twentieth centuries. It explains how the court averted a crisis during the Alaska gold rush days. These and many other illustrations of the court's role in western expansion make fascinating reading.

Wallace Stegner has written:

> There is something to the notion of western independence; there is something about living in big empty space, where people are few and distant, under a great sky that is alternately serene and furious, exposed to sun from four in the morning till nine at night, and to a wind that never seems to rest—there is something about exposure to that big country that not only tells an individual how small he is, but steadily tells him who he is.
>
> Wallace Stegner,
> *Where the Bluebird Sings*
> *to the Lemonade Springs* (1992)

The reader will have a rich and rewarding experience following the history of the largest and most diverse federal circuit in the "big country." Through it we can better learn who we are.

Justice Sandra Day O'Connor

Preface

I came upon this project somewhat accidentally. Looking for a way to accommodate the career of my wife, Susan, I discussed with Judge Joseph T. Sneed ways of spending an additional year in San Francisco after I finished my clerkship with him. Knowing of my interest in legal history, he suggested that I write a proposal to the Ninth Circuit outlining what I thought was a feasible historical study to be undertaken during the year after I completed my judicial clerkship. This book is the result of that proposal. When I say that this book would not have been possible without those two people, then, I am speaking the literal truth!

In my proposal to the Ninth Circuit I suggested exploring the role the court played in western development. Rather than engage in a straight-forward institutional study and chart personnel changes in the court, I hoped to examine how the court participated in the development process. I also wanted to feel free to make historical judgments about the court and the judges who served on it. Thus, I insisted on two precon-ditions from the Ninth Circuit before agreeing to write this book: first, that the court would exercise no control over the substance of the manuscript; and, second, that the study would conclude before the time when any judge now living had been appointed to the court. The present judges who were involved in this project, Chief Judge Clifford Wallace, former Chief Judges James Browning and Alfred Goodwin, and Judges Arthur Alarcon, Warren Ferguson, and Joseph Sneed, readily acceded to these requests, and I owe them a great debt of thanks for their encour-agement, support, and faith that my research would finally reach fruition. I make special note of this aspect of the book lest anyone unfairly attribute to the court or individual judges any criticism expressed herein. Judge Sneed was unstintingly generous both as a guide to the court and as a former academic whose own scholarly credentials made him an ideal adviser.

My full-time work on this project was limited because Justice Byron White hired me to serve as one of his law clerks, beginning in August of 1991. In addition to being a phenomenal experience in its own right, the Supreme Court clerkship gave me a different perspective on the federal court system. It also brought me into contact with Justice Sandra Day O'Connor, the circuit justice for the Ninth Circuit. I am very grateful to Justice O'Connor for enthusiastically agreeing to write a foreword for this book, and all the more because she produced it during June, the busiest time of year at the Supreme Court.

Financial support came from several different sources. The Ninth Circuit kept me on the payroll as a law clerk during the eleven months I spent full-time on this book. The Committee on the Bicentennial of the United States Constitution of the Judicial Conference and the Attorney Admission Fund Committee of the Ninth Circuit provided generous grants that I used for research assistance and travel to research sites throughout the country. I am very grateful for this assistance. I also wish it to be known that I renounced any claim to royalties and am not profiting from sales of this book.

In doing the research on this book, I attempted to be as comprehensive in my treatment of relevant materials as possible. I read all the known papers of the judges about whom I have written (and have included in the notes the libraries where the collections may be found); every law review article about the Ninth Circuit or a significant case the court decided that I could find for 1891–1941; and every newspaper article about significant cases that I could locate. I also read a large percentage of the first 10,000 of the court's reported decisions—the Ninth Circuit library kindly lent me a set of *Federal Reporters* and the early volumes of *Federal Reporter*, Second Series, for use in my office. This book is, however, a general survey of the court's history over a fifty-year period; researchers interested in a particular topic may find the sources referenced in the Notes useful only as a starting point.

Many individuals helped me in numerous ways during the course of my work on this book and it is a great pleasure to publicly acknowledge my thanks to them. Marcia Fay, Linden Hagans, Elizabeth Harris, Niall

Lynch, Susanna Pollak, Anna Marie Hagans, and Giselle Barth did a tremendous job of research, working diligently and uncovering more material than I ever thought possible in the brief time we had in which to work. The librarians at the Ninth Circuit headquarters were unfailing in their responsiveness to my many research requests, and each deserves special thanks: Helen Hill, Scott McCurdy, Cheryl Blare, Deborah Celle, Eric Wade, Sara Bacon, Sarah Bingham, Patricia Espinoza, Filiberto Govea, Lisa Larribeau, and Konrad Steiner. Librarians at the Bancroft Library at the University of California at Berkeley, the Huntington Library, the San Francisco Public Library, the Hastings Law School Library, the Los Angeles County Law Library, the Green Library at Stanford University, the University of Oregon Library, the Oregon Historical Society, the Alaska State Library, and the University of Alaska Library were extremely helpful, as were archivists at the National Archives in St. Louis and in Washington, D.C. Of the latter, Rod Ross deserves special thanks.

Other Ninth Circuit personnel who were particularly helpful in a variety of ways include Cathy Catterson, Mary Demarais, Rollins Emerson, Ellard Hill, Jim Hochstadt, Ted Peterson, Bob Pleasant, Bill Roberts, Mary Schleier, and Roger Tom. Judge Charles Merrill was kind to lend me Loris Eldredge's secretarial services during my time at the Ninth Circuit. Loris did a superb job, combining efficient skills with a wonderfully sardonic sense of humor. After I left the Ninth Circuit, Sheryl Farmer and Neth Arenas-Butler provided excellent typing assistance. At various stages of the project, I benefited from sound advice on numerous issues that was offered by William Burchill, Francis Gates, Michael Griffith, Craig Joyce, Bruce Mann, Roy Mersky, William Patry, Scot Powe, Rayman Solomon, Lois Weithorn, David Weisskopf, and Charles Alan Wright. Countless members of the Ninth Judicial Circuit Historical Society gave me their support and encouragement (and I owe thanks to Bradley Williams for favors large and small). I also appreciate the Historical Society publishing prior versions of Chapter Two as "Railroads, Robber Barons and the Saving of Stanford University," 4 *Western Legal History* 225 (1991), and of Chapter Five as "The Ninth Circuit and the Development of Natural Resources in the Early Twentieth Century," 6 *Western Legal History* (forthcoming Summer/Fall 1993). Finally, Naomi Schneider at the University of California Press was wonderful. I owe her special gratitude for sticking with me during the many months it took me to complete revisions while I was clerking for Justice White. Her colleague, Jane-Ellen Long, was a highly skilled copy editor. Rose Anne White, William Murphy, and Valeurie Friedman also made my dealings with the Press a real pleasure.

A number of friends read the entire manuscript—often in a very short amount of time—and made countless useful suggestions. It is impossible in this preface to convey the full extent of my thanks to those who spent long hours reading the manuscript in draft form and offering suggestions for making it better: Joe Franaszek, Christian Fritz, Ronald Mann, Maeva Marcus, Nancy Rapoport, and Judge Sneed. Still others, including Chris Eisgruber, Lanny Naegelin, Susan Simmonds, and Michael Sturley, read parts of the manuscript. These readers were immeasurably helpful to me in refining my analysis, challenging assumptions I had made, and broadening my perspective on the Ninth Circuit and the federal courts generally.

My wife Susan was as committed to this project as I was. She spent many hours helping with numerous mundane tasks, from photocopying to inserting data into a spreadsheet program. She also read the manuscript, helped to select the photographs, and served as an indispensable foil whenever I let the inevitable frustrations of a project this large get me down. One evening, as I sat reading over the manuscript for what seemed the umpteenth time, she deadpanned, "Haven't you read that book before?" Were she not put off by the sentimentalism of the gesture, I would dedicate the book to her.

D. C. F.
Washington, D.C.

Introduction

Three gentlemen meet quietly and unpretentiously, three
times a year in a red brick building, by no means an
example of architectural beauty, situated in an exceedingly
unbeautiful part of San Francisco, and constitute a high
court of the nation. This court is conspicuously
distinguished for its territorial jurisdiction, actual power and
the magnitude of the interests involved in its decisions. The
great mass of the citizens are, however, unaware even of the
existence of this tribunal and know nothing of its important
place in the judicial system of the Federal Government.

Austin Lewis, 1900

With Justice Stephen J. Field presiding and Circuit Judge Lorenzo Sawyer
in attendance, the United States Circuit Court of Appeals for the Ninth
Circuit held its inaugural session on June 16, 1891, in the Appraisers'
Building in San Francisco. Justice Field convened the court's first meeting
not to hear cases or to discuss issues of great legal import, but rather to
ordain the new western court that Congress had created through the
Evarts Act of March 3, 1891. An assemblage of distinguished members
of the bench and bar congregated in a "dismal, cheerless" courtroom
adorned with "dusty, faded draperies of red, its great square ugly corners
outlined in shadow by the faint light that glimmered through dirty
windows." The setting was not imbued with the splendor to be expected
from a court that "has all the dignity and not a little of the power of the
greatest tribunal in the land."[1]

The question that ran through most spectators' minds before the
judges took their seats on the bench belied the significance of the new
court's formation: Would the judges wear robes? District Judge William
W. Morrow laughed in response to a query whether he had bought his
gown by saying that "silk is too expensive to purchase on a contingency.
But . . . I think it an excellent idea, do you not, for the judges to wear

their gowns? It is expressive of great dignity and not repugnant to republican principles." Not everyone felt this way. For many, robes symbolized the tension between the character of monarchical and republican institutions. A similar controversy arose in at least one other circuit court of appeals that opted to don the "mystic gown."[2]

This concern was forgotten once Field called the court to order. The justice explained that the object of the law creating the circuit courts of appeals "was to relieve the Supreme Court of the United States from the vast accumulation of business which now crowds its dockets, and at the same time to bring nearer to suitors the judicial force required for the disposition of a portion of such business." To achieve this objective by staffing the court with needed judges, Congress had authorized the circuit courts of appeals to designate a district judge to sit on the court along with the circuit justice and two circuit judges. In the Ninth Circuit this assignment was particularly crucial. Advancing age and the Supreme Court's vast workload prevented Justice Field from hearing more than a few circuit cases per term. As the circuit judge from the preexisting system, Lorenzo Sawyer would hold one of the judgeships designated by statute. Another judge remained to be appointed. Moreover, at the court's first session, Field announced that Matthew P. Deady, the distinguished and long-serving federal district judge for the district of Oregon, would sit on the appellate bench by designation. Although Judge Ogden Hoffman of the northern district of California was senior to Deady, Hoffman's increasing age and ill health prevented him from assuming the duties of the new court.[3]

After Field had spoken, an uncomfortable silence filled the "gloomy courtroom" of the Appraisers' Building. At Judge Sawyer's whispered suggestion, Field inquired whether perhaps "some member of the bar would care to propose something to the court." Alfred Clarke, an attorney and counselor-at-law, broke another awkward silence by addressing the court. Somewhat nervously, with hands stuck deep in the pockets of his overcoat, Clarke began by congratulating the judges, congratulating California, congratulating the United States, and congratulating the civilized world. "He only ceased his congratulations to give a synopsis of universal history." Clarke then began an interminable oratory on the origins of law and criminal justice that surveyed the use of thumb screws and iron boots from Roman times up to the present day. Not surprisingly, the *San Francisco Chronicle* reported that everybody "seemed to be nervous." After the court and the audience recovered from this oration, Justice Field thanked Clarke and adjourned the court.[4] These inauspicious beginnings gave little hint of the contributions the court would make to western development during the ensuing decades.

The creation of this intermediate tier of federal courts accorded with the dual character of the lower federal courts established by Congress in the 1789 Judiciary Act. In both instances Congress ensured that the lower federal courts would be instruments of national power by vesting in them jurisdiction to decide cases involving crimes and offenses against the United States, causes in admiralty, and, eventually, cases arising under the Constitution and laws of the United States. These subaltern federal courts also assumed regional attributes. The 1789 act granted them subject-matter jurisdiction over suits between citizens of different states that arose under state law; it also delineated the territorial jurisdiction of these courts into "districts," which comported with the boundaries of states or parts of states.[5]

Congress preserved this territorial concept in its 1891 reform. It gave each circuit court of appeals jurisdiction to hear appeals from within a defined circuit composed of the districts of a number of states. Congress intended that these courts would render final dispositions in a great majority of cases from federal trial courts (and thereby relieve the Supreme Court of much work) and that they would also refine issues in appeals to the Supreme Court. The respective dockets of the fledgling circuit courts of appeals in the 1890s exemplified both the disparate levels of development throughout the country and the wide array of local concerns in the regions they served. These parochial issues at times paralleled concerns in other circuits, thus implicating questions of wider importance that, in certain circumstances, merited further review by the Supreme Court. From one perspective, therefore, the different circuits looked alike. At a deeper level, however, regional forces gave these intermediate appellate courts their defining characteristics.

When Congress established the United States circuit courts of appeals in 1891, it empowered the Ninth Circuit to hear certain appeals from trials in United States courts in California, Oregon, Nevada, Washington, Idaho, Montana, and the Territory of Alaska. Eventually, the circuit also included Arizona and Hawaii, both as territories and then as states, Guam and the Northern Mariana islands, and, for over fifty years, an extra-territorial court operating in China.[6] At its inception the circuit comprised states and territories at very different stages of development. From the sophistication of San Francisco to the barren desert of Nevada and Arizona, the West presented a range of problems and opportunities unmatched in diversity by any other circuit. Stretching from the Arctic Circle to the Mojave Desert and later to the tropics, the circuit boasted a wealth of natural resources and a host of natural wonders. These states and territories contained not only the sites for many of the country's national parks and monuments but also vast stores of hidden gold, silver, copper, and other valuable minerals; huge tracts of land suitable for lumbering and agriculture; and a long coastline for fishing and international sea trade.

To understand the U.S. Circuit Court of Appeals for the Ninth Circuit as an institution is impossible without attempting to know something about its judges and the legal problems they confronted. During the court's first half-century, the men who held circuit judgeships on the court embodied the same pioneering impulse as other newcomers to the West. Until the 1930s, when the first judges born in the region took office, the judges were also transplants from other parts of the country who had moved westward in search of opportunity. Some of the Ninth Circuit judges received appointments from political offices; others from state judgeships; and still others from private practice. Because Congress authorized only three circuit judgeships for the Ninth Circuit during the court's first four decades of existence, the administration of the court was quite informal and the character of the institution clearly reflected the personalities of its judges. For most of this period, the longevity of three judges gave the court an institutional solidity unmatched by any other federal circuit court of appeals. When these judges retired in the 1920s and early 1930s, the court fell into disarray, with a spate of new, inexperienced judges taking office just as the court's docket was increasing rapidly. How judges came to the court and how they coped with their judicial responsibilities provide two perspectives from which to view the Ninth Circuit in its first half-century.

The personalities of the court's judges, if studied alone, however, would scarcely bring to light the importance of the court in western development. Numerous issues of regional importance never drew the Supreme Court's attention, thus heightening the significance of the Ninth Circuit's work. On the most important issues facing the West between 1891 and 1941—transportation, labor, and natural-resource development—the Ninth Circuit issued key rulings. Exploring the context of its decisions is just as vital to understanding the Ninth Circuit as is an examination of the lives of its judges and the institutional pressures they confronted. This context was complex and distinct from that of the other circuits in the federal system. Much more so than in other, more industrialized parts of the country, the Far West depended on extractive enterprises for economic growth. Population patterns and the region's geographical diversity also set the Ninth Circuit apart.

The Ninth Circuit's significant role in various aspects of western development has been overlooked by historians, who have featured key rulings by the court in monographs on certain subjects but have neglected any concentrated study of the court itself. Because no detailed treatment of the Ninth Circuit exists, much of this book is devoted to a descriptive, roughly chronological account of the court's evolution through its first fifty years. The date of 1941 offers a convenient stopping point for this narrative, because in that year the judges publicly debated the circuit's role in the West and whether the geographical boundaries of the circuit should be altered. These debates occurred on the eve of the United States' entry into World War II, a conflict that presented the Ninth Circuit with difficult issues of a character qualitatively different from those confronted by the court in its first half-century. Thematically those issues seem better suited to a subsequent study.

At a different level, this book tries to say something about the nature of federal courts and the federal court system. First, I hope to demonstrate that key administrative developments arose out of substantive disagreements among the judges over the outcomes of cases. Intellectual conflict between judges is to be anticipated, especially when they are appointed by presidents of different political parties at different times. Perhaps less expected is that those jurisprudential disagreements will contribute to institutional changes. One development that emerges from this study is the specialization in roles performed by the federal judiciary. In the late nineteenth and early twentieth centuries, circuit and district judges were almost interchangeable in the performance of trial and appellate work. Over the half-century covered in this book, this flexibility of roles largely disappeared, at least in the Ninth Circuit. The chapters that follow will attempt to account for this transformation, which led to a much more hierarchical federal judicial system by the 1930s. As this role specialization was occurring, the disagreements among the circuit judges who performed appellate tasks sharpened. These substantive conflicts in turn forced the need for administrative reforms. What began in the 1890s as an almost informal system of assigning judges to hear cases rigidified as the court's caseload and its number of judges expanded. Ultimately, concerns arising out of substantive disagreements among the circuit judges led to the creation of a procedure to decide cases by an *en banc* panel composed of all the circuit judges on the court.

Second, I will try to show that the "federalization" of the law was occurring well before the New Deal era, when the conventional wisdom posits that a legal "revolution" took place in the nature of federal-state relations.[7] In some respects, the concentrated attention of legal scholars on the Supreme Court is partly responsible for the prevailing view, because many federal law cases never required plenary consideration by the Supreme Court in the pre–New Deal period. If the Ninth Circuit is any guide, the experiences of the various circuit courts of appeals and district courts, however, can well document the change in legal culture that was occurring in the early twentieth century; these subaltern federal courts are a rich and largely untapped lode for legal historians. As docket pressures on the Supreme Court escalated and Congress responded by vesting in the Court greater discretion to decide which cases it would hear, the influence of circuit courts of appeals rose correspondingly. And since many appeals of right to the appellate tribunals raised no important federal constitutional issues, the circuit courts of appeals functionally became the courts of last resort in the overwhelming majority of the cases they decided.

Issues involving federal law, and the federal government's "encroachment" upon matters heretofore left to the states, are particularly evident in the period from 1891 to 1941 in the Ninth Circuit, because of the dynamics of western development. Much of the land in the Ninth Circuit's constituent states was federal public land, and Congress enacted numerous statutes to regulate it. Issues that in other parts of the country were questions of state law became "federalized" in much of the West as a result of the existence of vast tracts of federal public land upon which westerners depended for the extraction of natural resources. Moreover, federal concern for domestic labor underscored certain immigration issues, such as the exclusion of the Chinese, a topic that occupied much of the Ninth Circuit's attention in the late nineteenth and early twentieth centuries. And in World War I, Congress even went so far as to authorize regulations on houses of ill repute within a certain distance from a military base. This regulation appears to have created significant litigation only in the Ninth Circuit, but there it displayed a palpable expansion in the role of the federal government in local affairs, as did national laws to prohibit the consumption and sale of liquor in the 1920s. In certain instances, the Ninth Circuit judges themselves debated the contours of this process of incursion by the federal government into state and local affairs, and their arguments have a familiar ring today. By attempting to develop these themes, therefore, this book seeks to improve understanding of the federal court system generally in this century.

From 1891 to 1941, major developments in western history provided work for the Ninth Circuit. Sometimes the Ninth Circuit's opinions affected people throughout the region; sometimes they touched only the immediate litigants. In many cases, how the court's judges viewed the law directly influenced the course of progress in the West. An exploration of this symbiosis between the social and economic forces that created work for the court and the impact of judicial decisions on those forces will uncover the importance of the court as it progressed through its first half-century. The theme of western development animated the life of the court, from the types of issues it decided to the pioneering qualities of the judges who served on it.

ONE

Origins and Early Years

The greatest despot of our land is the United States
circuit judge.

The Nation, *Jan. 6, 1881*

In the century between the 1789 Judiciary Act and the Evarts Act of
1891, efforts to reform the federal judicial system lagged far behind the
economic, social, and demographic transformations occurring throughout the country. Westward expansion in the mid-nineteenth century
served both to exacerbate the deficiencies in the federal court system and
to create opportunities for aspiring judges, who built the foundation for
the post-1891 Ninth Circuit.

I. ORIGINS OF THE FEDERAL CIRCUIT COURTS OF APPEALS

The creation of the United States circuit courts of appeals in 1891
changed the structure of the federal courts. The Constitution invested
Congress with unlimited discretion to establish "inferior Courts" of its
own design; and for over a century, Congress had periodically enacted
reforms designed to make the nation's judicial system more responsive
to litigants' needs. The 1789 Judiciary Act, for example, ordained a
system of courts in three circuits and thirteen districts. With the exceptions of Massachusetts and Virginia, the districts comported with the
geographical contours of each state. Congress provided for a single judge
to hold district court. The district courts mainly heard suits involving
admiralty issues, although they also had original jurisdiction over other
miscellaneous matters. The circuits, by contrast, comprised groupings of
districts. The eastern circuit, for instance, consisted of the districts of

New Hampshire, Massachusetts, Connecticut, and New York. In each district of the three circuits, Congress required that a circuit court be convened twice a year. Circuit courts had trial jurisdiction over suits involving issues of state law when the litigants were from different states, and limited appellate jurisdiction over the district courts.[1] Except from 1801 through 1802, the circuit courts retained their dual purpose until 1891, when Congress divested them of appellate jurisdiction and created the circuit courts of appeals. Circuit courts continued to exercise trial, or *nisi prius*, jurisdiction until Congress finally eliminated them altogether in the 1911 Judicial Code.[2] The confusing nomenclature of the federal court system thus dates from its earliest days.*

Because Congress expected that a light Supreme Court workload would free the justices to ride circuit in pairs, it made no provision for the appointment of separate circuit judges. Such inaction rankled members of the highest court, who found the expectations of their own workload too low and the burdens of circuit travel too high. Partly to address the problems created by the 1789 Act, which were readily evident within a decade, and partly to maintain Federalist control over one aspect of the national government machinery, the outgoing Adams administration enacted the infamous "Midnight Judges" Act of February 13, 1801. This statute regrouped the districts into six numbered circuits and authorized sixteen circuit judgeships: three judges for each of the first five circuits covering the eastern seaboard states, and one for the sixth circuit, which consisted of Tennessee, Kentucky, and the Ohio Territory. In addition to creating the circuit judgeships, the 1801 reform foreshadowed the 1891 circuit courts of appeals system in authorizing circuit court sessions for the entire numbered geographical region. Congress also continued to authorize circuit court sessions in each district of the circuit.[3]

Except for its retention of original jurisdiction in both circuit and district courts, the 1801 Act was a logical blueprint for the federal

---

*A *circuit* comprised the districts in a given geographical territory. A *circuit court* was the court convened in a district that, until 1891, exercised both trial and appellate functions. Between 1891 and the end of 1911, circuit courts had only trial jurisdiction, their appellate duties transferred to the circuit courts of appeals created in 1891 by the Evarts Act. A *circuit judge*, the office established temporarily in 1801 and permanently in 1869, had the authority to hear trials in circuit courts up through the end of 1911 and appeals in the circuit courts until 1891 and in the circuit courts of appeals after that date. Although the 1801 Act numbered the respective circuits, it was not until sometime in the twentieth century that the circuit courts of appeals came to be popularly referred to by their geographical territory—for example, the "Ninth Circuit," as opposed to the "Court of Appeals for the Ninth Circuit." The modern practice is followed here.

judiciary's growth as the country expanded westward. Distrust of the Adams administration's motives, however, obscured the tangible benefits of the reform. Within a year of assuming office, on March 8, 1802, the Jeffersonians rescinded the "Midnight Judges" statute. They were not wholly confident that this repealer legislation would win approval from the Federalist-dominated Supreme Court, however, and six weeks later they passed a statute canceling the upcoming August session of the Court. A section of this law also reconfigured the circuits but omitted any new authorization of circuit judges. Resumption of circuit-riding duty soon proved to be very onerous for the justices, but they acquiesced because they interpreted the 1802 statutes by implication to require such travel. As the burdens of travel in a growing country steadily increased, the justices gradually abdicated some of their statutory circuit responsibilities, and district judges filled the gap by holding circuit court.[4]

In midcentury, the addition of California as a state gave Congress the impetus needed to confront the undesirability of the country's highest judges failing to meet the strict requirements of the law. As one lawyer would later observe dryly, "It would seem that the Judges of the Supreme Court, at least, ought to be exempt from statutes enacted with an eye single to their disregard and violation." In 1855, Congress took its first tentative step since the ill-fated "Midnight Judges" Act to create intermediate-level judgeships. It established California as a separate, unnumbered circuit and authorized the appointment of a circuit judge to exercise authority analogous to that of a circuit-riding justice. The California circuit court thus had the same original and appellate jurisdiction as all other circuit courts, except that it covered two district courts, the northern and southern districts of California. The vast distance between California and Washington, D.C., made this a pragmatic solution to free a justice from riding circuit in the Far West. Although the sitting district judge for the northern district of California, Ogden Hoffman, coveted the new circuit judgeship, Matthew Hall McAllister received President Franklin Pierce's appointment.[5]

McAllister, a Georgian of distinguished background, was the son of Matthew McAllister, an eminent lawyer whom President Washington had appointed as district attorney for the district of Georgia. Matthew Hall McAllister himself followed in his father's footsteps, first as a student at the College of New Jersey (later Princeton), where he did not distinguish himself, and later as an attorney in Georgia, where he did. Politically active, the second McAllister served in a number of public offices, including district attorney for the southern district of Georgia, mayor of Savannah, and state senator. He was a fervent Unionist and an opponent of nullification. The political situation in Georgia, coupled with the riches to be made practicing law in California, undoubtedly influenced McAllister in 1850 to join his sons in San Francisco. Within two years he had earned enough to retire and travel to Europe. On a return visit to Georgia in 1853 he narrowly lost an election to become one of that state's United States senators. This defeat, and the imprudent expenditure of his retirement monies by one of his sons, caused McAllister to return to San Francisco, where he and his family were to leave a lasting mark.[6]

McAllister served as circuit judge for seven years, resigning on April 7, 1862, for reasons of health. This judgeship, which had possibly been intended as a surrogate Supreme Court justiceship, became just that with the exigencies presented by the Civil War.[7] By 1863 the Supreme Court confronted a number of important war-related cases, and the Republicans were naturally anxious for the Court to affirm the legality of the Lincoln administration's actions. Addition of a tenth justice, who would be vetted for sympathy to the Union cause, would solidify a precarious pro-administration majority.[8] The man who assumed this post, Stephen J. Field, had turned down the California circuit judgeship made vacant by McAllister's resignation, with the reply that he "preferred to remain Chief Justice of the Supreme Court of the State than to be a judge of an inferior federal court." He had generously hinted, however, that "if a new justice were added to the Supreme Court of the United States, I would accept the office if tendered to me." The administration evidently took no umbrage at this audacity: when in 1863 Congress authorized the tenth justiceship and abolished the circuit judgeship, Lincoln offered the Supreme Court position to Field. Even though Field was a Democrat, he appointed him on the assurance that Field was a fervent Unionist. Whether the intention was for Field to serve as a full-time justice in Washington or as a resident circuit-rider who would occasionally travel to the nation's capital is not entirely clear.[9] In any event, Field enjoyed a long tenure on the Supreme Court, but he continued to maintain close ties to the western federal courts.

When Congress abolished the California circuit judgeship in 1863, it formed a Tenth Circuit comprising the districts in California and Oregon. Three years later, Congress reconfigured the circuits ar d added Nevada to a new Ninth Circuit with California and Oregon. The legislature did not provide these circuits with any formal staffing until 1869, when it authorized appointment of a circuit judge for each of the country's nine circuits. This reorganization implemented a modified version of the Federalist plan of 1801. For the first time since 1801, Congress established a nationwide tier of circuit judges, who were to perform both trial and appellate functions. The 1869 reform commanded the justices to continue their circuit-riding duties, but their obligation was reduced to one circuit term every two years.[10] This law notwithstanding, the justices probably did not hold circuit court in more than one court in the circuit every other year, and Stephen Field, who may well have been the justice most diligent in performing circuit work, only infrequently held circuit court outside California.[11]

Congress commanded the far western circuit judge to hold court in each district of the three-state Ninth Circuit. The man who assumed this circuit judgeship, Lorenzo Sawyer, was confirmed by the Senate on January 11, 1870, when he was nearly fifty years old. A native of Jefferson County, New York, Sawyer at age twenty began to make his way westward. He stopped first in Ohio, where he read law with Judge Noah H. Swayne, a distinguished jurist who later was a colleague of Field's on the United States Supreme Court.[12] The discoveries of gold in California lured Sawyer to the West, but he arrived in July of 1850, too late to reap the immense riches of the earliest and luckiest miners. As he wrote after settling in California, "I would advise no man to come here," because the "risk of failure, and to life and health, far overbalance every prospect of success to those who come here with a view of returning." Sawyer himself was determined to stay, "not to make his pile and return, but to cast his lot with the new State, with her to sink or swim." He soon abandoned his mining pan to sluice the muddy waters of legal practice. After holding the offices of San Francisco city attorney and California district judge, he ascended to the California Supreme Court in 1863, serving as chief justice from 1868 to 1870. When he lost his reelection bid, he saw a great opportunity in the new circuit judgeship that Congress established in 1869. With the support of his mentor, Noah Swayne, who by then sat on the U.S. Supreme Court, Sawyer successfully secured a life-tenured judgeship.[13]

The two decades during which Sawyer served as circuit judge saw tremendous change in the federal court system. Even though Sawyer performed his duties as circuit judge with great industry and integrity and Congress enacted several reforms, litigants' needs outpaced these efforts. After the Civil War, a number of factors contributed to the inability of the federal courts to handle ever-expanding dockets. Adoption of the Thirteenth, Fourteenth, and Fifteenth amendments embedded in the

Constitution the transformation in federal-state relations that the North had won on the battlefield. Civil rights legislation enacted by Congress in the postwar period prompted another spate of federal lawsuits.[14] By explicitly providing for the vindication of federal rights, these laws inaugurated a fundamental alteration in the role of the federal judiciary.

In addition to these constitutional and statutory influences, Congress increased the load on federal courts by expanding their jurisdiction. Two statutes were instrumental to this growth. The first, enacted in 1863, portended significant changes by permitting removal from state to federal court of cases brought against United States officials for acts committed during the Civil War under the authority of the president or Congress. This statute was but an insignificant amendment compared to the revolutionary effects of the Removal Act of 1875. Until passage of the 1875 statute, litigants were able to bring a federal suit only in limited circumstances. The 1875 law gave federal tribunals full power, through original jurisdiction or removal from state court, to hear cases implicating federal rights arising under the Constitution and laws of the United States. The federal courts were no longer "subsidiary courts." Despite its revolutionary consequences, however, the statute's legislative history reveals very little of the drafters' intent, for floor debate on the bill was minimal.[15]

Concomitant with these structural factors, the natural outgrowths of business in a transcontinental society affected the work of the federal judiciary. Reconstruction unleashed involvement by the national government in such matters as transportation and commerce, issues in which the states had heretofore exercised primary influence. And although the South experienced an economic slump after the Civil War, the rest of the country was booming. These influences, combined with the growth in national population, contributed to an increase in business that the federal courts were ill equipped to handle. Between 1873 and 1890, the number of cases filed in circuit and district courts rose from 29,013 to 54,194.[16]

Partly by design and partly by default, therefore, the federal courts became repositories of a burgeoning number of suits that steadily increased in complexity. Efforts by Congress to maintain the proper functioning of the courts lagged far behind the developments that severely pressured the system. Although a step in the right direction, the 1869 reform was outmoded even at its adoption. This law added fewer new judgeships than had the 1801 "Midnight Judges" statute. For the vastly overloaded Supreme Court, the authorization of nine circuit judgeships did not go far to relieve the justices of their statutory responsibility to hear cases in circuit courts. Moreover, the enactment of the 1869 circuit-judge law lulled Congress into a complacency that militated against greater structural reform.

Practicing lawyers quickly felt the limitations of the 1869 legislation. In the more than two decades between the authorization of circuit judgeships and the creation of the circuit courts of appeals, the newly created American Bar Association worked hard to reform the federal judicial system. One major complaint lawyers made was that frequently only a single judge held circuit court. Congress had originally envisioned that a panel of judges would hold circuit court, but there were simply too few authorized judgeships for a panel to sit in every session of circuit court. Indeed, district judges handled approximately two-thirds of the circuit court work, and they assumed an even greater share of the circuit courts' appellate duty. By one estimate, in approximately eight-ninths of all cases brought in a four-year period during the 1880s, the same district judge heard and decided the appeal for rehearing or new trial.[17]

Burgeoning federal dockets and the perceived unfairness of the same judge performing trial and appellate functions in the same case constituted two fundamental issues in the continuing effort to reform the federal judiciary. An important political dimension was also involved. The reorganization contemplated by members of the American Bar Association struck at the heart of federal-state relations. Throughout its first century the federal court system was quite small; the low caseload inadequately foreshadowed what was to come. After the Civil War, several factors combined to increase federal court dockets: the effect of the Removal Act of 1875, the growth in interstate commerce and population, and the assumption by Congress of control of matters that had traditionally been left to the states. The circuit court system with nine circuit judges lacked sufficient personnel to handle this work. Yet because an expanded federal court appellate system would entrench power in the national government, certain interests in Congress resisted enacting further reforms. The sectional rivalries and concern for states' rights that had been prevalent in the Civil War era were not completely dead. These forces would attempt to dilute the power of federal courts during the debates over the Evarts Act of 1891, which established the circuit courts of appeals.[18]

By the 1880s, as reform efforts failed to accommodate social change, the system erected by Congress had fallen into disarray. The circuit-riding situation in the Eighth and Ninth Circuits was particularly disastrous. The great distances involved made coverage of these circuits by a circuit judge and justice impossible. Although the justice assigned to the Ninth Circuit, Stephen J. Field, traveled west frequently, the assignment was not completely satisfactory. Increasing age—by the 1880s Field was in his seventies—and a traumatic incident that left one man dead and himself no doubt badly shaken, served to restrict Field's circuit-riding still further.[19] Moreover, relations between Field and Judges Sawyer and Hoffman had deteriorated dramatically, the result of disputes both professional and personal.[20] Some of the tension between Field and the California federal judges stemmed from basic party differences: Field was a Democrat and Hoffman and Sawyer were Republicans. Democrats generally sought restrictions on federal courts and federal jurisdiction, whereas Republicans advocated maintaining the postwar growth in the power of the federal judiciary. The changing fortunes of the two parties in the post-Reconstruction era significantly affected the pace of federal court reform. The 1875 legislature that passed the Removal Act was the last overwhelmingly Republican postwar Congress. After 1875, the Democrats for the most part controlled the House of Representatives and the Republicans maintained precarious majorities in the Senate. Deadlocked in Congress, neither party was able to impose its vision of the role and structure of the federal court system on the other.[21]

In 1885, A. H. Garland, the new attorney general, advocated the creation of a court of appeals in each circuit. His proposal in many respects presaged the establishment of a separate tier of federal courts in 1891. Under Garland's scheme, each court of appeals would be composed of the circuit justice, a circuit judge, and two district judges. The new courts would have jurisdiction to hear appeals or writs of error from final judgments of district and circuit courts when the amount in controversy exceeded $500 or when the district or circuit judge certified a question as being of general importance for the appellate court's guidance. Instead of adopting Garland's proposal, Congress enacted more modest reforms by raising the amount-in-controversy requirement to $2,000 and limiting other grounds for invoking federal court jurisdiction. While this statute may have eased pressure somewhat on the lower courts, on the very same day Congress enacted another law with precisely the opposite effect, this one conferring on district and circuit courts concurrent jurisdiction with the court of claims in actions against the United States.[22]

The failure of the 1887 law to decrease the load on the Supreme Court led bench and bar alike to renew their pleas for reform. Their actions achieved some success at last on April 4, 1890, when Representative

John H. Rogers introduced a bill that attempted to address the Supreme Court's backlog problem. The bill essentially repeated many earlier proposals, including Attorney General Garland's plan of 1885. It went further, however, by advocating the fusion of district and circuit courts and the creation of nine intermediate courts of appeals that would have final decision in cases arising solely through diversity jurisdiction (subject to certification to the Supreme Court). It also authorized the addition of two circuit judges for each circuit, for a total of three, and repealed all existing laws requiring Supreme Court justices to perform circuit work. These proposals finally became politically acceptable after 1890, when, following Benjamin Harrison's presidential victory in 1888, the Republicans captured control of both the House and the Senate. Partisan considerations no longer impeded the creation of politically attractive patronage positions.[23]

On August 5, 1890, Senator William M. Evarts substituted a bill of his own for the House version. Evarts's bill modified the House proposal in several important respects. First, it divided the appellate stream from the district and circuit courts by transmitting the most important issues directly to the Supreme Court and diverting the more numerous but less difficult issues to the nine new appellate courts. The bill also proposed retaining original jurisdiction in both district and circuit courts and provided for direct appeals from these courts to the United States Supreme Court in certain classes of cases. All other cases were to go to the circuit courts of appeal for final decision, subject to review by the Supreme Court. Appellate jurisdiction in the circuit courts would finally be abolished. In a response as much to traditional sentiment as to political expediency, the Evarts bill retained the old circuit courts and permitted Supreme Court justices to attend them. This last provision was a bow to believers that the justices gained a better perspective—a common touch with the people—by continuing to ride circuit, if only in an abbreviated form. Finally, the Evarts proposal authorized only one additional circuit judge, for a total of two, for each circuit.[24]

The Evarts bill triumphed, becoming law on March 3, 1891. The Supreme Court felt the benefits of this reform immediately. According to reports by the attorney general, the Supreme Court reduced its backlog from 1,190 cases in 1890 to 313 by 1897, as docketings fell from 623 to 302. As then-Attorney General Joseph McKenna was able to report in 1897, "I think it is generally conceded that [the circuit courts of appeals] have justified their creation by accomplishing what was expected of them."[25]

II. THE NINTH CIRCUIT'S FIRST JUDGES

In the western states, formation of the circuit court of appeals in 1891 signaled more than the creation of a new judicial structure. It also symbolically represented the passing of the torch from an old generation of jurists who had served on the federal bench for decades to a new generation whose jurisprudence would light the way well into the twentieth century. Two seminal figures of the old generation, Lorenzo Sawyer and Ogden Hoffman, would die before the end of 1891. Two more, Justice Stephen Field and Judge Matthew Deady, would be dead by the end of the decade. This transformation in personnel augured significant changes for western litigants in the adjudication of numerous disputes, from mining law to Chinese rights, although it produced no greater comity among the federal judges.[26]

The Evarts Act authorized two judgeships for each circuit. One of these was to be assumed by the sitting circuit judge: in the Ninth Circuit, Lorenzo Sawyer. Before the court heard its first case in October of 1891, however, Sawyer and Hoffman both died; President Harrison was thus faced with the task of filling one district and two appellate judgeships. It went without saying that California, the largest and most populous state in the Ninth Circuit, would be represented on the court. But the informal practice of reserving judgeships for constituent states also dates from this period, and most observers correctly surmised that someone from Oregon or Washington would receive the other commission.[27]

The two leading candidates for the California "seat" on the Ninth Circuit and the northern California district judgeship were Joseph McKenna and William W. Morrow, who both coveted the more prestigious appellate seat. They had become friends during their service in Congress in the years before Harrison made his selections. When the president named Morrow to the district judgeship, the San Franciscan withdrew from consideration for the circuit judgeship, thus paving the way for McKenna's nomination. McKenna had been born in Philadelphia on November 10, 1843, and his parents had moved to Benicia, California, in late 1854. Originally hoping to become a priest, McKenna attended Catholic schools before changing his mind and embarking upon a career in the law. He graduated from Benicia Collegiate Institute in 1865; later that year he gained admittance to the California bar. Shortly after commencing his practice in Fairfield, California, he won sufficient recognition to become the county attorney for Solano County, California, from 1866 to 1870. McKenna served briefly in the California legislature, from 1875 to 1876, but ambition drove him to seek a seat in the United States Congress three times—in 1876, 1878, and 1880—without success. He persisted, however, and in 1884 he was at last elected. He served in Congress from March 4, 1885, to March 28, 1892, when he resigned to accept President Harrison's appointment as circuit judge for the Ninth Circuit.[28]

McKenna's tenure on the Ninth Circuit was short—approximately five years—and in that time he evinced a greater ability to maintain his political friendships than to attract the respect and admiration of his judicial brethren in the Far West. Rumors abounded that the principals of the Southern Pacific Railroad had been responsible for his appointment. It is impossible to evaluate the veracity of these rumors, but certainly fears that McKenna would prove to be a lackey of railroad interests were unfounded. Charges of dilatoriness and indifference to judging flourished, however, fed by his slow work style.[29] Despite these contentions, the Supreme Court rarely reversed McKenna and his opinions reflected competence, if not brilliance.

The main source of the ill feeling toward McKenna stemmed from his relationship with Judge William B. Gilbert, who was appointed to the Ninth Circuit in 1892 to fill the second judgeship created by the Evarts Act. Very little is known about Gilbert, despite his having served on the Ninth Circuit for nearly forty years. Born July 4, 1847, in Fairfax County, Virginia, Gilbert was named for his illustrious ancestor Colonel William Ball, who emigrated from England to Virginia in 1650 and was the grandfather of George Washington's mother, Mary Ball. The Gilbert family did not share the Confederate sympathies of other prominent Virginia families. A Unionist, John Gilbert relocated his family to Ohio sometime before the Civil War began, but his son William did not serve in the Union Army, instead attending Williams College, where he was graduated in 1866. After accompanying a scientific expedition in the upper Amazon, the future Ninth Circuit judge spent two years on a geological survey in Ohio.[30]

Abandoning these initial flirtations with science, Gilbert enrolled in the University of Michigan, where he received a Bachelor of Laws degree in 1872. The following year, he moved to Portland, Oregon, his home for the remainder of his life. A member of the Portland bar, Gilbert practiced law in a succession of partnerships from 1873 to 1892, when President Harrison announced his nomination of Gilbert as circuit judge. The nomination appeared to encounter little opposition until it was revealed that Wallace McCamant, one of Gilbert's associates in Gilbert

& Snow, had written to a friend that "Mr. Gilbert's appointment would be to my professional and pecuniary advantage." Unexplained, this message raised obvious questions about Gilbert's rectitude. McCamant hastily attempted to undo the damage by writing a series of letters to senators and the attorney general accounting for this statement. Apparently Gilbert's law partner, Zera Snow, had suggested to McCamant that he would be offered the partnership if Gilbert ascended to the bench. This explanation of "pecuniary advantage" was clearly more palatable than others, and the Senate gave its advice and consent to Gilbert's appointment on March 18, 1892.[31] Although Gilbert managed to avoid ignominy from his young associate's remarks, McCamant himself was less successful three decades later, when he would irrevocably damage his own nomination to the Ninth Circuit in 1925 through another imprudent choice of words.[32]

For nearly thirty-five years Gilbert was the ranking circuit judge in the Ninth Circuit, and for a considerable time before his death in 1931 he was the ranking circuit judge in the United States in length of service.[33] In his long judicial career, Gilbert's opinions were to span almost three hundred volumes of the *Federal Reporter*, including many of the most important decisions rendered by the Ninth Circuit. Tireless, industrious, and possessed of great charm, Gilbert was very much a nineteenth-century man, even though more than a third of his life was spent in the twentieth. He refused to ride in an automobile, an invention he decried as "a symbol of the new mechanical age." His anachronistic view of progress did not, however, dim the significance of his many contributions to the development of Ninth Circuit law. In the ensuing decades, Gilbert wrote for the court in the Stanford controversy, a notorious Alaska gold-mining scandal, one of the Teapot Dome suits, and the *Olmstead* case, which established the constitutional authority of the government to impose wiretaps without search warrants. Yet despite gaining nationwide prominence as a judge, Gilbert zealously guarded his privacy. His "passion for inconspicuousness" extended to never carrying a bundle on a street car, "fearing," he confided, "to attract attention."[34] He performed his judicial service with little fanfare, leaving the public spotlight to Erskine Ross and William Morrow, his colleagues of nearly a quarter-century.

III.   ROSS ARRIVES AND McKENNA MOVES UP

The available indications are that Gilbert's relations were strained not only with McKenna, but also with Judge Erskine Ross. Ross and Gilbert served together for over thirty years on the Ninth Circuit. Their judicial differences extended to a wide range of issues that arose in the federal courts. How far their diverse backgrounds shaped their judicial disagreements is difficult to say, but their contrasting family origins did little to promote comity between them. Ross too hailed from a prominent Virginia family, but his chose to stay in Virginia and fight for the South. Born June 30, 1845 at Bel Pré, his father's plantation in Culpeper County, Virginia, Ross was fifteen years old when war broke out. He had just enrolled at Virginia Military Institute when four companies of V.M.I. cadets were ordered to Camp Lee, Virginia, outside Richmond, under the command of Thomas J. ("Stonewall") Jackson. These young cadets served as drillmasters for the raw recruits who began to pour in after Virginia seceded in April of 1861. Not long after the war started, Ross saw battle at Cedar Run. His military service undoubtedly would have continued but for a conspiracy of three influences: his father insisted on his returning to V.M.I., his three older brothers were already in the Confederate Army, and Ross himself was barely sixteen years old at the time. He continued his education at V.M.I. and became cadet captain of A Company, which saw service at the Battle of Newmarket.[35]

The devastation in his home state at the conclusion of the war left few opportunities for Ross. After helping to found the Alpha Tau Omega fraternity in Richmond, Ross left Virginia in the spring of 1868. At the invitation of his uncle, Cameron E. Thom, Ross journeyed to Los Angeles, traveling by boat around South America just a year before the first overland railroad was completed. Only 5,000 persons of various nationalities inhabited Los Angeles when Ross arrived on May 19, 1868, but the city was to grow during Ross's residency there, passing 700,000 by the mid-1920s. Ross himself helped to establish the nearby city of Glendale, which by the time of his death in 1928 had a population of more than 23,000.[36] Ross wasted little time embracing the legal profession under the tutelage of his uncle, a practicing attorney in Los Angeles. Ross was admitted to the state bar in 1869 and practiced for ten years.

In 1879 Ross was elected a California Supreme Court justice for one of the truncated, three-year terms prescribed by the state's new constitution. At the end of his term, Ross was reelected for a full term of twelve years. After considering resignation in 1884 or early 1885, Ross was persuaded by a strong showing of public support to continue in office for another year. Then, despite a petition signed by more than one hundred leaders of the bar urging him not to step down, he announced his resignation effective October 1, 1886. Ross's reasons for relinquishing his seat on the state Supreme Court remain unclear. Even years after his resignation, Ross offered only that he resigned for "several good and substantial reasons." Two theories are plausible. One is that Ross left the court to take a more lucrative position in private practice. This theory does not seem entirely persuasive, given that Ross practiced law for no more than a year, taking a seat on the federal district court in 1887. The more likely reason for Ross's resignation is that he stepped down to move his sickly wife and child to the warmer climate of southern California.[37]

Ross's resignation from the California Supreme Court made him a tempting candidate for President Grover Cleveland to appoint to the judgeship for California's southern district. J. D. Bicknell, a distinguished Los Angeles lawyer whom Ross himself had recommended for the judgeship, was the early front-runner for the position, but friends of Ross enthusiastically pressed his nomination with the president and with Justice Field, who retained some influence in questions of California judicial politics. Francis G. Newlands, a lawyer in San Francisco and later a Nevada representative to Congress, for instance, sent a telegram to Justice Field on December 10, 1886, lauding Ross as the best candidate for the district judgeship. Newlands explained that Ross had resigned not from disinterest in public service, but due to his family's health, and he extolled Ross's virtues: "He possesses in an eminent degree the judicial faculty, and in point of character, reputation and general esteem is surpassed by no man in the State." Justice Field's response to the telegram showed that getting Ross nominated would be difficult. He pledged to bring Ross's great merits to President Cleveland's attention, but Field himself was already committed to another candidate. Despite the fact that most of the Democratic organization and California's congressional delegation, including Leland Stanford, had come out for Bicknell, Ross was held in such high esteem that when word of his availability for the district judgeship was made known, dignitaries throughout the state began to communicate their support to the Democratic administration. But it was no sure thing that Ross would accept the nomination if it were offered. Newlands telegraphed Ross's friend James de Barth Shorb: "Have received telegram that President has offered position to Ross. See him immediately & urge acceptance answer."[38] Though met with surprise by the press, the appointment of Ross was praised, and he earned a national reputation as district judge by his handling of several important cases. Most notable among these were his decisions in one of the 1894 Pullman strike cases and in the case of *Chum Shang Yuen*. This latter case led to a spat between Ross and Attorney General Richard Olney over whether the Justice Department would enforce the Chinese Exclusion Act, and it marked Ross as very strict on the issue of Chinese exclusion.[39]

When Congress established the third judgeship for the Ninth Circuit in 1895, therefore, Ross seemed an obvious candidate for elevation. Even after his appointment to the circuit court of appeals bench in early 1895, Ross well exemplified the flexibility in roles performed by federal judges in this era. The creation of circuit courts of appeals did not lead immediately to specialization of the federal judiciary. Ross, for instance, continued to hear trials regularly for more than a decade after becoming circuit judge. Indeed, he rendered some of his most important trial court rulings *after* his elevation, including his decision to strike down as unconstitutional California's irrigation law in *Bradley v. Fallbrook Irrigation District*, and his ruling to reject the United States government's suit to collect on the bond of Leland Stanford's estate in *United States v. Stanford*. Ross's handling of these cases more than validated his excellent reputation as a judge.[40]

The elevation of Ross brought the Ninth Circuit's contingent of circuit judges to three for the first time. But within two years, politics intervened to disrupt the court's composition and to present an intriguing circumstance that determined the career paths of two Ninth Circuit judges, Ross and McKenna. After McKinley won the 1896 election, he persuaded Joseph McKenna to relinquish a life-tenured judgeship on the Ninth Circuit to become attorney general. McKenna and McKinley had formed a warm friendship during their joint service on the House Ways and Means Committee during the 1880s. McKenna, touted as a possible secretary of the interior or attorney general, was prepared to accept either of the two positions. In the wake of a spirited controversy between Catholics and non-Catholics a few years earlier over the interior secretary's administration of Indian schools, McKenna's Catholicism aroused some opposition to the post at the Department of the Interior. McKinley shrewdly named McKenna for the top spot at the Justice Department, thus nullifying the religious issue.[41] President McKinley announced this appointment in February of 1897, a full month before he himself was to take the oath of office. Not insensitive to the political patronage involved, McKenna announced that he would delay submitting his resignation to prevent President Cleveland from filling his Ninth Circuit seat with a Democrat. McKenna did, however, publicly hint that he favored William Morrow for elevation to his seat on the Ninth Circuit when it became available.[42]

McKenna's appointment to the Cabinet was generally greeted with favor among Californians, who were proud to have their state represented for the first time in a president's Cabinet. Once ensconced in the office of attorney general, McKenna established a hearty work ethic that usually met with approval. He was regarded by the media as something of an anomaly—a Cabinet officer who rode his bicycle to work. "There is something quite interesting in the spectacle of an Attorney-General of the United States, a man of the greatest dignity and learning, scudding about at dewy morn on a racing-machine; but the interest grows to wonder when it is noted that he is quite capable of going along without using his handlebars!" McKenna frequently took lunch at his desk, one hand on his sandwich and the other on a book, much to the consternation of subordinates in the Department of Justice who struggled to keep pace. "'It is rather a wonder to me,'" one such official reportedly said, "'that he does not sleep in his office.'"[43]

Perhaps it was this dedication to hard work and physical fitness that enabled McKenna to enjoy a lengthy career, which reached a higher station when Justice Field finally announced his retirement. During the election year of 1896, Field had begun to intimate that he was ready to step down from the Supreme Court. A feud between Field and President Cleveland, however, led the justice to remain on the bench until a new president took office. Field's well-known intransigence may have prevented Ross's elevation to the Supreme Court, for the young California judge was widely rumored to be Cleveland's first choice. Field held on, however, despite Justice Harlan's by now legendary visit to persuade him to step down. During 1897, the justices had huddled to devise a way to persuade their enfeebled colleague to resign. They drafted Justice John M. Harlan to remind Field of the time he had gone to Justice Robert Cooper Grier to persuade him to step down. They hoped a retelling of the story would drive the hint home to Field that he should retire. When Harlan finished, Field burst out: "'Yes! And a dirtier day's work I never did in my life!'"[44]

Field's resistance weakened when the new president took office. In April of 1897, a month after the inauguration, Field privately communicated to the new president his plans to retire on December 1 of that year. Regional politics caused a buildup of pressure to fill the Supreme Court vacancy with another Californian. Thus Field's decision to resign while McKinley, and not Cleveland, was president opened the way for the appointment of the Republican McKenna. The California judiciary's leading Democrat, Erskine Ross, had missed his first opportunity for elevation to the Supreme Court. Ross was held in such esteem, however, that he also received prominent mention as a successor to Justice Rufus Peckham twelve years later.[45]

McKinley's nomination of McKenna to the Supreme Court sparked fierce opposition. His religious faith was one impediment, given the prevalence of anti-Catholicism in the late nineteenth century. A number of citizens from Maine, for example, presented petitions to their senators urging the president not to name McKenna as a successor to Field. These petitions contained inflammatory language:

> [T]here is now one Roman Catholic Judge upon the Supreme Bench of the United States; and whereas, the appointment of another papist will give the papist[s] two ninths of the members of said court, when they have but proximately one ninth of the population of the United States; and whereas, all papists owe their first and highest allegiance under the canon law, which is an article of their religious faith and binding upon their consciences under the penalties of their Church, which in all cases involving a conflict between their Church and the State, compels their obedience to the Supreme Pontiff and not to the Constitution of the United States and the laws of the land.[46]

President McKinley had attempted to insulate himself somewhat from anti-Catholic opposition by announcing from the outset of his campaign that he intended to represent all Americans, Protestant and Catholic alike. Such statements, however, failed to deter anti-Catholics from opposing McKenna's appointment to the Supreme Court.[47]

A second impediment to McKenna's elevation was more difficult to overcome: the candidate's detractors questioned his competence for the job. Instead of rallying behind their former colleague, both of McKenna's Ninth Circuit brethren opposed the appointment. Despite press reports that the nominee would easily be confirmed, Gilbert led an attack on McKenna in a futile attempt to prevent confirmation. The recognized ringleader of the McKenna protests, Gilbert went so far as to present a petition advocating the nominee's rejection by the Senate. Other prominent Oregonians signed the petition, including Judge Charles B. Bellinger of the United States District Court and a number of state judges.[48] Firsthand experience as McKenna's colleague sparked Gilbert's animus. In nearly five years' service with McKenna on the Ninth Circuit, Gilbert had had numerous opportunities to see firsthand the quality of Judge McKenna's mind and character. In his view, both came up lacking.[49]

He was more circumspect than Gilbert, but Ross too favored Senate rejection of McKenna, though he knew it was unlikely. Whether because he harbored a lingering resentment at his own lost opportunity or because he genuinely believed that McKenna was ill suited to the task, Ross indiscreetly shared his views with the press. "'I do not know of any concerted action to defeat his confirmation in the event he is appointed,'" Ross told them. "'But attorneys generally who are acquainted with Judge McKenna as a rule do not think the appointment is a wise one. He is not competent.'"[50] Unlike Gilbert, however, Ross did not actively lobby against the nomination.

Opposition to McKenna's appointment was marked; the daily San Francisco newspapers throughout early December, 1897, printed seemingly every rumor about his Supreme Court prospects. This intense press attention partly reflected the rivalry between California and Oregon. The California papers also perceived that the Oregon protest was animated by state jealousy. Although this opposition did not seriously threaten McKenna's promotion, the Senate delayed confirming him until January of 1898. The *San Francisco Call* confidently took credit for holding off McKenna's enemies and for preserving the appointment to the high court: "It is apparent that *The Call* has turned the attack on Judge McKenna and that its promoters are in retreat." McKenna was confirmed by the Senate on January 21, 1898, with opposition coming only from Senator William V. Allen, the populist from Nebraska, "whose hand seems to be against all men who do not believe in his peculiar doctrines."[51] McKenna served on the Supreme Court until his retirement on January 5, 1925, his long service overshadowed by the brilliance of colleagues such as Justices Harlan, Brewer, Holmes, and Brandeis. He died November 21, 1926.

IV. MORROW'S ELEVATION

The year before his appointment to the Supreme Court, McKenna's promotion to President McKinley's cabinet opened up a seat on the Ninth Circuit that was filled by McKenna's own choice, William W. Morrow, the United States district judge for the northern district of California. Born near Milton, Indiana, on July 15, 1843, Morrow was nine when his father died. In 1856 his mother apparently left their farm in Illinois, where the family had moved, to return alone to North Carolina to tend an inherited plantation. Three years later, at age sixteen, Morrow immigrated to California and settled in Santa Rosa, where he taught school and studied law. With the outbreak of the Civil War, Morrow made his way back east, for reasons that are somewhat obscure. According to one biographer, Morrow enlisted in the Union Army in

1862 and was attached to the Army of the Potomac. During his service there he was detailed to the office of the secretary of the treasury, where he served until the end of the war. Another biographer posits that Morrow went east during the first month of 1863 with the intention of attending college. While visiting Washington he was appointed by Secretary Salmon P. Chase to a position in the Treasury Department that he held for two years. During this time he also joined a local military unit and took part in army maneuvers near Washington. In January, 1865, he was appointed by the secretary of the treasury as a special agent carrying five million dollars to San Francisco.[52]

Regardless of Morrow's motivations for heading east, the Civil War undoubtedly had a major impact on him. Like many other families, the Morrows were deeply divided by the great issues posed by the conflict. As a young man in Illinois, Morrow became a devoted follower of Abraham Lincoln in spite of his mother's ties to the Confederacy. When the South seceded, Mrs. Morrow still lived in North Carolina. During the war Morrow attempted to get her through military lines, even going so far as to obtain a special pass from President Lincoln, but she apparently never received it and never saw her son again. In 1875, Morrow visited her grave in North Carolina and erected a monument to her memory. While there, he met up with a man who seemed to know a great deal about Morrow's maternal relatives. When they finally introduced themselves, the man said, " 'Why I used to belong to you.' " In her last will and testament Mrs. Morrow had left her slaves to her anti-slavery son. Morrow's reaction to the bequest is unknown, but it was starkly at odds with his Republican values.[53]

After the war Morrow returned to California. In 1870 he became the assistant United States attorney for California, a post he held for four years. In 1884 he was elected to Congress as a Republican from San Francisco and served three full terms, from March 4, 1885, to March 4, 1891. Intent on resuming the private practice of law after his congressional service ended, Morrow entered a partnership with Frederick S. Stratton, a union that lasted less than a year before Ogden Hoffman's death opened up the district judgeship in San Francisco. As district judge, Morrow earned a reputation for honesty and forthrightness on the bench, and, like Ross, Morrow presided over a difficult case that arose out of the famous Pullman strike of July, 1894. In the law of conspiracy this case, *United States v. Cassidy*, was important because it applied the rule that each person who furthers an unlawful scheme becomes a member of the conspiracy even if the person's role is a subordinate one or is executed at some distance from the other conspirators. Even three decades later, the charge to the jury in *Cassidy* was reputed to be the longest ever in a criminal case in the United States.[54]

Unlike his predecessor, Joseph McKenna, who had been somewhat reclusive and single-minded in his pursuit of work, Morrow was active in a number of political and civic roles. He helped incorporate the American Red Cross and held the presidency of its California branch. After the San Francisco earthquake of 1906, the national committee of the Red Cross commended him for distinguished service. Morrow was also a committed internationalist, serving as a trustee of the Carnegie Institution after 1900. He frequently gave speeches in various parts of the country on a wide range of international and domestic topics, and he won deep friendships through his involvement in noble causes, which he pursued with zeal and political savvy. As a judge, Morrow was very much the conservative, "leaning rather toward precedent than toward experimentation, and choosing the tried and beaten paths of conservatism rather than those which lead into unexplored fields." Morrow's long and distinguished career on the Ninth Circuit ran from 1897 to his retirement in 1923.[55]

These disparate origins shaped the values of the early Ninth Circuit judges—values that guided their judicial work. As succeeding chapters will seek to demonstrate, commonalities and differences in their backgrounds offer a reference point for evaluating their judicial philosophies and work together on the court. The Civil War, for example, affected far more than the individual personal circumstances in the early lives of Gilbert, Ross, and Morrow; arguably, it shaped their respective views about the function of the national government in a growing country and the evolution of federal-state relations. Perhaps because Morrow and Ross shared the experience of a district judgeship, they reviewed trial decisions much less deferentially at the appellate level than did Gilbert, who was appointed to the Ninth Circuit directly from private practice. Morrow tended to scrutinize trial decisions less critically than Ross, but he too occasionally fired off lengthy critiques of trial court proceedings. The political careers of Morrow and McKenna made them sensitive to public opinion, though never beyond the basic constraints inherent in their judicial role. Indeed, Morrow's political savvy and the understanding of the Southern mindset he had gained from his mother may have been crucial in keeping the court from rupturing under the competing influences of Ross and Gilbert, two men whose judicial philosophies were as different as the political sympathies of their families. Over the course of the next three decades, Ross and Gilbert were to disagree on issues large and small, and the outcomes of cases often depended on who sat on the panel with them.

Although McKenna was the first judge to be appointed to the Ninth Circuit after the creation of the circuit courts of appeals, his five-year tenure did not suffice to make a lasting impact on the court as an institution. The real stalwarts of the Ninth Circuit's early decades were Gilbert, Ross, and Morrow, each of whom served for more than twenty years and dedicated the bulk of his legal career to the court.[56] The longevity of these three jurists contributed greatly to the early development of the Ninth Circuit and provided stability in the handling of the court's work. From the 1890s to the 1920s (in Gilbert's case, to 1931), these judges laid a solid foundation for the court's jurisprudence in a rapidly changing West. During this period the court rendered judgments on a variety of key issues, from the consolidation of the railroads and the enforcement of anti-Chinese immigration laws to mining and the use of public lands. From its inception, the court faced a variety of difficult cases, the successful handling of which contributed to western development.

TWO

Railroads, Robber Barons, and the Saving of Stanford University

Stanford's testimony . . . convicts him of having been the most conspicuous criminal of the Century.

Lewis D. McKisick to Holmes Conrad, Dec. 10, 1895

Within five years of its creation, the court was presented in 1895 with a case of enormous and multifaceted dimensions: *United States v. Stanford*. The holding of the case established the liability of the railroad magnates, or "robber barons," who had reaped enormous profits from United States government subsidies for the unpaid loans of the railroad they owned, the Central Pacific Railroad Company. At a deeper level, the case illuminated the interplay between key government actors and railroad interests in influencing the course of litigation. It also provided a first comprehensive look at the court's internal procedures and the jurisprudence of two Ninth Circuit judges whose views would clash for three decades: William B. Gilbert and Erskine Ross. At the trial and appellate stages, these two jurists decided the case in favor of Mrs. Jane Stanford on grounds her attorneys did not argue. Her victory saved a fledgling university, Leland Stanford Junior University, which would not have survived if the government had prevailed.

Although the case did not have a significant effect on the development of law, it bears detailed attention for several reasons. First, the outcome of the case saved one of the most important institutions in the West, Stanford University. At a social level, the case highlights the importance of judicial decisions even when those decisions do not have long-lasting legal significance. Scholars of legal history often overlook the significance of judicial decisions that do not bear on the evolution of the law but which nevertheless mark federal judges as important actors in the development of the nation. Indeed, arguably the reason the case had no real precedential value was that the judges who decided it stretched so far to achieve the result they did. Second, the examination of a case as well-documented as this one casts light on how the judicial process operated in the 1890s, from mundane issues of procedure to questions of judicial ethics. Finally, the case illustrates the flexibility in roles performed by federal judges in this era. The assignments of judges that seemed natural in 1895 would have been totally contrary to administrative principles in practice four decades later.

I. BUILDING THE TRANSCONTINENTAL RAILROAD

The Civil War provided the crucial impetus for breaking a decision-making logjam over the construction of a transcontinental railroad. Although Congress had recognized its necessity for over a decade, squabbling between northerners and southerners over the preferred transcontinental route had impeded national legislation to assist private construction efforts. The secession of the southern states freed Congress to legislate the now urgently needed development of the northern route. In 1862 a detailed statute created the Union Pacific Railroad Company and conferred land-grant and bond subsidies to the Union Pacific and other railroad companies that participated in the construction of the route. This statute named the incorporators of the Union Pacific, spelled out its powers and functions, charted its organizational structure, and directed the time and place of its meetings. In addition, it specified detailed operating procedures for the other participating railroads, including rights of way, materials for construction, collection of subsidy bonds and patenting of land grants, and repayment of debts incurred by the railroads on the bonds.[1]

Congress entrusted construction to the Union Pacific for the eastern portion of the transcontinental route, which stretched from the Nebraska Territory to an unspecified point near the western boundary of Nevada. The Central Pacific Railroad Company, a corporation formed under California law, was to build the western segment, from San Francisco to the California-Nevada boundary and beyond until the railroads met. The 1862 statute recognized that the Central Pacific was "a corporation existing under the laws of the State of California," but it nonetheless provided that the Central Pacific should receive the same subsidy bonds and land grants "upon the same terms and conditions, in all respects, as are contained in this act for the construction of [the Union Pacific] line."[2]

The participating railroads received loans at 6 percent interest in the form of subsidy bonds for each mile of track completed: $16,000 per mile for the line west of the Sierra Nevada, $48,000 per mile for 150 miles through the Sierra Nevada, and $32,000 per mile for the sector east of the mountainous part. To induce speedy construction, Congress authorized loan payment on completion of each forty-mile segment of track. Over the course of its construction efforts, the Central Pacific received vast land grants and loan subsidies totaling $27,855,680. With interest at maturity, the Central Pacific's total indebtedness reached $60 million. Although historians have made much of the economic benefit conferred on the railroads by the land-grant policy, at least one economic historian has calculated that in real terms the loan subsidies brought twice as much aid to the Central Pacific as the land grant did.[3]

The 1862 statute also established the corporate bases of liability for loan repayment. Section 5 provided that "the Secretary of the Treasury shall . . . secure the repayment to the United States . . . of the amount of said bonds so issued . . . together with all interest thereon which shall have been paid by the United States." It authorized the government to secure repayment by holding a "first mortgage on the whole line of the railroad and telegraph, together with the rolling stock, fixtures and property of every kind and description, and in consideration of which said bonds may be issued." Congress empowered the secretary of the treasury to take possession of any railroad that defaulted on its bonds.[4]

Questions of repayment and liability, however, received little attention in the early days of construction. The four key shareholders of the Central Pacific—Leland Stanford, Collis Huntington, Mark Hopkins, and Charles Crocker—achieved considerable renown, being called "the Associates" or "the Big Four." As their designated foreman, Crocker, scouted to find adequate crews to lay track, the Big Four struggled to keep their investment viable. After months of negligible progress, Crocker began to use Chinese laborers. Their efforts succeeded in transforming a losing proposition into a profitable one. All told, thousands of Chinese toiled long hours to build the road. By late 1867, the Central Pacific's segment was approaching the California state line, some 278 miles east of Sacramento. The Central Pacific added 362 miles of track in 1868 and pushed into Utah early the following year. The Central Pacific and Union Pacific celebrated their link-up by driving a golden spike at Promontory Point, Utah, on May 10, 1869.[5]

Almost from the very beginning, legal controversies plagued the Union Pacific and Central Pacific railroads. Because the subsidies and land grants vested upon the completion of segments of track, the railroads received public funds before the line was finished. At an early stage, the government and the railroads clashed over payment of interest on the subsidy bonds, due semi-annually. The secretary of the treasury contended that the railroads owed the interest when it came due; the railroads interpreted the 1862 statute as amended in 1864 to require repayment of principal and interest upon expiration of the thirty-year loan period. Notwithstanding an official opinion from the attorney general validating the treasury secretary's view, Congress passed an appropriations bill requiring the secretary to pay out money withheld from the railroads for nonpayment of the interest.[6]

Throughout the 1870s and 1880s, scandals involving the Union Pacific and Central Pacific inspired concern in Congress over repayment of the subsidy bonds. As a government-created corporation, the Union Pacific received the most attention, but the Central Pacific did not escape scrutiny. In 1887 Congress established the Pacific Railway Commission to investigate wrongdoing by the railroads. The commission found plenty. It reported that the Central Pacific had defrauded the United States government, violated "[n]early every obligation which these corporations assumed under the laws of the United States," and "impelled the people of [California] to adopt amendments to the State constitution regulating railroads and creating a State commission to protect shippers against the discriminations of the Central Pacific Company." When the commission sought to compel Leland Stanford to answer questions or submit data, his close friend Justice Stephen Field held in the circuit court that such an investigation unconstitutionally invaded the power of the judiciary, states' rights, and Stanford's personal rights.[7]

By the 1890s, as the first of the subsidy bonds neared maturity, public attention focused anew on the railroads' liability for these loans. President Cleveland's administration expressed little interest in pursuing repayment from the two great railroads. In any event, by the middle of the decade both of them were either in receivership or on the verge of bankruptcy.[8] The shareholders of these behemoths, however, enjoyed great wealth and power, having stripped the companies of assets through payments of large dividends. For the Union Pacific this fact brought little solace. The 1862 statute incorporating the Union Pacific contained no provision holding shareholders liable for the corporation's unpaid debts in proportion to their number of shares. As a creature of California law, the Central Pacific seemingly stood in a different position. To the modern lawyer, schooled in the general principle that shareholders have limited liability for a corporation's debts, this rule may appear to defeat the purpose of incorporation. In the late nineteenth century, however, the rule of limited shareholder liability was not universal, and California was a very important exception.[9] In its original constitution of 1849, California law provided that "[e]ach stockholder of a corporation or joint-stock association shall be individually and personally liable for his proportion of all its debts and liabilities."[10] For the government to succeed in the *Stanford* suit, then, it would have to convince the courts that the California law applied, and the Central Pacific shareholders were liable for the company's debts.

By the mid-1880s, published reports of the Big Four's ostentatious lifestyle increased the attractiveness of pursuing the shareholder-liability theory. Former Governor and at that time United States Senator Leland Stanford lived particularly well, much to the chagrin of his partner Collis Huntington, who sought to shield the Big Four's personal wealth from the view of Congress and the public. In 1886, Stanford shattered Huntington's carefully crafted myth of the robber barons' poverty, when he announced the founding of Leland Stanford Junior University. This large endowment suggested that the Central Pacific stockholders had the financial means to repay the loans. Huntington viewed the gift with contempt, repeatedly referring to it as "Stanford's circus." When the benefactor died unexpectedly on June 20, 1893, reports that he had left an estate estimated at between $35 and $75 million combined with the current severe economic downturn to fuel demands that the government press its claims.[11]

The issue divided Congress. Senator George F. Hoar of Massachusetts introduced a resolution on June 8, 1894, directing the Judiciary Committee to inquire whether the government's claim against the Stanford estate "should be forthwith relinquished and put at rest." Hoar, whose feelings on the matter were surely influenced by his own service as an overseer of Harvard, believed that a government suit would threaten the existence of the young university, "one of the illustrious examples of munificence and public benefaction." Remarking that Hoar's resolution was "premature," Senator William A. Peffer of Kansas raised the salient political fact that "with millions of our people out of employment and with hundreds and hundreds of thousands of business men upon the verge of bankruptcy, we here in the Senate of the United States should not be talking about releasing a claim against a multi-millionaire's estate." Even given the possible adverse political consequences of Hoar's proposal, however, Attorney General Richard Olney endorsed it. In a letter to Senator Hoar, he wrote: "Whatever money may be due the Government, or might be collected by it at the end of a litigation, will probably be of more use to humanity at large, if applied to the charitable purposes for which Mr. Stanford designed it than if administered by the United States."[12]

Olney made no effort to hide his opinion from the public, which mirrored the divisions in Congress over the propriety of bringing suit. One member of Congress from New England observed that Californians were so angry at the Central Pacific syndicate that they might be willing to dismantle Stanford University to enforce the government's claim. And indeed the *San Francisco Call* demanded that the government follow through: "If the law makes the property of the four members of the syndicate responsible for its obligations, it will be no answer to the Government's suit to plead that part of that property has been put to beneficial uses." The *Call* editorialized that "this claim should be made, and its rightfulness determined." The newspaper advanced the "moral rather than [the] pecuniary grounds" of this position:[13]

> [I]t is of less importance to the people of the United States that this debt should be collected than it is that notice should be served that men shall not make free with public money and escape with the plunder. The people of the United States cannot afford to let a record be made that if a man gets hold of enough he may hold it in spite of court and Congress. . . . It is not well to establish loose precedents. The case of four rich but insolvent men has attracted the attention of the civilized world. People abroad do not understand how such things can be.[14]

While, during the summer of 1894, the public continued to debate the merits of bringing a suit, a group of senators prepared legislation to compel the attorney general to institute an action. Senator David B. Hill of New York introduced a bill requiring Olney to prosecute a suit "as rapidly as the interests of justice will permit." Even though Congress never passed the bill, the momentum to file suit built up. But it was not until the first of the bonds became due, in January of 1895, that the Justice Department's lawyers could initiate suit.[15]

II. THE GOVERNMENT'S SUIT

By early 1895, Justice Department lawyers had ruled out bringing suit against the Central Pacific itself, since they believed that the railroad lacked sufficient funds to pay the estimated $60 million judgment sought by the government. Of the Big Four, Crocker and Hopkins had already died and their estates had been distributed; Stanford's estate was still intact, and Huntington was still alive. Why the Justice Department elected to pursue the Stanford estate rather than the last living Central Pacific magnate remains a mystery, though Huntington's presence must have played a role. The most cunning of the four, Huntington had long been the leader of the Central Pacific. He reportedly had invested over $1 million to ensure the support of Congress for his various schemes.[16] Whether Huntington influenced Olney and the members of Congress, who in turn pressured the attorney general, or whether Huntington simply intimidated them, the government's decision to sue Jane Stanford as executrix of Stanford's estate freed Huntington from the expense of defending the suit. It also may have made the task more difficult. By going after a sympathetic widow who was struggling to keep a university afloat, the government lost the public sympathy it might have gained by pursuing a robber baron.

Accurately anticipating that the Stanford estate would refuse to pay on the claim, Olney appointed Judge Lewis D. McKisick as special counsel to prosecute the suit. McKisick had earned his honorific as a member of the Tennessee Commission of Appeals and later as a special judge of that state's Supreme Court. He moved to California in 1879 and soon gained a reputation as one of the best lawyers in the state. United States Attorney Henry S. Foote, whose later correspondence would cast serious doubt on his enthusiasm for the task, joined McKisick in preparing the government's case. If the Justice Department had been half-hearted in its effort to pursue litigation against the Stanford estate thus far, the appointment of McKisick represented a clear change in zeal. On March 15, 1895, the former judge filed the government's claim for $15,237,000 in the United States circuit court for the northern district of California.[17]

Jane Stanford well understood the threat presented by the complaint. An adverse decision would render her unable to sustain support payments for Stanford University, and the life of the institution would be in jeopardy. She put together a first-class legal team to defend the suit. Her lead counsel was a former justice on the Nevada Supreme Court, John Garber, of Garber, Boalt and Bishop. Russell J. Wilson and Mountford S. Wilson served as co-counsel, as did F. E. Spenser, who bore "a most striking resemblance to Justice Field." Russell J. Wilson filed one general and five special demurrers to the complaint on May 6, 1895, in an attempt to block the suit. The common-law demurrer pleading had the practical effect of denying the legal sufficiency of the complaint. Jane Stanford's lawyers based the demurrer on two theories: first, that neither Stanford nor his wife ever owed the amount demanded by the United States; and, second, that the suit failed because the government had never redeemed the bonds.[18]

A large crowd gathered at the Appraisers' Building in San Francisco on June 3, 1895, "in anticipation of oratorical efforts to be made" in the *Stanford* case. Judge Joseph McKenna disappointed the assemblage. He took the bench only to declare that he would not be hearing the case and to postpone it for "some judge" to hear. He did not explain that he had recused himself, but the onlookers learned through the court grapevine that McKenna and Leland Stanford had been close friends and that the senator had named the judge as a trustee of his estate. Although McKenna had resigned as trustee, "he felt a natural and commendable delicacy about sitting in a case where a decision in favor of the government would undoubtedly destroy the institution." McKenna's service in the circuit court as trial judge was not unusual. Until 1911, when Congress abolished the circuit courts and merged their original jurisdiction with that of district courts, the circuit judges appointed to the circuit courts of appeals routinely tried cases in the circuit courts.[19] After enactment of the Judicial Code of 1911, circuit judges tried cases in district courts and district judges sat on appellate panels with decreasing frequency.

Judge Erskine Ross replaced McKenna and on June 5, 1895, began to hear argument on the demurrers. Ross had been elevated to the appellate bench from the district court in southern California only two weeks before the government filed suit. Although he was junior to William B. Gilbert, the third circuit judge in the Ninth Circuit, Ross had a wealth of trial experience. His assignment to the circuit court for the *Stanford* case thus represented a sensible division of judicial labor, even if it foreclosed him from sitting on the panel for the almost-certain appeal in the case.[20] If the expected appeal occurred, Gilbert would preside over a panel with two district judges sitting by designation. These designations, which date from the first session of the court in 1891, formed an important staffing component of the circuit court of appeals during its first half-century. Panels composed of circuit judges were the most common, but district judges sat by designation much of the time.[21] This use of judicial personnel in the *Stanford* case theoretically meant that two district judges could reverse, over the dissent of one circuit judge, the trial decision of another circuit judge.

Such hypothetical outcomes seemed remote at the hearing in the circuit court. As counsel for the moving party on the demurrer, Garber spoke first. He spent an entire day developing his argument that Congress had not intended under the 1862 statute to create a personal agreement or liability on the part of the railroads' shareholders to pay the bonds. As an alternative position, Garber maintained that Stanford was liable under California law only for that portion of the Central Pacific debts incurred in California: action by the California corporation outside the state would be *ultra vires*, and thus outside the power authorized by law. After making this point, which rested on state law, however, Garber confusingly referred back to the 1862 congressional statute. A legal commentator berated the argument as "weak, rambling and inconclusive—the work of an evidently overrated lawyer."[22]

The local press was as critical of McKisick as the lawyer had been of Garber: "Judge McKisick open[ed] with an assortment of hard dry statement[s], utterly unpalatable to the few laymen present and not particularly refreshing to the assembled bar." The report continued in a similar vein: "Long passages from longer acts were read and deftly dovetailed with the theories of attorneys and the opinions of courts until everybody but the attorneys actually engaged were in more or less of a muddle on the entire proposition." McKisick's argument was that California law imposed liability on shareholders for a corporation's debts in the proportion to which they held stock ownership. Under this theory, the Stanford estate owed one-quarter of the debt issued to the Central Pacific. The legal observer who faulted Garber was not alone in his appreciation of McKisick's skill. Word quickly spread that "'McKisick is making a strong argument' [and t]he courthouse soon filled with attentive listeners; for lawyers like to hear a good argument in a great case." The gathered assemblage rewarded McKisick with an ovation at the close of his argument.[23]

Throughout these two days of argument, "Judge Ross sat unmoved as granite. Not a word dropped from his lips, nor an expression of his face, could be read as indicating what impressions the argument was making upon his mind." This imperturbable countenance reflected no lack of comprehension. Blessed with a razor-sharp intellect, he handed down a detailed decision a mere three weeks later. "[O]ne of the most capable and upright jurists who has ever adorned the wool sack of the State or Federal courts," Ross delivered his opinion sustaining the defendant's demurrer from the bench. It ran to some 13,000 words and paid Garber's argument "the left-handed compliment of deciding in favor of the demurrant on a ground neither raised by the demurrer nor discussed by Judge Garber in argument." Judge Ross focused almost entirely on the relevant provisions of California state corporation law, rejecting arguments that the issue required close analysis of the 1862 congressional statute.[24]

His opinion rested on four propositions. First, Ross wrote that statutory, and not common, law created individual liability of stockholders for corporate debts; he then analyzed California state law and determined that stockholders were not individually liable. Second, he interpreted a California Supreme Court decision as rendering nugatory the provision of the California constitution that assessed individual liability for corporate debt in the proportion of stock ownership. Third, Ross deemed California's general corporate statute invalid for vagueness, because it did not definitely assess liability on individual stockholders. "It is manifest," he said, "that the declaration that the stockholder is liable for all the debts and liabilities of the corporation 'in proportion to the amount of stock by him held' does not establish any rule by which any definite liability can be fixed." Finally, he held that the contract between the United States government and the railroad companies excluded any option for the government to seek indemnity from stockholders for the railroad companies' debts. Of this last proposition Ross observed that the congressional statute "embodying the contract" should speak to the question, yet he determined that the statute, though "drawn with great care, . . . is not as explicit as it should have been." Ross concluded that the statute contained no "absolute, unqualified promise to repay the bonds" and that Stanford thus assumed "no personal obligation . . . to repay them."[25]

III.   THE NINTH CIRCUIT DECISION

Ross's decision elicited a letter from Jane Stanford, who conveyed her gratitude with these words: "God in His mercy ruled that a just and righteous judge should pronounce judgment and you have graciously done more for me than save millions; you have by this decision vindicated the honor of my husband, the father of my sainted son—which is more precious to me than untold gold." The government's counsel saw it differently. Lewis McKisick fired off a spirited letter to Judson Harmon, Olney's replacement as attorney general, attacking the "lame and impotent conclusion that under the Constitution and laws of the State, the complainants have no remedy against the stockholders." With great care,

McKisick laid out precisely why he believed that Ross had misinterpreted California law. "By a bald assumption the Judge [had] confounded" the appropriate principle. "I say to you that the counsel for Mrs. Stanford were as much surprised at the result as I was, for Judge Garber did not argue that if there were a debt owing by the corporation, the stockholder was not liable for his proportion; on the contrary he admitted that he was, but did argue that he was only liable under" California law "for the reason no doubt that he wanted to avail himself of the increase of the capital stock to 1,000,000 shares." Accordingly, McKisick recommended that the Justice Department permit the bill to be dismissed and then to appeal the decision, even though Ross had given leave to amend. The judge's "error is so manifest that I doubt if the Circuit Court of Appeals will affirm the judgment, even without argument."[26]

A careful analysis of Ross's opinion that supported McKisick's assessment appeared in the well-respected *American Law Review* a few months later. "In a square, manly way," wrote the *San Francisco Call*, Seymour D. Thompson picked apart the circuit court judgment. "Judge Ross stands high in the professional and public estimation on the Pacific Coast. We share in that estimate of his character and talents. We have often had occasion to refer to his decisions in terms of commendation," Thompson wrote. "But we are in this case unable to follow his reasoning to the result which he reaches. We have regarded the question as a very important public question, and one suitable to be discussed in a legal journal. We have, therefore, investigated it with some care, in the light of a collection of rules and principles applied by the courts in determining the liability of stockholders in corporations, which rules and principles are not unfamiliar to us."[27]

Thompson's critique began at first principles. He disagreed with Ross's proposition that statutory law alone created stockholders' individual liability for a corporation's debts. Indeed, the original California constitution, which had been in effect when the Central Pacific incurred the bond obligations, provided for unlimited shareholder liability up to the proportion of stock ownership. Ross had deemed this constitutional provision unenforceable for vagueness under the California Supreme Court's ruling in *French v. Teschemaker*, which had held that section of the state constitution to be non–self-executing. Thompson attacked Ross for relying on this precedent, a decision that was "so extraordinary—so utterly opposed to common sense—that it has not met with much favor in other jurisdictions." Evidently, the California legislature, too, had viewed *French* with disfavor, because it had speedily enacted legislation to restore the rule of proportional shareholder liability for corporate debts. The principle of federal comity to the decisions of state tribunals interpreting state law did not, Thompson asserted, bind the federal courts "to unjust and monstrous results."[28]

Thompson's disagreement with Ross's expression of federal comity in following a state court decision exposed an important facet of Ross's jurisprudence. It also underscored a curious reversal in the continuing debate in legal circles over the exercise of power by federal tribunals. From the Civil War onward, Ross had resisted extensions of federal power into state affairs. The ex-Confederate soldier may have seen in the *Stanford* case an opportunity to chip away at doctrines that supported the discretion of federal courts to ignore state court precedents or to decide questions of state law under general principles.[29] Thompson's long recitation of contrary authority suggested that Ross might easily have devised his own interpretation of California statutory and constitutional law on this issue without following the state Supreme Court. Ross's decision to reject that course evidenced his enduring commitment to limitations on federal incursions into the state sphere. Ironically, the employment of the comity principle to *protect* a corporation and its stockholders departed from the historical circumstances in which the federal courts had extended their power. As corporations became larger and more powerful after the Civil War, they generally supported efforts by federal courts to devise general principles in diversity cases, because adherence to local law fostered uncertainty in interstate business. Consequently, federal courts developed a reputation as allies of big business.[30] Ross's support of corporate interests by resorting to local principles turned the conventional thinking on its head.

On the question of federal comity in adhering to state court precedent, therefore, the decision could have gone either way, as Thompson appeared grudgingly to concede. The commentator refused to grant as much in his third point of criticism: that Ross simply read out of existence the general California railroad statute, which made shareholders liable for corporate debts. Thompson chastised the judge's application of a state Supreme Court precedent to this provision when that decision did not address the salient statute.[31] Although Thompson did not say as much, Ross's reasoning on this issue differed fundamentally from the comity principle he had so carefully followed on the California constitutional question.

Thompson's last point addressed Ross's interpretation of the 1862 statute that established the government's "contract" for the construction of the transcontinental road by the Union Pacific and the Central Pacific. Ross had held that the congressional railroad statutes "unmistakably show that no personal liability of the individual stockholders was contemplated, either by the United States, on the one side, or the railroad companies and their stockholders, on the other side." Thompson reacted with total incredulity: "Lawyers need not be told that when a person gives credit to a corporation whose stockholders are individually liable for its debts, it is not necessary, to enable the creditor to enforce that liability, that either he, or the corporation, or its stockholders, should have *contemplated* such a result at the time when the credit was given." Examination of the "thousands of cases relating to the statutory liability of stockholders" revealed the novelty of Ross's approach: "not one can be found advancing such a doctrine."[32]

The historical justification for Congress's decision to subsidize construction of the railroad was subject to a wide variety of interpretations, as is shown by Thompson's scathing critique. Ross saw the 1862 and 1864 laws as an endeavor to extend public monies to private companies with the aim of advancing public aims. His critic interpreted the history in a much more sinister light:

> If [Judge Ross] had extended his researches downward through that public history, he would have discovered that the four co-adventurers who had received the aid from the government began by swindling the government, through a false representation made to a committee of Congress, as to the distance at which the foot-hills of the Rocky Mountains commenced from the City of Sacramento, out of double the amount of aid per mile that was really due under the terms of the statute, for a considerable number of miles; that they immediately organized an outside corporation composed of themselves, for the purpose of building the road, by contracting with themselves in the form of the railroad corporation, at a price enormously in excess of its real value, paying themselves in the bonds of the United States issued under the statute, and issuing to themselves stock composed of pure water and for which no value was ever paid by them. That they paid themselves thirty-four millions of dollars in dividends upon this stock; that they expended nearly five millions of dollars for purposes which their president, Leland Stanford, refused to disclose on oath, which purposes were not disclosed by any vouchers, and which expenditures a congressional committee reported as having been probably made in influencing legislation. . . . [33]

The truth arguably combined elements of both perceptions. Part of the history, mentioned by neither Ross nor Thompson but nevertheless lurking beneath the surface of the discussion, was the bequest Stanford had made to create the university named for his late son.

For Stanford University officials, the prospect of an appeal threatened disaster. On July 2, 1895, David Starr Jordan, the university's president, wrote to Attorney General Judson Harmon explaining the financial effect continued litigation would have on the institution. In agonizing detail he explained exactly where every penny from the Stanford legacy was needed to finance the university. "Should a decision be delayed long," he assured the attorney general, "the University would be obliged to live within its actual, not its prospective means. In other words it must close its doors and discharge most or all of its Faculty." The Justice Department recognized the university's predicament. It had no interest in unduly delaying the speed of litigation. Indeed, the disposition of the case was remarkably quick, especially considering its great complexity. From the initial filing in March, 1895, the case proceeded through arguments and final disposition at the circuit court, circuit court of appeals, and Supreme Court levels in just under one calendar year. By contrast, during this period the average time for a case to reach final decision in the circuit court of appeals alone was nine months from the date of docketing. Moreover, the Supreme Court at this time still had a backlog of cases.[34]

The Ninth Circuit convened on September 16, 1895, to hear argument in the appeal of Ross's decision. Judge William B. Gilbert of Oregon presided, with District Judges William W. Morrow of California and Thomas Hawley of Nevada sitting by designation. Although the audience was meager, the argument promised to be a good one. The court assented to McKisick's request for an unlimited time for oral presentations, and he began to read from the two-hundred-page book in which he had printed his argument. Delivered in a "quiet conversational tone," McKisick's exhaustive presentation placed heavy emphasis on Ross's alleged error in granting the demurrer for reasons emanating from California law. After dedicating well over half of his argument to an examination of the relevant California legal principles, McKisick developed an interesting argument in equity. If Ross was correct and the United States had no remedy at law, he argued, did it not have a viable remedy in equity? Surely the late railroad magnate owed something to the federal government for the generous loans that had facilitated his accumulation of wealth.[35]

McKisick closed by urging the circuit court of appeals to reconsider Ross's construction of the congressional statutes. The Union Pacific and Central Pacific *were* different types of entities and Congress must have intended to treat them as such. Whereas to the Union Pacific the United States government was both sovereign and creditor, to the Central Pacific it was only a creditor. That is, the United States government had not created the Central Pacific; it had merely lent it money. This detailed analysis, which took McKisick just over a day to deliver, elicited no questions from the bench. The local newspaper, however, reported a feature of the oral argument that differs from modern custom: "The plain level of [McKisick's] reading was occasionally broken into by remarks or questions equally quiet on the part of Judge Garber (representing Mrs. Stanford), which were answered or replied to by Judge McKisick with no change in the tone of voice."[36]

Garber himself, according to Seymour Thompson in his legal commentary, "had his case much better in hand than on his argument before Judge Ross, and it is fair to say that he made an argument worthy of his distinguished reputation." Despite Garber's efforts to advance the circuit court's analysis, McKisick's "powerful and learned argument" forced the appellate court to consider the "only debatable ground in the case": whether Congress, by creating a statutory scheme for the development of a transcontinental railroad, had intended to place the liability of the Central Pacific stockholders on an equal footing with that of the stockholders of the Union Pacific. Garber first addressed Congress's intent in holding the Central Pacific stockholders personally liable. The legislature's treatment of the Union Pacific offered the appropriate guide. The 1862 law that created the Union Pacific contained "no provision whatsoever for any individual liability on the part of the stockholders thereof." Because Congress had conferred the same rights and benefits of construction on the Central Pacific as it had on the Union Pacific, the legislature must have intended to relieve the Central Pacific shareholders of liability for the corporation's debts. The contract between the Central Pacific and the United States government, Garber asserted, was a contract in the fairest sense. It was the government's interest in completing the railroad at the earliest possible date that had inspired the deal. This argument had some persuasive appeal. If the government's aim during the Civil War had been to bridge the gap between the West Coast and the East Coast quickly, it could accomplish that goal either by building the road itself or by providing subsidies to private entrepreneurs willing to undertake the task. According to Garber, the government essentially traded an opportunity to hold the Central Pacific shareholders liable in order to achieve its short-term aim of improving communications and facilitating commerce with the West Coast.[37]

Garber concluded his argument the following day, "a remarkable effort, the two days' talk being made wholly without notes or memoranda, except the citations of law." When McKisick launched his rebuttal, he emphasized the equities on the government's side. In addition to large sums from the federal government, he noted, the railroads had received substantial subsidies from the major cities in California. San Francisco had paid $400,000, Sacramento nearly $300,000, and Santa Clara, San Joaquin, and Placer counties together had contributed hundreds of thousands of dollars more. "What has the appellee brought here? A demurrer supported by a rhetoric so brilliant and scintillating that it has illuminated the darkest continent, gone to Africa, and by a torrent of eloquence that poured out of this temple and resounded through the halls of this building as if a mountain had been lifted." Through his "torrent of eloquence," McKisick undoubtedly hoped to impress upon the judges that they owed the railroad no favors. Notwithstanding the railroads' receivership filings and poverty pleas, the fact remained that government subsidies had contributed substantially to the shareholders' wealth. Now was the time to repay the debt. When McKisick finally closed, Judge Gilbert in his courtly manner advised the litigants that the court would take the matter under "immediate study" and "render a decision as early as possible."[38]

Armed with this array of arguments, the Ninth Circuit might easily have reversed Ross's decision. As trial judge, he had ignored the arguments raised by counsel and devised a new theory of the case. An interested legal commentator had thoroughly criticized Ross's approach, and the government's counsel had comprehensively attacked it. But the circuit court of appeals affirmed. Judge William B. Gilbert wrote for the court, holding that Congress had not intended to impose liability on the Central Pacific stockholders under the contract terms created by the 1862 statute. Gilbert veered away from Ross's heavy reliance on California law and instead emphasized the special status of the Central Pacific under the laws of the United States. Whereas Ross's elaborate treatment of the state issues of corporation law and stockholder liability had been colored by his suspicion of national power, Gilbert took precisely the opposite tack.[39]

Although it might have done so, the Ninth Circuit did not devise its own interpretation of California law and thereby advance the power of the federal judiciary to decide issues involving state statutes. Rather, Gilbert looked to the congressional statutes, which he saw as embodying the "attitude of the United States." He concluded that "it was a matter of indifference to the government whether the Central Pacific Railroad Company or the Union Pacific Railroad Company built the road that was to be aided by the government bonds and subsidy." Premising his conclusion on this "indifference" and on the statute's omission of any imposition of shareholder liability, Gilbert contended that it was "impossible to conceive" that if Congress had "in view the ultimate liability of the stockholders of the Central Pacific Company it would not at the same time have imposed a like liability" on the Union Pacific's stockholders. He concluded that the government had thus "waived" its right to collect from the Central Pacific's shareholders the debts incurred by the company. Gilbert imputed the omission of shareholder liability provisions in the Union Pacific *statute* to the *contract* between the Central Pacific and the United States; he then inferred Congress's intent to waive its rights as a creditor. Gilbert's statutory analysis in this case underscored a wide contrast between his approach and that of Ross, who construed statutes strictly and eschewed attempts to infer congressional intent.[40]

In the *American Law Review*, Seymour Thompson commented that the "opinion of Judge Gilbert cannot be too highly commended as a good piece of literary work, if such an expression can properly be applied to a judicial opinion. It is well constructed, and is reasoned in a manner to make the conclusion very plausible, at least to one who is not well versed in the principles governing the liability of stockholders in corporations." Thompson explained Gilbert's seemingly radical departure from ordinary principles of corporation law, under which a creditor's rights did not depend on *intent* to hold the stockholders liable: "on the contrary, the charter or statute under which the stockholders are individually liable is conclusively deemed in law to enter into and form a part of the contract between the parties."[41]

If Gilbert's rendition of corporate law inspired objections, so too did his approach to statutory construction. He went a long way toward reaching his result through negative inferences and intentions by omission. His theory had a self-contained logic to it, but so did the opposite conclusion. Under an alternate approach, these omissions and inferences might have yielded a completely different outcome. The statutory omission of shareholder liability for the Union Pacific could instead be explained by Congress's control of the appointment of directors and the terms of the corporation's existence. If the Union Pacific acted contrary to Congress's intent, the legislature could then amend the original statutes and direct appropriate action.[42]

Congress had no such control over the Central Pacific, an entity incorporated under California law. If the terms of that railroad's incorporation or its actions raised concern in Congress, the national legislature could not redress the problem by statute. Congress reserved to itself only the right to amend the 1862 statute, which set out the terms of the land grants and subsidy bonds, "at any time, having due regard for the rights of such companies named herein."[43] Thus, Congress could alter the terms of the contract but could not change the Central Pacific as a corporate entity. Accordingly, Congress might well have intended *not* to hold the Union Pacific's shareholders liable for the corporation's debts and yet have retained its option of pursuing the Central Pacific stockholders. Given this view of the congressional legislation, Ross's concentration on the substantive basis for shareholder liability under California law made a great deal of sense, whether or not one agreed with his interpretation of that law.

IV. SAVING STANFORD UNIVERSITY

The day the Ninth Circuit rendered its decision, Lewis McKisick announced the government's intention to appeal to the Supreme Court. Although the special counsel had ably represented the government, now the Justice Department in Washington assumed control over the case. McKisick's post-hoc analysis of the circuit and appellate court opinions to Solicitor General Holmes Conrad fully expressed his bitterness at the judicial results: "The truth is that the decision of the Circuit Court and the Appellate Court, in so far as the law of the case is conserned [*sic*], has met the disapproval of every intelligent lawyer of the State, and has met the approval of only those who sympathize with Mrs. Stanford and with the Stanford University." In representing the estate, John Garber had followed a good strategy in omitting any reference to Leland Stanford's character, because "if he should have done so I should have replied that Stanford's testimony given before the Pacific Railway Commission and contained in the record, when read between the lines, convicts him of systematic corruption, and in fact convicts him of having been the most conspicuous criminal of the Century." Neither side had openly debated the suit's likely effect on the university, but McKisick believed that the "maudlin sentiment . . . manifested in its behalf" may have made a difference. The sixty-seven-year-old lawyer found this mysterious. He considered the university "the most astounding, vulgar, sepulchral monument to Egoism to be found in history, endowed with the largest race horse breeding establishment in the world, and with the largest vineyard in the world where is manufactured every year enough wine and brandy to debauch every misguided youth who attends the races to see the Stanford horses run or trot."[44]

If these sentiments fueled his commitment to the cause, the anger in them did not cloud his ability to analyze the legal problems confronting the department in its appeal to the Supreme Court. McKisick settled into a calmer tone in offering his advice to the solicitor general on how best to prepare. The "rather anomalous condition" of the case before the Court intensified the difficulties of preparation. While the circuit and appellate courts had decided the case on different theories, neither had relied on the arguments made by Mrs. Stanford's counsel. The Supreme Court itself might devise yet another theory. Having invested so much of himself in the case, McKisick relinquished his role with great reluctance: "This is submitted without desiring to thrust myself into the case, but I feel deep interest in it and believe that I am and always have been right."[45]

Beginning on January 28, 1896, the Supreme Court heard argument in the case. McKisick and Garber had been replaced by lawyers of higher official standing, with Assistant Attorney General J. M. Dickinson and Solicitor General Holmes Conrad representing the government, and Joseph H. Choate of New York arguing Jane Stanford's cause. The government's attorneys followed the structure of McKisick's arguments in the courts below. They emphasized Stanford's liability under California law and the irrelevance of congressional statutes in determining the Central Pacific stockholders' liability for the debts incurred by the company. When Conrad concluded, Choate began by "saying the magnitude of the claim was wholly unparalleled." He proceeded to cover the range of possible theories for resolving the case in Mrs. Stanford's favor, from the intent of Congress in forming the contracts with the railroads to the absence of shareholder liability under California law.[46]

On March 2, 1896, the Supreme Court rendered a unanimous decision. Writing for the Court, Justice John M. Harlan affirmed the decision of the Ninth Circuit. With only a few minor embellishments, the Court essentially adopted Gilbert's view that the 1860s statutes did not impose personal liability on the railroad stockholders. Harlan's analysis of congressional intent also mirrored Gilbert's: "[I]t cannot be inferred from the legislation of Congress that it intended, for the protection of the interests of the United States, to impose a heavier liability upon the stockholders of the California company than was imposed upon the stockholders of the Union Pacific Railroad Company. Why should it have so intended? Why should it be supposed that Congress would purposely make it more difficult to construct one part of the proposed national highway than another?" Harlan posed these questions without explaining how the Central Pacific construction effort would have been more difficult if Congress had intended to hold the company's stockholders liable. He then made no effort to offer an objective answer. Instead, the Supreme Court proceeded from premises that, if believed, led inexorably to the result it reached. In this respect, Harlan's opinion was far less impressive analytically than the lower-court opinions by Gilbert and Ross.[47]

For Stanford students, who closely followed the results if not the analysis, the Supreme Court's decision set off a spontaneous celebration. Word of the Court's ruling reached the campus late on the morning of March 2, 1896. Students streamed out of lecture halls at the blaring of horns and train whistles. Undeterred by a steady rain, a thousand students marched excitedly toward the president's house. David Starr Jordan made a half-hearted attempt to urge restraint until the news could be confirmed, but as the throng moved on to the chapel, he was overheard to say, "If it is as we hope, the students are at liberty to paint everything cardinal except the statues in the museum." Appropriately, the sun peeked through in the early afternoon as word spread that the initial rumors had been true. The Supreme Court's ruling saved the university. After years of delay, the assets in Leland Stanford's estate— well over $3 million—were to be distributed to the university.[48]

The potential effects on the university had hovered above the proceedings without playing any official part. Absent from the lawyers' briefs and the judges' opinions was any mention of Stanford's bequest. Yet the beneficence of the gift undoubtedly affected the outcome. The day after the Supreme Court announced its decision, Justice Field, who sat on the case, sent a telegram to Jane Stanford: "Heaven's care and overflowing kindness never fail." The sentiment stemmed from a long-standing friendship between Field and the Stanfords, yet the justice's telegram perhaps gave an appearance of impropriety. According to Field's biographer, "He wrote none of the court opinions, [but he] gave every possible assistance to Mrs. Stanford in protecting her interests." A later attorney general of the United States, Homer Cummings, added to the legend of Field's behind-the-scenes efforts: "Although Justice Field did not sit in the case when it was argued in the circuit court in California, it was said that he consulted with the judge who heard it and that he was responsible for the selection of Joseph H. Choate as Stanford's counsel before the Supreme Court."[49]

Even stronger evidence of the unspoken effect of the bequest on the litigation came from one of the government's lawyers involved in the case. Were it not for McKisick's vigorous prosecution of the government's claim, a letter from United States Attorney Henry S. Foote to Mrs. Stanford would cast serious doubt on the sincerity of the government's effort. Within a week after the Supreme Court's decision, Foote wrote: "Circumstances of course compelled me to appear for the Govt. against you, in your noble and heroic effort to preserve for yourself, and the State of California the University that bears the name of your dear son. . . . But not for one moment . . . had [I] any other feeling than that you ought and would succeed, in preserving to the young men and women now living, and to those yet unborn the blessings entailed by the preservation of the institution so beloved in this State."[50]

The very magnitude of the claim may also have shaped the outcome. The Supreme Court has never again relied on the *Stanford* case, arguably because it departed so far from ordinary principles of law.[51] United States Representative James G. Maguire of San Francisco noted the anomaly created in California's corporations law by the decision, which he summarized as, "in effect, that a stockholder in a corporation under the laws of California is not liable for his proportion of the debts of the corporation unless at the time of the contraction of the debts the creditor had in mind the stockholders' liability and intended to hold them for the debt." Because the Court's judgment appeared to nullify the existing California rules, Maguire bemoaned the fact that cases such as *United States v. Stanford* "have arisen in judicial procedure to obstruct the regular current of decisions, because the failure to apply ordinary rules of construction and decision to them tends to bring our judicial system into disrepute." He believed that the claim's size—$15 million—had distorted the judicial process. Maguire's proposed solution was to divest the courts of jurisdiction to decide any claim above $5 million.[52]

While the generosity of the bequest and the magnitude of the claim may have affected the outcome of the case, a third possible influence was the climate of railroad success in the Ninth Circuit between 1891 and 1906, when nearly one-quarter of all appeals heard by the court involved a railroad. As appellees, railroads prevailed 82 percent of the time over non-railroad appellants. Given the general tendency of appellate courts to affirm, this figure is not altogether surprising: the average rate of affirmance in the Ninth Circuit during this period was 69 percent. When data for the railroads' record as appellant is included, their success before the Ninth Circuit was not markedly better than non-railroad litigants'. As appellant, railroads succeeded 33 percent of the time, as against 31 percent for non-railroad appellants.[53] Whether these figures show the legal correctness of the railroads' contentions, the skill of their lawyers, favoritism by the court, or some subtle combination of all three, they establish that as either appellant or appellee, railroads won their appeals at a higher than average rate. It is untenable to attribute the result in the *Stanford* case to the railroads' general success during this period, but Jane Stanford's good fortune was no surprise in the context of railroad litigation victories.[54]

The *Stanford* case had the highest stakes of any litigation that came before the Ninth Circuit in its first decade of existence. The Supreme Court's decision did not dim the crucial role of the appellate court in constructing the legal framework upon which Justice Harlan's opinion chiefly relied. Through their opinions Judges Ross and Gilbert implanted in the law the seeds of their own views about the power of the central government and the place of states in the federal system. In the *Stanford* case their competing theories achieved the same outcome. In many other cases, it would not. For the next thirty years, Gilbert and Ross clashed frequently on issues ranging from property disputes to search-and-seizure law. The *Stanford* case provided a glimpse of the foundations for their jurisprudence. It also highlighted the extent to which the railroads succeeded in the federal courts. The case presented very complex issues upon which reasonable minds could differ. Yet the government's position secured not a single vote at any of the three levels of the federal judiciary. Even if Foote was something of a quisling to the government's cause, McKisick certainly dedicated great energy to winning the suit; his arguments were thorough and, to many, persuasive. Arguably the guaranteed calamity a government victory would have been to Stanford University contributed to unanimity among the federal judges and justices who decided the case. The legal issues upon which they concurred originated in Congress's Civil War–era goal of building a transcontinental railroad. Another facet of this construction—the use of Chinese laborers—produced legal problems of a different type over the last three decades of the nineteenth century and into the twentieth. Concurrently with its handling of the *Stanford* matter, the newly created circuit court of appeals for the Ninth Circuit was facing a multitude of cases associated with Chinese immigration.

THREE

Testing Tolerance

Chinese Exclusion and the Ninth Circuit

Judge Ross may not be an expert billiard player but he has demonstrated his ability to handle the cues adroitly.

Unattributed newspaper article, scrapbook of Erskine M. Ross

Westerners responded to the massive wave of Chinese immigration in the late nineteenth century by pressing Congress into adopting a series of ever-stricter exclusion laws. In the first decade of exclusion, which began in 1882, the western federal courts did much to protect Chinese litigants from unjust application of the law. After the creation of the circuit courts of appeals in 1891 and the passage of stricter anti-Chinese immigration laws in 1888 and 1892, this somewhat favorable judicial treatment of the Chinese ended. No longer did the western federal courts release hundreds of Chinese on writs of habeas corpus. The Ninth Circuit played the paramount role in adjudicating cases arising under national anti-Chinese laws. The Ninth Circuit may have had a greater impact on the enforcement of anti-Chinese legislation than any other court, arguably including the Supreme Court itself. The court's jurisprudence on exclusion, and its apparent shift from the tendencies of earlier western federal judges, had a direct effect on restricting the arrival of the Chinese during the late nineteenth and early twentieth centuries. A combination of factors produced this result: the altered legal context in which cases arose; the new jurisprudence of judges appointed in the 1890s; and the institutional setting of the circuit court of appeals.

I. THE CHINESE "INFLUX" AND CONGRESS'S LEGISLATIVE REACTION

From the time gold was discovered in California in the 1840s, Chinese immigrated to the West in search of the same riches and employment opportunities that attracted settlers from all over the United States and the rest of the world. After the first three disembarked in February of 1848, the Chinese arrived in ever-growing numbers. By 1850 the census listed 1,000 Chinese immigrants; by 1860, 35,000. By 1880, when the total reached its nineteenth-century peak, more than 100,000 Chinese lived in the United States, almost all of them in the Far West. From the beginning the Chinese suffered numerous indignities at the hands both of white Americans and of other immigrants, indignities that ranged from cruel vigilante justice to harsh municipal ordinances that singled out persons of Chinese descent.[1]

Much of this early "legalized" racism occurred in the mining camps of the Sierra Nevada, where by 1860 nearly two-thirds of all the Chinese in California resided. Part of the intolerance undoubtedly stemmed from competition for ore; part from basic differences in appearance and manner that alienated non-Chinese. Some of it also derived from a crucial difference between the experience of the Chinese and that of other recent arrivals. Having arrived with no intention of returning, the Irish and Germans, Catholics and Protestants, all experienced the displacement and frustration of uprooting their lives on a false promise of hope in a new country. For these groups the bond of a shared fate helped to transcend language and religious barriers. All immigrants suffered the disappointments and harsh realities of mining life, of course, but the psychological impact may well have been less severe for the Chinese, at least in the early years, since most had immigrated with the intention of returning to China. The perception of these differences, real and imagined, hardened in the rough-hewn social organizations that evolved in mining camps. White miners foreclosed the most advantageous opportunities to the Chinese but permitted them second-class status, whether as cooks or as purchasers of purportedly spent claims. Because the Chinese were willing to take on these less-desirable tasks, total exclusion was economically untenable.[2]

As the mines of the Sierra Nevada ceased to yield enough even for those Chinese who lingered to work low-grade sites, a new financial opportunity surfaced with the construction of the transcontinental railroad. The Central Pacific's initial labor problems evaporated when Charles Crocker hired thousands of Chinese who efficiently and economically tunneled mountains and laid track. From a project that seemed destined to ruin the Central Pacific, the road to Promontory Point turned into a major triumph. Impressed by Crocker's success with Chinese construction crews, another of the Big Four, Collis Huntington, decided to use Chinese labor in the 1870s to construct a southern transcontinental railroad through Arizona.[3] Western states also offered the Chinese alternatives to the hard labor associated with mines and railroads: many early Chinese settlers worked in service sectors, including mercantilism, laundries, restaurants, and agricultural produce sales. These opportunities combined with mining booms in the West to lure Chinese immigrants.

Nationwide, the Chinese numbered 105,465 in 1880, 95 percent of whom resided in states or territories that would compose the Ninth Circuit in its 1891 configuration. And there would have been even more had the economic decline of the 1870s not caused significant repatriation. Between 1877 and 1880, the number of Chinese leaving the United States nearly equaled the total arriving. Moreover, those Chinese who remained in the country were increasingly subjected to harsh discrimination on the theory that their willingness to work for lower wages deprived whites of jobs—a complaint that animated anti-Chinese sentiment for the next fifty years. Without empirical data to support or refute this argument, proponents of Chinese immigration struggled unsuccessfully to combat chauvinism.[4] One nineteenth-century description captured the prevailing assessment of the Chinese "problem" and the racist feelings that motivated it:

> As a class, [the Chinese] were harmless, peaceful and exceedingly industrious; but, as they were remarkably economical and spent little or none of their earnings except for the necessaries of life and this chiefly to merchants of their own nationality, they soon began to provoke the prejudice and ill-will of those who could not see any value in their labor to the country.[5]

Californians expressed their resentment of such behavior in a series of discriminatory laws enacted by the state legislature. In 1879, the Golden State went so far as to pass a referendum against Chinese immigration by the overwhelming majority of 154,638 to 883. Anti-Chinese movements also flared up in Nevada and in other communities throughout the West.[6]

With the national economic downturn of the 1870s, these statewide sentiments spread throughout the region, and Congress began to debate the drastic measure of excluding the Chinese from the United States. Business and Protestant clerical interests, who had favored Chinese immigration, began to withdraw their support in the face of fears that China's vast population would migrate en masse to the North American continent. President Rutherford B. Hayes, however, feared that unilateral action by Congress would force an abrogation of preexisting treaty relations with the Chinese and expose American citizens in China to retaliation. In 1880, the United States negotiated a treaty with China to establish terms for regulating future Chinese immigration. Article I provided that "[w]henever in the opinion" of the United States the arrival of Chinese laborers "affects or threatens to affect the interests of that country . . . the Government of the United States may regulate, limit, or suspend such coming or residence, but may not absolutely prohibit it." Upon ratification of the treaty, Congress promptly passed a bill to ban Chinese immigration for twenty-five years, but President Chester A. Arthur vetoed it on the ground that it exceeded the treaty's mandate.[7]

In 1882 the executive and legislative branches compromised to enact the first exclusionary immigration law in the country's history. This statute suspended all immigration of Chinese laborers for ten years and prohibited federal and state courts from admitting any Chinese person to citizenship. By procuring a certificate at the port of departure, Chinese residing in the United States could safely return to their homeland without losing the right to reenter the United States. Congress purported to justify these measures in a cruelly ironic preamble to the law, which declared that the presence of Chinese laborers "endangers the good order of certain localities within the territory thereof." The legislature thus blamed the *victims* for inciting, by their very existence, the anti-Chinese attacks.[8]

Though popular, the 1882 exclusion law proved difficult to administer; charges of corruption, graft, and ease of evasion pervaded the certification process. In response to these complaints and criticisms that the restrictions did not go far enough, Congress enacted further exclusion legislation in 1884. The new law retained the prohibition on citizenship and the suspension on Chinese-laborer immigration, and where the 1882 law excluded unskilled laborers, the 1884 amendment added skilled workers and miners as well. These discriminatory laws fueled vigilantism by whites throughout the West. In the mid-1880s, mass anti-Chinese demonstrations were staged in Tacoma, Portland, Santa Barbara, Pasadena, Santa Ana, Los Angeles, Sacramento, Chico, Nevada City, and Oakland. In 1886 an anti-Chinese state convention convened in Sacramento to petition the United States Congress for an absolute prohibition on Chinese immigration. In these and other western cities, locals hustled Chinese into the countryside or shoved them onto boats headed for China.[9]

The intensity of this widespread vigilantism convinced the Chinese government of the need to reach an agreement with the United States about the restriction of Chinese immigration. In an 1886 draft treaty, China tentatively consented to prohibit its laborers from emigrating to America. Before this pact was consummated, Congress drafted comprehensive exclusion legislation, and when the Chinese government failed to formalize its initial agreement with the United States, Congress passed the exclusion bill anyway. Apparently yielding to popular support for the measure, President Grover Cleveland signed the 1888 Chinese Exclusion Act, thus breaking precedent, for his predecessors had vetoed legislation that exceeded the scope of treaties in force. Two northern California legislators who strongly advocated this law, Joseph McKenna and William W. Morrow, would later serve as federal judges charged with interpreting it.[10]

The 1888 statute excluded all Chinese from entering the United States except those deemed to be in privileged classes, such as officials, teachers, merchants, or travelers. Congress authorized entry of these persons if they provided a certificate from the Chinese government confirming their classification. This certificate requirement also effectively prohibited Chinese laborers who had been legally admitted under earlier laws from reentering after 1888. The 1888 law did not alter the ten-year duration of the original exclusion, due to expire in 1892. With the Geary Act of 1892, however, Congress extended the immigration ban for another decade and further tightened the restrictions on Chinese laborers by requiring those lawfully in the United States to hold certificates proving their right to remain. Unless good cause were shown and proper proof of residence provided by at least one non-Chinese witness, any person found without such certificates was to be deported. Congress also provided for a grace period of six months during which Chinese residents were expected either to obtain their residence certificate or to leave the country.[11] In court, Chinese litigants failed to defeat the resident certificate requirement. After the grace period elapsed with substantial numbers in noncompliance, Congress extended the registration period for another six months rather than confront the administrative costs and burdens of strictly enforcing the deportation provisions of the 1892 law.

Perhaps out of concern for its natives who were subjected to draconian measures in the United States, perhaps because of antipathy expressed by judges such as Ross, the Chinese government assented to the harsh measures imposed by the 1888 and 1892 acts, signing a treaty with the United States in 1894. This treaty stayed in force until 1904, when the Chinese government declined to renew it. By the turn of the century, therefore, the Chinese exclusion acts had imposed a comprehensive statutory framework for halting the flow of Chinese into the country.[12] The realization of Congress's apparent aims would depend on how the federal courts, and particularly the Ninth Circuit, adjudicated questions arising under these laws.

The Chinese exclusion laws enjoyed widespread support throughout the late nineteenth and early twentieth centuries, and U.S. attorneys and immigration officials enforced them zealously. After the Supreme Court in 1889 rendered a popular decision by sustaining the constitutionality of the 1888 Chinese Exclusion Act, the numerous issues associated with administering the anti-Chinese laws came to demand a great deal of the Ninth Circuit's attention.[13] Although these cases established few enduring constitutional principles, they significantly affected the lives and livelihoods of thousands of Chinese. As the *San Francisco Examiner* wrote:

> The Chinese have always had a warm affection for the Federal courts and an equally marked dislike for the Custom House. If they could have their way every coolie who tried to enter the country in violation of the Exclusion Act would have his case passed upon by the Supreme Court of the United States. The courts have become weary of having their calendars blocked by the applications of On Dek, Wah Fat Lung and their various cousins for admission as California pioneers, and have decided to leave the work of sifting where Congress put it. In the course of thirteen years of experiments we have succeeded in making the Golden Gate pretty nearly coolie-tight. If we could be equally successful on the British Columbia and Mexican borders the Chinese problem would cease to disturb us.[14]

II. THE WESTERN FEDERAL COURTS AND THE CHINESE

Passage of the 1880s Chinese exclusion acts meant more work for the federal judiciary, and not just because of the "warm affection" the Chinese had for it. A variety of circumstances combined to put the "Chinese problem" primarily before federal tribunals. State courts interpreted the Commerce Clause of the United States Constitution to impede early state restrictions on the Chinese. The California Supreme Court upheld one discriminatory measure—an alien miners' license fee of twenty dollars per month—but it generally struck down state laws aimed at restricting Chinese immigration.[15] None of these cases ever reached federal court, however, because the California Supreme Court's invalidation of these state laws as unconstitutional infringements of Congress's commerce power made such review unnecessary. The California judiciary's obeisance to federalism was surely an impetus for local political pressure on Congress and the president to enact national anti-Chinese discriminatory laws.

State efforts were further preempted by the exercise of national power through treaties with the Chinese government and through congressional statutes. The first treaty between the United States and China set out basic principles of friendship in 1844. A more important pact concerning immigration, the Burlingame Treaty, followed in 1868. This agreement recognized a free right of expatriation and emigration between China and the United States. For its part, the United States guaranteed the Chinese "the same privileges, immunities and exemptions in respect to travel or residence, as may there be enjoyed by the citizens or subjects of the most favored nation." The codification of this anti-discrimination principle formally superseded state efforts to single out the Chinese for harsh treatment. Finally, the Civil Rights Act of 1870 banned states from discriminatorily taxing certain immigrants and not others, and it mandated that states tax all persons without regard to national origin.[16]

These state court decisions and national laws thus served both as partial impediments to discriminatory state laws and as seeds for federal litigation involving the Chinese. Despite these strong federal obstacles, however, states and municipalities continued to enact anti-Chinese laws, especially in communities with large Chinese populations, such as San Francisco. The "Queue Ordinance," for example, required San Francisco County jailers to cut the hair of every prisoner to within an inch of the scalp. The ordinance did not specifically refer to the Chinese, but its discrimination was clearly aimed at Chinese men, who wore their hair braided in a long queue. Riding circuit at the time, Justice Stephen Field struck down the ordinance in 1879.[17]

The federal courts in California also adjudicated challenges to the infamous San Francisco ordinances regulating Chinese laundries. One such regulation, enacted in 1880, required laundries to be one story tall, with twelve-inch walls of brick or stone and metal fittings or metal covering wood. It prohibited use of any other type of material without the Board of Supervisors' consent. Two years later, an amended ordinance forbade laundries in certain sections of the city except with the express consent of the Board of Supervisors, which refused to grant permission without the approval of twelve citizens and taxpayers within a block of the proposed laundry. These ordinances, like the "Queue Ordinance," took direct aim at the Chinese, who operated three-quarters of all laundries in San Francisco. Under the board's administration of the ordinance, all Chinese applications for licenses were denied. In a decision of enduring significance, the Supreme Court held that the Fourteenth Amendment prohibited the discrimination against aliens caused by enforcement of the "Chinese laundry" ordinances.[18]

Passage of the 1882 Chinese Exclusion Act shifted the focus from state and local legislation to federal laws that discriminated against Chinese. This act entrenched in federal courts the primary responsibility for adjudicating issues involving the Chinese. Whether sitting singly in district or circuit courts or in circuit court panels, western federal judges had tremendous power to shape the practical effect of the anti-Chinese laws. Unlike prior federal suits, which had challenged the federal constitutionality of state and local ordinances, cases arising after the passage of the Chinese exclusion acts involved routine criminal and civil issues. Popular acclaim for these statutes spurred the San Francisco customs officer to interpret them rigidly and to arrest the vast majority of Chinese seeking entry. To gain release from custody, they filed petitions for habeas corpus, which required federal-court attention.[19]

This litigation flooded the federal courts in San Francisco. By one estimate, District Judge Ogden Hoffman of the northern district of California heard over 7,000 Chinese habeas corpus cases between 1882 and 1890. The burdens of this immense litigation fell on Hoffman and Circuit Judge Lorenzo Sawyer, both of whom attempted to decide these cases fairly and quickly, a task made more difficult by prevailing public anti-Chinese sentiment. To his credit, Hoffman did not let his personal lack of sympathy for the Chinese interfere with his judicial responsibilities; he released hundreds of Chinese under writs of habeas corpus.[20]

Despite the restrictive actions taken by the San Francisco customs collector, who often arrested Chinese lawfully entitled to enter, Hoffman and Sawyer read the 1882 statute to exclude only Chinese *unskilled laborers.* Hoffman recognized the economic rationale of the law: "The evil which the treaty and the law were intended to remedy, was the unrestricted immigration from the teeming population of China of laborers, whose presence here in overwhelming numbers was felt by almost all thoughtful persons to bear with great severity upon our laboring classes, and to menace our interests, our safety, and even our civilization." This opinion, which announced the discharge of a Chinese merchant on a habeas writ, sparked public disenchantment with Hoffman, who chafed under the public opprobrium but did not succumb to it.[21]

Procedurally, the case is interesting also for the anachronism that both Hoffman and Field, the latter as circuit justice, wrote opinions at what was the trial level. In this period, circuit courts retained both original and appellate jurisdiction; a pair of judges—drawn from among the corps of district and circuit judges and circuit justice—sometimes still heard a trial in circuit court. This was one such case. Since Field and Hoffman concurred on the outcome and general interpretation of the law, the reason for writing separately is unclear. The existence of the two opinions, however, sheds light on how the thinking of Hoffman and Field evolved. Field later recanted and all but advocated the permanent suspension of Chinese immigration of any possible classification, not just laborers. Field apparently drifted more and more toward the popular sentiment of restricting Chinese immigration to an extent not approved by the 1880 treaty, which recognized Chinese teachers, students, merchants, and tourists as "privileged classes" to "go and come of their own free will." Hoffman and Sawyer, by contrast, persisted in their belief that the 1880 treaty should guide judicial interpretation of the 1882 statute.[22] Matthew Deady, United States district judge in Oregon, concurred in the Sawyer-Hoffman view, but Deady's impact was much less significant than Hoffman's, because the northern district of California heard the preponderance of the Chinese cases.[23]

Hoffman's sympathetic treatment undoubtedly elevated his workload still further. Assured of a hearing in his court, huge numbers of Chinese petitioned for habeas writs throughout the 1880s, far outstripping Hoffman's ability to immortalize each case with a written opinion. Sensitive to the public outcry that accompanied his discharge rulings, however, he periodically wrote opinions in an attempt to vindicate his collective decisions.[24] Hoffman's colleague Sawyer held similar views but managed to deflect public criticism. Unlike Hoffman, who apparently never made a public speech after 1852, Sawyer was a popular orator who achieved a reputation for fearlessness. Sawyer's public speaking gave him opportunities to explain his decisions outside the judicial context. He also handled fewer cases at the trial level than Hoffman. And in Oregon, Deady won the grudging respect of the white community, notwithstanding the unpopularity of his pro-Chinese rulings.[25]

As the opinions of Hoffman, Sawyer, and Deady crystallized in the mid-1880s on the principle of guaranteeing due process to the Chinese, they began increasingly to disagree with Justice Field, who still rode circuit in California. Field's attitude about Chinese immigration hardened after 1884, for reasons that remain obscure.[26] The subordinate federal judges had to respect the justice's views, not only because of his acknowledged brilliance, but also because his vote counted more than theirs. Under the 1802 statute that reconfigured the federal judicial system after the repeal of the "Midnight Judges" Act of 1801, the opinion of a circuit-riding justice controlled even when the justice was in a minority on a circuit-court panel. An 1872 statute reiterated this archaic hierarchy, and its application in 1884 sundered the court. In the case of *In re Chew Heong*, Field's opinion denied reentry to a Chinese laborer who had resided lawfully in the United States and then departed before the enactment of the 1882 Chinese Exclusion Act. The justice held that Chew Heong could properly be excluded for failing to present a certificate. In dissent, Sawyer sharply contended that Field's position conflicted with many earlier decisions of the California federal courts, which had refused to apply the 1882 Chinese Exclusion Act retroactively. Hoffman and Nevada District Judge George M. Sabin, also on the circuit court panel, joined in Sawyer's opinion. The sting of the public reprobation suffered by Sawyer, Hoffman, and Sabin was surely alleviated when the Supreme Court reversed Field's decision by a seven-to-two margin.[27]

Enactment of the 1888 Chinese Exclusion Act rendered the Supreme Court's ruling a nullity and defused the disagreement among the western federal judges and their circuit justice on this issue. This statute prohibited reentry even to Chinese laborers who had been lawfully admitted prior to passage of the 1882 law. Certificates would no longer gain Chinese laborers entrance. The ink of President Cleveland's signature on the bill was barely dry when customs officials and federal judges in San Francisco received notice by telegram to enforce the act immediately. Through such swift action the administration sought to enforce the new law against the approximately eight hundred Chinese who were expected to arrive in the Bay Area the following day. The circuit court for the northern district of California readily upheld the constitutionality of the 1888 act, and the Supreme Court unanimously affirmed in an opinion written by Justice Field. The broad sweep of the 1888 act and the decisions sustaining it produced still more habeas corpus cases. By one estimate, thirty thousand Chinese had left the United States with pre-1888 reentry certificates but had not yet returned.[28] They had little chance of eluding the harsh effects of the law, because the judicial system in which they would challenge denial of entry was undergoing significant change.

Historians have argued that up until the 1890s, western federal judges—especially Sawyer, Hoffman, and Deady—did much to treat Chinese litigants justly. Appropriately, scholars consider this early period of exclusion as crucial for understanding the judiciary's treatment of the Chinese. Adjudication of Chinese exclusion cases clearly entered a new phase, however, after the Supreme Court upheld the 1888 act.[29] The greater restrictiveness of the federal courts in the 1890s was a function of several factors. One explanation is that a new generation of federal judges took over from Sawyer, Hoffman, and Deady. Another is the legal context in which cases arose. The statutory language and precedents interpreting key provisions closed loopholes through which Judges Sawyer, Hoffman, and Deady had permitted Chinese entry in the 1880s. Though the post-1891 judges certainly had no sympathy for the Chinese, in many instances expression of their personal feelings was constrained by their role in applying the facts at hand to strict statutory language in light of controlling precedent. Constrained though they may have been by the legal context in which cases arose, the Ninth Circuit judges of the 1890s nevertheless were rarely predisposed to construe ambiguous provisions in favor of Chinese litigants. Prior to their tenure on the court, three future Ninth Circuit judges were establishing anti-Chinese track records that help to explain their later thinking.

III. McKENNA, MORROW, AND ROSS ON THE CHINESE

While Field, Sawyer, Hoffman, and Deady were interpreting the Chinese Exclusion Acts of the 1880s, two of their successors were in Congress helping to write more restrictive legislation. Both Joseph McKenna and William W. Morrow, who served in Congress from the mid-1880s to the early 1890s, responded to the passionate public outcry of Californians for even further constraints on Chinese immigration. Both actively supported strict enforcement of the 1882 and 1884 acts, as well as the more stringent 1888 measure.

On August 9, 1888, for example, Morrow requested immediate action on the 1888 bill, contending that the "present law and . . . treaty, by reason of inherent defects, do not prevent Chinese immigration." He took this strong stand because the "people of the Pacific coast ask—ay, they demand—that Congress shall relieve them of the difficulties" posed by Chinese immigration. Two weeks later, Morrow delivered a lengthy oration in which he surveyed a range of Chinese-related issues. He left no doubt that Judges Sawyer and Hoffman were disserving his San Francisco constituency. Without resorting to disrespectful rhetoric, Morrow nonetheless stated his belief that the Supreme Court decision in

Chew Heong, which mirrored Sawyer's dissenting analysis at the circuit court level, "destroyed the value of the [1884] amendment." Morrow pressed the White House for stricter enforcement of existing laws, advocated prohibition of the prior-residence exception to exclusion, urged absolute exclusion of all Chinese laborers, and expressed skepticism concerning the exception for Chinese merchants. In colorful language that verged on demagoguery, he concluded: "Because this Asiatic tramp forces his way through the western gate of the continent contrary to the spirit and purpose of our laws[,] are we going to ignore his persistent invasion of our territory, or at most toy with the question, and forgetting the rights and demands of American labor, surrender to the vice and demoralization of Chinese labor? This is the whole question, turn it as you will, and our duty appears to me to be plain."[30]

If his views on Chinese labor were not already clear, within two years of the 1888 act's passage, Morrow issued a report on behalf of the House Committee on Foreign Affairs that foreshadowed tension with his future position as federal judge. Morrow frankly acknowledged that some Chinese "are inoffensive, temperate, and law-abiding, and peculiarly subject to the influences of Christian civilization." But despite the "doubtless many individual cases tending to justify such a partial estimate of the Chinese character," Morrow refused to reopen the policy debate underlying the exclusion principle. Instead, he introduced a sweeping bill to exclude all Chinese permanently. The promise this bill offered was clear: it would obviate the need for Congress to decide in 1892 whether to renew the restriction on Chinese laborer immigration originally passed in 1882; moreover, it saved federal courts from the continuing difficulty of deciding whether to admit Chinese individuals seeking entry under the exceptions for merchants, tourists, and transit travelers.[31] If successful, Morrow's proposal would have eliminated much of his later work as a district and circuit judge. It failed, however, and as a federal judge Morrow assumed the responsibility of interpreting the very provisions he had so vigorously attacked as a legislator.

Morrow and his colleague and friend, Joseph McKenna, stood shoulder to shoulder on the exclusion issue, which both viewed as crucial to preserving jobs for whites. Morrow and McKenna never served together on the Ninth Circuit—Morrow was in fact appointed to take McKenna's place in 1897—but they did hear cases on the same panel when Morrow sat by designation as a district judge. McKenna made plain their unity of thought in a partisan remark, "My colleague [Mr. Morrow] showed that during the time the Democratic House waited and wasted, 20,000

Chinamen came to the country to compete with those already here against our wage-earners. . . . Let Chinamen come as they are coming, and will come if not restrained," he added, "and you will as surely destroy this free Government as though, to use a figure of Wendell Phillips, you should put gunpowder under the Capitol." McKenna felt compelled to add his observation that the Chinese "are purely a clannish, selfish, grasping people, totally devoid of all moral instincts and endowed with an endurance unequalled by any other class of laborers."[32]

These comments suggest that the future judge, whose responsibilities would include fairly adjudicating issues involving the Chinese, was capable of delivering the most scathing *ad hominem* attacks on them. Occasionally he linked these barbs to legal issues, urging at one point the deletion of a provision that permitted entry of Chinese laborers if they were owed debts of one thousand dollars or more. For McKenna, this exception to exclusion constituted political apostasy, because it allowed a Chinese laborer falsely to claim a debt to another Chinese: "The productive perjury of Chinese witnesses which so easily invents a place and a time and the circumstances of a prior residence will invent without straining a debt of a thousand dollars pending settlement." McKenna's support for labor was so strong and his antipathy for the Chinese so total that he supported both Democratic and Republican bills aimed at Chinese exclusion.[33]

Like McKenna and Morrow, a third Ninth Circuit judge also left an extensive track record on the Chinese exclusion issue. Before his elevation to circuit judge in 1895, Ross served as district judge for southern California. In this office, which he held from 1886 to 1895, Ross tried numerous cases involving Chinese who were seeking entry at the Port of Los Angeles. The most spectacular indication of his views on the subject was a political battle he fought with the Democratic Cleveland administration over enforcing restriction laws. The incident revealed that despite their different political affiliations—Ross was a Democrat; Morrow and McKenna were Republicans—they shared similar views on the Chinese labor question.

The episode grew out of the failed effort by the Chinese to obtain a ruling that the Geary Act of 1892 was unconstitutional. From the Chinese perspective, the most nettlesome provision of this law was section 6, which required Chinese laborers to register with their local internal revenue collector for a residence certificate within a year of the law's effective date of May 5, 1892. Rather than urge Chinese laborers to comply with the law, the Chinese Legation retained prominent attorneys to challenge its constitutionality. The Chinese minister sought assistance from the United States government to expedite a test case from the lower federal courts up to the Supreme Court before the expiration of the law's one-year registration period. Although Attorney General Richard Olney readily agreed, the grace period had elapsed by the time the Supreme Court rendered its decision. The Court's adverse ruling left thousands of Chinese laborers in technical violation of the law, including between seven and nine thousand in southern California. Tensions in Los Angeles grew so great that United States Attorney George J. Denis cautioned authorities to keep arrests to a minimum to avoid "any trouble or bloodshed."[34]

Denis undertook this prudent step on the direct instructions of Attorney General Olney. On September 2, 1893, Olney sent a telegram to Denis that sparked the dispute with Ross:

> I am advised by the Secretary of the Treasury that there are no funds to execute the Geary law, so far as same provides for deportation of Chinamen who have not procured certificates of residence. On that state of facts, circuit court of United States for southern district of New York made following order: "Ordered, that _____ be, and he hereby is, discharged from the custody of the marshal, and ordered to be deported from the United States whenever provision for such deportation shall be made by the proper authorities." Ask court to make similar order in like cases.[35]

Olney, who must have believed that strict enforcement would exhaust his department's resources and flood the federal courts, seriously miscalculated Ross's response. Unlike federal judges in New York, who responded pliantly to Olney's request, Ross lashed out at the attorney general, both for attempting to interfere with his judicial independence and for a gravely flawed reading of the relevant law. In a published opinion, the judge first ordered the deportation of Chum Shang Yuen, a Chinese laborer convicted of failing to register under section 6 of the Geary Act. He then quoted Olney's telegram to Denis and dedicated the rest of the opinion to refuting the attorney general's legal reasoning.[36]

Shortly thereafter, in a letter to the president who appointed him, Grover Cleveland, Ross complained that because this "practical annulment of the laws and of the orders of the Judicial Department regularly made in pursuance of them, strikes at the foundation of our system of Government, and cannot be permitted to pass unchallenged, I therefore respectfully call your attention to it for such action as you deem proper." To the attorney general Ross was far less courteous. In a letter released to the press, the judge told Olney that he had made himself look "ridiculous." The attorney general's legal analysis was totally unfounded, he continued, because Congress had not bifurcated appropriations for enforcement of the Geary Act by allocating funds to enforce some provisions and not others. Ross contended that if the law was constitutional, as the Supreme Court said it was, Olney's job was to enforce the whole statute, not just the provisions he favored. Impressed by this public reprimand, one newspaper conjectured that Olney would henceforth confine his attention "more strictly to the affairs of his department and less to those of the judicial arm of the government."[37]

Whether Ross's action reflected "magnificent courage" or prescribed unmitigated disaster depended entirely on where one stood on the underlying question of Chinese exclusion. Ross left no private papers explaining his view of this episode, but if the newspaper clippings he saved fairly indicate his thinking, "judicial independence" was merely the vehicle for strict exclusion enforcement. The West Coast newspaper editorials that Ross assiduously pasted in his scrapbook hailed the judge's action for its effects on exclusion: "Judge Ross has given the Geary act the requisite efficacy in spite of influences sedulously exerted at Washington"; "the decision of Judge Ross in regard to the Chinese cases will do wonders to encourage people who are anxious to see coolie labor abolished in California"; and "Judge Ross has shown himself an able, upright and fearless Judge, and one not overshadowed in any degree by a pro-Chinese President and his Cabinet." Public pressure for enforcement of the Geary Act, especially by labor groups, made Ross "probably the most popular man in Los Angeles."[38]

Just as Ross's anti-Chinese action increased his public standing in the Los Angeles area even before his elevation to the Ninth Circuit, Morrow and McKenna gained similar renown during the late 1880s and early 1890s, when they represented northern California in Congress. Given the public positions espoused by these men before their appellate court appointments, Ninth Circuit litigants during the 1890s could not be faulted for anticipating stricter enforcement of anti-Chinese exclusion laws than when Sawyer, Hoffman, and Deady had held judicial office. To some extent, the judicial performance of McKenna, Morrow, and Ross fulfilled their worst expectations. But precisely because of the differences between judicial and legislative work, assessing the *outcomes* of cases alone is an inadequate method of determining judicial attitudes.[39] Many of the cases appealed to the Ninth Circuit on the Chinese question involved statutory interpretation, and thus the strict wording of the statute invariably produced harsh results. Arguably a better way to assess the legal significance of the Ninth Circuit's jurisprudential change after 1891, therefore, is to analyze several classes of cases in the context in which they arose.

In assessing this context, it is important to keep in mind how the flexibility in judicial roles in this period colored the development of anti-Chinese doctrine. The internal administration of the Ninth Circuit contributed to the greater restrictiveness of the court's rulings on Chinese issues. In the 1880s, since Congress had authorized so few judges for West Coast states, Hoffman, Sawyer, and Deady had handled the vast bulk of Chinese-related cases. Hoffman and Deady sat predominantly in the districts for which they were appointed. Except when Circuit Justice Field sat with them, these judges had great influence in building precedent, because they had the opportunity to express their views in case after case. By 1895 the pool from which to draw judges for circuit court of appeals panels had expanded greatly. In addition to three circuit judges (compared to only one in the 1880s), the court brought in district judges from throughout the Ninth Circuit to compose appellate panels. This internal administrative procedure had the effect of diluting the doctrinal influence of any single judge. A closer examination of the Ninth Circuit's Chinese-exclusion jurisprudence casts light, therefore, on the development of the court's internal politics and its corresponding relation to judicial administration. The flexible panel-assignment system could last only so long as no single judge or pair of judges dominated doctrinal development in a manner deemed unacceptable by the other judges in the circuit. The Chinese exclusion cases illustrate how this system worked and why no pressure built up to reform the internal administration of the court.

IV. NINTH CIRCUIT JURISPRUDENCE

The American public demanded tough anti-Chinese restrictions, and Congress willingly obliged it by enacting steadily harsher immigration measures. In most appeals, the Ninth Circuit routinely affirmed convictions of Chinese for exclusion act violations or denied requests for habeas writs. Notwithstanding their very able counsel, the Chinese frequently lost appeals to the Ninth Circuit.[40] These results generally had less to do with racial animus on the part of the judges than with the anti-Chinese sentiment reflected in the Chinese exclusion acts themselves. Unlike the earlier western federal judges who interpreted more leniently drafted exclusion laws, the 1890s-era judges faced legal challenges to highly restrictive statutes, which left little latitude to achieve pro-Chinese outcomes even had the judges been so inclined. More often than not, either the statute or precedent spoke directly to the question. In more difficult cases requiring creative analysis by the judges, however, signs of racial animus appeared only in selective contexts. Sawyer, Hoffman, and Deady had bravely ruled in favor of Chinese litigants when the circumstances and their sense of justice required such results, but their successors tended to be harsher. To be sure, important exceptions to this generalization occurred, exceptions which warrant the conclusion that the Ninth Circuit confronted Chinese immigration issues with a certain ambivalence. Cases involving three issues—entry questions, the merchant exception, and citizenship by birth—illustrate the judicial tension that marked the court's treatment of the Chinese during this period.

As amended in 1884, the original 1882 Exclusion Act prohibited Chinese laborers from entering the United States. To enforce this restriction, the statute required incoming Chinese to produce a certificate from their government attesting that they were not laborers. This seemingly simple requirement, however, presented a legal issue on which opinion differed: were documents issued by consuls who represented the Chinese government in other countries sufficient evidence of valid certification? When the question first arose, the Chinese government informed the State Department that it had authorized its consuls in other countries to issue such certificates. The Treasury Department and the State Department disagreed over whether the United States should accept consul-endorsed certificates, and the Justice Department was asked to render a formal opinion. Attorney General Richard Olney determined that certificates "issued by the duly authorized consular officers of China in foreign countries and accurately conforming in their contents to the requirements of section 6 are the certificates contemplated by the law."[41]

This opinion accorded with Olney's generally lenient stance on the Chinese question. In keeping with their prior legislative preferences, however, McKenna and Morrow as judges took a much stricter line than the attorney general. Sitting as the Ninth Circuit panel shortly before Olney issued his opinion, McKenna and Morrow ruled that a certificate signed by the Chinese consul in Yokohama, Japan, did not have the same effect as one issued by the Chinese government and that the petitioner had failed to prove that the Chinese government had authorized its consuls to issue such certificates. Writing for the court, McKenna stated: "It is undoubtedly competent for the Chinese government to authorize its consuls to give the certificate prescribed by section 6, but there is no proof in the case that it has done so."[42]

If the Ninth Circuit's decision in *United States v. Mock Chew* signaled strictness in the handling of Chinese-entry questions, it was not a decision of enduring significance. The court merely remanded for proof that the Chinese government had authorized its consuls to issue certificates. Though the court was not privy to the Chinese legation's communications with the State Department, clearly such proof existed. Upon presenting the evidence in court, the petitioner would gain entry. The significance of *Mock Chew* lies less in its erection of a barrier to Chinese immigration than as an early indication that on close questions, McKenna and Morrow would adhere to their views as legislators in construing the exclusion acts unfavorably for Chinese immigrants, and especially laborers.[43]

By contrast, cases arising under the merchant exception to the exclusion acts exposed the difficulty of applying a legislator's mode of analysis to judicial decision making. These cases also revealed how the various combinations of judges comprising Ninth Circuit panels prevented any single judge from dominating the doctrinal development of the law.[44] District judges sitting by designation on appellate panels contributed significant opinions as the Ninth Circuit struggled to adjudicate the statutory exceptions to the anti-Chinese exclusion laws. Congress did not intend the 1882, 1884, and 1888 exclusion acts to prohibit Chinese in privileged classes, such as merchants, teachers, and students, from gaining entry. But to achieve its aim of excluding laborers, Congress required exempted persons to present certificates attesting to their status. If enforcement of the anti-Chinese immigration statutes had been left to the sole discretion of federal immigration officers and single-judge district courts, the potential for widespread abuses would have been great. The wording of the exclusion statutes left unclear whether the Chinese litigants would ultimately have recourse to the newly created circuit courts of appeals. In an important ruling that displayed the continuing vigor of the 1880s old guard of federal judges into the next decade, Deady wrote for William Gilbert and Thomas Hawley to uphold the right to appeal decisions of the district court involving immigration orders.[45]

Once this right-to-appeal question became settled precedent in the Ninth Circuit, Chinese litigants vigorously exercised that right. In the years following the creation of the circuit courts of appeals, the Ninth Circuit decided a number of cases testing the outer limits of the merchant exception to the exclusion acts. This litigation promised to be a fascinating legal battleground. As a legislator Morrow had favored eliminating the exemption, and now he was called upon to judge the government's vigorous efforts to limit claims by immigrants alleging to be merchants. For their part, Chinese litigants adroitly picked apart as many government arguments as they could. Unlike the many Chinese discharged on writs of habeas corpus by western federal courts in the 1880s, Chinese litigants of the 1890s won few litigation victories. The merchant exception was one of them.

In an 1894 opinion for the Ninth Circuit, McKenna uncharacteristically opened a doctrinal door for many subsequent Chinese claiming the merchant exception. Lee Kan, who worked as a merchant in San Francisco from 1880 to 1893, was arrested by port officials in 1894 when he attempted to land after a brief trip to China. He applied for a writ of habeas corpus, which the district court denied. In a ruling by Morrow, the district court held that Lee did not qualify as a merchant because he did not conduct business in his own name. He was one of eight partners doing business under the title "Wing Tai Lung." In a bow to business reality penned by McKenna, the circuit court of appeals reversed. "The construction contended for by the government would not only forbid the Chinese this practice," McKenna wrote, "but forbid them . . . the common practice of this country, and of all commercial countries. The designations of very few business houses contain the names of all of the partners."[46]

Lee Kan was not, however, a doctrinal gateway through which Chinese claiming to be merchants could traipse with impunity. The opinion contained an important caveat: Chinese merchants had to prove their ownership interest in the firm by producing the articles of incorporation or partnership. Nevertheless, *Lee Kan* was an important triumph for Chinese merchants from both immediate and long-term perspectives. When McKenna announced the court's decision, one hundred merchants were waiting in Bay Area jails for rulings on their habeas corpus writs, and another forty remained aboard the steamer *Rio*, which lay in port. These merchants won their freedom with the court's decision in *Lee Kan*.[47] From the larger perspective, the decision signaled some willingness by the court, as expressed through one of its most fervently anti-Chinese members, at least to evaluate the circumstances in which Chinese merchants conducted business.

Sometimes these circumstances redounded to the Chinese petitioner's detriment. In 1895 the court employed restrictive interpretations of business activity to foreclose the entry of Chinese claiming to be merchants. For example, the court affirmed the denial of a habeas writ to a person who admitted to having served as a house servant for short periods during the year before he left the United States. Because such activity fell within the definition of manual labor, McKenna concluded that the statute required federal officials to prevent the man's reentry, despite his partial ownership of a business. The court also denied reentry to a Chinese man who cut and sewed garments retailed by a firm of which he was a member. The court concluded that although he owned part of the firm he was not a "merchant" under the statute, because he had performed manual labor to fabricate the merchandise. McKenna reasoned that a " 'merchant' may not . . . 'engage in the performance of any manual labor except such as is necessary in the conduct of his business as such merchant,'—that is, in buying and selling merchandise."[48]

Despite these setbacks, Chinese litigants generally benefited from the merchant exception. As the court's doctrine on this exception developed, the significance of McKenna's opinion in *Lee Kan* loomed ever larger. Other judges began to build on the precedent, thus giving the merchant provision real protection for the Chinese who invoked it. In *Wong Fong v. United States*, for example, the court reviewed the deportation order of a person alleged by the government to be a Chinese laborer. Wong Fong contended that he had been a merchant for seven years before fire destroyed his business on August 1, 1893. Wong left the United States after passage of the McCreary Act of November 3, 1893, which provided an additional six months for Chinese to register, but before a registration office opened on January 1, 1894. The district court dismissed a stipulation of facts underlying Wong's assertion that he was a merchant after the fire of August 1, 1893. In an opinion by William Gilbert, whose prior thinking on the Chinese labor issue is unknown, the Ninth Circuit reversed. The court held that the articles of partnership established Wong's contention that he was in business with a Chow Kee. In Gilbert's view, *Lee Kan* controlled. Contrary to the district court's reasoning, the fire did not close out the partnership if the corporate records revealed a continuing enterprise—and, indeed, the partners had pooled their resources to erect a new building on the site of the old one.[49]

The *Lee Kan* rule was further elaborated in 1906, when Gilbert again wrote for the court in a challenging case with a number of factual twists. Ow Yang Dean was arrested for being a manual laborer without a residence certificate and was ordered deported. The government acknowledged that in 1890 Ow had become a member of the mercantile

firm of Hung Tai and Company in Walnut Grove and of Sang Wo Sang
and Company in San Francisco. In 1900, while still retaining his interests
in these concerns, Ow purchased a stake in the San Pablo Bay Shrimp
Company, a co-partnership. With this firm he performed such manual
labor as was necessary to keep the company in business. The district
court affirmed the deportation order, but the circuit court of appeals
reversed. Gilbert opined that because Ow's name was inscribed on the
corporate books, he was a merchant within the meaning of the Geary and
McCreary acts, and thus not deportable. The McCreary Act of 1893
required a person applying for reentry as a former merchant to show, by
testimony of two credible non-Chinese witnesses, that he was indeed a
merchant. The court found that the evidence introduced against Ow
lacked credibility. Persons in a rival shrimping firm purportedly had
written dishonest letters contending that he was a laborer. The court gave
much greater credence to evidence that he worked principally as a
bookkeeper for Sang Wo Sang and Company. Nevertheless, evidence
existed that Ow had also picked shrimp and crabs and delivered them.
Under McKenna's strict interpretations of merchant activity and manual
labor, Ow quite possibly faced denial of reentry. But Gilbert distinguished McKenna's earlier opinions for the court on the theory that Ow's
manual work was only a small component of his job. By this somewhat
selective use of precedent, Gilbert permitted entry of a merchant whose
claim raised several factual and legal difficulties.[50]

The merchant exception, therefore, proved to be more readily available to the Chinese than they might have anticipated in light of McKenna
and Morrow's legislative backgrounds. This more favorable treatment—
when compared to entry questions involving Chinese laborers—stemmed
from the perception that merchants did not threaten whites' jobs. It also
derived partly from Gilbert's more expansive reading of a key earlier
decision in the merchant-exception line of cases. But the court's treatment
of those Chinese who invoked the merchant exception was inconsistent,
as is indicated by some of the court's stricter interpretations of "merchant"; it depended on the panel composition and the opinion-writer. The
influence of the opinion-writer should not be understated—he provided
nuance to the explanation of the outcome. But the composition of the
panels, drawn from the three circuit judges and numerous district judges
of the Ninth Circuit, also played a key role.

The fluidity of panel composition and the flexibility of judicial roles
also delayed the development of an overt circuit politics. No single
judge or small group of judges could impose a certain viewpoint doc-

trinally on the others through the development of circuit precedent. Had McKenna and Morrow, for example, sat on every appellate court panel where a Chinese question was raised, the law of the circuit might well have developed far more harshly than it did. Because the scheme of assigning district judges to circuit court of appeals panels served to dilute the power of any single circuit judge, overt disagreements over doctrine were minimized and the system of administration was kept informal. Cases arising under the merchant exception illustrated the early workability of a judicial administrative system that put a premium on role flexibility.

This amalgam of contextual and administrative factors also helps to explain a third set of cases related to Chinese immigration: those determining whether the exclusion acts applied to children allegedly born in the United States of Chinese parents. The Fourteenth Amendment declared that "[a]ll persons born or naturalized in the United States . . . are citizens of the United States and of the State wherein they reside." The exclusion acts prohibited the Chinese from becoming naturalized citizens; the issue therefore arose of whether the citizenship provision of the Fourteenth Amendment applied to the American-born children of Chinese immigrants. Two competing theories attracted powerful advocates. The first posited that the language of the Fourteenth Amendment adopted common-law doctrine, thereby establishing citizenship for anyone born in the United States irrespective of their parents' citizenship. According to a second theory, the Fourteenth Amendment codified international law doctrine, under which parents' national status fixed that of the child, regardless of birthplace.[51]

The Ninth Circuit gave little credence to the international-law theory of citizenship, even though it had obvious exclusion implications. The law of the circuit, as enunciated by Justice Field in 1884, was that persons born in the United States were citizens, irrespective of their parents' nationality. In 1898 the Supreme Court formally sanctioned this position in the landmark case of *United States v. Wong Kim Ark*. The Court itself acknowledged that the western federal courts of the Ninth Circuit had "uniformly held" this common-law view for fifteen years and that "we are not aware of any judicial decision to the contrary."[52] The law of the Ninth Circuit had recognized the constitutional right of citizenship by birth beginning in 1884; the invocation of this right in the Ninth Circuit had thus provided a theoretical means of escaping the exclusion restrictions long before 1898. But although this circuit doctrine anticipated the Supreme Court's articulation of the applicable rule, in practice it provided little relief for children who claimed to have been born in the United States of Chinese parents.

In cases brought before and after *Wong Kim Ark*, the Ninth Circuit rejected numerous claims of citizenship on technical grounds. A succession of Ninth Circuit judges shared McKenna's view that testimony by the Chinese was made suspect by their alleged proclivity for perjury. In the first such case it decided after its creation in 1891, the court rejected the testimony of two Chinese witnesses who purported to have knowledge of the petitioner's birth in San Francisco in 1877. The court's rulings became a standard litany: "Under the circumstances stated by him, but little, if any, credence should be given to his own evidence as to the place of his birth, and he is corroborated on this vital point only by the testimony of other Chinese persons, who confessedly have seen him but a few times, and can give only hearsay evidence." The court also employed presumptions of proof to deny a person's citizenship claim. If a claimant produced credible proof and the government offered rebuttal evidence, the court sided presumptively with the government. As Morrow wrote in one such case, "The certificate of the court is that, after the defendant had introduced evidence to prove his nativity, the plaintiff (the United States) introduced evidence, both oral and documentary, in rebuttal. The presumption is that this evidence in rebuttal was sufficient to justify the findings." And when the Chinese presented credible evidence but were rebuffed in the district court, the Ninth Circuit upheld such rulings under a deferential standard of review, of "whether the evidence is so clear and satisfactory upon that point as to authorize this court to say that the court erred in refusing her [permission] to land."[53]

The erection of these evidentiary impediments in the citizenship cases is difficult to square with the court's adjudication of the merchant cases. The Ninth Circuit frequently reversed district court decisions excluding Chinese merchants, thus evidencing little of the deference to trial court proceedings it displayed in the citizenship cases. Moreover, in the merchant cases the court accepted as credible the testimony of Chinese witnesses and carefully scrutinized the trial record for error.[54] Explaining these apparent inconsistencies is difficult. Perhaps the judges legitimately found testimony of birthplace hard to evaluate because it rested on decades-old documents or distant recollections. The immediacy of statements about type of work were easier to assess. The judges may also have feared an onslaught of returning laborers claiming citizenship and believed that the economic status of merchants posed less of a threat to the American work force. McKenna and Morrow were, after all, products of elective politics. Morrow remained closely tied to Republican party politics in California throughout his judicial career. And although he was much less politically involved than McKenna or Morrow, Ross was not oblivious to the social consequences of his rulings, as the Olney episode revealed. By contrast with the 1880s cadre of Sawyer, Hoffman, and Deady, therefore, the core of Ninth Circuit judges who decided Chinese entry and citizenship questions in the 1890s and 1900s were much less willing to rule against domestic labor interests.

V. "HARD" CASES

Chinese immigration issues occupied a large segment of the western federal courts' dockets in the last two decades of the nineteenth century and the early years of the twentieth. The establishment of the circuit court of appeals in 1891 occurred in the midst of personnel changes in the western federal judiciary and the enactment of stricter statutory controls on Chinese immigration. The stricter statutes limited the latitude of the later judges. Moreover, whereas the judges of the 1880s appeared pre-disposed by judicial temperament or racial tolerance to rule in favor of Chinese litigants in the early years of the exclusion acts, for the most part the 1890s judges were not. The anti-Chinese sentiments of at least three of the 1890s judges—McKenna, Morrow, and Ross—can be traced in actions of theirs that preceded their tenure on the circuit court of appeals. A third possible explanation for this jurisprudential change lies in the legal and factual context of the cases appealed to the court. Under this view, the composition of panels (except insofar as they comprised group-ings of an array of different circuit and district judges) mattered far less than the circumstances facing the court.

A fourth theory is also plausible: that the later judges saw the role of law and of their court in a different light than their predecessors had. Ogden Hoffman and Lorenzo Sawyer, for example, dealt with the thou-sands of Chinese who came through their courtrooms on an individual basis. Hoffman's biographer has written that the district judge "ex-pressed his personal delight at being able to avoid separating Chinese children from their parents" and that the multitude of separate hearings forced him "to see and hear them as human beings with distinct expla-nations and histories that had to be dealt with on a case-by-case basis."[55] The later judges expressly eschewed this approach. In two deportation cases decided in 1899 and 1905 by the circuit court of appeals, Gilbert, Ross, and Morrow unanimously rejected arguments by Chinese parties in factually compelling circumstances. These decisions revealed much about their level of detachment from the plight of Chinese litigants and illustrated their limited faith in the law's ability to redress individual injustices.

In the first case, two young boys aged thirteen and fifteen arrived in the United States to live with their father and to attend school in Eugene, Oregon. They landed in May of 1896 and immediately presented a certificate from William E. Hunt, the United States consul for China, along with a letter to Hunt from two Americans who said that the boys' father intended to bring his sons to the United States for schooling. Though they did not present any other certificates, the immigration officials permitted the boys to land. Two years later, the United States attorney for Oregon filed a criminal information charging them with being laborers not entitled to reside in the United States. The district court found that the boys had been students in English schools in Eugene since their arrival and thus had not violated the law. The court permitted them to stay, but the Ninth Circuit reversed. The court held that even though United States immigration officials had erred in permitting their entry and the boys had not performed any manual labor, they had to be deported because the certificate they had obtained from the United States consul was invalid under the exclusion acts. Writing for the court, Morrow reasoned that the boys could not overcome their illegal entry merely by showing that they were engaged in a lawful pursuit in the United States. Whereas the district court applied a lenity principle, the appellate court employed a strict construction of the statute to order the boys back to China. No authority existed for either position. Morrow's ruling certainly applied exclusion more restrictively and thus advanced one of the expressed aims of the exclusion legislation. However, these boys were students, a group that was permitted to enter under the 1888 Exclusion Act.[56] By giving the entry-certificate provision greater weight than a consideration of the targeted group, Morrow's technically correct opinion arguably did little to advance the policies underlying exclusion.

A factually different yet similarly moving case involved a young Chinese woman slave who escaped to the United States and arranged a marriage of convenience to avoid being returned to her slave master in China. The district court analogized to the Thirteenth Amendment's prohibition on slavery and concluded that her deportation would essentially remand her to a life of slavery. In one of his very rare opinions reversing a district court ruling, Gilbert found that the Thirteenth Amendment did not apply in this case. Washington District Judge Cornelius Hanford had conceded that this amendment was not directly implicated, but he nevertheless believed that equitable considerations emanating from the amendment justified his ruling. Gilbert disagreed. "The case is one which, from its nature, enlists the sympathy of the court," Gilbert concluded, "and we regret that the law is so written that it does not permit us, as we view it, to yield to the humane considerations which actuated the court below." The appellate court was surely correct that the Thirteenth Amendment did not proscribe deportation under these facts, but Hanford's opinion had a persuasive quality: "[I]t is shocking to contemplate that the laws of our country require the court to use its process to accomplish such an unholy purpose."[57]

The "unholy purpose" achieved by the court's deportation of the Chinese slave exemplified an approach to the adjudication of Chinese exclusion issues in the 1890s different from that which the judges in the previous decade had advanced. With the exception of the merchant provision, the circuit court of appeals interpreted the exclusion acts strictly and firmly against Chinese interests. The reasons for this jurisprudential shift from the previous decade are by no means clear, but the results were. Despite representation by skillful counsel and active remonstration by Chinese government representatives in the United States, the restrictive immigration laws and the court's adjudication of them achieved their desired results. Whereas between 1870 and 1882 approximately 200,000 Chinese immigrants had arrived in the United States, after the 1882 and 1884 exclusion laws took hold the numbers dropped off precipitously, from 39,579 in 1882 to a mere 22 immigrants in 1885 and 10 in 1887. Largely because of the statutory exceptions for merchants and other "privileged" persons and the judicial interpretations that strengthened them, the numbers of Chinese immigrants rebounded, averaging about 2,000 per year from 1890 to 1920. During World War II, when the Chinese were allies against the Japanese, Congress finally repealed the array of Chinese exclusion acts it had enacted over the years. After decades of systematic, legalized discrimination, Congress finally instructed that the Chinese be treated the same as other immigrants.[58]

FOUR

Intrigue at Anvil Creek

[T]he high-handed and grossly illegal proceedings initiated
almost as soon as Judge Noyes and McKenzie had set foot
on Alaskan territory at Nome . . . may be safely and
fortunately said to have no parallel in the jurisprudence of
this country.

Judge Erskine M. Ross, 1901

By the turn of the century, the volume of appeals involving the Chinese
had begun to decline and the circuit courts of appeals were ready to
celebrate their first decade of existence. The Ninth Circuit had faced
unique challenges in the *Stanford* matter and had handled the vast
majority of the Chinese-related appeals percolating in the nation's federal courts. Its jurisdiction covered the largest tract among the nine
circuits and included the last of America's great frontiers, Alaska. From
this Territory emerged a crisis that threatened the appellate court's
authority over its constituent subordinate courts and imperiled development, not only in Alaska, but potentially throughout the West.

I. ALASKAN GOLD

Although Russians had unearthed small amounts of gold in Alaska
before it became part of the United States in 1867, full-fledged gold
rushes to the region did not begin until the 1880s. Discovery of gold in
Canada around Dawson, near the Alaska border, set off a stampede to
the Klondike region during 1897 and 1898 and inspired gold-digging
elsewhere in Alaska. During the autumn of 1897, prospecting began in
earnest on the Seward Peninsula, a far western spot just below the Arctic
Circle, across the Bering Strait from Siberia. Accessible only by boat and
only during the part of the year—typically, between June and October—

when the seaward passageway was free of ice, this region attracted a group of eight men who discovered gold placers in March, 1898, on two tributary streams of the Niukluk River. Rather than dig deep holes or tunnels, the prospectors worked the placer mines by gathering ore from surface gravel and washing away unwanted dirt to retain the valuable mineral particles. After a month of panning, the men organized the first mining district on the Seward Peninsula. Before long the *Federal Reporter* would be studded with their names: Melsing, Tornanses, Anderson, Libby, Mordaunt, Hultberg, Blake, Kittilsen. These prospectors staked their claims near Council City, where John Brynteson, a coal miner, Erik O. Lindblom, a tailor, and Jafet Lindeberg, a reindeer herder, met by chance in August, 1898.[1]

Brynteson, Lindblom, and Lindeberg all were originally natives of Scandinavia: Brynteson and Lindblom from Sweden, Lindeberg from Norway. By the time they met, Brynteson and Lindblom were already naturalized American citizens, but Lindeberg was not—a status he would change before long. These native Scandinavians briefly prospected in the Council City district but soon became dissatisfied with that location. They made their way up the coast to the mouth of the Snake River, then followed it to a tributary known as Anvil Creek, named for an anvil-shaped rock that stood on the summit of a nearby mountain. On September 21, 1898, these three greenhorn prospectors discovered gold in large quantities, and the next day they began staking claims. They called the first one Discovery Claim, a collective claim later held under the corporate name of the Pioneer Mining Company. Each prospector also staked out an individual claim along Anvil Creek. In late September and mid-October of 1898, the prospectors filed their notices of location, a step necessary to preserve their claims. Under United States law, mineral deposits on public land were open to exploration and purchase by United States citizens and persons who had declared their intention to become citizens. Although Lindeberg was not at that time a citizen of the United States, he had formally applied for citizenship to the commissioner at St. Michael on July 22, 1898.[2]

The placer discoveries on Anvil Creek in September of 1898 set off a new gold rush. The first prospectors to arrive were other natives of Scandinavia who lived nearby. They quickly staked the whole district by posting notices of location and boundary markings, tasks made easy by the area's small size. Approximately half of Anvil Creek's six-mile-long streambed appeared to contain "pay gravel." The average claim was 660 feet wide and 1,320 feet long. Thus, four such claims extended a little over a mile along the creek and twelve covered the entire gold-rich area. These prospectors also liberally exploited the right to secure claims for others through powers of attorney.[3]

Despite efforts by the locators to keep their bonanza a secret, word of the discovery reached the outside world just as the autumn ice began to block seaward traffic to Nome. Anticipation grew over the winter as the news spread throughout the region and along the Pacific Coast. Thousands traveled north during the spring thaw. But when the first newcomers arrived in mid-1899, they discovered that the original locators held a virtual monopoly on the small, rich area around Anvil Creek. The first response was to stake the entire surrounding district in hopes of a lucky strike. By the end of December, 1898, 300 claims were recorded; by April of 1899, 1,200; by July, 2,000; and by December, 4,500. Most of the claims were of dubious legality, for few of the miners concerned themselves with the legal requirements of staking a valid gold discovery claim, which included the performance of assessment work. The more enterprising and devious of the later arrivals sought to "jump" the native Scandinavians' claims by filing competing claims and challenging the legality of the original locators' claims in quiet title suits. In December of 1898, the first group of claim-jumpers targeted claims obtained through the original locators' use of allegedly illegal powers of attorney. Other claim-jumpers asserted that the Scandinavian-born locators were not citizens and therefore could not legally hold a claim. Although these objections were completely unfounded in fact and in law, a number of people attempted to steal the claims of Brynteson, Lindblom, and Lindeberg.[4] Louis Melsing, a jumper from Council City, attempted in February of 1899 to take legal control of Anvil Creek Claim No. 10, which belonged to Johan S. Tornanses. On June 5, 1899, another determined jumper, Robert Chipps, contested Lindeberg's claims. His suit challenged the citizenship of the three Scandinavians and asserted that their location was void on the ground that aliens could not establish a valid mining claim.[5]

Since the laws of the Alaska Territory in fact permitted aliens to hold mining claims, the late arrivals to the area decided to take matters into their own hands. In July of 1899, a town meeting was called in Nome, where within two months the population had mushroomed from 250 to 2,500. On the agenda was a resolution declaring all existing mining claims to be void. When the resolution passed, the conspirators who conceived the ordinance planned to light a series of signals to awaiting comrades who would immediately restake Anvil Creek. An army officer named Lieutenant Oliver Spaulding somehow got wind of the plan and determined to prevent this travesty of justice. Backed by only a few soldiers, Spaulding bravely ordered the resolution to be withdrawn, on threat of clearing the hall at bayonet-point. The meeting broke up after a two-minute stalemate. Although Spaulding's action exceeded his authority, it and some good luck prevented rioting and bloodshed. The immediate crisis passed when a miner discovered gold on the beach sands adjacent to Nome a few days later. The Anvil Creek claims were momentarily forgotten as nearly 2,000 men and women worked side by side to pan gold amounting to $2 million.

Not all sought riches through illegal means. Charles D. Lane soon arrived from the West Coast, where he had earned a reputation for his business savvy and fair dealing. Instead of jumping claims or filing lawsuits, he negotiated with the original locators and secured four of their claims for a reported $300,000. Some of the original locators were undoubtedly fed up with the competition, the litigation, and the threats to their lives. As a bona-fide purchaser with experience in litigation, Lane planned to fight off the claim-jumpers in court and develop the claims with state-of-the-art equipment. He eventually brought in modern appliances, established a line of steamers from San Francisco to Nome, erected warehouses and other buildings, and built and equipped a railroad from Nome to the mines. He named his company the Wild Goose Mining and Trading Company. This was one wild goose whose chase would not prove to be in vain.[6]

Lane's arrival elevated the struggle to wrest control of the rich Anvil Creek claims to a higher level of sophistication. Undaunted, the claim-jumpers retained the Nome law firm of Hubbard, Beeman, and Hume to press their actions against the Pioneer and Wild Goose companies. As one of the first steps in this representation, Frank Hubbard went to Washington in 1899, where he met the claim-jumper Robert Chipps and a man named Alexander McKenzie, an influential political boss of Minnesota and the Dakotas. With a capital of $15 million, McKenzie had formed a corporation known as the Alaska Gold Mining Company. Its purpose was to procure titles held by jumpers of the Nome mining claims—including Chipps's location on Discovery Claim at Anvil Creek—by trading shares for the jump-claims. McKenzie would keep a majority of the stock and would parcel out minority rights to the claim-jumpers.[7]

The actions of Hubbard, Chipps, and McKenzie in Washington posed a distinct threat to the original locators' claims. At that time, Congress was considering legislation to provide a civil government for Alaska. Few realized that "the 1900 civil code was put together in the middle of a conspiracy designed to steal the richest claims in the Nome district." Among other provisions, the bill copied an Oregon law guaranteeing aliens the right to acquire and hold lands in Alaska on the same basis as citizens of the United States. This provision met immediate opposition from Senators Henry Hansbrough of North Dakota and Thomas H. Carter of Montana, both thought to be in cahoots with McKenzie. Carter moved to amend the provision to prohibit aliens from holding or conveying mining claims in Alaska. This amendment would reverse a Supreme Court decision that upheld the right of aliens to hold title to a mining claim by conveyance. Senator Hansbrough frankly admitted that his amendment targeted the Scandinavian prospectors.[8]

That such a provision would have violated the Fifth Amendment by taking property without just compensation was not lost on Senators William M. Stewart of Nevada, Henry M. Teller of Colorado, John C. Spooner of Wisconsin, William B. Bate of Tennessee, and Knute Nelson of Minnesota. A series of ugly debates on the Senate floor scarcely concealed the influence of McKenzie behind Carter and Hansbrough and of Charles Lane behind Stewart. Nelson, himself a native of Norway and a man of high integrity and intellect, tersely countered the pro-McKenzie forces by stating that "the object of this amendment is not to legislate for the future. It is to legislate in the interest of those who have jumped these claims." After vigorous debate the amendment was withdrawn, and the bill establishing a civil government for Alaska became law on June 6, 1900. This same statute established a federal district court for the district of Alaska and authorized the appointment of three judges to reside in various divisions of that territory. Though defeated in his initial bid to shape the law to his liking, McKenzie was not about to give up the fight to gain control over the Anvil Creek claims. He worked behind the scenes to induce his friend President McKinley to appoint Arthur H. Noyes of Minnesota as judge for Division No. 2, which included Nome.

The statute required the Division No. 2 judge to reside in St. Michael and to hold at least one term each year there, beginning the third Monday in June. The law also permitted the judges to hold special terms of court at such times and other places in their district as they deemed appropriate, provided that notice was given at least thirty days before such a special term was held.[9] These statutory requirements would provide an important basis for judging the propriety of Judge Noyes's future actions. A second element of future importance was the authority under which Noyes was appointed. Unlike justices of the Supreme Court and judges of the "inferior" federal courts designated by Article III of the Constitution, the Alaska district judges appointed under the 1900 law did not enjoy the same removal protections. Article III judges may be removed by impeachment and conviction by Congress. Judges of the territorial courts, by contrast, were removable at will by the president. Some chief executives freely exercised this authority to exploit patronage opportunities. The territorial judges had frequently evoked complaints, especially in regions that fell within the Ninth Circuit's geographical boundaries. Early Nevada territorial judges, for example, were accused of maintaining financial interests in the mines that were litigated in their courts, and one Arizona territorial judge refused to hold court in the town of Globe unless its locals provided a residence for him.[10] Noyes easily topped these indiscretions. His scheming with McKenzie presented the Ninth Circuit with its first major crisis.

II. INTERLOPERS

Enactment of the Alaska Civil Code signaled the growing significance Congress attached to the Territory. Due to the Klondike and Nome gold rushes, Alaska's population nearly doubled between 1890 and 1900, from 32,052 to 63,592. But this "mild but unenlightened interest" in the Territory's affairs did not stop McKenzie's scheming to take control of the rich Anvil Creek claims. He saw Noyes's appointment as simply the next step in an alternate plan. For the unsuspecting miners at Nome, the judge's arrival offered the promise of law and order in a town brimming with gamblers, prostitutes, and more than fifty saloons. But the circumstantial evidence suggests that Noyes never intended to serve as an honest judge in his division.[11]

Noyes and McKenzie, who were old friends, traveled with Chipps from Seattle aboard the steamer *Senator*, arriving at Nome on July 19, 1900. Chipps and McKenzie disembarked, but Noyes did not touch land until two days later. By then the time fixed for holding a term of the court at St. Michael had elapsed—the statute having provided for such term to begin on the third Monday in June. And, under the law, Noyes had no authority to hold a special term of court until thirty days after posting notice. When McKenzie left the ship on July 19, he had gone immediately to the office of Hubbard, Beeman and Hume. The law firm had a 50 percent contingent interest in the Anvil Creek litigation. McKenzie told W. T. Hume that he "controlled the appointment of the judge and the district attorney." If the firm wanted to press its clients' claims against the original locators in the district court, the partners had better transfer their interest to McKenzie's corporation and receive in lieu thereof certificates of stock. Left with little choice, they accepted these terms. Shortly thereafter, McKenzie also insisted that the lawyers give him an additional one-fourth interest in their firm. Hume initially protested, but when McKenzie threatened to ruin Hume's legal practice and sabotage his clients' interests, he consented.[12]

The claim-jumping suits provided legal cover for McKenzie's real goal of controlling the rich Anvil Creek mining claims. In theory, so long as the true ownership was in doubt, neither the original locators nor the claim-jumpers could work the claims. Having displaced the law firm that represented the claim-jumpers, McKenzie had them prepare papers for the appointment of receivers in four actions in which Hubbard, Beeman and Hume were attorneys for plaintiffs. As judge, Noyes could then appoint McKenzie himself as the receiver of the property. A receiver in a property dispute typically serves to ensure preservation of the property, preventing either side from depriving the other of mineral wealth and thus allowing the court to adjudicate competing claims to title in a fair and just manner. The cliché that this was hornbook law, which should have been well known to Noyes and McKenzie, underscored the correct principle: "The business of a receiver of a mining property is to preserve the property and to close out the business turned over to him, and a court of equity has no authority to direct its receiver in charge of mines to carry on a general mining business."[13] McKenzie's conception of what a receiver should be, however, was quite different. Just how different was not immediately evident to the miners at Anvil Creek.

On the morning of July 23, McKenzie bustled around Nome preparing to put his plan into effect. While the lawyers were readying papers to request the appointment of a receiver, McKenzie was rounding up wagons to transport his men to Anvil Creek. In the late afternoon, Hume called on Judge Noyes at his hotel to present the papers. The lawyer began reading the affidavit setting out the facts purporting to justify the receivership appointment, but Noyes cut him off. A reading was unnecessary. Noyes accepted their arguments without deigning to hear from the other side, and said that as a stranger to the territory, he preferred to appoint someone he knew. Noyes then named McKenzie receiver, but with instructions to take immediate possession of the relevant mining claims, to work them, and to preserve the gold dust and proceeds of the claims subject to further orders of the court.[14]

Noyes took this action a scant two days after leaving the ship. The court had not yet been organized, nor had it issued notice of a special term. Moreover, Noyes had failed to comply with the statute requiring a term of court to be held in St. Michael beginning the third Monday of June. All this seemed quite irrelevant to the judge at the time, as did the necessity of having some legal or equitable justification for the appointment of a receiver, which Hume's papers failed to posit. Had a compelling case been made for placing a receiver at the mines, in all probability the lesser step of ordering an injunction would have sufficed to protect the claims of the rightful owners, because it would have halted all activity at the mines. Instead, within minutes of the official receivership appointment and before the papers were filed with the clerk, McKenzie was whipping his teams toward Anvil Creek. The miners of the Wild Goose and Pioneer mining companies first learned of the receiver's appointment when McKenzie and his men arrived at Anvil Creek bearing official papers.[15]

The following day, Samuel Knight, an attorney for the original locators, requested a hearing. Noyes at first refused, stating that he would take up the matter when he returned from St. Michael, but Knight persisted. Noyes reluctantly agreed and heard arguments at three o'clock that afternoon, after which he announced that he would render his decision the following Monday, six days later. In the meantime, another attorney for the original locators, W. H. Metson, challenged the broad sweep of Noyes's July 23 order, which permitted the receiver to take possession not only of the mine but also of the miners' tents and personal property. Metson's appearance before Noyes gave the judge an opportunity to upbraid the lawyer for his clients' actions up at Anvil Creek: "'Your people are preventing the receiver from working the Discovery claim. I am going to tie your people up all around. I am going to make an order which will take everything away from them.'" Noyes then enlarged McKenzie's powers as receiver by explicitly directing him to "take possession of all sluice boxes, pumps, excavations, machinery, pipe, plant, boarding houses, tents, buildings, safes, scales, and all personal property, fixed and movable, gold, gold dust, and precious metals, money boxes, or coin, and all personal property upon said claim." McKenzie immediately implemented the order. His men took possession of the original discoverers' personal property, their gold dust, and the business records for their mines.[16]

Noyes then left for St. Michael. He had promised to return to Nome on July 30 to render a decision on the motion to rescind the receivership, but that day expired without a ruling. Noyes managed to stall on this pivotal issue until August 10, when he denied the original locators' motion. By now it was becoming clear to them that McKenzie was hardly the disinterested receiver contemplated by ordinary legal process. But they did not know the depth of his corruption. They were unaware that McKenzie had purchased Robert Chipps's claimed title to the Discovery Claim, that he had muscled into a one-fourth contingent interest in the litigation, and that he exercised influence over Judge Noyes.[17] Although the original locators were not privy to McKenzie's devious scheme, the complaints instituted by the claim-jumpers gave notice to lawyers of even average caliber that something was amiss. The complaints not only misrepresented the facts and the law on their face, but they also failed to plead the necessary elements for the appointment of a receiver.[18]

Moreover, Noyes's requirement of a $5,000 bond for each claim was grossly inadequate to protect the parties. When Noyes appointed the receiver, the Discovery Claim was yielding $15,000 in gold dust per day. On adjoining claims, the Wild Goose Mining Company was collecting between $5,000 and $10,000 daily. Instead of protecting both sides and deterring the receiver from wrongdoing, the assessed bond was a trifle—the equivalent of what the miners could produce in a matter of hours. Indeed, within weeks of taking possession of the mines, McKenzie's men extracted gold dust valued at more than $100,000. By mid-September he had accumulated a total of $130,000 in ore. McKenzie also allegedly confiscated more than $200,000 in gold dust that belonged to the original locators, who later sued McKenzie for $430,000 in damages, consisting of the value of the claim, their mining rights, and ruined mining tools.[19]

Having failed to persuade Noyes to rescind the receivership appointment, counsel for the original locators next requested orders allowing them to appeal to the circuit court of appeals for the Ninth Circuit. Noyes denied their motion.[20] At the time, the Ninth Circuit was not in session, but Judge Morrow in San Francisco entertained their emergency motions and issued writs of supersedeas for the purpose of overriding Noyes's rulings. Based on the "shocking record" presented to him, Morrow ordered McKenzie to restore the mining claims to the original locators, together with the gold, gold dust, and other personal property he had received under Noyes's orders.[21] Because Morrow was the only circuit judge whose chambers were in San Francisco, where the court was headquartered—William Gilbert and Erskine Ross kept their chambers in Portland and Los Angeles, respectively, and traveled to San Francisco for the court's sessions—he acted alone in issuing these orders.

Attorneys for the Pioneer and Wild Goose companies attempted to execute Judge Morrow's writs of supersedeas and proper citations, but McKenzie refused to comply with the orders and Noyes would not enforce them. The judge explained unconvincingly that " 'I can do nothing about this order; this litigation has caused me a great deal of worry. My hands are tied; the court has taken the whole matter out of my hands. You gentlemen have got to fight this thing out among yourselves.' " He added, " 'I shall make no order; it is not my duty to do so; it is not within my province or right to do so.' " Cornelius L. Vawter, the United States marshal assigned to Noyes's court, later testified that the judge said he " 'was not going to do anything and McKenzie could do as he pleased.' "[22]

Tension in the community escalated as word of Morrow's action leaked out. The Wild Goose and Pioneer companies' miners threatened to enforce the Ninth Circuit orders themselves. In a face-off with McKenzie, W. H. Metson reportedly forced the issue to near-violence at the mine site—a decision of dubious wisdom, for although the receiver presented an enormous target at 6'6", McKenzie had a reputation as the fastest draw in Dakota. Bloodshed was averted only by the timely arrival of soldiers.[23]

As the situation unraveled, Noyes continued to display his contempt for the appellate court's orders: " 'I have got a right to interpret those writs,' " Vawter recalled Noyes as saying. " 'I don't know whether [the bonds] are genuine or not; I don't know who Frank Monckton is; I am not going to take any clerk of the court's word for it. . . . In any event,' " Noyes allegedly added, " 'the Supreme Court will knock them out when it gets there.' " Noyes also spurned assistance from military officers who offered to enforce the Ninth Circuit writs. The soldiers fretted that vigilantism would ensue, especially if McKenzie refused to heed the appellate court's order. Noyes cautioned that "matters should rest [as they are], and peace and order be preserved, and I therefore request that you render such assistance to the marshal as may be necessary to maintain that peace and quiet." Maintaining the status quo, of course, meant McKenzie's continued plundering of the Anvil Creek claims.[24] Noyes's unwillingness to implement the Ninth Circuit orders forced the Wild Goose and Pioneer lawyers once again to seek emergency assistance from San Francisco. Even with counsel in the Bay Area, the long delay gave the McKenzie gang appreciably more time to carry out its scheme.

Nevertheless, by early October the original locators had recaptured their mines by somehow persuading McKenzie to relinquish his control. But when the Pioneer and Wild Goose miners began to dig for gold and transport it out of Nome, Chipps, one of the original claim-jumpers, applied to the court for an injunction prohibiting the original locators from shipping gold dust outside the territorial jurisdiction of the court. Not surprisingly, Noyes granted the motion. He issued this order without requiring a bond, once again ignoring the original locators' interests. Meanwhile, two United States marshals were on their way to Nome from San Francisco, where Morrow had dispatched them to arrest Alexander McKenzie for contempt of court. The Ninth Circuit judge had acted quickly, mindful of the fast-approaching autumn freeze. The marshals arrested McKenzie on October 15, 1900, and charged him with contempt of court for disobeying the writs of supersedeas.[25]

The receiver would not give in without a struggle. The marshals discovered that McKenzie was holding more than $200,000 in gold dust at the Alaska Banking and Safe-Deposit Company. McKenzie rebuffed their demand to hand over the keys to the deposit vaults that held the stolen dust. Moreover, he threatened violence if the marshals executed the Ninth Circuit orders. Undaunted, the deputy marshals secured military support, broke open the vaults at the bank, took the gold dust, and delivered it to the original locators as directed. They then proceeded to San Francisco, where McKenzie was brought to the bar of the court.[26]

III.   A JUDICIAL RESCUE

Nome rejoiced over McKenzie's arrest. "'It is seldom that a calamity happening to a single individual is productive of such universal joy as when McKenzie the boss, McKenzie the distributor of patronage, McKenzie the messiah, McKenzie the all seeing, the all wise, the all powerful, had become plain Mac the prisoner.'" McKenzie's arrest shifted the struggle from Nome to San Francisco, where the authority of the circuit court of appeals would be tested. It also sent a signal his co-conspirators could not fail to notice. The next day, as the *Valencia* sailed with the prisoner aboard, the original locators moved to dissolve the October 10 injunction. Hume, counsel for the claim-jumpers and a key figure in the incident, stated in open court that he believed it incumbent on his clients "to dissolve the injunction of their own motion, or for the court to dissolve it." Judge Noyes took the hint and so ordered.[27] The damage had been done, however, and this last-ditch effort to comply with Ninth

Circuit orders would be met with the reprobation it deserved. The court dealt with Noyes in due course; its first task was to handle the McKenzie matter.

The proceedings began on November 7, 1900, before United States Commissioner E. H. Heacock. Heacock's duties as commissioner were generally akin to those of a justice of the peace or magistrate: he had the authority to issue search warrants and to hold preliminary hearings on criminal matters.[28] Because the complicated web of events in Nome required the taking of testimony, the circuit court of appeals deputed Heacock to serve as a kind of trier of fact in McKenzie's contempt proceedings. Heacock's permissive conduct of the trial raised numerous objections from McKenzie's distinguished legal team, which included Frank Kellogg of St. Paul, Milton S. Gunn, and ex-Congressman Thomas J. Geary, as well as R. B. Beeman of the Nome law firm McKenzie had shanghaied. The commissioner followed "his usual procedure of allowing the witness to answer all the questions, whether objected to or not, and leave to Judge Morrow the task of striking out or allowing the answers to remain in the record." This procedure enabled the court to elicit all the facts, particularly under the intense and skillful questioning of E. S. Pillsbury, whom the court appointed special prosecutor. A famed San Francisco attorney and leader of one of its most prominent firms, Pillsbury carried out his role with zeal and the aid of the original locators' lawyers, including W. H. Metson from Nome, J. C. Campbell, and the firm of Page, McCutchen, Harding and Knight. Morrow's assignment to the case, as the judge who would review the evidence prior to its consideration by the full Ninth Circuit panel of himself, Gilbert, and Ross, was perhaps as much a function of his keeping chambers in San Francisco as of his being the junior member of the court. He was also a very experienced trial judge.[29]

The evidentiary phase of the contempt trial took several weeks and preparation for oral argument and consideration of the case several more. When the court decided the case on February 11, 1901, it was in a difficult position. The court had compiled an extensive record of illegality by an officer of the court who was also one of the most powerful political bosses west of the Mississippi. McKenzie had a legion of supporters from Capitol Hill to the White House. At the same time, the miners in Nome were angry beyond description at what McKenzie had done. His arrest by the marshals may well have prevented a lynching.[30] Whereas McKenzie's political allies in Washington undoubtedly would have applauded leniency by the court, the Nome miners wanted a harsh penalty. And these were merely the parochial political considerations that clouded the judicial environment. In addition, the court's handling of Noyes and other participants in the scheme would shape larger issues of development and of respect for the judiciary.

Erskine Ross's opinion for the court downplayed the grander themes. But by carefully analyzing the narrow legal issues involved, the court rendered a decision with far-reaching significance. Before the court proceeded to the merits, it considered whether the defendants could appeal from the order appointing the receiver. Noyes had denied a right of appeal on the ground that receivership orders were not included in the Alaska Civil Code provision pertaining to interlocutory appeals. Ross chose not to dispute this characterization of the law, which Noyes probably construed correctly. Instead, he cleverly reasoned that Noyes's decision was a "final judgment" appealable under the general provision governing appeals of district court rulings: "[A]n order by which a placer mining claim, whose proper preservation in no respect requires it, is taken from one who is in the actual possession thereof, and turned over to a receiver, with instructions to extract from it its only value, is, in effect, a final decree, and appealable as such; for its entire value may be thus destroyed by improper working or extravagant management, or by the extraction of all its mineral, while he from whom it is taken, and who asserts a right to it, may prefer to work the claim to a limited extent only, or in a particular manner, or not at all." The restrictiveness of this elaborate holding indicated that the court devised the rule solely for this case. With a candor that reflected many of his judicial opinions, Ross conceded that authority for this position was difficult to find: "Surely, the authority, by whatever name called, under which such a result may be wrought, is, in effect, a final judgment."[31]

The court next considered whether a single judge of the circuit court of appeals could grant a writ of supersedeas. This issue posed no great difficulty, because section 11 of the Evarts Act provided that "any judge of the circuit courts of appeals, in respect of cases brought or to be brought to that court, shall have the same powers and duties as to the allowance of appeals or writs of error, and the conditions of such allowance, as now by law belong to the justices or judges in respect of the existing courts of the United States respectively." In its first case construing the Evarts Act, the Supreme Court had upheld the authority of a justice to grant a writ of supersedeas under this provision. The same principle applied to circuit judges.[32]

On the merits, the court rejected McKenzie's claim of "sincerity" in refusing to obey the supersedeas writs. McKenzie's conduct, the court concluded, "so far from impressing us with the sincerity of the pretension that his refusal to obey the writs issued out of this court was based upon the advice of his counsel that they were void, satisfy us that it was intentional and deliberate." The "grossly illegal proceedings initiated almost as soon as Judge Noyes and McKenzie had set foot on Alaskan territory at Nome . . . may be safely and fortunately said to have no parallel in the jurisprudence of this country." Accordingly, the court sentenced him to one year's imprisonment in California's Alameda County jail. McKenzie immediately filed a writ of habeas corpus in the Supreme Court. The Ninth Circuit had rendered its decision on February 11, 1901. The Supreme Court heard argument on February 26 and handed down its decision on March 25, 1901—speedy review for an influential politician. For this result, though, McKenzie undoubtedly would have preferred to wait. The Court rejected his application for a writ and upheld the Ninth Circuit's ruling on all grounds. In a short opinion by Chief Justice Fuller, the Court held that the Ninth Circuit had properly invoked jurisdiction and exercised its power without abuse.[33]

Proceedings against Noyes and other members of the Nome gang were held in abeyance while the Supreme Court decided McKenzie's fate; a reversal would effectively terminate this corollary litigation. Other alleged co-conspirators included McKenzie's attorney Thomas Geary, United States Attorney Joseph K. Wood, and a Department of Justice attorney, C. A. S. Frost. Back in Nome, Noyes and Wood continued to hold office throughout the winter of 1901, although the judge did little to dent the backlog of cases that had built up over the past two years. On May 25, 1901, the momentum accelerating toward a juridical resolution of the controversy took a curious political turn when President McKinley commuted McKenzie's term to the time he had served, a little more than three months. The ostensible reason for the pardon was McKenzie's deteriorating health. The press reported that the prisoner was "too weak to leave the jail," but one historian has written that "McKenzie's debility did not keep him from sprinting from the jail door to the train station or from continuing to exercise his political power for twenty more years before he died." Health issues aside, the pardon underscored the political influences still at play. Meanwhile, the Ninth Circuit cited Noyes for contempt, and the Justice Department suspended him from further work pending the outcome of the case and assigned his docket to the very able and upright James Wickersham, the district judge for Division No. 3.[34]

Winter's end opened access to Nome, and Noyes received the court's contempt citation on July 5, 1901. But he still held some hope that powerful political allies would find a way to transfer the investigation from San Francisco to Washington, where he would stand a better chance of evading punishment. Noyes traveled to Minnesota and to Washington, presumably to lobby for himself, before arriving in San Francisco in October for the contempt proceedings, which followed the same format as the McKenzie case. Commissioner Heacock presided at the evidentiary phase, with Pillsbury again serving, for no fee, as the court's special counsel.[35] After taking several thousand pages of testimony, the court rendered its decision on January 6, 1902.

The court charged Noyes with contempt for refusing to enforce the supersedeas writs ordering McKenzie to relinquish the gold dust taken from the Anvil Creek claims. Noyes alleged in defense that he believed that all matters pertaining to the receivership had passed beyond his control. Writing for the court, Judge William B. Gilbert suspected otherwise. Although it expressed no official opinion on the existence of a conspiracy, the court left little doubt about its view: "Much of [the evidence] tends strongly to show the existence of a criminal conspiracy between some of these respondents and McKenzie and others to use the court and its process for their private gain, and to unlawfully deprive the owners of mines who were in possession thereof of their property under the forms of law." The taint of conspiracy colored the proceedings; and the court seemed intent on punishing other misconduct under its authority to discipline contempt. Gilbert acknowledged as much when he stated that "[r]eference to the evidence of their misconduct will be made only for the purpose of finding the animus which actuated them in the commission of the acts with which they stand charged." This approach guided the court's summary of Judge Noyes's offense, which focused more on the squalid deeds of the Nome ring in stealing gold than on the specific actions that justified a contempt conviction. Indeed, much of Gilbert's rendition of the facts bore little on the contempt charge, and he included elaborate dicta to expose other schemes by Noyes and McKenzie.[36]

Framing the contempt conviction in these terms may have been unnecessary for deciding the narrow legal issue presented by the case, but it served a useful function. By including the full scope of Noyes's wrongdoing in its opinion the court insulated itself from attack by Washington

politicians who were sympathetic to McKenzie and Noyes. In this politically charged litigation, the opinion itself was the most logical forum
for the court to anticipate and answer its Capitol Hill critics. At the same
time, the opinion reinforced the position of those Justice Department
officials who sought to punish Noyes, Wood, and others. The court
resoundingly adjudged Noyes guilty of contempt, but the judges disagreed on the appropriate punishment. Gilbert and Morrow fixed the
penalty at a fine of $1,000. Ross, however, urged that Noyes be sen-
tenced to eighteen months' imprisonment. Neither Gilbert nor Morrow
believed that the Ninth Circuit had authority to impose this sentence,
which would constitute a "removal" from office.[37] Accordingly, they
entrusted such action to the Executive Branch.

The court also decided contempt charges brought against Thomas J.
Geary, McKenzie's lawyer in Nome. A decade earlier Geary had written
the infamous 1892 Chinese Exclusion Act. A well-known member of the
San Francisco bar, he now persuaded the court that the evidence was
insufficient to establish his guilt beyond a reasonable doubt. Geary
testified that he "never at any time advised McKenzie to disobey the
writs." He sincerely believed that the orders appointing McKenzie receiver were not appealable and that the writs themselves did not require
surrender of the gold dust. Geary testified that he did not directly advise
McKenzie on the appropriate course of action. Uncertain as to the proof
of contempt, therefore, the court dismissed the charge against him.[38]

The other officers of the court were not so fortunate. United States
Attorney Joseph K. Wood, who first arrived in Nome with McKenzie and
Noyes and who, at McKenzie's instigation, became a silent member of
Hubbard, Beeman and Hume, was also charged with contempt of court
for his actions regarding the enforcement of the supersedeas writs issued
to McKenzie. The charge stemmed from Wood's response to the marshals' demand for the bank vault keys where McKenzie had deposited
the gold dust. McKenzie told the marshals he had given the keys to
Wood. To United States Marshal Shelley Monckton's request that Wood
hand over the keys, Wood allegedly responded: "'Do you understand I
have the keys to those boxes? Understand nothing; I don't care what you
understand.'" After Monckton made a formal demand for the keys,
Wood simply said, "'See you later'" and left. For his conduct in the
incident, Wood received a sentence of four months' imprisonment in the
Alameda County jail.[39]

The last defendant was C. A. S. Frost, an attorney deployed by the
Justice Department as a special examiner to advise the clerk and the

marshal of the fledgling Alaska district court regarding their duties and accounts. Frost was a less conspicuous figure in the conspiracy. He had served as special examiner to the court until September 15, 1900, when he resigned to become assistant U.S. attorney under Wood, after Hume resigned that post. After seven months, on April 15, 1901, he stepped down, this time to become Noyes's private secretary. Frost's offenses included tampering with names submitted for jury duty and assisting in the contempts of McKenzie and Noyes. In its final act concerning the Nome scandal, the court sentenced him to twelve months' imprisonment in the Alameda County jail.[40]

IV. CONSEQUENCES

The intrigue at Anvil Creek was more than an exciting incident that provided the plot for Rex Beach's best-selling novel and for films starring Gary Cooper, John Wayne, Marlene Dietrich, Randolph Scott, and Anne Baxter.[41] The episode threatened to upset order not only at the fledgling Nome camp but also at mining sites elsewhere in Alaska and the continental West. Unchecked, the insubordination by district court officials would have posed a serious challenge to the Ninth Circuit's authority as the most powerful federal court in these states except the Supreme Court. At a different level, the episode imperiled the court's independence, forcing its judges to rule on narrow legal issues in a politically charged environment. In these circumstances, the court's handling of the incident had significance far beyond the narrow parameters of the contempt cases themselves.

In Nome, the immediate effects of the Ninth Circuit's action were great. Mining activity had ceased during the year and a half between the arrival of Noyes and McKenzie in mid-1900 and the contempt conviction of the judge in early 1902. Distrust of the judiciary dried up capital investment in mining development and construction. Because the stakes were so great, investors' hesitation to commit financial resources was understandable. Between 1898 and 1906, more than $37 million in gold was produced from the Seward Peninsula. It is impossible to say how much higher this figure would have been if the miners had trusted the local judicial process during the McKenzie-Noyes affair: a contemporary report placed the estimated value of gold in the region at $325 million. As the population of the Nome area mushroomed in the summer of 1900 from 3,000 to 20,000, thousands of inexperienced miners suffered significant deprivation from this chilling effect on normal economic activity.

Miners closed down their operations and waited, fearful that claim-jumpers or court-appointed receivers would steal their ore. By November of 1900, squatters and jumpers had filed more than five hundred suits, for which Noyes had appointed more than one hundred receivers, usually friends of McKenzie or McKenzie himself. The institution of these suits, the struggle to rescind receivership orders, and Noyes's own dilatoriness in attending to his docket meant severe hardship even for the original locators, who had to pay the high cost of living and expensive litigation without confidence that they could legally work their claims. The Ninth Circuit's firm handling of the McKenzie ring and Judge Wickersham's able stewardship of the district court restored the Nome miners' faith in the judicial process.[42]

That message gained greater significance when vast quantities of gold were discovered in 1902 in the Tanana Valley, where in ensuing years the town of Fairbanks grew up. Unlike the situation in Nome under Noyes's tenure, in Tanana Valley property disputes involving mining claims were litigated in the district court and appealed to the Ninth Circuit as a matter of routine. In the first decade of this century the circuit court of appeals considered numerous cases on a wide range of issues. As gold production increased in the Fairbanks area, so did appeals to the Ninth Circuit. Indeed, nearly one-fifth of the mining cases decided by the Ninth Circuit between 1900 and 1910 originated in Alaska, evidence of the extent to which prospectors placed their faith in dispute resolution by judicial process rather than self-help.[43] Many of these cases raised lingering issues from the Nome region that remained unresolved until after the Noyes scandal was put down.[44] The property disputes that were the stuff of high drama in Nome became rather more mundane under the Ninth Circuit's jurisprudence. Mining litigants steadily gained confidence that the appellate court would reverse if the district court had erred and that disagreements among the Ninth Circuit judges related to the uncertainty of law and not to furtive scheming.[45]

The Ninth Circuit came under heavy fire for its actions in the Nome episode. Miners viewed the punishment meted out as too light. After the Ninth Circuit convicted Noyes of contempt, the grand jury in Nome wanted to indict the judge for criminal offenses. Neither the Justice Department nor Judge Wickersham was anxious for this development to occur, and both persuaded local authorities that the disgrace of a contempt conviction was punishment enough. Others, too, believed that the punishments amounted merely to a slap on the wrist. One respected historian has characterized the $1,000 fine of Noyes and four months' imprisonment for Wood in very unflattering terms: "Such light penalties indicated that Washington, D.C. was still looking after the Spoilers." This conclusion may not be wholly fair. The context of the ruling was a contempt proceeding, and although a court had discretion, prison terms for contempt were typically not severe. As Ross stated in his separate opinion, "For those shocking offenses it is apparent that no punishment that can be lawfully imposed in a contempt proceeding is adequate." He thought that Noyes, Frost, and Wood should be imprisoned for eighteen, fifteen, and ten months respectively. Noyes avoided a jail term because Morrow and Gilbert reasonably believed that the judiciary could not "remove" a colleague by ordering imprisonment for contempt.[46]

After the court rendered its decisions, some politicians in Washington accused the Ninth Circuit judges of wrongdoing for imposing penalties on the Nome ring. Loose talk posited that Lane's people had bribed the court. Characterizing the penalties as "monstrous," Senator Porter J. McCumber stated on the Senate floor that Gilbert, Ross, and Morrow "are intensely biased; . . . they are prejudiced beyond all reason and all sense." To this calumny Senator Benjamin R. Tillman, a farmer from South Carolina, responded that McCumber "owes it to himself to quit attacking this court or prove something against it otherwise than by mere assertion." A charge of corruption against the court seemed similarly ill-advised. After Morrow had issued the writs of supersedeas, Noyes himself allegedly declared: "'Our company made a great mistake not to have had someone to look after the San Francisco end of this litigation; if it had these writs would never have been issued.'"[47]

As the senators debated the Ninth Circuit proceedings, the Justice Department wrapped up its investigation, which culminated in Noyes's removal. Led by Attorney General Philander C. Knox, the department's probe went over much the same ground as the Ninth Circuit's proceedings and received a presidential nudge, if not an outright order, in February of 1902. David H. Jarvis, the collector of customs at Nome and a confidant of McKinley's successor, wrote to President Theodore Roosevelt in early 1902 that only "the immediate removal of everybody connected with this conspiracy will give the people confidence in the good intentions of the administration, and restore confidence and stability to the business of that part of Alaska." Roosevelt scrawled at the bottom of this memorandum, "Atty Gen'l, This is from Jarvis, who certainly knows Alaska. TR." Knox got the message. In February, 1902, he conducted a hearing to which he invited E. S. Pillsbury to testify.

Pillsbury, who had served the court without pay for three months, saw the Justice Department investigation as an ill-conceived review of the Ninth Circuit's action. Explaining his refusal to appear at Knox's hearing, the venerable San Francisco lawyer stated, "I do not consider that the Court has need of vindication from any source."[48]

As mining activity continued in Alaska and other states in the circuit during the early part of the century, the court's handling of the Anvil Creek incident served as a reminder of the importance of law and orderly process. No one could doubt that the court stood resolutely against similar lawlessness in its other tribunals throughout the circuit. The court would treat contempt of its orders with firmness and dispatch. This message spread throughout the West at a time when the court's authority was still uncertain. Although by this time it had already decided seven hundred cases, it had heard few appeals from the territories of Alaska, Arizona, and Hawaii. The far-flung Ninth Circuit demanded a powerful, if not an omnipresent, force for law and order. The court's action in the Anvil Creek incident signaled, not only to the frontier miners of Alaska but to the settlers of Arizona, the farmers in Hawaii, and all persons throughout the circuit, that it would handle disputes by process of law without succumbing to corruption or political pressure.

FIVE

The Judicial Faultline

Battles over Natural Resources

[The West] is a new and rapidly developing region,
gradually becoming populated, and exceedingly rich in the
precious metals; . . . suddenly there has arisen an entirely
new condition of industrial affairs in that region,
and . . . consequently legal problems of a correspondingly
novel type will demand solution.

Austin Lewis, 1900

In their first few years together on the court, William Gilbert and Erskine Ross had articulated different approaches to judging. The discerning observer could predict, from their divergent party affiliations and dissimilar upbringings, possible sources of conflict on the bench. On the great problems that confronted the court in its first fifteen years—the *Stanford* case, the Chinese exclusion issues, and the Nome scandal—their disagreements typically embraced only subtleties that did not affect outcomes. After the Anvil Creek incident, however, disputes over natural resources—especially mining, timber, and oil—unlocked the potential for serious discord. By disposition and intellect, Gilbert and Ross competed for preeminence on a court that significantly affected the ability of westerners to exploit the region's natural resources.

Through the vicissitudes of congressionally conferred jurisdiction, the Ninth Circuit became the court of last resort for over 96 percent of the cases it handled. Through a quirk of geography, a large proportion of the nation's mineral and timber resources rested in the territorial configuration of the Ninth Circuit. And through the evolution of the region's history, the United States government held title to much of the land in the circuit, thus giving federal rather than state courts the predominant role in adjudicating disputes involving these lands.[1] What the Ninth Circuit had to say about resource disputes, therefore, took on great importance for the people who sought to tap the West's natural wealth.

And what Erskine Ross and William Gilbert thought mattered even more, because they approached these problems from very different perspectives. Whoever gained a majority for his view affected the course of land development, of investment in extractive enterprises, and of the United States government's ability to enforce public-land laws.

I. COMPETING JUDICIAL PHILOSOPHIES

Shortly after he became circuit judge in March, 1895, Ross rendered a decision that illuminated his thinking on the sanctity of property. As trial judge in the circuit court in *Bradley v. Fallbrook Irrigation District*, Ross held that a California statute establishing irrigation districts impaired a landowner's property rights without due process. As he eloquently stated in his conclusion to that opinion, "Unfortunate as it will be if losses result to investors, and desirable as it undoubtedly is, in this section of the country, that irrigation facilities be improved and extended, it is far more important that the provisions of that great charter, which is the sheet anchor of safety, be in all things observed and enforced."[2]

For jurisdictional reasons, the appeal in *Bradley* bypassed the Ninth Circuit: until 1925 the circuit courts of appeals' jurisdiction did not extend to questions involving the construction of the Constitution, the constitutionality of a United States law or treaty, or the alleged contravention of the Constitution by state constitutions or laws. On direct appeal, the Supreme Court reversed Ross's decision. But neither this ruling nor jurisdictional limitations on the circuit courts of appeals dampened the veneration of property rights that Ross articulated in a range of disputes over natural resources.[3] His chief intellectual counterweight on the Ninth Circuit, William B. Gilbert, held a substantially different view of property and a philosophy of judging that clashed sharply with Ross's. While their different approaches to judging readily emerge, in key respects their judicial philosophies defied such labels as "laissez-faire conservative" or "traditional conservative."[4]

Statutory construction presented a classic battleground for Ross and Gilbert, as they disagreed over how far judges should go in attempting to ferret out Congress's intent. For his part, Ross interpreted statutes literally. If the statute did not speak directly to a question, he saw his role as ended. In one such case, Ross wrote for the majority in construing a statute that prohibited a person from locating "any placer-mining claim in Alaska as attorney for another unless he is duly authorized thereto by a power of attorney in writing." Ross's construction required the miner or agent to file the power of attorney before either person knew whether a discovery warranted the filing of location papers. Gilbert dissented, because he found no logic in a statute construed to require miners to file a power of attorney before locating a potentially lucrative site. In the natural rhythm of events, he contended, a miner would use the power of attorney only after making the discovery. In Gilbert's opinion, a simpler and more sympathetic interpretation of the statute would permit the agent for the locator to file the power of attorney concurrently with the location certificate. "The act of Congress does not say that the power of attorney must be recorded before the initiation of any of the acts of location," Gilbert maintained. "It is a harsh and narrow construction that gives to the act that meaning, and it is a construction which is contrary to the liberal teaching of . . . numerous other decisions."[5]

These two jurists clashed heatedly over even the seemingly simple question of whether a statute required two witnesses to the filing of a deed by an original locator. Writing for himself and William W. Morrow, Gilbert held that a conveyance witnessed by only one person satisfied the requirements of a statute that appeared to require two. For a strict constructionist like Ross, this interpretation eluded reason. He contended in dissent that the statutory requirement of two witnesses "meant what it said." Ross deemed irrelevant that Congress intended a subsequent statute to cure other defects of the conveyance. If the statute required two witnesses, it was "an essential part of the execution." Because the court had openly acknowledged the failure of the parties to obtain two witnesses, Ross refused to endorse the conveyance.[6]

The two judges' conflicting choices between what Congress said literally and what it must have intended reasonably extended to their approaches to contract disputes. The same principles applied; the same battle lines were drawn, as an appeal from Alaska demonstrated. In *Alaska Treadwell Gold Mining Company v. Alaska Gastineau Mining Company*, the court reviewed a decree of specific performance. Alaska Gastineau had sued for specific performance on a written contract between its predecessor in interest, Oxford Mining Company, and Alaska Treadwell. Oxford Mining Company had leased certain mining property to Alaska Treadwell along with a sawmill, a boarding house, and other appurtenances to the mine. As part of the arrangement, Alaska Treadwell had promised to build a water power plant to generate electricity and to supply "a current of not to exceed three hundred (300) horsepower." The district court interpreted the contract to include starting surges of up to three or four times the normal amount for one of Alaska Gastineau's special machines.[7]

In an opinion by Ross in which Morrow joined, the Ninth Circuit held that the contract was not specific enough to demonstrate a commitment by Alaska Treadwell to deliver this amount of power. Ross wrote that the court should certainly consider the parties' intent when construing the written document, but in so doing it could not add to or take away from any of the contract's provisions: "To read by construction into the written contract of the parties such a requirement is therefore to read into it a most important provision not there found." Gilbert dissented, agreeing with the trial court's finding that the parties intended to include the disputed item. In a sentence that said much about his judicial philosophy, Gilbert explained, "Where a contract is susceptible of a construction in accordance with justice and fair dealing, the court should adopt it."[8]

These different approaches to interpretation also showed themselves in deed and recordation disputes. In the first two decades of this century, the Ninth Circuit heard numerous appeals from decisions adjudicating property issues. In this context, Gilbert's reasonable-interpretation approach usually prevailed over Ross's literal constructionism. In one such case, the court considered whether miners had properly marked their mining claim and sufficiently recorded notice of that location. Gilbert's opinion for the court rested on the reasonableness of the description. He attempted to understand the customary mode of describing mines so that he could assess whether a person with this information could find the location in question, for "[i]f he could, the notice is sufficient." Ross found this approach unsatisfying. He complained that the notice was vague and urged a remand for more fact-finding because the description said nothing about the location of a stake in relation to a key landmark. His attention to detail and insistence on precision would not accept a lesser description.[9]

The exactness Ross demanded of Congress in writing statutes and of parties in drafting contracts applied no less forcefully to the standards employed by federal courts in the conduct of trials: he evaluated trial court proceedings rigorously. Gilbert, however, deferred to the trial court's fact-finding and application of legal standards. He believed that if a jury found certain facts to be true, the appellate court should not upset those findings. The same pattern of deference developed for abuse-of-discretion issues. Ross, by contrast, suffered no angst as he discovered and articulated the trial court's errors. The hands-off approach he favored in construing written documents did not at all apply to his review of trial court proceedings. Gilbert's activism in searching for the intent behind the written language did not foreshadow a more intrusive approach to reviewing errors on appeal.[10]

On general mining disputes, Gilbert's position prevailed most of the time. With his view on recordation and other property disputes ascendant, litigants might anticipate that the court would attempt to infer the parties' intent from their actions. Yet Ross's occasional victories taught potential litigants that they risked losing in the Ninth Circuit if they failed to abide by the strict requirements of the property statutes. After the initial uncertainty caused by his invalidation of such "incomplete" conveyances, Ross's position forced litigants to become more sensitive to legal requirements. Had he consistently captured a majority, Ross's formalistic rule might eventually have created more certainty, but Gilbert's approach arguably suited the times better, especially in Alaska, where the skill of the bar was uneven and access to current legal opinions limited.[11] A harsh interpretation of conveyancing principles or recordation law would have penalized many enterprising miners. By interpreting their actions and their intentions with greater flexibility, Gilbert captured the commercial realities of the region during that era more accurately than did Ross.

II. THE BUTTE COPPER WARS

For the first two decades of the twentieth century, disputes over land and mining claims, particularly in Alaska, composed a large segment of the court's docket. Many of these lawsuits meant financial riches or ruin for the individuals and small companies who appealed to the Ninth Circuit. But during this same period, the court was addressing legal issues involving much larger companies. Toward the end of the nineteenth century, as technology became more sophisticated and minerals more difficult to extract, the need for large infusions of capital led to the concentration of mining properties into fewer hands and to the development of mining companies. This consolidation occurred throughout the mining West, from Alaska to Arizona. The court played a particularly prominent role in the struggle to gain control over Montana's copper, a struggle that eventually resulted in the agglomeration of the Anaconda Copper Company. While historians acknowledge the federal courts' key role in the Butte copper wars and the successful development of Anaconda, they shy away from explaining the contextual importance of key judicial decisions.[12] The consolidation of this great copper behemoth occurred amidst Ross and Gilbert's ongoing jurisprudential disagreement on natural resources issues.

The idea of creating a great copper company originated with Henry H. Rogers, who, as one of John D. Rockefeller's powerful associates, had helped to raise the Standard Oil Company to a position of preeminence. Rockefeller apparently disapproved of Rogers's plan and refused to invest Standard Oil funds in the copper venture. Rogers's opponents nevertheless persistently, if incorrectly, attacked his copper dealings as an outgrowth of the oil company, a demagogic claim with great popular appeal among Montana miners. During the 1890s, when Rogers launched these efforts, Montana's most powerful copper concerns included the Anaconda, the Boston and Montana Consolidated Copper and Silver Mining Company, the Butte and Boston Consolidated Mining Company, and the Montana Ore Purchasing Company.[13] Fritz Augustus Heinze, a young entrepreneur who controlled Montana Ore Purchasing, resisted Rogers's bid to control Montana's copper properties. Heinze instituted massive litigation against the Boston companies, which prevented Rogers from implementing his initial strategy of purchasing them before acquiring the Anaconda. Heinze's battle against the other copper giants required a lot of gumption, particularly in light of Rogers's clear capacity and intent to crush anyone who stood in his way. Unfazed, Heinze used his keen understanding of state and local politics to ensure that his efforts were backed by widespread public support and a compliant state bench composed of elected judges. His success in these endeavors frustrated the Boston and New York controllers of the other copper companies. To establish the basis for diversity jurisdiction to avail themselves of a federal forum, the other copper companies attempted to reincorporate in New York. Heinze partially obstructed even that stratagem. After having associates purchase stock in the rival companies, Heinze financed their minority shareholder lawsuits to challenge the reincorporations when the directors attempted to act without obtaining consent through a shareholders' meeting. The minority shareholders won victories in state and federal courts that required the companies to restart the reincorporation process from scratch.[14]

When the Butte and Boston and Boston and Montana companies finally established federal diversity jurisdiction through legitimate reincorporation, they found an audience more receptive than the Montana state courts. One of the earliest federal cases, *Morse v. Montana Ore Purchasing Company*, illustrated some of the extralegal dynamics that shaped the outcome of the copper wars. Morse, a manager of the Boston companies, sued Heinze's Montana Ore Purchasing, claiming that the latter's mine intruded into one of Butte and Boston's mines. Although the jury found for Heinze, U.S. District Judge Hiram Knowles set aside the verdict and ordered a new trial, on the ground that the pro-Heinze newspapers in Butte had improperly influenced the jury. The case illustrated Heinze's wide support among the people of Butte, who viewed him as the underdog in his struggle against the great copper companies. It also demonstrated why the Boston companies clearly preferred federal court.[15] Led by Gilbert over Ross's dissent, the Ninth Circuit favored the forces of consolidation that attempted to put the upstart Heinze out of business.

In one such case, *Heinze v. Butte and Boston Consolidated Mining Company*, Butte and Boston alleged that it owned a one-half interest in one claim and a two-thirds interest in another. Heinze intervened to protect his own rights in the remaining divided interests in the claims. Butte and Boston asserted that Heinze was operating the mines illegally, extracting thousands of dollars' worth of ore each month and preventing a receiver from operating the mine properly. Heinze challenged Butte and Boston's underlying claim of ownership by contending that the company had purchased its interests from a man who was insane and therefore could not legally make a sale. The case raised only issues of state law, but the Boston company had by this time succeeded in transferring its corporate citizenship to New York, thus enabling it to invoke the federal courts' diversity jurisdiction. On appeal, the Ninth Circuit considered whether the circuit court in Montana had acted correctly in appointing the receiver and in its rulings on the possession issues. Barely two years after the Ninth Circuit had sharply rebuked the use of receivers in the Nome gold scandal, Gilbert wrote for the majority in upholding the appointment of the receiver. He conceded that the Nome cases stood for the proposition that extraction of ore from a mine "by a receiver is not to be permitted, except upon convincing proof of the necessity of such mining operations." Gilbert confessed that his deferential approach to trial proceedings contributed to the decision; he felt that the "record does not show that under all the circumstances" the trial court "so abused its discretion as to entitle the appellants to a reversal of its orders."[16]

In a very lengthy dissent, Ross disagreed with much of Gilbert's analysis. He first challenged the majority's unwillingness to remand for a legal proceeding to determine the sufficiency of Butte and Boston's title. He favored more fact-finding on Heinze's allegation that the company had purchased its interest from an insane person. Ross next disputed the court's conclusion on the receivership issue: he held that few situations justified appointment of a receiver with power to operate a mine, and this case was not one of them. If an injunction was insufficient to keep the property in its prior state, as the majority apparently believed, Ross asserted that the court could have appointed a receiver without conferring power to extract ore from the mine. The receiver's role should have been limited to enforcing the injunction. The Nome episode hung eerily over Ross's opinion and fueled his hostility to the notion of appointing receivers to work mines. Demonstrating his willingness to correct perceived errors by closely scrutinizing district court proceedings, Ross would have rejected this claim, which was important in protecting the Anaconda's growing empire.[17]

While Heinze struggled with the Boston companies in state and federal courts, Rogers and his colleagues began to buy shares in Montana's major copper companies, in an attempt to corner the market. After purchasing the Anaconda company outright in 1899, the Rogers group formed the Amalgamated Copper Company as a holding company to control Anaconda and the companies they planned to add to the stable, which included the Washoe Copper Company, the Parrot Silver and Copper Mining Company, the Colorado Smelting and Mining Company, the Boston and Montana Consolidated Copper and Silver Mining Company, and the Butte and Boston Consolidated Mining Company. By November, 1900, Amalgamated had indeed acquired a majority of the Parrot stock and all of the Washoe and Colorado companies' stock; by 1901, they also held a majority in the Boston and Montana and Butte and Boston. Heinze's Montana Ore Purchasing Company remained the largest Montana mining company outside Amalgamated's control.[18]

By 1903, after losing another series of state court proceedings to Heinze, Amalgamated ordered its own mines shut down. Amalgamated's management, recognizing that its workers were enamored of their charismatic opponent, evidently hoped that closing the mines, ostensibly because of the litigation, would turn its 15,000 miners against Heinze. The gambit nearly worked. Only a dramatic public oration by Heinze soothed the restless workers. This small rhetorical victory, however, could not compensate for the financial drain on Heinze caused by the protracted litigation war. In a desperate bid in 1904, he flouted a federal injunction by secretly mining a disputed passageway. Heinze attempted to intimidate local U.S. District Judge Knowles, but Ninth Circuit Judge Morrow speedily dispatched Idaho District Judge James H. Beatty to sit in the Montana district court by designation and reestablish the court's authority. Beatty held Heinze in contempt of court and the Ninth Circuit refused to review the order, thereby upholding the fine of $20,000. Had the federal courts protected Heinze's interests with the same vigor as the Montana state courts, the upstart copper magnate might well have succeeded in unjustly taking ores and mining claims from his competitors. Instead, Heinze's defeat in federal court effectively forced him to sell out to Amalgamated in 1906 for an estimated $10.5 million. He also agreed to dismiss 110 lawsuits that were tying up property worth $70–100 million.[19]

The man who succeeded in bringing the pugnacious Heinze to the negotiating table was John D. Ryan, who went on to lead the Anaconda Copper Mining Company into its final stages of consolidation and through a long period as one of America's largest corporations. Throughout his long and successful business career, Ryan had a penchant for consolidation and won recognition as the leader of both the copper and brass industries. He also headed Montana's largest power company. While negotiating with Heinze, Ryan had bought a majority of the stock in the Alice Gold and Silver Mining Company, one of the last of the independent Montana mining companies. Nearly a decade later, this acquisition sparked major litigation. Minority shareholders, taking a page from Heinze's book, challenged the sale of Alice's assets to the Anaconda.

On Ninth Circuit review, Ross saw the facts as a classic squeeze-out. The Alice majority shareholders, controlled by Ryan, had voted to sell the company's assets to Anaconda at a bargain-basement price in exchange for Anaconda stock. A recent decision of the Supreme Court prevented the minority stockholders from invoking antitrust laws.[20] Accordingly, Ross wrote an opinion annulling the sale on the ground that it had fetched an inadequate price and that the directors had failed to protect the interests of *all* the stockholders. In a highly unusual disposition, Ross's opinion was reported first, with the notation, "Ross, Circuit Judge, dissenting in part," followed by a short opinion of Gilbert's that District Judge Charles Wolverton of Oregon joined. Ross had evidently lost his support on the panel for annulling the sale to Anaconda. With his customary deference to the district court, Gilbert maintained that the trial judge correctly followed a Supreme Court decision requiring corporate property to be sold to the highest bidder upon dissolution. Just as he had in the earlier Heinze suit, Gilbert was able to pull another member of the court to his side, thus permitting the consolidation of the Anaconda over Ross's dissent.[21]

Anaconda's eventual victory was expedited by Heinze's miscalculation in violating the injunction. Nevertheless, Heinze's combative litigation strategy, which at times required the services of a veritable army of thirty-five lawyers, did tie up Anaconda for so long that it never achieved its goal of controlling the national copper market. By the time the Montana copper wars ended in 1906–1907, Arizona's mines were booming, and Heinze's litigation efforts had helped to prevent Anaconda from buying up the copper mines of the Southwest. In this sense, the Butte battle may well have impeded the national consolidation of copper interests.[22] Moreover, even if Ross's opinions in these crucial cases had prevailed, the Montana copper war might have had the same outcome, given Anaconda's vast financial resources. The controlling influence of Gilbert's position, however, helped to facilitate Anaconda's victory in Montana.

III.   TIMBER DEPREDATION ON PUBLIC LAND

Lumber, water, and coal were needed for the mining process, and as part of its gambit to control Montana's copper mining industry, the Anaconda Company's chief backers launched a concerted effort to gain inexpensive, plentiful supplies of these resources. The company particularly required vast quantities of lumber to shore up its shafted or tunneled mine walls. In 1888, Anaconda used 40,000 board feet per day in its deep-shafted mines alone. Marcus Daly, a miner's miner who developed the Anaconda Company from a small operation to a great copper enterprise, gained a tremendous competitive edge over his mining competitors by entering into partnership agreements with lumber magnates, including the great lumber baron Andrew B. Hammond. However, Hammond and others were accused of obtaining some of their lumber illegally. In 1878 Congress had enacted legislation conferring the right to cut timber "on the public domain for mining and domestic purposes."[23] The United States brought civil suits against Hammond and other commercial loggers to recover the value of timber allegedly obtained in violation of the statute. The stage was set for another clash between Ross and Gilbert, though the battle lines were not drawn immediately. This time Ross would prevail.

In 1904 and 1905 two of the timber trespass suits made their way to the Ninth Circuit. In the first, *United States v. Bitter Root Development Company*, the court reviewed a Montana circuit court decree that the United States had improperly brought a bill in equity when a remedy existed at law. The substance of the government's claim was that Daly had used Bitter Root to defraud the government of timber worth $2 million. The case proved easy for the court to decide, and Gilbert's majority opinion masked the disagreements that were to come. The court dispatched the government's theory that the legal remedy was inadequate because of "the trouble and difficulty of unraveling before a jury the devious and confusing methods adopted by the appellees in creating corporations." The "greater convenience of the equitable remedy is no ground," wrote Gilbert, "for depriving a party of his constitutional right to a jury trial."[24]

The next important case, *United States v. Clark*, opened the breach between Ross and Gilbert on the timber trespass issue. The government sued W. A. Clark for fraudulently procuring public land that contained plentiful timber. The scheme purportedly relied on homestead claims by fifty persons who were retained by Clark's operatives. The homesteaders allegedly had violated the terms of the congressional statute prohibiting procurement except in good faith and for their own exclusive use, for when they secured the patents to the lands, they sold them, and their property rights ended up in Clark's hands. Clark, who was one of Daly's cronies, failed to persuade the trial court to sustain a demurrer to the government's bill. The Ninth Circuit reversed. In an opinion by Ross that Morrow joined, the court held that "the evidence in the present record falls far short of establishing that [Clark] knew, or had reason to know, of any such frauds at the time of his respective purchases." Gilbert sided with the government; he believed that Clark had had sufficient notice of potential wrongdoing to have been able to inquire about how the lands he bought had been obtained from the United States. *Clark* well illustrated a pattern in these two jurists' approaches to civil suits brought by the United States to recover for timber depredation. Ross consistently struck down the government's interests, whereas Gilbert tended to view its claims in a sympathetic light. The judgment in the case also reiterated their dichotomous views on issues of contract and deed interpretation: Gilbert generally tried to ferret out the ill intent of the parties to the purported scheme, whereas Ross construed the written documents more narrowly, without attempting to divine the parties' aims.[25]

The greatest of the Montana copper and timber cases involved Andrew Hammond. One student of his life has written obliquely that Hammond's "logging crews cut timber from land he had purchased from the railroad, but there is little doubt that his woodcutters also strayed onto adjacent federal lands." In its largest suit in the Ninth Circuit, the United States attempted to establish that the "straying" of Hammond's workers was part of a more nefarious scheme to defraud the common weal of 21,000,000 board feet of timber taken from public lands in Montana. At trial, the jury returned a verdict against Hammond, but only for one-quarter ($51,040) of the damages sought by the government. In the context of its general lack of success in pressing such actions in the West, however, this verdict represented a major victory for the federal government.[26]

In an opinion by Ross that District Judge Frank Rudkin joined, the Ninth Circuit reversed and remanded for a new trial. "[A]fter a very attentive examination of the record," Ross ruled that the verdict could not stand. The district court had instructed the jury to find as a matter of law that, if the government prevailed, it should receive interest on the award. Because the government delayed filing suit for seventeen years, the accrued interest exceeded the value of the lumber as uncut timber. The court remanded the case for the jury to determine the propriety of such an award. In dissent, Gilbert objected to what he viewed as Ross's heavy-handedness in devising an objection and then reversing on that ground. "It is not to be doubted," he said, "that, if the precise objection had been pointed out and the authorities cited, the court below would have given appropriate instructions. Counsel at the conclusion of a trial ought not to be permitted to hold back an important point of objection to an instruction, and thereby mislead the trial court and secure a reversal on appeal." After remand, the case apparently ended in settlement, the government accepting a modest $7,000 of the $211,854.10 it had originally sought from Hammond.[27]

The outcome in *Hammond* accorded with the federal government's general failure in the timber depredation suits it brought in the Ninth Circuit during the early twentieth century. The Ninth Circuit typically decided these cases with a single opinion, but this unanimity flowed from two fundamentally different judicial tenets. Ever suspicious of exercises of federal power, Ross sided against the government in case after case, though without ever articulating any specific animus or bias.[28] Gilbert responded more favorably than Ross to U.S. interests on timber issues, but he did not let this position override his generally deferential approach to reviewing appeals. These divergent perspectives merged to produce unanimity on public-land-timber cases where juries had ruled in favor of the government but had awarded very low damages.

In one of the earliest of these cases, the United States sued for $630, the manufactured value of 90,000 feet of lumber at $7 per thousand feet. The jury evidently believed that the timber was cut in "good faith," for they returned a verdict awarding only $35. On appeal, Gilbert wrote for the court in an opinion joined by Ross and Morrow. Unsurprisingly, Gilbert briefly articulated his philosophy of deference to trial courts' fact-findings and evidentiary rulings. At the same time, the unstated message was a ringing defeat for the United States in its effort to recoup timber depredation damages. This result accorded with Ross's general distrust of assertions of national authority, especially against persons attempting to develop the West's resources. In two factually similar cases, the court upheld jury verdicts of $300 and $6,102 when the United States sought $2,500 and $17,751, respectively. Of the $84,346.38 the Justice Department recovered in timber depredations during 1909, slightly more than a quarter was from litigation in the Ninth Circuit. Except for a few large recoveries against mining companies, the government had very little to show for its litigation efforts. In 1910 alone, the Justice Department filed sixty-six timber depredation suits alleging a total of $436,350.86 in money damages, yet received awards of only $8,851.26, of which it collected a mere $4,318.13.[29]

Suspicious as he might have been of efforts by the United States to collect damage awards against loggers who allegedly had violated public land laws, Ross nonetheless took a dark view of attempts to defraud the government of title to public lands. Thus, the government had far greater success in acting to revoke land patents obtained by fraud than it had in depredation suits. In cases involving proper patents under the mining laws, for example, the court upheld findings of fraud when people acquired claims to public land by asserting falsely that they had found paying quantities of minerals. The court also cracked down on a purchaser who had known that the patentee had obtained the land by fraud. Homestead laws permitted a person to get a patent to public land only for the purpose of establishing a homestead, not for mining. In a series of land fraud suits brought by the United States attorney in Oregon, the Ninth Circuit spoke with a unified voice in upholding the government's position to rescind patents obtained illegally under homestead laws.[30] These cases presented straightforward questions that were relatively easy to decide. In other major patent-revocation litigation involving oil lands, the government took on the Southern Pacific Railroad and sparked a series of cases as contentious as any the court has ever seen.

IV. CALIFORNIA OIL DISPUTES

The Ninth Circuit's handling of Alaska gold mining, Idaho and Montana copper mining, and Pacific Northwest forestry issues provides the doctrinal moorings for assessing the court's work in the 1910s in a series of lawsuits over California oil. The oil controversies combined aspects of mining law, the congressional land grants to the railroads, and a decision by the president to reserve certain oil-rich lands for use by the navy. These disputes stemmed from the land-grant subsidy of the 1860s, which provided that the railroads would receive alternate tracts of public land, in a checkerboard layout, as they completed segments of railroad track. The original grants had been subject to the proviso that title would not pass to lands containing minerals. Long after the government issued the land patents, oil was discovered on some of these lands. The government faced the question of how to regain title to the lands it had deeded prior to the discovery of oil. A second concern was how to protect lands reserved by executive order from the "drainage" caused by the railroads drilling on their adjoining tracts. As they had on many other natural resource disputes, Gilbert and Ross differed in their approaches to these questions. Their previous opinions offer a glimpse into the nature of their disagreement.[31]

In one of the earliest of such suits, private mining speculators sought to uphold their claim to title against the Southern Pacific Company. The miners contended that the land-grant statute prohibited the transfer of mineral lands to the railroads, the normal rules of mineral discovery applied, and the court should uphold their claim to title. Sitting as trial judge in circuit court, Ross disagreed. In a significant victory for the railroad, he held that absent a finding of fraud or mistake on the railroad's part in securing the land patent, the court would not entertain a collateral attack against the title. This decision, which the Justice Department followed closely, elicited a written expression of approval from Attorney General George Wickersham. Wickersham's letter caused an uproar when the railroad, having obtained it surreptitiously, produced it during the appeal. Recognizing the importance of a ruling on these issues by the nation's highest court, the Ninth Circuit certified the questions presented without rendering its own judgment on them. The Supreme Court upheld Ross's decision in *Burke v. Southern Pacific Railroad Company*.[32]

The *Burke* ruling required the government to prove fraud by the railroad to invalidate title to oil lands obtained under the land-grant subsidies. In a suit against the Southern Pacific to recover 6,000 acres of land situated in Elk Hills, California, and valued at $18,000,000, the government first attempted to meet this proof-of-fraud requirement. The government alleged that "the lands are mineral lands and were known to be such to the defendant railroad company at the time they were listed and patented." In a major victory for the government, the trial court ruled that the railroad had procured the patent to the public lands in Elk Hills by fraud. Meanwhile, the attorney general had also announced plans to file a series of suits to challenge patents to 165,000 acres, of which 20,000 acres lay in Naval Petroleum Reserves No. 1 (Elk Hills) and No. 2 (Buena Vista Hills). The value of these lands exceeded $500,000,000. The suits were later consolidated, and in an important ruling in 1915 the district court denied Southern Pacific's motions to dismiss.[33]

While the railroad's appeal in the Elk Hills suit and discovery in the consolidated reserves case were pending, the Ninth Circuit addressed a related question in the case of *Consolidated Mutual Oil Company v. United States*. This suit challenged the viability of drilling leases in the reserves. *Consolidated Mutual* sketched out the lines along which the court would battle in the government's bid to wrest control of the naval reserve lands from the railroad. The United States sued to block drilling on the reserves created by executive orders and to reclaim title to the land. Under an executive order in 1909, President Taft had set aside certain lands as an oil reserve for the navy's use. The order contained an important caveat: "All locations or claims existing and valid on this date may proceed to entry in the usual manner after field investigation and examination." Congress had subsequently enacted a statute validating the order.[34]

In an opinion that exemplified the hallowed place of property rights in his jurisprudence, Ross wrote an opinion reversing the district court's decree for the United States. Joined by Judge William H. Hunt, Ross observed that the oil companies "then had in the lands here in question valuable rights of possession and conveyance, which the courts of the country would protect and enforce, . . . rights, too, acquired by the license, if not by the invitation, of the government, and in the pursuance of which the lessee of this property had then, according to the records, already expended more than $20,000." Ross felt certain that President Taft, whom he respected a great deal, intended the executive order "to apply to all locations and claims existing at the time of the making of the withdrawal order to which the locators or claimants had some valid right" and thus to exempt those particular claims.[35]

Gilbert dissented in an opinion that reiterated his deference to trial courts and his obeisance to United States national interests as he perceived them to have been articulated by the president and Congress. For Gilbert, the appeal presented the solitary issue of "whether the court below, in appointing a receiver, abused the discretion which was vested in it." Having framed the issue thus, what Gilbert would answer was readily evident to even the most inexperienced follower of the court's decisions. After criticizing the majority for presuming to infer Taft's "intent" in framing the executive order, Gilbert offered a ringing affirmation of the federal government's power to protect the oil reserve: "Lands which have ceased to be public lands, by reason of the initiation of pre-emption and homestead and other claims, are still so far public lands that the United States may protect them from waste."[36]

In one important ruling, then, Ross had required the government to carry the difficult burden of proving fraud to rescind a railroad land grant, and in another he had permitted an oil company to continue its leasing operations in petroleum reserves that had been set aside by executive order and act of Congress. Both decisions were major defeats for the government, but if the Justice Department could win the Elk Hills and consolidated naval reserves suits, it would be able to forestall the massive drilling that was sure to occur if the railroad retained its land patents. Shortly after the *Consolidated Mutual Oil* judgment, the Ninth Circuit handed down its decision in the Elk Hills case. Although Ross was not on the panel, his viewpoint was well represented. In a decision that one historian has described as "a little hard to believe," the court reversed the district court ruling that the Southern Pacific had fraudulently obtained title to the land.[37] Idaho District Judge Frank Dietrich, who eight years later would be elevated to the Ninth Circuit, wrote for himself and Hunt. In a lengthy opinion that canvassed the facts and scrutinized the trial record, Dietrich conveyed no small uncertainty in ruling against the government:

> Without further discussion, our general conclusion is that the lands were not, in 1903–1904, known to be valuable for their mineral. The conditions were such only as to suggest the probability that they contained some oil, at some depth, but nothing to point persuasively to its quality, extent, or value. Or, putting it in another way, the conditions were such as to suggest the possibility of oil in paying quantities, and to induce the more venturesome—such as were willing to take chances—to prospect the field; but we are satisfied they were not "plainly such as to engender the belief" that any given section or other legal subdivision contained oil of such quality and quantity, and at such depth, as would render its extraction profitable.[38]

Perhaps because the decision seemed certain to advance to the Supreme Court, Gilbert dissented without opinion, a practice much more common in the early twentieth century than it is today.[39]

While the government appealed the Ninth Circuit's decision in the Elk Hills case to the Supreme Court, the district court finally closed discovery in the massive consolidated naval reserves case. Required by the *Burke* decision to prove that the Southern Pacific had obtained the lands through fraud, the government alleged that "the 'Big Four' of the Central and Southern Pacific Companies . . . were all parties to a deliberate, long-enduring, and wide-embracing scheme to acquire from the government wrongfully vast areas lying on the west side of the San Joaquin Valley, involving some of the richest oil lands that the world has ever known." Judge Benjamin Bledsoe of Los Angeles expressed shock that the government could accuse "some of the most prominent, most forceful, most far-seeing men that our state has produced [of engaging] in the diabolical plan of consummating one of the greatest frauds of the age." Bledsoe's incredulity surely would have drawn a spirited rebuttal from Lewis Mc-Kisick, who, when representing the United States against the Stanford estate twenty-four years earlier, had described one of the Big Four, Leland Stanford, as "the most conspicuous criminal of the Century."[40]

Bledsoe's ruling was less a surprise than was the tenor of his language. The government's case appeared to be weaker in the consolidated reserves case than in the Elk Hills litigation, which the Ninth Circuit had decided in the railroad's favor. But the Supreme Court reversed the Ninth Circuit in the Elk Hills case, thus vindicating Gilbert's view and renewing hope that the government might yet prevail in an appeal in the consolidated case upon which Bledsoe had just ruled. Incredibly, Attorney General A. Mitchell Palmer announced that the government would not appeal Bledsoe's decree. Palmer's decision "utterly ruined" the naval petroleum reserve at Buena Vista and, according to one historian, "has remained incomprehensible, outside of possible aspersions on Palmer's integrity." As for the Elk Hills reserve, the Supreme Court's decision saved it for the moment, but a new threat surfaced within two years, when the Harding administration took office. The fate of Elk Hills at that time became inextricably linked with a place in Wyoming called Teapot Dome. Appropriately, William Gilbert was to have a major say in the final disposition of the Elk Hills reserve, but he would have to wait nearly a decade for his chance.[41]

V. ECONOMIC DEVELOPMENT AND THE ENVIRONMENT

Gilbert's view of the government's national interests in natural resource litigation did not prevail in the most important cases decided by the

Ninth Circuit during the first two decades of the twentieth century. Ross's position garnered a majority in critical cases that went against the government's interests.[42] For reasons they did not memorialize, Morrow and Hunt, the two judges who most frequently completed the Ninth Circuit panels that decided these cases, sided with Ross. Some of these disputes involved giants of the commercial world and corporations of great regional and national significance. Gilbert and Ross disagreed sharply on the federal government's position in many cases that were critical to the development of natural resources. But on the question of exploiting those resources at the expense of the environment, these two independent-minded jurists came down on the same side. However starkly their philosophies contrasted, both judges strongly believed in the importance of capitalizing on the West's natural resources for development. They differed on the choice of means to this end, but they both held fast to the objective. Cases raising issues with distinctly environmental effects brought this conjunction of views into sharp focus.

In 1906, Ross and Gilbert united to decide a significant case, *Mountain Copper Company v. United States*. The United States brought suit against the copper company, claiming that the plant's mining, roasting, burning, smelting, and refining caused undue harm to timber on public land that adjoined the plant. Bolstered by extensive trial testimony of allegedly irreparable timber damage on public lands, the government requested a permanent injunction against Mountain Copper's smelting operations. Reasoning that no known means existed to smelt copper without discharging sulphurous and arsenical fumes, the circuit court issued a decree permanently enjoining the copper company from roasting, burning, and smelting copper or other ores at its works at Keswick, Shasta County, California.[43]

In an opinion for himself and Gilbert, Ross reversed the circuit court's decision. These two judges, among the most experienced in the entire United States, agreed that in striking the balance between the harm done to the United States by the discharges and the detriment to the company that resulted from enjoining its activities, the weight of interests fell on the side of the copper company. Ross carefully courted Gilbert's vote in the opening paragraphs of the opinion by discounting any notion that national sovereign power, to which Gilbert regularly deferred, was at stake. Ross observed that the government had sued "not in its sovereign capacity, but as a landowner, to enjoin alleged injuries to its property, not directly, but indirectly, through the maintenance of an alleged nuisance by the defendant on its own property." Ross thus downgraded the government's position to that of any ordinary landowner. He then recited the general rule that "when the government comes into a court asserting a property right, it occupies the position of any and every other suitor. Its rights are precisely the same; no greater, no less." Once he had dispelled the special aura of the complainant, Ross then belittled the value of the property upon which the alleged nuisance had purportedly wreaked havoc. The 4,000 acres in the "damaged zone" was "mountainous in character, with little or no soil, practically worthless for agriculture or horticulture." To protect this land the government asked the court to shut down a smelting plant that produced an average of 600 tons of copper ore per day. The court rejected the proffered less harmful alternative, erection of a condensation chamber, as far too costly for the negligible benefit it would produce. Such a device would make only a modest dent in the amount of sulfuric acid released and would cost $3–5 million. Ross concluded, and Gilbert agreed, that the "maximum injury" to the United States was a "mere trifle" compared to the harm that would be done to Mountain Copper if the injunction stayed in force.[44]

The dissenting opinion of Nevada District Judge Thomas Hawley expressed an eloquent concern for the environment. He contended that Judge Lorenzo Sawyer had crafted the relevant controlling principle in the seminal case of *Woodruff v. North Bloomfield Gravel Mining Company* two decades earlier. In *Woodruff*, Sawyer had granted a permanent injunction to stop a mining company from causing a nuisance to downstream landowners by discharging debris into a river. Hawley deemed *Woodruff* indistinguishable and asserted, "Unless the doctrines therein announced are erroneous, it should be followed. If the ruling in that case was wrong, it should be overruled." He admonished Ross's ledger-balancing approach and maintained that a profitable corporation "has no right . . . to destroy the property of the individual landowners in the vicinity or seriously to impair and injure the health of those living upon their own lands in the vicinity of its works."[45]

Despite the plaintive appeal by Hawley, a court dominated by Ross and Gilbert would rule consistently in favor of business interests that exploited natural resources to the detriment of the environment. Two years after *Mountain Copper*, the court decided a case that closely paralleled the facts of *Woodruff*. In *McCarthy v. Bunker Hill and Sullivan Mining and Concentrating Company*, landowners sought an injunction against a copper smelting operation run by a number of copper mining companies in Idaho, whose operations had irrevocably polluted the streams from which the landowners drew water. Relying on *Moun-*

tain Copper, the circuit court in Idaho refused to grant the requested injunction.[46]

The Ninth Circuit affirmed in an opinion by Ross in which Gilbert and Montana District Judge William Hunt joined. In *McCarthy*, Ross took a new tack to defeat the landowners' interests against the polluting smelter companies. Deviating from his usual jurisprudence, Ross deferred to the trial court proceedings: "[A]n appellate court will not ordinarily interfere with the action of the trial court in either granting or withholding an injunction in cases in which the evidence is substantially conflicting, and especially where the trial judge, at the request of the respective parties, has had the benefit of a personal inspection of the premises." Ross made no attempt to explain this departure from his typical intrusive approach to reviewing trial errors, the approach he had employed two years earlier in *Mountain Copper*. Because the court in *McCarthy* reviewed a ruling that rejected an injunction, Ross rested the decision on the deferential approach he often eschewed. This case also marked some movement by Ross away from his earlier position of fealty to the individual property owner's concerns to the exclusion of the community's interests. In the celebrated *Fallbrook* case, Ross had struck down a state irrigation district law because it allegedly infringed on a landowner's due-process property rights. No constitutional issue arose in the copper smelting cases, and Ross's concern for the small landowner in them was similarly lacking.[47]

The trial court in *McCarthy* had determined that the high value of the mining activity far outweighed the detriment to the landowners' property. In the Coeur d'Alene region, where 12,000 people lived, the mines produced approximately 40 percent of the lead extracted in the United States and an estimated $13 million yearly in lead and silver. Testimony in the case had revealed that the mining operators would lose their capital investment of $12 million and a total of at least $25 million. Estimated losses to the region's inhabitants and other property owners totaled over $50 million if the court enjoined these mining activities in Idaho. The court might have followed Lorenzo Sawyer's lead in the *Woodruff* case by enjoining the smelting operations until protective technology redressed the problem. Such a remedy, however, would have struck Idaho's principal business interests a potentially irreparable blow. The Ninth Circuit instead viewed its decisional locus in absolute terms. Either the mining activity continued, or it ceased.[48]

If expressing greater concern for the environment or the adjoining landowners entered into the thinking of Ross or Gilbert, they never articulated it in a judicial opinion. The closest Ross came was in a 1911 case involving the mammoth Washoe smelter in Montana. Ross counseled the complaining farmers that the "court is always ready and willing" to protect them against wealthy mining corporations "in all proper cases." After all, he continued, he himself was "a farmer, and [had] been for more than 40 years." Although Ross did in fact own over a thousand acres in southern California, his projection of the court's consequent willingness to protect landowners against mining companies was somewhat disingenuous.[49] Ross was indeed committed to upholding the rights of property owners in most situations. The mining-pollution context was, however, an exception.

When weighing the respective interests of the parties involved, Ross and Gilbert invariably sided with the mining companies. As the great copper-smelting companies gathered strength in the first decade of the twentieth century, environmental concerns mounted. By 1913, legal commentators observed that the issue of smelting pollution had "assumed serious importance in recent years." The Supreme Court had not yet directly addressed the question, but it had ruled that the great importance of the mining industry was not necessarily enough to cut off all the complainant's rights: "[T]he right of the lesser interest is not thereby subordinated to the greater," though that "is sometimes a consideration when a plaintiff seeks relief by injunction rather than by an action at law."[50]

The Ninth Circuit's copper smelting cases well demonstrated its laissez-faire approach to developing the West's natural resources. The position of Gilbert and Ross seemed to be that the West was large enough to accommodate polluting smelting operations, even if adjoining landowners suffered as a result. This view, however fervently expressed in the discharge cases, was not so ironclad that it clashed with the fledgling conservation movement, which in the 1910s was struggling to protect certain public lands from development.[51] In 1918, the Ninth Circuit issued an important pro-conservation opinion that helped to preserve the Grand Canyon. In *Cameron v. United States*, the court ruled unanimously that the United States could restrict mining and logging activities on land that Congress had expressly set aside to become the Grand Canyon National Forest. The court swept aside Ralph H. Cameron's contention that the secretary of the interior lacked authority to deny his application for a mineral claim located near the rim of the Grand Canyon. Cameron doubtless hindered his cause by charging a toll to everyone who used the trail leading into the canyon and by maintaining a hotel and refreshment stand on the rim of the canyon. He also attempted to prevent the government from constructing certain land improvements such as walks, railings, and seats that were needed for the convenience and protection of the public in its enjoyment of the Grand Canyon. District Judge William H. Sawtelle, who more than a decade later would himself be elevated to circuit judge, entered a decree for the government enjoining the toll-taking and ordering Cameron's buildings to be torn down. In an opinion by Ross, the Ninth Circuit upheld this decision, which the Supreme Court also affirmed.[52]

The decision in the *Cameron* case represented a major victory for the conservation movement and evinced a more overt concern for the environmental consequences of development than the Ninth Circuit had demonstrated in the copper smelting context. In the pollution discharge cases, the Ninth Circuit under Gilbert and Ross was far more deferential to business interests than was at least one other circuit court of appeals.[53] By upholding the government's authority to protect the Grand Canyon, however, the court signaled some willingness to support the nascent conservation movement. These disparate cases involving environmental concerns indicate that Gilbert and Ross finally found common ground on a natural resource issue, after years of disagreement on so many others.

Drawn to the West in the mid-nineteenth century by visions of wealth, people from all over the world arrived in search of gold, silver, and copper. Exploiting these natural resources required great infusions of labor and capital. In many instances, extraction irreparably scarred the land. Throughout its history the Ninth Circuit has been confronted with the tensions between preserving the environment and permitting the exploitation of the resources within its territorial jurisdiction. Ross and Gilbert contributed to western development by carrying on a dynamic dialogue on resource issues for the three decades of their joint service on the Ninth Circuit. Cautious by nature, deferential to trial court decisions, and respectful of the federal government's litigation interests, Gilbert favored an approach rooted in the common sense of trying to deduce what the parties intended and deferring to the federal government when it sought to regulate the use of public lands. Undeniably brilliant, Ross espoused a different set of values and a different style of judging. Ross fought for the Confederacy at a tender age and from these experiences perhaps developed the suspicion of national power that he expressed in his judicial opinions. The United States government fared very poorly when Ross reviewed its attempts to protect the public lands. Such suits, he intimated, attempted to extend the power of the central government too far into the affairs of individuals and corporations. Notwithstanding a few smelter cases, Ross displayed a marked willingness to chide mistakes at the trial court level and to reverse decisions when he believed that the court had erred either in its fact-finding mission or in its application of the law.

Ross and Gilbert differed in the weight they gave to the written expressions embodied in contracts, deeds, and property records. Ross was a lawyer's lawyer, insisting on exactness and adherence to the strict confines of the written word. Gilbert was much more of an interpretivist, seeking fairness and justice as he perceived it in the expressed intentions of the parties. Ross was not above sending the parties back to the drafting table if an agreement was imprecise. Gilbert intuitively understood that the commercial enterprises of gold seekers, miners, and others in a still-wild West did not readily lend themselves to the practice of the high state of law demanded by Ross. Gilbert prevailed in the great copper consolidation war that broke out in Montana. But when the United States accused timber operators of illegal logging on public land and charged railroad and oil companies with improperly exploiting the naval petroleum reserves, Ross succeeded in pushing the court in the direction of corporate interests.

The two complemented each other well. In most of the smaller-scale resource cases Gilbert's view prevailed. But in his sometimes acid dissents Ross undoubtedly signaled the need for westerners to be more meticulous in their affairs, particularly if they cared about the outcome in federal court. Had Ross's view consistently prevailed in property and contract disputes, the results would have been unduly harsh. Because Gilbert's opinion triumphed more often, the court worked to decipher the parties' intentions and to render just, if not always the most technically accurate, decisions.

These judicial disagreements arose in the context of an increasing federalization of the development process and the growth of the lower federal courts' importance. The railroad subsidies and mining laws of the 1860s and 1870s continued to produce significant litigation in the Ninth Circuit well into the second decade of the twentieth century, as new minerals were discovered and extracted throughout the West. The existence of large tracts of federal public land contributed to the Ninth Circuit's significance in deciding questions spanning the economic spectrum. Growing confidence in the circuit courts of appeals and the Supreme Court's increasing exercise of discretionary jurisdiction meant that many important Ninth Circuit cases went unreviewed. This steadily swelling power would continue unabated through the 1920s, as a federal criminal law emerged, and through the 1930s, as the New Deal dramatically enlarged the federal government's role in local affairs. Although many legal historians trace the federalization of law to the New Deal, in fact its antecedents may readily be seen in prior decades. The disputes over natural resource development in the Ninth Circuit provide one illustration of that phenomenon.

The Ninth Circuit's natural resource cases also show early signs of an evolution toward a more specialized federal judiciary and the development of a more explicit circuit politics. Unlike the era of the Chinese Exclusion acts, in which the full panoply of circuit and district judges in the Ninth Circuit contributed important rulings, by the 1910s judicial roles were becoming specialized. What made the jurisprudential disagreements between Ross and Gilbert so fascinating was that the swing vote often emerged from the ranks of district court judges drawn on to complete circuit court of appeals panels. These two judges led the way toward appellate specialization, as they sat with decreasing frequency as trial judges, especially after abolition of the old circuit courts in 1911. It is impossible to say for certain, but their frequent disagreements over natural resource questions may have sparked this role specialization. Suspicious that the other might be able to impose his views on a panel completed by two other judges, Ross and Gilbert may each have decreased his trial court duties to ensure that his counterpart was unable to take Ninth Circuit doctrine in untoward directions. If they sat together on the circuit court of appeals, each had at least a chance to influence the course of circuit law. Thus, the *Federal Reporter* reveals a vast number of Ninth Circuit cases in which Ross and Gilbert sat with a third judge, either one of the other two circuit judges, Morrow and Hunt, or pulled from the ranks of the district courts. Ross and Gilbert were apparently content with the ad hoc system of drawing a third judge to fill out a panel, for no administrative reform movement arose within the Ninth Circuit in this era, as it would during the 1930s. The relative parity between these two judges in their achievement of results may have accounted in part for the absence of an overt attempt by one or the other to capture doctrinal control over the Ninth Circuit through an administrative gambit. Such a delicate judicial détente could last only as long as these two judges stayed on the court, and as the country moved toward World War I, hints of a changeover in Ninth Circuit personnel were beginning to emerge.

SIX

Replacing the Vanguard

"Did you publicly, in a public speech, characterize Justice
Brandeis, of the United States Supreme Court, as an
'avaricious mountebank'?"

> *Senator Hiram Johnson questioning Ninth*
> *Circuit Judicial Nominee Wallace McCamant, 1926*

The struggle between William Gilbert and Erskine Ross for judicial
supremacy on the Ninth Circuit spanned three decades. During their last
ten years together, from 1915 to 1925, as the country entered the European war and imposed liquor prohibition, these judges at last seemed to
grow old and to cede some of their dominance to new judges on the court.
In many respects, the judges who replaced the vanguard of Gilbert, Ross,
and Morrow shared the same pioneering impulse that had lured the
court's early judges to the West. Like the miners, lumbermen, and oil
drillers who came to exploit the West's natural resources, the lawyers who
moved westward and later served the region as circuit judges sought material advancement and professional opportunity. As the federal judiciary
played an expanding role in the development of the region, the politics
of appointment to the Ninth Circuit grew more heated, with a wider array
of interest groups struggling to make their views known. In some respects,
the period between the late 1890s and the early 1920s had been quietly
apolitical for the Ninth Circuit. Gilbert and Ross, both taciturn men,
expressed their jurisprudential disagreements in judicial opinions but
took few steps to alter the internal administration of the court. The
departure from the bench of Morrow and Ross in the 1920s left a void
on the Ninth Circuit at a time of great expansion in the court's docket.

I. JUDICIAL REFORM AND THE TRANSFER OF WILLIAM HUNT

By the end of fifteen years together, the court of Gilbert, Ross, and
Morrow had achieved national prominence. When Woodrow Wilson

became president in 1913, the Ninth Circuit had the longest uninter-
rupted composition of any circuit court of appeals in the federal system.[1]
Presidents Theodore Roosevelt and William Howard Taft both left office
without having appointed a judge to the Ninth Circuit. During the period
between 1897 and 1913, significant developments occurred. At a parochial level, just before the 1906 earthquake and fire the court moved
into a building at Seventh and Mission streets in San Francisco, one of
the finest facilities of its kind in the country.[2] In these new quarters the
court witnessed a growth in appellate litigation that increased the Ninth
Circuit's docket from 72 to 129 appeals per year between 1897 and
1913.[3]

Moreover, Congress enacted legislation in 1911 to gather scattered
provisions of statutes relating to the federal judiciary into a single comprehensive code. This legislation abolished the circuit courts and merged
their original jurisdiction with that of the district courts. The elimination
of the old circuit courts contributed to the decline in dual role-playing
by circuit judges in the Ninth Circuit. Between 1891 and 1911, circuit
judges had routinely tried cases in circuit or district court and heard
appeals (except in the cases they had tried) in the circuit court of appeals.
After the Judicial Code of 1911 was enacted, old-time circuit judges such
as Gilbert, Ross, and Morrow continued occasionally to hear trials in
district court, but case reports indicate that this was a declining phenomenon. Role specialization by circuit judges evolved first, as the number and complexity of appeals steadily increased. District judges continued to staff circuit court of appeals panels even into the 1930s, when
Congress finally provided for a sufficient number of circuit judges to
handle the Ninth Circuit's caseload.[4]

A third development during this pre–World War I period was Congress's creation of a special Commerce Court. This court, composed of
five judges, had jurisdiction over orders of the Interstate Commerce
Commission, with review of its decisions by the Supreme Court.[5] The
statute creating the Commerce Court authorized the chief justice to
"temporarily assign" the five judges to any circuit court or circuit court
of appeals when the business of the Commerce Court did not require the
full complement of judges. Chief Justice Edward Douglas White accordingly dispatched William Henry Hunt of Montana to the Ninth Circuit,
with the apparent expectation that he would commute between San
Francisco and Washington to perform his various judicial assignments.
On October 22, 1913, Hunt's judicial career took an unexpected turn
when the Democratically controlled Congress legislated the Commerce

Court out of existence. Congress debated whether to abolish the judgeships too, but the need for judicial personnel and the constitutional
uncertainty of terminating life-tenured positions persuaded a majority to
adopt a creative solution. Congress authorized the original five Commerce Court judges to serve as ambulatory circuit judges until their
death, retirement, or resignation, at which time the position would
expire. As in the original Commerce Court statute, Congress empowered
the chief justice to assign the judges among the circuits; White again sent
Hunt to the Ninth Circuit, where he served until his resignation in 1928.[6]

Hunt was born in New Orleans on November 5, 1857. His father,
William H. Hunt, had a long and distinguished career in which he held
the posts of attorney general of Louisiana, United States secretary of the
navy, and minister to Russia. Like his father, William Henry Hunt
attended Yale briefly before studying law at the University of Louisiana
(later Tulane). At the age of twenty-one Hunt moved north. He served
in a number of public capacities in the Dakota Territory and then went
on to Montana, where he lived for the next twenty-two years. Hunt held
the office of attorney general of the Montana Territory from 1885 to
1887 and that of associate justice of the Montana Supreme Court from
1895 to 1900. In 1897, when Joseph McKenna resigned from the Ninth
Circuit to become attorney general, Hunt received widespread support
as a candidate to fill the vacancy. McKinley instead chose William W.
Morrow, but he did appoint Hunt governor of the Puerto Rico Territory.
Hunt held this office from 1901 to 1904 and then accepted President
Theodore Roosevelt's nomination to become district judge for the district of Montana. He served in this capacity with distinction until 1911,
when Taft appointed him as a judge on the newly created Commerce
Court.[7]

With the abolition of the Commerce Court the Ninth Circuit gained
in Hunt a high-caliber jurist who worked hard to maintain good relations
with his colleagues. On a court composed of people as diverse in background as Gilbert, Ross, and Morrow, Hunt's own experiences and
personality undoubtedly helped to build bridges on a personal level
between the judges. Hunt's arrival certainly seemed to have affected
Erskine Ross, who included a number of Hunt's letters in his scrapbook.
One of these letters, written in 1915 on the occasion of Ross's seventieth
birthday, said much about the esteem in which Hunt held his colleague:

> It is not given to many men to have lived so interesting a life as yours has been,
> and I know of no man who can at seventy think with greater satisfaction of
> his career in life than you. To have been a soldier, enlisted for a cause which

in your heart and mind you conceived to be your highest duty to country, and then to have followed with distinction the profession of the law; to have been a pioneer in moulding sentiments of virtue and rectitude in a new community; to have been called upon as a judge of the highest court of your State to blaze trails by which enlightened principles of justice would be illumined, and to have been an honored judge of the national courts of your country for these many years, mark unusual activities in those directions. But above everything your friends value your splendid character and your gentle disposition and that modesty which has distinguished you above all gentlemen whom I know.[8]

Not only Ross, but Morrow and Gilbert, too, were leading full lives. Morrow had reached seventy in 1913; Gilbert, in 1917. All three seemed ready and able to carry out their duties well past that age. Beginning in 1911, however, Congress determined that judges should strongly consider retirement when they turned seventy, and the 1911 Judicial Code included a provision to award a pension equivalent to full salary for judges who had reached the age of seventy after having served at least ten years.[9] No provision was made for any sort of partial retirement, which would have been an ideal solution for all three of these active Ninth Circuit judges.

In the spring of 1913, Attorney General James C. McReynolds received word that both Morrow and Ross were contemplating retirement. William Kent, a member of Congress from California, keenly followed these rumors and proposed a list of Californians to fill the potential vacancies. Among others, Kent recommended William Denman of San Francisco, a well-respected admiralty lawyer who was active in civic affairs. Denman would eventually get his chance to sit on the circuit bench, but not for another two decades. As Republicans, neither Gilbert nor Morrow wanted to vest the appointment power of their successors in President Wilson. Ross was a Democrat, but his interest in continued service outweighed his fealty to Democratic succession, and the rumors of his impending retirement proved false.[10] He served for another ten years, despite the onset of a physical disability so severe that he needed an aide to lift him up to the bench.

This disability may have been one of the factors that led Congress to enact more extensive judicial-retirement legislation in 1919. In the House debate on a proposal to grant the president the power to remove incapacitated judges, Andrew Volstead of Minnesota observed: "During the years past it has been very difficult to get rid of men unable to do the work but who were unwilling to resign and who continued on the bench, obstructing and interfering with the administration of justice." The congressional debates never singled out a specific judge to illustrate the need for a new law, but enough legislators evidently believed in the wisdom of the measure that a bill was passed to add two important elements to the existing retirement system. One amendment provided that a retiring judge could "be called upon by the senior circuit judge of that circuit . . . to perform such judicial duties" as the retired judge "may be willing to undertake." The second change authorized the president to appoint an additional circuit or district judge "if he finds that any such judge is unable to discharge efficiently all the duties of his office by reason of mental or physical disability of permanent character."[11] Even with these added inducements to step down, both of which authorized payment of full salary to the departing judge, none of the Ninth Circuit judges relinquished their office during Wilson's tenure as president. By the time Wilson himself left office in 1921 in a debilitated condition, Morrow was seventy-eight years old, Ross was seventy-six, and Gilbert was seventy-four.

II. MORROW STEPS DOWN

Morrow stepped down first. Despite the obvious benefits conferred by the 1919 law and the rumors that announced his impending resignation from active service, Morrow refused to retire while a Democrat had the power to choose his successor. Morrow's ties to the Republican party were strong, both personally and professionally. He was a close friend of Senator Hiram Johnson of California, and his daughter Eleanor was married to Colonel H. L. Roosevelt, a cousin of Theodore Roosevelt's. Morrow's friendship with Johnson ran so deep that on several occasions in the 1920 presidential campaign Morrow publicly defended the senator from attack. Morrow even went so far as to compare Johnson to Abraham Lincoln, pointing out that both had been called radical during their presidential bids. The judge claimed firsthand knowledge to support his statement: as a young man, he said, he had attended the Republican convention that first nominated Lincoln for the presidency. Morrow's involvement in presidential politics reflected his commitment to public affairs, his party loyalty, and a conception of judicial propriety that gave judges the right to speak out on partisan issues.[12]

By the early 1920s Morrow had become an elder statesman in northern California political circles. In October of 1921, when he passed the thirty-year milestone of service on the federal bench, he basked in the warm glow of public adoration for his kindliness and civic spirit. A popular orator on a wide range of topics, Morrow gracefully aged into a role as the Grand Old Man of San Francisco, whom the locals loved to honor. In a sense, the talk of his retirement reflected his advanced age more than it did any deterioration in ability. Even at seventy-eight, his "carriage is erect and his step firm: his gray hair lends dignity to his rugged features; his mouth is firm and his square jaw denotes determination and tenacity of purpose; his eye is honest and kindly." His only expressed professional regret was that he had never developed a special "knack" or "interest" in a particular aspect of the law.[13]

After nearly thirty-two years of service on the federal bench as a district and circuit judge, Morrow finally relinquished his Ninth Circuit seat on January 1, 1923. Under the 1919 act, Morrow retired at full pay with the freedom to accept such judicial duties as Senior Judge William Gilbert chose to authorize. This provision enabled Morrow to fulfill his often expressed desire to "die in harness." In the final six and a half years of his life, Morrow sat on a number of cases. A judicial conservative, Morrow rarely reached far beyond existing doctrine to decide cases, which added an ironic touch when his own participation in an appeal set an important precedent for the court. While serving as a "senior status" judge shortly after his retirement, Morrow wrote an opinion affirming the conviction of several bootleggers under the Prohibition acts. The convicted rum-runners challenged Morrow's authority to serve and requested a reversal in a petition for rehearing. In the first recorded opinion addressing this statute, the Ninth Circuit upheld the validity of the provision authorizing retired judges to hear cases. District Judge Paul J. McCormick wrote that Senior Judge William B. Gilbert had complied with the relevant procedures and that "Judge Morrow was eligible and qualified to participate in, to consider, and to decide this case." In a curious conclusion that confirmed the *ex parte* discussions that must have occurred in chambers, McCormick wrote: "We are authorized to state that Judge GILBERT [who was not on the panel] concurs in the foregoing opinion and decision." This decision became a venerable precedent for the continued service of judges after retirement.[14]

Morrow's retirement made the first vacancy on the Ninth Circuit since 1897. Following the partisan trend of his predecessors, President Warren G. Harding selected a Republican as Morrow's replacement. Frank Rudkin was born in Vernon, Ohio, on April 23, 1864, and attended common schools in Ohio before going to college in Ontario, Canada, where he took honors in mathematics, Latin, and Greek. He then matriculated at Washington and Lee University, in Lexington, Virginia, next door to Erskine Ross's alma mater, Virginia Military Institute. After completing his law course at Washington and Lee, Rudkin settled in North Yakima, Washington, where he practiced law for fourteen years before winning an election as state superior court judge in 1901. He was elevated to the Washington Supreme Court four years later by popular vote, and rose to become chief justice in 1909. In 1911 Rudkin accepted President William Howard Taft's appointment to become United States district judge for the eastern district of Washington. During his rise in the professional ranks Rudkin earned a formidable reputation for his powerful legal mind and judicial instincts. The first member of the Ninth Circuit from Washington, Rudkin won notice as a possible successor to Judge Morrow as early as 1921. As one proponent put it at that time, he "has the clearest insight and the quickest and most diligent application of any judge that I have ever had the honor of appearing before." Rudkin was confirmed by the Senate on January 9, 1923, only eight days after Morrow's resignation became effective, and only five after his appointment by President Harding.[15]

A certain "contrariety and contradiction" marked Rudkin. Although a companionable person, Rudkin lived as a bachelor until he was fifty-seven, when he married Ellen Rose Doty. Even those best acquainted with him commented on Rudkin's rise to fame within his profession when only a very few persons knew him well. Notwithstanding his quiet demeanor and modesty, during his eight years on the Ninth Circuit Rudkin made an impression on his colleagues. "Those of us," Judge William H. Sawtelle said of Rudkin, who "trudge to our conclusions with pedestrian pace marveled at the rapidity with which he grasped the controlling principle of a case." Judge Curtis D. Wilbur felt that Rudkin had distinguished himself both by his congeniality and by his steadfastness in plowing through the work of the court. Although he became very ill in the last months of his life, Rudkin sat on the court almost constantly from October 10, 1930, until April 13, 1931, when he heard his last case. Death came a mere three weeks later, on May 3, 1931.[16]

Although Rudkin's Ninth Circuit service lasted for only eight years, he contributed much to the intellectual life of the court. He was the second of the new crop of judges who replaced those who had led the Ninth Circuit through its first three decades. Despite his junior status on the court, Rudkin often challenged the reasoning of the well-established judges, especially Gilbert's. In a number of cases that raised difficult questions of criminal procedure, Rudkin applied an innovative thinking that the court had before seen only in Erskine Ross. Problem-solving was his forté. Undoctrinaire and non-ideological, Rudkin analyzed cases with creativity and insight. Several Ninth Circuit decisions show signs that Rudkin "stole" the majority from the judge who had originally been assigned to write the court's opinion.[17] Although he formally assumed Morrow's seat on the court, Rudkin in many ways filled the intellectual gap created by Erskine Ross's resignation in 1925.

III. ROSS RETIRES

Ross's retirement, like that of William Morrow, had long been rumored, but even after Morrow retired in 1923, Ross stubbornly refused to yield his place on the bench, despite failing health. Nationally famous for his decisions in numerous cases, Ross clearly enjoyed his power and prestige. But, early in 1925, a cabal of sorts formed on the Ninth Circuit to secure Ross's retirement. Gilbert informed William Denman, the man who, coincidentally, would be chosen ten years later to fill Gilbert's own seat: "You will be interested to know—and this is way down deep sub rosa— that from recent correspondence I have had, a movement is on foot to appoint a successor to Judge Ross. Of this I will tell you more when I see you."[18] On the same day, Morrow wrote to Attorney General Harlan Fiske Stone with more details of the plan. Morrow explained that he had written to Oscar Lawler, a friend of Ross's,

> to the effect that Judge Ross' physical condition and limited attendance upon the Circuit Court of Appeals for some time had been brought to the attention of the Department of Justice, and I suggested that as he had made a faithful and honorable judicial record on the Federal Bench by service for a period of more than thirty-five years, he had won an honorable retirement, and that he voluntarily avail himself of that privilege rather than leave it to the possible action of the President under the Act of February 25, 1919.[19]

Several different considerations may have motivated Morrow's "suggestion." The most obvious concern was that Ross would be dishonored if President Coolidge had to invoke the disability provision of the 1919 statute. Morrow also undoubtedly believed that Ross's infirmity damaged the court's ability to handle cases. Ross's output of opinions did decrease in number after 1923. But to his last day on the bench, Ross produced opinions that validated his reputation as one of the country's finest circuit judges. Although Morrow and Gilbert disagreed sharply with Ross in many Prohibition cases, no evidence exists that differences on substantive issues played any part in their attempt to secure his retirement. Gilbert and Morrow's plan clearly involved some tricky maneuvering and placed in an uncomfortable position those of Ross's friends who urged him to resign. Oscar Lawler elliptically informed Morrow that he had contacted another close friend of Ross's, Frank Flint, who agreed that "some plan must be devised whereby there will be time and opportunity for adaption [*sic*] to the changed situation. If it were possible to arrange so that the date of retirement could be a year hence, opportunity would be afforded to so adjust personal affairs as to avoid the difficulties of an abrupt change." This time frame caused some discomfort to Attorney General Stone, who in those same weeks was preparing to assume new responsibilities on the Supreme Court. He therefore wrote to Flint that "everybody will be satisfied if matters can be so managed that Judge Ross will retire in six months from this time."[20]

Whether these machinations had any effect on Ross is unclear, although the seventy-nine-year-old jurist did submit his letter of resignation to President Calvin Coolidge on March 16, 1925.[21] Coolidge, in a letter that he invited Ross to share with the press, graciously testified to Ross's valuable service to the country:

> It is now approaching the end of the half century since you were called to the Federal Bench. During that long period, your performance of many and difficult duties has been marked by an ability, courage and determination which have repeatedly won the highest testimonies. It has been your fortune to confront on different occasions conditions which required, in the discharge of your duties, the highest qualities of learning, wisdom, moderation and great firmness. In these you have never failed, but rather have repeatedly demonstrated a particularly exalted character and a thorough-going realization of the place which the judiciary must occupy under our system of government.
>
> As you are now retiring after so long and distinguished a career, I wish you to know of my regret that your service is to be terminated, and of my confidence that your record will long stand as a memorial to a just, and fearless and able Judge. That you may be privileged for many years to enjoy the rewards which such service has so well earned for you, is my earnest wish.[22]

Ever conscious that he should complete the task at hand, Ross asked that his resignation be made effective June 1, 1925, so that he could finish writing opinions in pending cases. Unlike Morrow, who had taken the modern-day equivalent of "senior status" and who occasionally still heard appeals, Ross's retirement more closely accorded with the term *resignation* in the 1919 act because he never sat on another case. When he retired, Ross had put in more years of service on the federal bench than any other judge.[23]

Throughout his long career, Ross had won the confidence of the public and the respect of his peers on the bench. Touted as a possible Supreme Court justice, a candidate for the United States Senate from California, and even as a prospective presidential nominee, from a relatively early age Ross instead dedicated his talents to the Ninth Circuit. In a letter written shortly after Ross announced his retirement, William Hunt captured the sentiments of many:

> What more comforting thought can one have than that he has for many, many years devoted his mind and heart to the doing of justice by his fellow men! Surely a life of unselfish fealty to the noblest work earns that reward which comes in the unstinted respect of all good men; that honor which goes with the unqualified esteem of one's fellows.

Nearly four years later, on December 10, 1928, Ross died in Los Angeles.[24]

IV.   McCAMANT'S MISFORTUNE

The campaign to succeed Ross was fierce. Numerous candidates from throughout the circuit sought the job, submitting an extensive series of endorsements and supportive petitions. Geographic and communications constraints made the written record compiled on behalf of each candidate the most critical aspect of the nomination process; the Justice Department screeners relied heavily on letters of recommendation and protest to advise the attorney general of possible nominees to present to President Coolidge. In a memorandum for the attorney general that was dated April 25, 1925, William J. Donovan, assistant to the attorney general and later director of the Office of Strategic Services, surveyed the seven most likely candidates to succeed Judge Ross: Frank H. Norcross of Nevada; Kenneth Mackintosh of Washington; Garret W. McEnery of California; Wallace McCamant of Oregon; William P. James of California; Frank S. Dietrich of Idaho; and Gavin W. Craig of California. This briefing memo excerpted recommendation letters and attempted to flesh out these applicants for the attorney general's benefit. About Judge Norcross, for instance, Donovan added both endorsements and protests, the latter including the statement that "Judge Norcross is so persistently and actively against the Eighteenth Amendment that it would strongly influence his action against the enforcement of the law if he were put on the bench." A few of the candidates, such as Mackintosh and McEnery, had slim files, and the statements by Donovan suggested that the absence of other endorsements of these candidates essentially spoke for itself.[25]

Perhaps because he himself had participated in the letter-writing process during William Gilbert's bid to secure a nomination in 1891–1892, Wallace McCamant's file was exemplary in its completeness. The voluminous record compiled on his behalf included endorsements from many prominent lawyers throughout the West and virtually every public figure of note in Oregon. Although Donovan's Justice Department memorandum does not reveal his own view of McCamant's qualifications, he did paraphrase the Oregon secretary of state's assessment of McCamant: "Judge McCamant is eminently qualified, his integrity is unquestioned, . . . he is a clear thinker, a logical reasoner and thoroughly versed in the law, and therefore would bring with him to the bench all those qualifications so essential in order that the dignity and strength of that most important position may be maintained." In a precursor of a battle to come, Donovan also excerpted a protest letter in which the author stated that she opposed McCamant's appointment "to any office under the United States" because it would be "a reward for the treachery to the people of Oregon."[26]

Frank Dietrich of Idaho received strong endorsements from the elected officials of Idaho. Donovan's memorandum excerpted the most flattering statements, including Senator William Borah's observation that "Judge Dietrich would be good timber for the Supreme bench of the United States. He is one of the ablest Federal judges, in my opinion, on the bench, and back of it all, is a man of exemplary character." But Donovan added: "It has been considered a fixed rule that no appointments would be made to any Federal Court of a person over the age of sixty years." The memorandum listed the age of each district judge in the Ninth Circuit and noted that Dietrich, the only formal candidate for promotion on the list, was sixty-two at the time of the report, January 23, 1925.[27]

The internal records of the Justice Department do not indicate whether the attorney general's advisers formally downgraded Dietrich's candidacy on account of age or upgraded McCamant's as a political reward for his strong support of Calvin Coolidge in 1920. In this sense the official records mask the importance to McCamant's bid for a judgeship of his role in stopping Hiram Johnson's presidential bid in 1920 and in placing Calvin Coolidge's name in nomination as vice president on the Republican ticket with Harding that year. These Justice Department documents do not record for posterity McCamant's role in Coolidge's career or the deep appreciation the president felt for McCamant's aid, but McCamant's personal papers offer an intriguing glimpse into the subterranean politics of the appointment.[28]

McCamant met Coolidge for the first time at a Republican Club of Massachusetts meeting shortly after the 1920 Republican convention, and thereafter they conducted a regular correspondence that continued throughout Coolidge's presidency. Despite offers of positions on the district court, on the United States Court for China, and as assistant attorney general, McCamant steadfastly pursued his ambition to become circuit judge. In one letter to President Coolidge, he spurned a judgeship in China with these words: "So far as my own inclinations and qualifications are concerned, I would enjoy appellate judicial work. I greatly prefer to remain at the bar rather than do judicial work in a court of original jurisdiction." Far from taking umbrage at McCamant's response, Coolidge communicated its content to Attorney General Harry M. Daugherty. Not long thereafter, Daugherty wrote that McCamant was "fortunate in having the good friendship of the President, and I shall be glad to serve him and at the same time be of service to you."[29] When Daugherty left the Justice Department under the cloud of the Teapot Dome scandal, McCamant was considered to be a likely successor. However, perhaps in response to McCamant's apparent lack of interest in any government position other than a circuit judgeship, Coolidge instead appointed Harlan Fiske Stone. As it turned out, McCamant may have done himself a disservice in failing to pursue this position, for Stone went on to be named to the Supreme Court.

During the early part of 1925, the Justice Department appointment machinery geared up to address the Ninth Circuit vacancy created by Ross's retirement. After a month of deliberation, Assistant Attorney General John Marshall recommended McCamant to the attorney general on May 25, 1925. Marshall thought the department had a winner:

> Judge McCamant has served as an Associate Justice of the Supreme Court of the State of Oregon, during which time he has displayed great ability, and attained a reputation for the clarity and soundness of his decisions. There is abundant testimony that he is a man of ripe experience, and judgment; keen of mind and clear of expression, endowed with a natural sense of justice, is courageous in his convictions, and follows the right as he understands it regardless of criticism from any source.[30]

The Senate had adjourned for the summer, but the Constitution empowers the president to fill vacancies during recesses. Any commission granted under the Recess Appointments Clause is temporary, however, and the Justice Department historically has interpreted the clause to require the president to resubmit the nomination to the Senate for confirmation prior to the end of the next session or segment of a session. President Coolidge appointed McCamant under the Recess Clause on May 25, 1925, and he took the oath of office on June 4, 1925.[31]

McCamant knew that his final confirmation would not be easy, and he had been laying the groundwork for senatorial confirmation a full two years before he received the appointment. This preparation appeared to pay off. Toward the end of 1925, when his name was submitted to the Senate for its advice and consent, the nomination sailed through the initial stages of the Senate process. McCamant received endorsements from the subcommittee that handled such nominations and from the full Senate Judiciary Committee. When the nomination reached the full Senate for consideration, however, the politics of confirmation took center stage, with Hiram Johnson of California in the starring role. Johnson first requested an open executive session to debate McCamant's merits, but he lost two close votes.[32] When Johnson spelled out his objections in closed session, the nomination might have failed on the spot but for the intervention of Oregon Senator Charles McNary, who won a vote to refer it back to the Judiciary Committee.[33] McNary requested that McCamant come to Washington to defend himself against Johnson's charges.[34]

On January 29, 1926, the Judiciary Committee convened a hearing to consider McCamant's fitness for the job. Such hearings were highly unusual for judicial nominations, and this fact perhaps accounts for the rather unfocused beginning of the proceedings. The morning hour seemed pointless until Johnson gave a tantalizing taste of what was to come in the afternoon session. Just before noon, Johnson launched this colloquy:

> Senator Johnson. Do you intend to continue during the noon hour? I will ask one more question, unless you intend to continue during the noon hour.
>
> The Chairman. That will depend on the wishes of the Committee.
>
> Senator Johnson. Did you publicly, in a public speech, characterize Justice Brandeis, of the United States Supreme Court, as an "avaricious mountebank"?
>
> Mr. McCamant. I am unable, Senator Johnson, to recall the language I used. I did deliver a political speech in Seattle, on Lincoln's birthday, 1916, in which I criticized the appointment—
>
> Senator Johnson (interposing). You do not recall the exact characterization?
>
> Mr. McCamant. No, sir; I do not. . . .
>
> Senator Johnson. May I ask one more question. Did you publicly say, in a public speech, that Theodore Roosevelt was worse than an anarchist because of his views regarding the recall of judicial decisions?
>
> Mr. McCamant. I never said that; no, sir.[35]

The Committee recessed for lunch. When it reconvened two hours later, Senator Johnson began with a series of benign questions about McCamant's law practice, a line of inquiry seemingly geared more toward giving his colleagues an opportunity to get resettled from lunch than toward eliciting any useful information. When Johnson reintroduced the colloquy regarding Justice Brandeis's appointment to the Supreme Court, McCamant's answers betrayed a lack of understanding about the committee's difficulties with his nomination.[36] By attempting to address aspects of his legal practice that had raised questions in the morning session, McCamant's testimony completely missed the point. It was his earlier *political*, and not his *legal*, activities that worried the committee. Half of the hearing had elapsed before Johnson coyly permitted Mc-Camant himself to broach the subject. The senator asked whether Mc-Camant had "any statement that you desire to make to the Committee at all on any other subject?" McCamant replied carefully: "Well, with reference to the charges that have been made against me because of my conduct at the Republican National Convention of 1920, I am ready to discuss that subject, Senator Johnson."[37] In the closed executive session of the full Senate, Johnson had charged McCamant with duplicity in the 1920 presidential campaign. How the nominee responded to this allegation would determine the likelihood of his confirmation.

Revisiting his memories of the 1920 Republican campaign was undoubtedly bitter for Johnson, who had jockeyed in a large field for the presidential nomination. By contrast to the California senator, McCamant's role barely earned a mention in subsequent accounts of the race. A solid Republican of long standing, McCamant ran, uncommitted to any candidate, as a delegate-at-large to the Republican National Convention. His campaign pledge contained a statement that proved to be his undoing: "I have avoided committing myself to any candidate for President in order that I might be in a better position to support the candidate who wins out at the Oregon Primary."[38]

Hiram Johnson had won a plurality in the Oregon primary, but McCamant had refused to vote for him at the Republican National Convention. Senator McNary of Oregon, who attempted to pilot Mc-Camant's nomination through the minefield laid by Johnson, wanted his colleagues to understand McCamant's rationale for seemingly breaking his pledge to Oregon's Republican voters. With a deference to the cold logic of law that was greater than his understanding of the politically charged environment, McCamant responded that the state laws did not require a delegate-at-large to vote for the candidate who carried the

Oregon primary. The senators might have conceded McCamant this much, in spite of his apparent pledge to support the victor, but the judicial nominee had uttered statements that seemingly went beyond typical electioneering. Senator Thomas J. Walsh of Montana pinpointed an example. McCamant's campaign slogan was "For President, an American, a Republican, and a statesman." Walsh believed it to be fairly self-evident that the president had to be an American and that a Republican would support another Republican. He therefore inquired about the significance of these words in the slogan. McCamant's reply contained the seed of his later demise: "Well, the significance was that there are many men, Senator Walsh, who are eligible for the Presidency of the United States by the fact that they were born in the United States, who in my mind are not Americans. They are not in accord with the fundamental principles of our American government."[39]

When pressed to describe one such candidate who was not an American according to McCamant's definition of the term, McCamant replied, "I am frank to say that I had Senator Johnson in mind." When Johnson wanted to know why McCamant did not pronounce this position publicly during the 1920 primary campaign, McCamant averred that he "did state it with very great frequency during the campaign, Senator Johnson."[40] Despite the apparent lack of any published sources to buttress this allegation, McCamant contended that he "talked as freely on that subject before the primaries as [he] did after the primaries with newspaper men who had authority to publish it." When McCamant presented numerous affidavits supporting his claim, Johnson sought to elicit an expression of remorse or recognition of wrongdoing: "Did you consider yourself under any promise, express or implied, legal or moral, by virtue of what you said in the voters' pamphlet, to support any candidate?" "No, sir." McCamant reiterated that his use of this language indicated to people that he had not committed himself and that he had reserved his "freedom of action." A multitude of affidavits, including one from Johnson's Oregon campaign manager, established that interested citizens throughout the state had understood this position.[41]

But McCamant fell victim to the legalese of his 1920 campaign literature. By pledging in writing to support the winner of the primary, he had opened the trap in which the senators snared him in the 1926 hearing. The voluminous affidavits he brought forward could not save the nomination no matter how unambiguously they testified to his honesty and forthrightness in presenting his position. As McCamant stated in the hearing, "You can interpret [the affidavits]. It is up to you. I think on the whole record it is impossible for anybody to say I endeavored to mislead the public."[42] He quoted a letter written during the campaign that explained his position:

> I should dislike to vote for Hoover: but if his name goes on the ballot and he receives the endorsement of the Oregon electors, I will come across and vote for him if I am a member of the convention. I refuse, however, under any and all circumstances to vote for Hiram Johnson. I notice in the press reports this morning that he had the support of the Non-partisan League in North Dakota. He is an advocate of the recall of judicial decisions. This means that he does not believe in the form of constitutional government which has come down to us from the fathers. In other words, he is not an American. Under no circumstances will I vote to send to the White House a man who is not an American.[43]

McCamant's "proof" that the California senator advocated putting judicial decisions to a popular vote was that Johnson had run as Theodore Roosevelt's running mate on the Bull Moose Party platform of 1912, which contained such a plank.[44] Johnson now took the opportunity to highlight the full implications of McCamant's position:

> Senator Johnson. In that letter you said I was not an American?
> Mr. McCamant. Yes; I did.
> Senator Johnson. Theodore Roosevelt was not an American then?
> Mr. McCamant. He was not a good American.
> Senator Johnson. He was not a good American. I stand on this man's statement. If any man can be confirmed in the Senate for judge when he says Theodore Roosevelt was not a good American, I will want to know why.
> Senator Carroway. I suppose the colonel's son, Quentin, who died in France for his country, was also un-American?
> Mr. McCamant. I have never heard that he declared for the recall of judicial decisions.
> Senator Carroway. You heard that he stood pretty close to his father, and he loved him, and his father loved his son?
> Mr. McCamant. Yes, sir.
> The Chairman. The Chair is of the opinion, unless corrected by the committee, that the attitude of Mr. McCamant toward Colonel Roosevelt, or toward Senator Johnson, or whether he was justified in that attitude, is not material to this inquiry. The question is whether these letters or affidavits modify the statement that he published in the State publication.

Despite the best efforts of Albert B. Cummins, who chaired the hearing, to refocus the questioning on the truthfulness and integrity of McCamant's conduct during the 1920 campaign, Johnson had secured the requisite fodder to defeat McCamant. McCamant attempted to resurrect himself, but to no avail.[45]

Not once during the hearing did the subject of McCamant's judicial record arise. Although as a recess appointee McCamant had heard appeals and issued opinions for seven months, the senators never questioned him on a single matter directly related to judging. Three Ninth Circuit judges sent telegrams to the Judiciary Committee on McCamant's behalf, but they only succeeded in boosting his cause slightly. One telegram, from William H. Hunt and William W. Morrow, said: "As associates of Judge McCamant, it is a pleasure to say that we find him able, diligent, and fair-minded and think his work on the court is highly creditable." Another telegram, from Judge William B. Gilbert, McCamant's longtime friend and former boss from the law firm of Gilbert and Snow, commented: "There can be no question of Judge McCamant's ability. He has done excellent work on the federal bench."[46] Cordial, courtly, and polite, the telegrams did not elaborate on these statements to shed any additional light on what the judges actually thought of McCamant or his ability.

The judges' reluctance to go further in lauding McCamant may have stemmed from several different factors. One was the political circumstance. The judges sent both telegrams after the Senate had referred the nomination back to committee; the contentiousness of the fight to come perhaps dampened the enthusiasm of their recommendations. Second, McCamant had not completely settled in as a federal appellate judge. During the eleven months he served under the recess appointment, McCamant wrote forty opinions. Few posed difficult questions, and in only one did a judge dissent. After such a short time on the bench McCamant had not yet fully proved himself. Whatever the reasons for their somewhat lukewarm recommendations, the incumbent Ninth Circuit judges' assessments of McCamant became mere footnotes to the proceedings.[47]

Coolidge stuck by McCamant despite calls to withdraw the nomination. Six weeks after the hearing ended, the Senate Judiciary Committee issued an adverse report on McCamant, with an official tally of fourteen members voting, ten to four against the candidate. The following day, March 17, 1926, without a record vote or debate, the Senate rejected the nomination of Wallace McCamant. "I may say, without egotism," Hiram Johnson wrote to his son, "it is the greatest personal victory that has been won here in many a day and is so regarded." For Senator Robert N. Stanfield of Oregon, McCamant's rejection constituted the most "shocking or oppressive" political experience in his career. Stanfield saw the defeat as his colleague from California had cast it, in purely political terms: "In this instance it was the fear that the press had aroused a prejudice in the mind of the public against you because you had mentioned the name of Roosevelt in a way they thought would be interpreted by this same public mind as an effrontery to one they revere, and that it must be avenged," he wrote to McCamant. "This same vindictive public would exact the scalps of those Senators who had the temerity to support you."[48] A month later, McCamant scrawled a one-sentence resignation letter to President Coolidge. So ended the brief judicial career of the only circuit judge in the country's history to suffer rejection by the Senate after serving under a recess appointment. He lived out the rest of his days as a practicing attorney in Portland and died on December 17, 1944.[49]

V. THE ELEVATION OF DIETRICH

For the Ninth Circuit, the failed nomination of McCamant could not have come at a worse time. Ross had written twenty-four opinions in his last year on the court, a not unimpressive figure given his advanced age, but after his retirement he would write no more. Morrow was slowing appreciably. As a senior status judge, he averaged just over six opinions per year after 1925. The sudden rise in docketings, from 225 in 1924 to 359 in 1925, exacerbated the need for new judges. Even though Rudkin was well on his way to compiling his impressive average of over sixty-three opinions per year, he could not handle the increasing workload of the court by himself. To be sure, Gilbert was a stalwart even in old age, averaging over forty-five opinions annually after he reached the age of seventy-nine, and Hunt did his share, averaging approximately forty-five opinions per year from 1925 until he left the court on November 30, 1928.[50]

Despite the great need for a fourth Ninth Circuit judge to join Gilbert, Hunt, and Rudkin, Coolidge and his Justice Department advisers moved slowly after the Senate rejected McCamant in March of 1926. Reportedly to punish Hiram Johnson and California for the Senate's rejection of McCamant, Coolidge ignored calls by southern California lawyers to fill the vacated slot with one of their own. On December 22, 1926, the president nominated Frank S. Dietrich, who must have believed that his best chance for elevation had eluded him in 1925. The California press saw the Dietrich appointment as another patronage plum for Idaho Senator William E. Borah, one of Dietrich's chief backers.[51] Born January 23, 1863, on a farm near Ottawa, Kansas, Dietrich attended local schools before receiving his bachelor's degree from Brown University. He graduated in 1887 and returned to Kansas to teach history, Latin, and political economy at Ottawa University. While teaching, he began to read law with a man named Stewart. Dietrich followed his mentor to Blackfoot, Idaho, and was admitted to practice there in 1891. Dietrich served as counsel to the Union Pacific Railroad from 1899 to 1907, when President Roosevelt appointed him as district judge for the district of Idaho, a post he retained until Coolidge elevated him to the Ninth Circuit.

Dietrich had earned the respect of attorneys throughout the circuit. Attorney General John G. Sargent's report to the president included endorsements from Senator Frank Gooding of Idaho, Governor C. C. Moore, Chief Justice William A. Lee, and others, "all of whom speak in the highest terms of Judge Dietrich's learning, ability and experience." And Senator Gooding's words surely comforted the Executive Branch officials bruised by McCamant's defeat: "I have never heard [Dietrich] criticized, and it seems to me that this is a most remarkable thing to say of any man."[52] Less than two weeks after Coolidge submitted the nomination, the Senate confirmed Dietrich to the Ninth Circuit bench. Renowned more as a trial than as an appellate judge, Dietrich's opinions for the Ninth Circuit nevertheless exhibited sensitivity to trial errors without sacrificing common sense. Logic sometimes counted more than precedent. His tenure on the Ninth Circuit was so brief—not quite four years—that he arguably never hit his stride on the appellate bench. He died of a heart attack while in his automobile on October 2, 1930. In his last year on the court Dietrich wrote ninety-one opinions, a quantity reflecting both the immense pressure felt by the judges to keep up with the workload and Dietrich's growing efficiency in doing more than his share of it.[53]

As the court underwent these personnel changes, it was also experiencing other dramatic transformations caused by a docket increasingly composed of cases that raised questions of social order, from the unrest associated with World War I to the Teapot Dome scandal. Earlier in the century, cases involving issues of economic and natural resource development had dominated the docket of a stable court. But the original vanguard of Gilbert, Ross, and Morrow, who served side-by-side for nearly three decades with only the addition of Hunt, had retired within a few years of one another. From the departures of Morrow and Ross came the additions of the highly able Rudkin, the unfortunate McCamant, and an as yet untried Dietrich. Amid the uncertainty created by this personnel turnover, the court would face some of its most critical challenges, occasioned first by the onset of World War I.

1. Stephen J. Field, appointed to the Supreme Court in 1863, sat as circuit justice for the Ninth Circuit until his retirement in 1897. (U.S. Court of Appeals, Ninth Circuit)

2. Lorenzo Sawyer was appointed circuit judge for the Ninth Circuit as it was configured in 1870. He died in 1891 prior to the court's first oral argument. (Stanford University Archives).

3. In 1892, Joseph McKenna was the first Ninth Circuit judge appointed under the Evarts Act. McKenna later served as attorney general before being appointed by President McKinley to the Supreme Court. (U.S. Court of Appeals, Ninth Circuit)

4. The Appraisers' Building in San Francisco, the first headquarters of the Ninth Circuit. (Courtesy of the Bancroft Library, University of California)

5. The U.S. Court of Appeals and Post Office Building, which served as the Ninth Circuit's headquarters from 1905. The building survived the 1906 earthquake but was badly damaged by the 1989 Loma Prieta earthquake. (U.S. Court of Appeals, Ninth Circuit)

6. (left to right) William W. Morrow, William B. Gilbert, Erskine M. Ross. This trio filled the three authorized judgeships for the Ninth Circuit between 1897 and 1923. (U.S. Court of Appeals, Ninth Circuit)

7. Jane Stanford, widow of Leland Stanford, successfully fought the United States government to preserve her late husband's estate and save Stanford University from bankruptcy. (Stanford University Archives)

Judge McKisick's Variety in Listening to Judge Garber's Closing.
[From courtroom sketches by Homer Davenport.]

8. Lewis D. McKisick served as the government's counsel in the suit against Leland Stanford's estate. Here he is depicted by the cartoonist for the *San Francisco Examiner*. (Stanford University Archives)

The Leader of the San Francisco Bar in Action.
Ex-Judge John Garber read cold law, threw points into the teeth of the Court with the vigorous action of a baseball pitcher, warmed to his peroration and hastily brushed aside technicalities like cobwebs from the face of the law. As sketched by Homer Davenport.]

9. John Garber was retained by Jane Stanford to represent the Stanford estate. (Stanford University Archives)

10.   Leland Stanford served as governor of California and United States senator and helped to build the first transcontinental railroad. His legacy to Stanford University, however, may have been his greatest contribution to western development. (Stanford University Archives)

11.   Workers laying track in the West. Railroad cases composed a large portion of the Ninth Circuit's docket in the 1890s. (National Archives)

12. Chinatown, San Francisco, late nineteenth century. Merchants who owned businesses like the Sing Fat Company were exempt from immigration restrictions in the 1882 and 1884 Chinese exclusion acts. The man on the right, with his hair knotted in a queue, would have been subject to the infamous "Queue Ordinance" of the 1870s. (San Francisco Public Library)

13. These Chinese students were in theory exempt from exclusion and deportation, but the Ninth Circuit sometimes issued quite harsh rulings about such persons. (Reproduced by permission of the Huntington Library, San Marino, California)

14.   The No. 5 Claim at Anvil Creek, near Nome, Alaska. The struggle to gain control over this placer mine sparked the greatest crisis to order in the Ninth Circuit's history. (B. B. Dobbs Collection, Photo number 12-217, Alaska State Library)

15.   Barges jammed with would-be millionaires headed for Nome during the gold rush of 1899–1901. In the summer of 1900 alone, the population of Nome grew from several hundred to over twenty thousand. (Oregon Historical Society, #cn 004605.)

16. Arthur Noyes, the Alaska district judge who manipulated the court system in an apparent conspiracy to steal gold from the Anvil Creek mines. (Historical Photograph Collection, Accession number 86-003-23N, in the Archives, Alaska and Polar Regions Department, University of Alaska Fairbanks)

17. Alexander McKenzie was one of the toughest and most astute political bosses west of the Mississippi. When Noyes appointed him receiver of the Anvil Creek mines, he immediately set about extracting as much gold as he could, in violation of normal receivership practice. (North Dakota Institute for Regional Studies & NDSU Archives)

18. When the Ninth Circuit successfully quelled the Anvil Creek conspiracy, Jafet Lindeberg was able to mine the claims he had discovered in 1898. He is shown here with some of his gold bars. (Lomen Collection, Accession number 72-71-3112, in the Archives, Alaska and Polar Regions Department, University of Alaska Fairbanks)

19. Loggers in Oregon, circa 1900. The government brought numerous timber depredation suits against loggers who felled trees on public lands, but the Ninth Circuit typically sided with the loggers. (Oregon Historical Society, #OrHi 49096)

20. Erskine M. Ross, a federal judge for four decades, three of them as circuit judge. This brilliant jurist disagreed with his colleague William Gilbert on numerous issues, and these judicial disagreements helped to shape western development. (U.S. Court of Appeals, Ninth Circuit)

21. William B. Gilbert served as an active circuit judge for thirty-nine years, the longest tenure of any circuit judge in American history. He wrote for the Ninth Circuit in the *Stanford* case, the Teapot Dome scandal, and the *Olmstead* wiretapping case. (U.S. Court of Appeals, Ninth Circuit)

22. The I.W.W. was a tough and lawless organization before its demise in the mid-1920s. (Oregon Historical Society, #OrHi 77730)

23. Roy Olmstead, pictured with his wife and mother-in-law. Federal wiretapping of Olmstead led to a landmark search-and-seizure case. (San Francisco Public Library)

24. The Prohibition era produced widespread lawlessness and a dramatic increase in the federal courts' dockets. (San Francisco Public Library)

25. Curtis Wilbur (at right), then secretary of the navy, looking at the checkerboard pattern of land grants made to railroads. This map concerned the Elk Hills naval petroleum reserve implicated in the Teapot Dome scandal. (San Francisco Public Library)

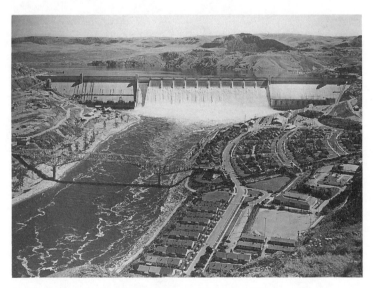

26. Great water projects in the New Deal era such as the Grand Coulee Dam (shown here) brought water conservation and electrical power to the West. (Oregon Historical Society, #OrHi 85433)

27. The swearing-in ceremony of Homer T. Bone, appointed to replace the deceased Bert E. Haney on the Ninth Circuit. (left to right) Clifton Mathews, Francis A. Garrecht, Curtis D. Wilbur, Homer T. Bone, William Denman, and William Healy. (San Francisco Public Library)

SEVEN

War, Liquor, and the Quest for Order

It is our duty to see that the law is executed and uphold those whose duty it is to enforce it.

Judge William W. Morrow, 1916

In the summer of 1916, with the war in Europe approaching the end of its second year and an American presidential campaign just beginning, San Franciscans experienced a tragedy that symbolized a breakdown in social order and foreshadowed a range of issues the Ninth Circuit would confront in the ensuing years. On July 22, 1916, a bomb exploded during a massive Preparedness Parade in San Francisco. Business interests and Republicans had sponsored the parade to show San Francisco's support for America's war preparation efforts. Members of the city's strong labor movement and ethnic communities, which were deeply ambivalent if not flatly opposed to the country's entry into war, made no secret of their opposition to the Preparedness Parade. The blast itself, which occurred shortly after the parade began, killed six persons and injured forty-four others. Operating on the assumption that radical groups were responsible, police arrested a member of the Industrial Workers of the World (I.W.W.), Osmond Jacobs, on July 24, 1916, after he allegedly remarked, "It's a damned good job. . . . It might have been better if—"[1]

Two days later, at the Exposition Auditorium in San Francisco, William W. Morrow, the "venerable jurist of the United States Court," captured the feelings of an outraged public: "A monstrous, unprovoked and cowardly crime has been committed in our midst; a crime against innocent human beings; a crime against society; a crime that strikes at the very foundation of our government; a crime perpetrated in broad daylight in the presence of thousands of witnesses." "The protection of life depends entirely upon law," Morrow continued, "but the execution

141

of that law is in the hands of its officers. . . . It is our duty to see that the law is executed and uphold those whose duty it is to enforce it."[2]

This theme—the strict and sure enforcement of the law—dominated the court's work from World War I to the end of Prohibition in 1933. Beginning in 1917, as the nation marched to war, the court's docket increasingly reflected issues concerning the draft, the rights of citizens to speak freely in opposition to America's involvement in the conflict, and war-related labor disputes. When the aftermath of war produced widespread anti-liquor sentiment and government corruption, the court faced the challenges of Prohibition enforcement and the adjudication of a major civil suit arising out of the Teapot Dome scandal. For the court as an institution, the period signaled the need for fundamental reforms that Congress failed to appreciate until the mid-1930s. As it had with much substantive legislation, including the Chinese Exclusion acts, Congress enacted laws that significantly increased the federal courts' work without authorizing the appointment of additional judges to handle the expanded caseload. The power of federal courts continued to grow, as the national government extended its influence into heretofore local concerns. At a societal level, the Ninth Circuit served an important balancing function in the West, between radicals who tested the outer limits of the law and zealous law enforcement officials and district judges who occasionally overstepped the bounds of constitutional propriety. For the first time in the Ninth Circuit's history, civil liberties required frequent judicial attention. As the judges developed a greater familiarity with these issues, fissures on the court emerged, sparking debates that went to the heart of historical notions of rights.

I. WORLD WAR I AND THE NINTH CIRCUIT

The onset of World War I presented the court with problems of a sort it had never before encountered. Judge Morrow, who continued to speak often in public, displayed an uncompromising patriotism and strongly hinted at how the court would respond to war-related legal issues. At a "monster mass meeting" to demonstrate the support of San Franciscans for universal military training that was held on March 29, 1917, a little more than a week before Congress formally declared war against Germany, Morrow "made a stirring speech explaining the absolute need for an adequate and thoroughly trained armed force for the defense of the country." He sharply rebuked those who sought strict neutrality even after the Germans sank the *Lusitania*: "[W]e know also that the time will come when designing nations will try to destroy this country. We owe a duty to our posterity." Despite his opposition to Wilson on many political issues, the Republican judge stood alongside the Democratic president on the proper response to aggression. "As American citizens we are all confronted with a great responsibility," he declared. "We are the keepers of the future of the greatest republic the world has ever known. We must get together to make this a great, powerful organization in support of the President, who stands for American rights."[3]

Not all westerners shared such views. Morrow's unabashed public support for the war effort presaged a certain juridical tension with his duty to administer the law fairly. As it turned out, whether as a result of reluctance on his part to judge those charged with violating war-related measures or of his workload decreasing as he grew older, Morrow had little judicial impact on the Ninth Circuit's war jurisprudence.[4] Nevertheless, his public statements about the war paralleled the sentiments expressed by his judicial colleagues in their dispositions of war-related appeals. The court consistently upheld the military's interest in two distinct classes of cases in the court's "war" docket: implementation of draft laws, and enforcement of anti-prostitution provisions. These categories of cases generally accorded with the military's goals of obtaining soldiers and keeping them healthy.

Getting soldiers was the first priority. On April 1, 1917, the army was 184,000 enlistees short of its goal of 287,000 soldiers. That month, only 36,000 responded to the declaration of war by signing up. By the end of June, the army still needed 50,000 soldiers, and enlistment records lagged far behind those of the Civil War and the Spanish-American War. Enlistment figures in the Far West were among the highest in the country. Oregon ranked first, with 90.11 percent as of April 1, 1918; the first draft there pressed only 717 men into service. By June of 1918, Nevada topped the "honor roll." But precisely because other states did not approach these figures, the president and Congress agreed on a Selective Service Act that authorized the raising of a 500,000-man army. The statute originally subjected to the draft "all male citizens, or male persons not alien enemies who have declared their intention to become citizens, between the ages of twenty-one and thirty years."[5]

In one of its first war legislation cases, the Ninth Circuit upheld the conviction of a man for failing to register for the draft. He contended that he exceeded the lawful age of thirty, but Ross skeptically reviewed his proffered evidence and upheld the district court's finding of fact that the defendant was under thirty-one. This case foreshadowed a pattern in

which the Ninth Circuit deferentially scrutinized district court determi-
nations of fact and conclusions of law, rarely reversing convictions for
Selective Service Act violations.[6] Sometimes men went to great lengths
to avoid the draft, such as the time two defendants claimed an exemption
from the draft because their "wives" depended on their labor. Their
claims failed when the local draft authorities discovered the salient fact
that neither man was married; the women purporting to be their wives
had participated in the scam. The only time the Ninth Circuit reversed
a conviction for a failure to register occurred two years after the war
ended. According to the district court, the man who was accused of draft
evasion fell within the range of eligible draftees, which Congress had
extended on August 31, 1918, to all men between eighteen and forty-five
years of age. The defendant himself did not know for certain whether he
was forty-five or forty-six, and the Ninth Circuit gave him the benefit of
the doubt.[7]

The Selective Service Act draft cases illustrated the court's firm commitment to upholding the military's prerogatives in obtaining soldiers.
This act also contained provisions that underscored the growing power
of the temperance movement in America; one prohibited liquor consumption by soldiers, and another authorized regulations on "houses of
prostitution." The latter provision aroused action by law enforcement
officials and drew the Ninth Circuit's scrutiny of the military's goal of
keeping the men disease-free. Section 13 of the Selective Service Act
empowered the secretary of war "to do everything by him deemed
necessary to suppress and prevent the keeping or setting up of houses of
ill fame, brothels, or bawdy houses within such distance as he may deem
needful of any military camp, station, [or] fort." Pursuant to this statutory authority, the secretary issued a regulation prohibiting such es-
tablishments within five miles of a military base.[8]

If the reported cases are any guide, the ban caused few problems
anywhere in the country and none in the Ninth Circuit except in San
Francisco. But there the restriction severely cramped business. Numerous
bawdy-house proprietors operated within the five-mile zone of the Pre-
sidio and Fort Mason. When the first convicted defendant challenged the
constitutionality of the regulation, Judge William H. Hunt explained
that Congress's powers "'to raise and to support armies,' and also 'to
make rules for the government and regulation of the land and naval
forces'" validated the anti-prostitution regulations. The court thus upheld a sweeping exercise of national power on an issue traditionally left
to the states. In much the same way, a decade and a half later the New

Deal was to effect similarly expansive extensions of federal power into the local sphere. Interestingly, although these incursions of federal power over traditionally local concerns produced considerable rancor on the Ninth Circuit, the legality of the anti-prostitution regulations drew no dissent from Erskine Ross, who in many economic contexts had resisted such extensions of federal power.[9]

Having thus resolved the constitutional objections to the regulations, the court readily affirmed the convictions of numerous bawdy house proprietors on the facts proved at the district court. Federal officials cracked down on bordellos on Broadway, Geary, Eddy, Third, and Stockton streets in San Francisco. Moreover, specific rulings facilitated enforcement efforts. The court permitted the physician of the City Board of Health to testify about the "diseased physical condition of certain women found on the premises," such evidence being admissible "to prove the character of the house." The court also allowed evidence that an Oriental woman had stood in a doorway on Stockton Street and said, "Come on in," to a white man walking by. Judge William Gilbert held that the "evidence was clearly admissible for the purpose of showing that prostitution was being practiced on the premises."[10]

The judges disagreed in only one case. Hunt and Gilbert affirmed the conviction of a woman for prostitution, but Ross dissented, because he believed that Congress had unintentionally repealed the provision of the Selective Service Act under which the United States attorney had charged the defendant. This subtle distinction well illustrated Ross's insistence that statutes be read and applied with the utmost precision. Under the 1917 statute, Congress empowered the secretary of war to issue orders and regulations prohibiting prostitution, and the district court convicted the defendant of violating one of those orders. But in 1918, when Congress amended the bawdy-house provision, it directly banned solicitation without authorizing an administrative regulation to that effect. Although this glitch in the statute appeared to have been unintentional, Ross reasoned that the new statute stripped the secretary of authority to issue the order under which the defendant had been convicted. Had the defendant been prosecuted for violating the statute, Ross would undoubtedly have upheld his conviction. But because the indictment invoked only the order, Ross believed the conviction could not stand. He also candidly stated that the court's decision in a previous bawdy-house case had been wrong for the same reason.[11]

The Ninth Circuit's strict enforcement of the Selective Service Act solved two problems. It enabled the United States to conscript able-bodied men, and it aided the armed forces in keeping the men able-bodied. These cases presented few difficult legal problems; the court simply reviewed the evidence and affirmed. But the cases highlighted an unprecedented extension of federal power and presaged similar developments that arose in the Prohibition and New Deal eras.

II.   OPPOSITION TO THE WAR

Another important class of war-related cases raised a more complex set of issues. Under the Espionage Act of 1917 and subsequent amendments, the Justice Department prosecuted more than 2,000 cases, over half of which resulted in convictions, including those of senatorial nominee J. A. Peterson of Minnesota, Eugene V. Debs, and more than 150 I.W.W. leaders. None of these convictions apparently involved a bona fide spy or saboteur. Instead, the Justice Department employed the Espionage Act to suppress anti-war opinion and anti-recruitment efforts. Groups sympathetic to Germany received special attention from the department as German spy hysteria swept the country.[12] Federal prosecutors went after these "subversive" groups with a potent weapon, section 3 of the Espionage Act, which provided:

> Whoever, when the United States is at war, shall willfully make or convey false reports or false statements with intent to interfere with the operation or success of the military or naval forces of the United States or to promote the success of its enemies and whoever, when the United States is at war, shall willfully cause or attempt to cause insubordination, disloyalty, mutiny, or refusal of duty, in the military or naval forces of the United States, or shall willfully obstruct the recruiting or enlistment service of the United States, to the injury of the service or of the United States, shall be punished by a fine of not more than $10,000 or imprisonment for not more than twenty years, or both.[13]

Under this statute the court confronted the third major set of war-related issues: those associated with freedom of expression. The court's jurisprudence in these cases demonstrated that the Ninth Circuit was not willing to go very far to protect important rights of expression, although a few of the court's rulings laid a groundwork for enhanced protection of defendants' trial rights.

The Justice Department's administrative style under President Wilson magnified the importance of the Ninth Circuit's work. High officials in the Justice Department purportedly opposed the draconian measures prescribed by the Espionage Act and its amendments, but they failed to police United States attorneys in far-flung districts of the country who enforced the act with unremitting zeal. The Ninth Circuit had more than its fair share of these prosecutors. According to statistics gathered by the attorney general, in numbers of prosecutions brought under the Espionage Act the district of Arizona ranked fourth with forty-seven in 1918 and second with forty-six in 1919. Districts in the Ninth Circuit tried 16.9 percent of all Espionage Act prosecutions in 1918 and 24.4 percent in 1919. In the latter year, the Ninth Circuit contained three of the top five districts in numbers of such criminal prosecutions: northern California with fifty-two (first), Arizona with forty-six (second), and southern California with thirty-nine (fifth).[14]

Confronted with this swell of cases, the federal judiciary reacted in a "hysterical" manner, according to Justice Oliver Wendell Holmes, who himself perhaps contributed to the hysteria. In *Schenck v. United States*, Holmes's opinion for the Court had upheld the Espionage Act's constitutionality by stating that the "question in every case is whether the words used are used in such circumstances and are of such a nature as to create a clear and present danger that they will bring about the substantive evils that Congress has a right to prevent." As one historian has described it, the federal judiciary "proved to be highly immoderate in passing on Espionage and Sedition Act cases. Jurymen were reported by one judge to have regarded verdicts of guilty as a means of demonstrating their own loyalty." The Ninth Circuit faced a great challenge in protecting defendants' rights in this climate.[15]

In the wake of *Schenck*, the Ninth Circuit heard many appeals concerning freedom of speech, in such areas as obstructing recruitment, inciting insubordination, uttering abusive language about the military, and hindering the operation of the armed forces. The Justice Department targeted German-Americans for these prosecutions under the Espionage Act, and the Ninth Circuit routinely upheld their convictions. Thus, the court affirmed the conviction of a German-American who made public speeches in Sherman County, Oregon, to the effect that moneyed interests in the United States had caused the country to go to war, that Germany was in the right and the United States was in the wrong, and that "one German could lick ten Americans." The court took very seriously the opposition of German-Americans to the United States war cause, even a year and a half after the war ended. The court showed greater tolerance for subversive speech by non-Germans. It reversed the conviction of a Swede who had made certain statements supportive of the Kaiser in a private conversation with a person not of draftable age.

But on the whole the Ninth Circuit had little patience with attempts to obstruct recruiting efforts. The court tended to uphold these Espionage Act convictions because it detected a link between the speech uttered and obstruction of recruitment.[16]

One discernible trend of the Ninth Circuit's jurisprudence on freedom of expression, then, was that German-Americans were subjected to stricter enforcement of speech laws than were other anti-war speakers. These cases also exhibited a few tentative forays into the relation between prosecutions for speech and defendants' rights, but far more often than not, the military's interest prevailed over the speaker's, as one celebrated case illustrated. The film *The Spirit of '76* depicted a British soldier during the War for Independence "impaling on a bayonet a baby lying in its cradle and then whirling it around his head so impaled." It also portrayed "[o]ther unspeakable atrocities committed by British soldiers, including the shooting of harmless women, the dragging off, sometimes by the hair of the head, of young American girls." At a private screening of the film before the censor, the director deleted the objectionable scenes, only to reinsert them after the censor approved the film's release to the public. The district court convicted the filmmaker and confiscated the film because it tended to "arouse our revenge and to question the good faith of our ally, Great Britain, and to make us a little bit slack in our loyalty to Great Britain in this great catastrophe or emergency."[17]

On appeal, the Ninth Circuit affirmed, finding that the film "might be a truthful representation of an historical fact, and yet the nature of it, the circumstances surrounding the exhibition thereof, the time, the occasions when the public exhibitions are had, may well tend to . . . be calculated to foment disloyalty or insubordination among the naval or military forces." Federal prosecutors had not proved that any military personnel had seen the film, thus raising the question of whether the defendant had incited any actual insubordination. Judge Hunt's opinion held simply that the "exhibition to the public at a public place, if given with the evil intent described, is sufficient." Both district and appellate court opinions appear to have assumed the director's "evil intent," perhaps not an illogical inference from his film editing, but nevertheless one the government did not prove. In this decision, then, the court announced that it would affirm the convictions of speakers who told the truth, whose "evil intent" had not been proved, and whose message had not reached the audience protected by the statute.[18]

Judge Hunt, who wrote the court's opinion in the *Spirit of '76* case, elaborated on his strict law-and-order approach to speech-related issues in a case involving distribution of a book, *The Finished Mystery*. The book contained passages questioning the purpose of going to war and suggesting that the British were as culpable as the Germans.[19] Hunt's opinion affirmed the conviction with a ringing condemnation of what, by late twentieth-century standards, would seem to be an innocuous book:

> It is difficult to gather any purpose other than a disloyal and wicked one on the part of one who, knowing the contents of the book described, deliberately offered the same for sale. The book rails at love of country, calls the prosecution of the war a crime, denies the truth of the fact that the war was a last resort, where other methods failed, and generally in other ways endeavors, not only to foment suspicion and hatred of the cause of the United States, but also to engender respect for the position of Germany as against the United States.[20]

In contrast to these harsh rulings, in the case of *Shilter v. United States* the court gave seed to the notion that overzealous prosecution of antiwar speakers might implicate defendants' rights. The court reversed an Espionage Act conviction because the indictment failed to show the connection between the defendant's acts and the military. Gilbert's opinion held that the United States attorney had neither pleaded nor proved that Shilter intended his alleged seditious statements to cause insubordination or disloyalty among the military. Gilbert's opinion does not disclose why the court chose this occasion, rather than the *Spirit of '76* case it decided just two weeks later, to focus on the link between the speech and its intended consequences. The court seemed wedded to Erskine Ross's aphorism that "[f]ree speech in times of war is by no means the same thing as free speech in times of peace." *Shilter* did, however, signal to overzealous federal prosecutors that the court would not rubber-stamp improperly conceived indictments.[21]

When viewed through the lens of late twentieth-century First Amendment doctrine, the court's jurisprudence of free speech cases arising under the Espionage Act on the whole appears draconian in its severity.[22] By modern standards, most of these cases would be summarily reversed if indeed prosecuted at all. But when viewed in the context of the times, the Ninth Circuit deserves credit for sometimes acting slightly more protective of defendants' rights than did the district courts whose opinions it reviewed. The Ninth Circuit was neither the most civil libertarian nor the most enforcement-conscious among the circuit courts of appeals. On the one hand, the Eighth Circuit reversed a number of Espionage Act convictions, including one of a man named Von Bank who, as president of the local school board, had refused to put the American flag above the district schoolhouse. He had stated that "he would just as soon see a pair of old trousers hanging over the schoolhouse as the United States flag." The Eighth Circuit threw out his conviction on the ground that he had been prejudiced by "the passions of the times" when charged with the crime and that "there was no evidence from which the jury had the right to find or infer that the defendant used the language quoted above with the intent to cause . . . insubordination, disloyalty, mutiny, or refusal of duty in the military." The Sixth Circuit, on the other hand, almost invariably upheld Espionage Act convictions.[23] It may have been, then, that the zealousness of certain western United States attorneys and the xenophobia pervading the region prevented the Ninth Circuit from taking a stronger stand against the hysteria that swept the country.

If the context provided one constraint upon a more libertarian approach, the prevailing Supreme Court precedents supplied another. After the exposition of Holmes's "clear and present danger" test in *Schenck v. United States* in 1919, a majority on the Supreme Court began to uphold the position that the "bad tendency" of a person's speech, rather than the actual threat of danger, justified punishment. Throughout the 1920s, the Supreme Court took a restrictive view of speech in the context of subversion. Under the Supreme Court's judicial regime, the Ninth Circuit had little room to advance the cause of civil liberties even if the judges had been so inclined. When the court reversed, it did so on procedural, rather than free speech, grounds. Ross, Rudkin, and Hunt, the judges who would be among the most solicitous of a defendant's procedural rights during Prohibition, evinced no similar interest in First Amendment protections. Morrow and Gilbert viewed both clusters of rights narrowly. Ross and Morrow may have derived their protective view of military interests from their Civil War experiences, but opinions by Hunt and Gilbert, who never served in the military, display similar attitudes. This combination of context, precedent, and inclination merged to advance strong restrictions on speech in the Ninth Circuit during and immediately after World War I.[24]

III. LABOR UNREST

The Espionage Act proved to be a much less successful weapon in the Ninth Circuit when it was directed at labor groups, many of which viewed the war as capitalistic exploitation of the working class. Although hardly sympathetic to the radical labor message, the Ninth Circuit judges shielded defendants from many federal prosecutorial excesses. The court did not extend free-expression doctrine beyond the limits imposed by the Supreme Court, but the trial procedures it required had the effect of protecting speech by labor leaders. These labor-related cases played an important part in the development by the Ninth Circuit of a less rigid conception of order.[25]

The labor group most responsible for this altered approach, the Industrial Workers of the World, or "Wobblies," was in some respects an unlikely beneficiary of this jurisprudential change. The I.W.W. rose rapidly in the West after its formation in Chicago in 1905, and it quickly gained a reputation for "unbeatable militancy." The Wobblies launched a massive free-speech battle in 1909 to win the right to disseminate their pro-labor views. Throughout the 1910s, the Wobblies attempted to organize workers in communities from Washington to Pennsylvania, Montana to Missouri, and South Dakota to southern California. They rarely backed down from a fight, and they seemed particularly drawn to labor struggles where violence appeared imminent: "Without question they were tough and lawless in any tough and lawless situation." When the war in Europe began in 1914 and the economy responded with an upsurge, the I.W.W. saw an opportunity to win higher wages and lower hours. By 1917, the Wobblies had attracted approximately 60,000 dues-paying members, and several hundred thousand more held membership cards. But this success in winning adherents came at a high price. It polarized popular opinion, particularly in the West, and encouraged business groups, who had the most to lose from the success of the Wobblies, to incite a number of attacks on the radical labor group. In March of 1917, for example, police broke up a fund-raising dance in Miami, Arizona, that was being held for striking miners and their families. Two months later, 600 men torched the I.W.W. hall in Oakland. And in the summer of 1917, vigilantes intimidated Wobblies following a strike against the Anaconda Copper Company in Montana.[26]

Meanwhile, state and federal prosecutors throughout the country were filing criminal charges against the Wobblies for various acts of vandalism, property destruction, and anti-war militancy. The most spectacular incident of the federal government's campaign against the I.W.W. took place in the summer of 1917, when United States attorneys and special agents of the Justice Department from Chicago westward investigated the labor organization for suspected acts of sabotage. On September 5, government officials raided I.W.W. headquarters in Chicago and offices throughout the West. The government brought criminal charges in Chicago, Sacramento, and Wichita based on the papers seized and other signs of subversion. The Chicago trial attracted the most notoriety, because the principal defendant was I.W.W. leader William D. (Big Bill) Haywood. The authorities originally intended the September 5 raid on the California headquarters of the I.W.W. in Fresno to gather evidence for the impending prosecution of the group's leaders in Chicago. They found little evidence suggesting violent subversion, but the United States attorney in Sacramento nevertheless brought a separate indictment in February, 1918, against fifty-four men and one woman. Pre-trial detention facilities were harsh: the jailers provided inadequate food and crowded the prisoners, forcing them to take turns resting while the others had to stand. Five defendants died before trial. The government dropped some of the other indictments and eventually brought forty-six defendants to trial.[27]

At the trial itself, over which Frank H. Rudkin presided, forty-three of the forty-six defendants refused to defend themselves. They sat mute in the courtroom, represented by no counsel. To draw Rudkin as the trial judge was a fortunate break for the defendants, but their defense strategy poorly exploited the opportunity. Rudkin was one of the best district judges in the Ninth Circuit, and his elevation to the appellate bench in 1923 brought to the court a judge who fearlessly bucked the popular hysteria and ensured fair procedures for criminal defendants. One reporter at the scene described Rudkin as "a powerful man, overtopping all others in the courtroom. Though he is past middle age, his vigor and keenness are unabated, and one feels instinctively that he will see justice done or know the reason why." But without experienced trial counsel to point out the many weaknesses in the government's case, the defendants had little chance to prevail. Even with Rudkin's "moderate instructions," the jury convicted most of the defendants. By the time the case came before the Ninth Circuit, the I.W.W. was on a downhill slide after its numerous battles with federal officials. Thirteen Wobblies from Sacramento appealed, but after carefully scrutinizing the trial record, the court could find no error. In an opinion by Erskine Ross, the Ninth Circuit affirmed on all counts.[28]

The outcome in the Sacramento Wobblies case derived more from dubious legal strategy than from hostility on the court's part. Early in its jurisprudence of I.W.W. cases, the Ninth Circuit displayed a willingness to strike a balance between overzealous prosecution of I.W.W. radicals and just punishment of law-breakers. Even before the end of World War I, the Ninth Circuit reversed convictions of I.W.W. defendants charged with violating provisions of the Espionage Act. The court ruled in two cases that the indictments had failed to provide notice to the defendants of the facts that purportedly constituted the crimes. These rulings were particularly significant because the Wobblies had polarized public opinion in western Washington. The United States attorney there deployed the Espionage Act, often with very little evidence, to bludgeon the I.W.W. The Ninth Circuit served as an important check on violations of the Wobblies' rights of due process. As William Gilbert stated in one of these cases: "The plaintiffs in error had the constitutional right to be informed of the nature and cause of the accusation against them. To furnish them with that information it was necessary to set forth in the indictment the particular facts and circumstances which rendered them guilty and to make specific that which the statute states in general."[29]

Not only did the Ninth Circuit check the work of overreaching prosecutors, it also restrained excesses by district judges handling I.W.W. trials. In one case the court reversed a conviction brought against a Wobbly who had been indicted in Oregon and convicted for saying that liberty bonds were "not worth the paper they were written on" and "To hell with the government." The Ninth Circuit found no fault with the indictment; the problem lay in District Judge Charles E. Wolverton's instructions to the jury. The judge had imprudently added to the jury instructions the following: "The I.W.W. is a disloyal and unpatriotic organization. Adherents thereof owe no allegiance to any organized government, and so far as the government is concerned the organization itself is thoroughly bad." In striking down this jury instruction and reversing the conviction, Judge Hunt walked the delicate line between protecting the defendant's rights and bowing to popular sentiment. "Of course," he wrote, "where it is proven that an organization has such purposes, it should be held to be disloyal and unpatriotic. But without some further evidence to show that the pamphlet was issued by some one whose position in the order was such that the writing should be regarded as an authoritative statement of the attitude of the organization as a whole toward the government of the United States, . . . we are not satisfied that it justified the conclusion that, as a matter of law, the organization is disloyal and unpatriotic, and that its adherents owe no allegiance to any organized government." Contemporaneously with this decision, he wrote for the court in another case that the government need not prove the falsity of statements accusing the United States of entering the war against Germany for capitalist reasons. As these and other statements by Hunt show, Wobblies fared much better under his scrutiny of procedural rights than did other Espionage Act defendants.[30]

After the Ninth Circuit, in spite of popular anti-Wobbly sentiment, reversed a number of I.W.W. convictions under the Espionage Act, the Justice Department tried a new tactic, this time invoking the 1917 Immigration Act to smash the I.W.W. That statute provided that "any alien who at any time after entry shall be found advocating or teaching the unlawful destruction of property, or advocating or teaching anarchy, or the overthrow by force or violence of the Government of the United States or of all forms of law or the assassination of public officials . . . shall, upon the warrant of the Secretary of Labor, be taken into custody and deported." Since many Wobblies were aliens, this immigration statute augmented the government's arsenal of prosecutorial weapons. The immigration office in Seattle acted with special diligence, arresting one hundred aliens in a two-week period in January of 1918.[31]

The Seattle labor situation fueled the antagonism underlying the deportation proceedings. Ordinarily, the city each year absorbed anywhere from 5,000 to 13,000 migratory workers. After a successful lumber strike by the I.W.W. in 1917, these displaced workers began to join the Wobblies. "To already nervous and frightened Seattle citizens, therefore, the 1917 migration cityward seemed more like a seditious invasion than the normal backwash of the rural proletariat." Prosecutions under the 1917 immigration statute succeeded for a time, but Judge Frank Rudkin, then eastern Washington's federal district judge, dealt a harsh blow to these efforts to criminalize guilt-by-association. Most of the deportation cases occurred in the western district of Washington, but Rudkin heard several such cases in Spokane and in his district effectively prohibited the government from deporting foreign-born Wobblies for being members of the labor organization.[32]

In one such case, Rudkin rejected the government's theory that the organization's views could be imputed to the defendant even when no evidence existed that the defendant had ever uttered such views: "From this conclusion there is no escape unless a person can advocate and teach by silence and I am clearly of the opinion that such was not the sort of advocacy or teaching that Congress had in mind." However much this position must have heartened I.W.W. members who faced prosecution, because Rudkin's counterpart in the western district of Washington, Judge Jeremiah Neterer, held a different view, attempts to halt use of the immigration law as an anti-Wobbly weapon did not succeed easily.

Neterer generally upheld a broad interpretation of the 1917 immigration law that permitted deportation of any I.W.W. member who supported the organization. Years later, in a celebrated case, the Ninth Circuit itself was decisively to reject Neterer's position.[33]

The western federal courts often ruled against the popular anti-I.W.W. sentiment in an attempt to maintain adequate procedural protections for Wobbly defendants. The Justice Department's take-no-prisoners attitude made the federal courts' task all the more difficult. After assuming office in June, 1919, Attorney General A. Mitchell Palmer launched a campaign of "summary arrests, brutal interrogations, and arbitrary mass deportations" to wipe out radicalism. He was responding in part to a massive outbreak of labor activity. Workers in Seattle had walked out in February of 1919, and over the next six months nearly 2,000 strikes erupted across the nation, from a low of 175 in March to a high of 388 in May. The Justice Department's crusade against the Wobblies, coupled with a lack of sympathy among the general public for the group's radicalism, contributed to the eventual extinction of the I.W.W. One historian attributes its swift downfall after World War I to attacks by federal, state, and local governments that "gave it no quarter."[34]

The demise of the I.W.W. occurred despite its victories in the Ninth Circuit. Historians of the American labor movement have recognized the I.W.W.'s importance in the evolution of employer-employee relations. In terms of the Ninth Circuit's legal history, federal prosecutions of the I.W.W. served as a vehicle for the court's close scrutiny of criminal procedure in an important, if somewhat subtle, departure from the court's jurisprudence of other anti-war radicals. Undoubtedly a law-and-order court during this period, the Ninth Circuit was not so strict as to enforce order at the expense of law. Even in 1918, in the midst of intense war-related popular hysteria, the court coolly reversed convictions of Wobblies on narrow procedural grounds.[35] This approach failed to save the I.W.W. from extinction, but it did highlight the linkage, in the court's nascent jurisprudence, between two fundamental rights: free speech and freedom from unreasonable searches and seizures. The court's predominant tendency in Espionage Act cases was to uphold the strictest and narrowest interpretation of free-expression rights. When it reviewed convictions of I.W.W. members for expression-related actions, however, the court became increasingly protective of defendants' rights, and this attitude ripened when the court faced judicial challenges posed by Prohibition.

IV. PROHIBITION AND THE COURTS

The court spoke with a single voice in all but a handful of war-related and I.W.W. cases, even as its approach shifted perceptibly for the latter group. Fissures opened when the court confronted the next great challenge to social order: enforcement of laws prohibiting the manufacture, distribution, and sale of intoxicating liquor. By the early 1920s, when Prohibition cases began to flood the federal courts, the Ninth Circuit jurists openly disagreed on a range of issues that directly affected the ability of officials to enforce the law. Even with increasing dissent, the court as a whole did not perceive the same kind of menace to social order in the Prohibition cases that it did in those relating to the I.W.W. and the Espionage Act. Party affiliation cannot explain these differences, because Ross was the lone Democrat on the court. Whereas patriotism might explain the unanimity in non-I.W.W. Espionage Act cases, it does not add any particular insight to the court's treatment of the I.W.W. and Prohibition issues. Nativism and chauvinism appear also to be inadequate explanations, since the court seemed to treat I.W.W. aliens more favorably than aliens (particularly Germans) prosecuted under the Espionage Act. Although no documentary evidence exists for such a conclusion, a possible reason for the differences in these law-and-order approaches is that the level of social consensus on the underlying substantive law subtly influenced the court's jurisprudence. Public support for Prohibition varied from state to state, from class to class, and between gender groups.[36] The judges' divergent approaches to Prohibition enforcement arguably mirrored these social divisions. Their perception of a lessened threat to order, then, may have influenced the doctrinal development of key defendants' rights.

Congress enacted the first wartime alcohol ban shortly after the end of hostilities, on November 21, 1918. The act prohibited the manufacture of intoxicating liquors after May 1, 1919, and outlawed sales after June 30, 1919. On January 16, 1919, Nebraska's ratification of the Eighteenth Amendment provided the requisite three-fourths majority to make Prohibition the supreme law of the land. The amendment took effect in January of 1920, but its prohibition on "the manufacture, sale, or transportation of intoxicating liquors" required passage by Congress of enforcing legislation. The Volstead Act, sponsored by Minnesota Republican Andrew Volstead, became law over President Wilson's veto on October 28, 1919.[37]

During the years leading up to passage of the Eighteenth Amendment and the Volstead Act, every Ninth Circuit state except California had passed a statewide prohibition referendum. This early enthusiasm began to wane during the 1920s. In 1928, according to one commentator, Montana and Nevada were "wet" and Idaho and Arizona were "dry"; northern California was "fiercely wet," southern California, "fiercely dry"; west of the mountains in Oregon and Washington, citizens were, "if not as yet publicly wet, potentially very much so." Divisions within these geographical demarcations also surfaced. The ambivalence of labor unions toward the Prohibition movement reflected public opinion. Some labor leaders believed, rightly, that heavy drinking damaged the general welfare of workers and sparked a backlash against organized labor. At the same time, many people saw little harm in drinking beer or liquor after work. In the words of Samuel Gompers, the president of the American Federation of Labor and a confirmed wet, Prohibition made us "a nation of grouches." Enforcing the new law proved extremely difficult. In Nevada, for instance, which in 1918 had passed its own anti-liquor referendum, state officials nevertheless found they lacked the fiscal and physical resources that would have been needed to enforce the Volstead Act, and, after repeatedly asking in vain for federal aid, they effectively abandoned the attempt.[38]

Enforcement of the Volstead Act was in any event chiefly the responsibility of federal officers. Their investigations led to federal prosecutions, which in turn overwhelmed the federal courts.

> A vice inherent in the 18th Amendment, arising from its legislative phraseology, is that it burdens the Federal courts as guardians of the Constitution, for, unless the Constitution is to become as easily susceptible to amendment as a Congressional enactment, it will, whenever current public opinion fails to lead to "appropriate" legislation even as regards the Amendment's more radical reaches, throw the burden on the courts themselves enforcing it. Their alternative, of allowing the Constitution to come into disrepute through neglect, is unthinkable.[39]

In 1913, the federal district courts tried an estimated 52,618 cases. In 1920, as Prohibition took effect, this figure escalated to 140,000 cases, more than half of which were criminal matters. The Ninth Circuit's docket mirrored the national trend. In 1892–1893, criminal appeals constituted about 2 percent of the court's docket. By the 1908–1912 period, between 5 and 10 percent of the court's work involved criminal appeals. And by 1925, the high-water mark of Prohibition, nearly 40 percent of the Ninth Circuit's caseload was criminal, the vast majority of which involved Prohibition problems.[40]

The Ninth Circuit unanimously upheld the constitutionality of the Volstead Act in 1922, but soon afterward the judges began to disagree on enforcement and criminal procedure. At one extreme sat William Gilbert, for whom the aim of the criminal process was simply to establish guilt or innocence. The system should not permit criminals to use minor technicalities to escape punishment. A 1925 dissent captures his general approach to criminal appeals: "Where the other evidence . . . clearly establishes the guilt of the accused, I can see no justification for setting aside the judgment obtained thereunder, merely because of the erroneous admission of evidence of the prior activities of the accused in the line of illicit distilling, and I submit that to do so is to exalt unduly a mere technicality."[41]

Gilbert's hard line extended beyond evidentiary questions to issues of far greater significance. Search and seizure issues came to the forefront during Prohibition because the Volstead Act required officers to obtain a warrant for searches of dwellings. Gilbert, who rarely voted to reverse convictions, dissented vigorously in two prominent cases when the court threw out convictions based on warrantless searches of distilleries set up in the defendants' homes. Gilbert did not believe that the warrant requirement should apply in such clear cases of circumvention: "I still maintain that the owner of a distillery, in which intoxicating liquor is unlawfully manufactured on a large scale for commercial purposes, cannot, by making the distillery his dwelling place, or by constructing his dwelling above or adjacent to the distillery, claim for the latter the protection and immunity from search which the law accords to a dwelling house."[42]

Just as they had disagreed with each other on natural resource issues, so too did William Gilbert and Erskine Ross clash on the proper approach to criminal matters. Both judges exemplified an unbending individualism and a confidence in their own rightness, occasionally to the point of self-righteousness.[43] Ross steadfastly denied the power of the government to invade the sanctity of the home without a warrant: "The home of every person in this country," he wrote in one dissent, "whether it be a hut or a palace, and whether it embraces only a few feet of ground, or as many acres, is secure against invasion without his consent, unless made under and by virtue of a legal warrant of search and seizure." Ross found that Congress had exercised "extreme care" in "secur[ing] the constitutional rights of our people in authorizing the issuance of search warrants."[44] And for the Volstead Act's statutory warrant requirement, Ross argued that the term *dwelling* encompassed both the home itself and the surrounding fenced-in property, or curtilage. As he commented in a dissent in *Forni v. United States*, "[The agent] had, in my opinion, no more right to 'climb' over the inclosure of a residence than he would have had to break open its front door, and any evidence so obtained would, if the premises constituted the [defendant's] home . . . , be clearly inadmissible." Advancing age had not dimmed the power of Ross's pen. The court handed down *Forni* on January 5, 1925, when Ross was seventy-nine years old. It was to be one of his last opinions. Within two months, the long struggle to ease him off the court would be accomplished and the old jurist would retire from all judicial service.[45]

The judge who inherited Ross's intellectual place on the court, Frank Rudkin, wasted no time placing his own stamp on the court's jurisprudence. Within five months of his elevation to the court, Rudkin animatedly opposed Gilbert's exaltation of order over process. Gilbert had written a majority decision permitting third-party statements that the defendant had employed a man to transport liquor. Admitting such statements, wrote Rudkin in dissent, was "manifest error, in any conceivable aspect of this case."[46] As a former trial judge, Rudkin found particularly objectionable the prejudicial statements of judges. He would vote to reverse a conviction when the district judge had made what he believed to be improper comments to the jury, either in summations or in instructions. In one bootlegging case, Rudkin joined an opinion to reverse when the district judge had instructed the jury: "'You are not to be hoodwinked and bamboozled by anybody; not by unreasonable testimony, if it is unreasonable.'" When lawyers fell below Rudkin's expectations, he bluntly told them: "The information in this case is a complex mass, slovenly thrown together." And if his colleagues on the court themselves overreached, Rudkin upbraided them in the published reports. In an otherwise typical Prohibition case, Rudkin believed that Judge Frank S. Dietrich had analyzed issues that he should have avoided. "I concur in the judgment," he wrote, "but am opposed to the practice of discussing or considering questions not properly before us, because the inevitable tendency is to encourage loose practice, mislead the bar, and embarrass the court in the future."[47]

The celebrated case of *Olmstead v. United States* perhaps best illustrates the depth of Rudkin's convictions, the occasional acerbity of his writing style, and the extent to which he and Gilbert disagreed on fundamental principles. Roy Olmstead, the youngest lieutenant in the Seattle

Police Department in 1920, was well on his way to becoming the most respected police officer in the city when the temptations of corruption got the better of him. Upon discovering the monetary value of his badge, Olmstead embarked on a career in the illicit liquor trade. The local authorities detected Olmstead's sideline and dismissed him from the police force in March, 1920. His bootlegging business then took off. He insisted on the highest-quality merchandise and refused to let his men carry firearms. The locals venerated Olmstead, whose flamboyance increased along with his power. Exasperated by the renowned rum-runner's success, Prohibition officials relentlessly pursued him, but found only scanty evidence of wrongdoing. In 1924 a free-lance wiretapper approached Olmstead and offered to sell him a transcript of his own telephone conversations. Believing the transcripts to be inadmissible in a court of law, Olmstead refused to pay the extortionist, but, now knowing that federal officers were eavesdropping on his conversations, he occasionally took advantage of the wiretaps to convey false information and flaunt the apparent foolishness of the federal authorities. Olmstead's arrogance proved to be his undoing: federal officials gathered enough evidence to convince a grand jury to indict him and ninety other defendants for conspiracies to violate the Volstead Act. The trial promised to be the biggest the nation had seen under the Prohibition amendment.[48]

The government's case turned on the legality of the wiretap. At trial, Judge Jeremiah Neterer permitted a number of witnesses to refresh their recollections of the telephone conversations by consulting papers that a secretary had retyped from handwritten notes taken by agents who had listened in to Olmstead's conversations. This procedure raised at least two questions. One was the permissibility of this use of a written document to refresh the recollection of the witnesses; the second was the constitutionality of the wiretap under the Fourth Amendment. Neterer ruled against the defendants' arguments on both issues, and Olmstead's lawyers appealed.[49]

Whether the Ninth Circuit would affirm or reverse depended a great deal on the composition of the panel drawn to hear the case. During these years, the three judges most likely to find Olmstead's arguments persuasive were Rudkin, Hunt, and Ross. Of these three, Ross and Rudkin viewed search-and-seizure challenges with the greatest sympathy, but Hunt occasionally joined them when the violation seemed particularly egregious. Together they had reversed a conviction in 1925 when the evidence given to the magistrate for a search warrant was insufficient to establish probable cause. Gilbert, by contrast, rarely discerned an unreasonable search and seizure, and the district judge who had recently been elevated to the circuit court of appeals, Frank Dietrich, was reputed never to have touched liquor. Given this array of potential judges, the panel of Gilbert, Rudkin, and Dietrich must have given Olmstead little reason for optimism. In a split decision, with Rudkin dissenting, the court affirmed the convictions of those who had appealed.[50]

In his majority opinion, Gilbert rejected both the evidentiary and constitutional challenges. On the evidentiary point, he held that the district court properly allowed the witnesses to consult the typed notes, under the rule that witnesses may refresh their recollection by examining a document. On the larger issue, the one upon which the Supreme Court later granted certiorari and that legal scholars and public officials have debated for decades, Gilbert considered whether wiretapping constituted an unreasonable search under the Fourth Amendment. As a historical matter, he correctly reported that the protection of the Fourth and Fifth Amendments "has never been extended to the exclusion of evidence obtained by listening to the conversation of persons at any place or under any circumstances." This case raised the question of whether such novel technology abridged constitutional rights. Gilbert said no: "Whatever may be said of the tapping of telephone wires as an unethical intrusion upon the privacy of persons who are suspected of crime, it is not an act which comes within the letter of the prohibition of constitutional provisions." Furthermore, he continued, the illegality of the method of collecting evidence " 'is by no means condoned, but is merely ignored.' "[51]

Rudkin disagreed with both contentions. He argued first that the process of note gathering, compilation, and retyping sufficiently distorted the process that the witnesses "who made use of the compilation in testifying had no part in its preparation and had no knowledge whatever as to the truth or accuracy of the matters therein contained, except such recollection as they might have from hearing the original conversations. . . . In the present case," Rudkin continued, "witness after witness, day after day, testified to names, dates, and events, so numerous and with such unerring accuracy, that it becomes at once apparent that the book, and not the witnesses, was speaking. A better opportunity to color or fabricate testimony could not well be devised by the wit of man." Rudkin's more pressing objection, however, concerned the constitutionality of this evidence-gathering practice. Quoting Justice Field in a late-nineteenth-century Supreme Court case, Rudkin made an analogy between wiretapped conversations and posted letters, which the Supreme Court had held were " 'as fully guarded from examination and inspection . . . as if they were retained by the parties forwarding them in their own domiciles.'" He surveyed the differences between the mail and the telegraph, but concluded that they were "distinctions without a difference." In a plea that persuaded the defendants to continue their appeal to the Supreme Court, Rudkin concluded: "If ills such as these must be borne, our forefathers signally failed in their desire to ordain and establish a government to secure the blessings of liberty to themselves and their posterity."[52]

In a landmark decision, the Supreme Court affirmed by a five-to-four vote. Chief Justice William Howard Taft's majority opinion upheld the constitutionality of wiretapping. Adopting the strict construction that Gilbert had favored at the appellate court level, Taft's opinion interpreted the Fourth Amendment narrowly to concern "material things— the person, the house, his papers or his effects." Taft reasoned that Congress had the authority to restrict such use by direct legislation. The courts, he wrote, "may not adopt such a policy by attributing an enlarged and unusual meaning to the Fourth Amendment."[53] Justices Holmes, Brandeis, Butler, and Stone dissented. Although Justice Holmes was not prepared to say that the "penumbra of the Fourth and Fifth Amendments" covered the defendants in this case, he did find much merit in Olmstead's argument. "We have to choose," he declared, "and for my part I think it a less evil that some criminals should escape than that the Government should play an ignoble part." Justice Brandeis spoke powerfully of the protections conferred by the Fourth and Fifth amendments, in the process flattering Rudkin's opinion with two quotations from it. Constitutional protections should keep pace with technological advances, argued Brandeis: "Discovery and invention have made it possible for the Government, by means far more effective than stretching upon the rack, to obtain disclosure in court of what is whispered in the closet." And in a statement directed perhaps as much to the Tafts and Gilberts of the world as to law enforcement officials, Brandeis added that the "greatest dangers to liberty lurk in insidious encroachment by men of zeal, well-meaning but without understanding."[54]

The *Olmstead* case closed an important chapter in the war on liquor. The tenuous majorities in both the Ninth Circuit and Supreme Court decisions and the passion of the dissenters reminded citizens how inherently difficult it was to enforce legislation of this type. Brandeis had cautioned that if the government "becomes a lawbreaker, it breeds contempt for law." Prohibition itself sometimes blurred these social roles. If Olmstead, a somewhat happy-go-lucky police officer turned bootlegger, could so readily flout the law, he was not alone. The Ninth Circuit handled several large-scale corruption cases involving municipal officers. Indeed, illegal liquor sales were taking place less than a block from the Ninth Circuit's headquarters at Seventh and Mission streets in San Francisco.[55]

The boom of the 1920s appeared to many people to bear out the middle-class perception that banning alcohol would promote a healthy economy. Investment soared as many laborers established savings accounts for the first time, truancy declined, and alcohol-related crimes plummeted. The initial euphoria over Prohibition, however, faded as a determined wet segment of the population made enforcement of the laws difficult and expensive. And with the onset of the Great Depression, the economic justification for Prohibition no longer seemed salient. By 1933, the movement to repeal the Eighteenth Amendment had gained overwhelming strength. Between April and November of 1933, thirty-seven states held elections on repeal of national Prohibition. Nearly 73 percent of the twenty-one million voters nationwide favored repeal. On December 5, 1933, Utah became the thirty-sixth state to ratify the Twenty-first Amendment. Prohibition was finally dead.[56]

V. TEAPOT DOME

Despite the efforts Rudkin and Ross made to move the court toward a more civil libertarian posture, Gilbert's view of order prevailed among a majority of the circuit and district judges who composed Ninth Circuit panels during the 1920s. Gilbert's clear sense of right and wrong usually tipped in the government's favor. Questionable actions by federal officials were usually outweighed by the defendant's own criminal conduct. As was made clear in a celebrated civil case that emerged from the 1920s Teapot Dome scandal, Gilbert's indignation reached its zenith when public officials themselves breached the public trust. Ironically, although posterity has immortalized Teapot Dome, the Elk Hills facet of the scandal was more important legally and historically. The Teapot Dome reserve in Wyoming, estimated to hold twenty-five to thirty million barrels of oil, paled in comparison to the reserve in Elk Hills, California, which contained approximately eight times as much oil. Moreover, the Elk Hills litigation took place first and established the precedent for deciding the Teapot Dome case.[57]

The Ninth Circuit's role in the episode provided a source of ultimate vindication for Gilbert, who had dissented in 1918 when the government unsuccessfully sought to void the Southern Pacific Railroad's claim to the oil rights on the land. The Supreme Court had upheld Gilbert's dissenting view, but that victory proved fleeting. The incoming Harding administration abruptly changed government policy in 1921 and leased the naval reserves at Teapot Dome to the Mammoth Oil Company and that at Elk Hills to the Pan American Petroleum and Transport Company. When the scandal finally erupted, the Ninth Circuit was called upon to determine the legality of the Elk Hills lease to Pan American, valued in excess of $100,000,000.[58]

Two people bore the lion's share of the responsibility for the policy change that erupted into scandal. When Harding took office in March, 1921, he named his old crony, Senator Albert B. Fall of New Mexico, as his secretary of the interior, and Edwin Denby as secretary of the navy. By an executive order dated May 31, 1921, Harding transferred responsibility for the administration and conservation of oil- and gas-bearing lands in naval reserves from the Department of the Navy to the secretary of the interior. This transfer itself raised suspicion, since Fall was well known to advocate development of the oil resources on naval reserves. With this newly gained authority, Secretary Fall worked out of public view with several oil companies to make contracts and leases regarding the naval reserves. Under certain contracts, the Pan American Petroleum and Transport Company agreed to furnish 1,500,000 barrels of fuel oil to the navy and to construct storage facilities at Pearl Harbor. As compensation the company would receive crude oil from naval reserve lands at Elk Hills, California. If this oil production decreased, the contracts stipulated that the government would grant additional leases in the Elk Hills reserve to maintain total deliveries of 500,000 barrels per year.[59]

Several months elapsed before government insiders became suspicious of Fall's actions. Then an extensive Senate investigation was begun, but on January 2, 1923, before much public attention had focused on the new government policy, Fall announced his resignation. More than a year later, President Coolidge approved Congress's joint resolution calling for legal action by the federal government to recover public lands that had been leased and to rescind the contracts involving the storage facilities. The resolution stated that the contract of April 25, 1922, and a subsequent lease entered into on December 11, 1922, had been executed under circumstances "indicating fraud and corruption . . . without authority on the part of the officers purporting to act" for the United States and "in defiance of the settled policy of the Government . . . to maintain in the ground a great reserve supply of oil adequate to the needs of the Navy."[60]

During the course of the investigations leading up to the joint resolution, President Coolidge had become suspicious of Attorney General Harry Daugherty's role in the contracts and leases. Instead of relying on Justice Department lawyers, Coolidge commissioned Owen J. Roberts and Atlee Pomerene to serve as special counsel for the United States. Roberts, who in 1930 would be appointed to the Supreme Court by Herbert Hoover, led the team that brought suits in equity against the Pan American Petroleum and Transport Company in the southern district of California and against Mammoth Oil Company in Wyoming. Judge Paul J. McCormick of Los Angeles ruled first. On May 28, 1925, he held that the president of Pan American, Edward L. Doheny, had obtained the Elk Hills lease in part by making an unsecured loan of $100,000 to Secretary Fall. McCormick also decreed that this fraud required rescission of the contracts and leases but that the company was entitled under equitable principles to compensation for the storage facilities it had constructed at Pearl Harbor pursuant to the agreement. The decision of his Wyoming counterpart, Judge T. Blake Kennedy, could not have been more different. A month after McCormick rendered his decision, Kennedy ruled against the government on every point. He upheld the legality of the contract, the validity of the lease, and the power of President Harding to transfer reserves from the Department of the Navy to the Department of the Interior. Moreover, he found no evidence of fraud or corruption in the transactions involving Fall and the Mammoth Oil Company.[61]

These conflicting district court rulings cast great uncertainty on the government's attempt to rescind the contracts. The Ninth Circuit handled the appeal from McCormick's decision first, a fortuitous break for Roberts and Pomerene. As he had with many of the most important decisions in the court's thirty-five-year history, Judge William B. Gilbert took charge writing the opinion. The case brought Gilbert full circle from his 1918 dissent supporting the government's argument that the Southern Pacific had procured these same Elk Hills lands by fraud under Congress's land-grant subsidy of the 1860s to build the railroads. By reversing and accepting Gilbert's position in the *Southern Pacific* case in 1919, the Supreme Court had preserved the government's claim to these oil reserve lands. Now Gilbert had the opportunity for complete vindication in his own court by ruling to rescind the allegedly fraudulent contracts and to protect the naval reserves from private exploitation. In a lengthy opinion that carefully canvassed the record, the Ninth Circuit affirmed in part and reversed in part. The court affirmed the findings that the contract had been made fraudulently and that the president did not have power under a congressional statute to transfer control over the naval petroleum reserves from the Department of the Navy to the secretary of the interior. Gilbert's opinion reversed that part of McCormick's decision that required the United States to pay fair compensation for the purported benefit it received from the construction of the fuel storage facilities at Pearl Harbor. The judge applied the maxim that "he who seeks equity must do equity." Gilbert ruled that the company had not come with clean hands. By conspiring to defraud the United States, the company was not in the ordinary position of a defendant in an action at equity. To receive compensation, the company needed to establish that it had been an innocent trespasser and not an active wrongdoer.[62]

The week before the Supreme Court heard arguments in *Pan American Petroleum*, the Eighth Circuit handed down its decision in the *Mammoth Oil* case. In one crucial respect the Eighth Circuit disagreed with Gilbert's analysis in *Pan American Petroleum*. Gilbert had found that the secretary lacked statutory authority to make contracts regarding the reserves. "With great respect for the ability and learning of that distinguished court," Judge William S. Kenyon's opinion for the Eighth Circuit stated, "we find ourselves unable to arrive at the same conclusion as to this lease and contract." The Eighth Circuit did, however, reverse the Wyoming district court decision regarding fraud in the making of the contract and lease. The court also rejected the argument in equity that the United States was indebted to the oil company for benefits accrued under the contract. Accordingly, the Eighth Circuit reversed and remanded with instructions to cancel the lease and contract, enjoin the oil company from further trespasses, and account for the value of oil taken under the lease and contract. The decisions of the circuit courts of appeals for the Eighth and Ninth Circuits, therefore, were similar in that they both found fraud in the creation of the contracts and leases and they both rejected claims for equitable compensation based on the benefits derived by the United States government. They differed, however, in the purported authority of the secretary to act under the 1920 statute. The Supreme Court ultimately adopted the Ninth Circuit's view, affirming Gilbert's opinion on all grounds and thus making review of the *Mammoth Oil* case somewhat anticlimactic, since the Court had no new ground to break.[63]

A side note to the Teapot Dome scandal of interest for the Ninth Circuit's history concerned Denby's successor as secretary of the navy.

In March, 1924, President Coolidge appointed Curtis D. Wilbur, chief justice of the California Supreme Court, to restore order and integrity to the Department of the Navy. Wilbur immediately announced that he would not approve any leases or contracts without the express authorization of Congress unless they were essential to prevent drainage by nearby oil drilling. As secretary of the navy from 1924 to 1929, Wilbur did much to polish the department's tarnished reputation. He then received President Hoover's appointment to the Ninth Circuit. Partly because of Wilbur's stewardship and partly because the government's control over these oil properties was inviolable, as announced by judicial rulings, the Elk Hills and Teapot Dome oil reserves remained free of private drilling until 1976, when Congress authorized "emergency" pumping. During President Ronald Reagan's terms of office, the government received nearly $8 billion in revenue from the oil in these reserves.[64]

Changes occasioned by the onset of World War I and the employee-employer struggles that preceded it upset social order in the West. The first manifestation of these divisions was the anti-war protest movement. This movement arose from elements of the working class, many of whom were foreign-born, to what was perceived as a capitalist war. A nativist response directed against aliens or naturalized citizens from Europe (especially Germany and Austria) inspired a spate of federal prosecutions that eventually made their way to the Ninth Circuit. These cases forced a comprehensive examination of free speech by the federal courts. And although the Ninth Circuit's support for rights of expression in this period was small, these cases laid a foundation for the diverse conceptions of social order that would frame debates on constitutional and statutory questions of defendants' rights. The often overzealous federal prosecutions of I.W.W. activists provided a crucial link between the doctrinal development of free speech rights, on the one hand, and procedural protections for defendants, on the other. United States attorneys prosecuted Wobblies for their anti-war statements. The Ninth Circuit, in turn, developed more stringent procedural requirements to protect these defendants. This concern for defendants' rights underscored the court's consideration of search-and-seizure issues during Prohibition and divided the court. Gilbert stood at one extreme, frequently supporting the government's position; Ross and Rudkin held more expansive views of freedom from warrantless searches. If Gilbert correctly anticipated the Supreme Court's jurisprudence of Fourth

Amendment protections in the mid-1920s, positions taken by Rudkin and Ross have been vindicated by subsequent judicial rulings.[65]

In addition to shedding light on the Ninth Circuit's evolving conception of social order, the cases in this era demonstrate the increasing federalization of the law and the growing power of the federal judiciary. Although draft and Espionage Act cases did not encroach upon state sovereignty, the prostitution cases surely did. And regulation of liquor, traditionally a matter of local concern, became federalized through the states' ratification of the Eighteenth Amendment and passage of the Volstead Act. Prohibition dramatically increased the criminal side of the federal courts' docket and created administrative havoc for the Ninth Circuit, which was ill prepared for the explosion in case filings.

This period played a smaller role in the development of an internal Ninth Circuit politics primarily because the personnel of the court was in such a great state of flux. District judges continued to sit on appellate panels, although by this time the circuit judges rarely tried cases alone in district courts. During the early decades of the twentieth century, it will be recalled, the disagreements between Ross and Gilbert over natural resource questions had arguably contributed to role specialization among the Ninth Circuit judges, as these two jurists competed for influence over the court's doctrinal direction. The postwar era produced some jurisprudential disagreements but no impetus for the development of a discernible circuit "politics," since no single judge or pair of judges could impose a viewpoint on the court as a whole. The judges who had borne the brunt of the court's load during the war and Prohibition died within three years of one another; a new core of judges was to face the legal challenges posed by the Great Depression and the New Deal, challenges that would transform the federal courts generally and the Ninth Circuit in particular.

EIGHT

Different Paths to the Bench

You might be interested in knowing that we lawyers now
look upon the [Ninth Circuit] as a very weak court. Any
new appointment in my opinion ought to be made for the
purpose of strengthening the personnel of the court as much
as possible.

Frank E. Holman of the Seattle Bar Association, 1935

The problems of social disorder that characterized the Ninth Circuit's
work between 1918 and 1933 had not entirely subsided when the court's
personnel underwent another dramatic transformation. Between January of 1928 and June of 1931, the composition of the court changed
completely. In that three-and-a-half-year period, one judge retired and
three died. President Herbert Hoover had a golden opportunity to place
an enduring stamp on the Ninth Circuit's jurisprudence. But when he left
office in March, 1933, the court had only two judges; two positions
remained vacant. From being the circuit court of appeals composed of
judges with the most experience on the federal bench, the Ninth Circuit
in a few short years became the one with the least. When Frank Rudkin
died on May 3, 1931, Curtis Wilbur, with only two years of experience
on the federal bench, assumed administrative responsibility as the court's
senior judge.[1] The remaining vacancies and the addition of more judgeships enabled President Franklin D. Roosevelt to reshape the court.
Roosevelt's Ninth Circuit appointees in turn contributed substantially to
western development through their adjudication of the New Deal. During this period the appointment process came into sharp focus, highlighting the paths taken to gain a seat on the court and the caprices
inherent in the selection of federal judges.[2] Understanding the backgrounds of these new appointees also sheds light on their divergent

approaches to the New Deal and on the emergence of a distinct circuit politics.

I. THE APPOINTMENT OF WILBUR

When William H. Hunt took senior status by retiring from active service on January 31, 1928, the number of judges authorized for the Ninth Circuit fell to three. Congress had specifically provided in 1913 that Hunt's position, which it originally established for the Commerce Court, was not to be filled upon his death, resignation, or retirement. The court, however, desperately needed a fourth, and arguably a fifth judge. Congress attempted to redress this personnel shortage by creating a fourth judgeship on March 1, 1929, in the dying days of the Coolidge presidency. For reasons its records do not elucidate, Congress displayed deep ambivalence, despite a steadily increasing caseload, about the Ninth Circuit's need for four judges. As originally drafted, the House version provided simply for the authorization of one additional judge, but the Senate Judiciary Committee appended a second section to the bill the full Congress eventually passed. According to the final version, "When a vacancy shall occur due to the death, resignation, or retirement of the present senior judge of [the Ninth Circuit] such vacancy shall not be filled unless authorized by Congress."[3] This provision singled out Judge Gilbert, who was eighty-one at the time and in deteriorating health. As a whole, the statute sent conflicting signals: it provided stopgap help to the court while abolishing a badly needed position. On the one hand, the legislative history suggests that the House intended to keep the number of judges at four. On the other, the Senate report that accompanied the bill contained no explanation for the elimination of Gilbert's seat. The Republicans held a majority in both houses of Congress, so the Senate's insistence on this provision was apparently *not* a partisan political gambit to keep a political appointment out of the incoming Hoover's hands. Nevertheless, Congress's action exposed its complete lack of appreciation for the growing burdens on the sitting judges: the court's caseload had already more than doubled since 1920.[4]

The day after Congress passed this law, Coolidge announced a number of "midnight" judicial appointments, including that of Curtis D. Wilbur for the new Ninth Circuit seat. Wilbur, the outgoing Coolidge's secretary of the navy, fell victim to the political uncertainty occasioned by the transition between the two Republican administrations. Word leaked out in mid-January of 1929 that Hoover intended not to retain any Californians for his cabinet, which some observers interpreted as a slap at Wilbur. The press speculated that Hoover did not want to overrepresent California in the new government. Wilbur's nomination to the Ninth Circuit lapsed when the Senate announced that it would take no action on most of the judges Coolidge had sent to Capitol Hill. Hoover gave no immediate indication of whether he would resubmit the Coolidge nominees. In the meantime, Wilbur announced his intention to practice law in San Francisco. No sooner had he opened his office, however, than Hoover renominated and the Senate confirmed him for the Ninth Circuit.[5]

Curtis Dwight Wilbur's long career in public life was similar in some respects to the pre-appointment backgrounds of his predecessors. Like McKenna, he had held a Cabinet post; like Ross and Hunt, he had served as a state judge. Born in Boonesborough (later shortened to Boone), Iowa, on May 10, 1867, Wilbur came from a family with a strong pioneer streak. Wilbur's grandfather was an Andrew Jackson Democrat, but his six sons were Lincoln Republicans, a party affiliation shared by two prominent grandsons, Curtis and Ray. Curtis Wilbur earned his bachelor's degree from the United States Naval Academy in 1888, but he left the navy soon thereafter, fearing that the paucity of available officer positions would stymie his career. Wilbur moved to Riverside, California, where his parents had relocated during his stint at the academy. He taught school for two years while studying law at night. After gaining admittance to the California bar in 1890, he began practicing law in Los Angeles.[6] During the next twenty-eight years Wilbur held a number of county and state posts, including chief deputy district attorney of Los Angeles County, county superior court judge, and finally, in 1918, associate justice of the California Supreme Court. Wilbur ascended to the chief justiceship of the California Supreme Court in 1922 but resigned in 1924 when Coolidge named him secretary of the navy.[7]

Wilbur's service in Coolidge's Cabinet came at a troubled time. In addition to the Teapot Dome and Elk Hills oil reserve scandals that rocked the Harding administration and led to the resignation of Secretary of the Navy Edwin Denby, Wilbur had to confront the international problems associated with post-war demilitarization. Under Denby, the United States had agreed to the 1922 Washington Treaty, which set basic limits on the naval forces of the United States, Great Britain, Japan, and Germany. Wilbur assumed the responsibility for seeing that the United States Navy both abided by and built up to the limits guaranteed in the treaty. Given the pacifism sweeping the country in the 1920s and the attendant calls for naval demobilization, Wilbur faced a great challenge in balancing competing forces to ensure that the navy remained strong. Secretary Wilbur appreciated the importance of naval aviation and submarine warfare, and he accurately perceived the dangers posed by Imperial Japan and international communism. These views placed him in the mainstream of the Republican party.[8]

The Republicans' long run of success in presidential politics had translated into domination of the federal judiciary as a whole and the Ninth Circuit in particular. Within two years of Wilbur's appointment, this supremacy swiftly ended when all three of his original colleagues— Gilbert, Dietrich, and Rudkin—died: Dietrich on October 2, 1930; Gilbert on April 27, 1931; and Rudkin on May 3, 1931. As the judge with the most seniority on the court, Wilbur essentially succeeded Gilbert, whose death had ended the era of the Evarts Act judges appointed by President Harrison in 1892. Gilbert's tenure—thirty-nine years of active service, thirty-five of them as the senior Ninth Circuit judge—stands as the longest in the Ninth Circuit's history, and quite possibly the longest in the history of all the federal circuit courts of appeals. His career on the court spanned a period of significant social and economic change, to which his opinions contributed greatly. It was perhaps fitting that he lived to see Stanford University's most famous alumnus, Herbert Hoover, occupy the White House, for he had written the Ninth Circuit's opinion that saved the university from bankruptcy in 1895. Nor was that alone among his judicial contributions to western development. Gilbert's Ninth Circuit decisions covered virtually every facet of social and economic enterprise, from immigration and natural resource extraction to issues related to World War I and Prohibition. A man with a "passion for inconspicuousness," he spent his adult life in Portland out of the public spotlight.[9] Although the influence of Gilbert's judicial opinions affected the lives of people throughout the West, few knew his name.

Wilbur's de facto replacement of Gilbert as senior judge occurred when Wilbur himself was still learning the job of circuit judge. Wilbur had the least experience of any Ninth Circuit judge ever to assume this post, which involved the administration of the court and participation in the Judicial Conference of Senior Judges, a body created in 1922 to increase administrative efficiency in the United States court system.[10] Wilbur's assumption of this responsibility and honor so early in his tenure as circuit judge reflected the enormous disarray into which the court had fallen. The new senior judge faced the formidable task of administering the court during the great social tumult brought on by the Depression. His ideological opposition to Roosevelt and the New Deal made the challenge all the greater. After a wave of Roosevelt-appointed Democrats joined him on the Ninth Circuit, Wilbur became the lone Republican. Only one Democratic judge had served on the court in its forty-year history, Erskine Ross. By the 1930s the political representation on the court would be reversed. Attempts to replace the Old Guard of Gilbert, Ross, and Morrow with long-serving Republicans had failed. The three Republican administrations of the 1920s and early 1930s had seven opportunities to appoint judges, but their only Ninth Circuit appointee who held office for any significant length of time was Curtis Wilbur.[11]

II. SAWTELLE'S BRIEF, UNHAPPY TENURE

With the death of Frank Dietrich on October 2, 1930, and the continued illness of Senior Judge William Gilbert, the Hoover administration moved quickly to fill the vacancy on the court. Between the presidencies of Grover Cleveland and Franklin Roosevelt, only William Howard Taft patronized his party less often than Herbert Hoover in appointing federal judges. Hoover named a Democrat, William Henry Sawtelle, to fill the vacancy left by Dietrich. The son of a Presbyterian minister, Sawtelle was born on August 27, 1868, in Tuscumbia, Alabama. He attended school in his hometown and set up his first law practice there. After more than a decade in private practice and in state attorney positions, in 1903 Sawtelle moved to Tucson, Arizona, in response to the health needs of his family. Before long he had become a leader of the Arizona bar.[12]

After ten years of private practice in Arizona, Sawtelle was appointed United States district judge for the new state. He served for nearly two decades in that capacity and often sat by designation on the Ninth Circuit. Sawtelle was sixty-two years old when Hoover appointed him to the court, and his short service there proved to be unhappy.[13] He died on December 17, 1934, when he fell down the stairway in his home after having complained of weakness earlier in the day. He had served on the court for less than four years, but in that brief time he wrote 239 opinions, an average of nearly 60 per year. Sawtelle's colleagues believed that he literally worked himself to death. He assumed his duties when the short-handed court was attempting to handle a sharply rising docket. After an initial decrease in the number of cases pending—from 150 in 1929 to 99 in 1930—by 1932 the number of cases in arrears had climbed back up to 159. The deaths of Gilbert and Rudkin and an increase in docketed appeals put great pressure on Wilbur and Sawtelle. As Wilbur later explained, "Judge Sawtelle felt the heavy burden very much, but bent every effort to do his full share of the work of the court." This load exacted a high toll on Sawtelle, who increasingly looked forward to retirement. According to Wilbur, "[h]e often said that as a man grows older he should be relieved of work rather than have the heavy burden greatly increased as was the case in our court. Nevertheless, he worked faithfully, constantly, and effectively. I believe he spent many, if not most, of his evenings on the preparation of opinions. Because of his burden of work, Judge Sawtelle looked forward eagerly to the time when he could retire, saying, with a smile, that he would telegraph his application for retirement on his seventieth birthday."[14]

Francis Garrecht, who joined the court not long before Sawtelle died, went some way toward exposing the nonfeasance of Congress and the president in failing to redress the personnel shortage on the Ninth Circuit. He pointed out that in the year after he joined the court, that is, from May, 1933, to May, 1934, Sawtelle and Wilbur had each written more than twice as many majority opinions as the average United States circuit judge. William Denman, who joined the court a few months after Sawtelle's death, assessed the effect of the court's caseload crisis on Sawtelle even more bluntly:

> My own opinion of Judge Sawtelle's death is that it was unnecessary. There was no need for those sixty opinions he wrote that last year. The responsibility lies with the Congress. It is its constitutional duty to afford the country a judiciary sufficient in numbers to care for a litigation constantly and rapidly expanding under its own legislation. The bench would have been vastly better off if he had written forty [opinions] and saved to the circuit his wisdom and experience. Sawtelle had another viewpoint. He had seen Dietrich and Rudkin die under a similar call to what they felt their duty, and went out as a soldier in the trenches, under the drive and strain of helping keep clear this court's calendar. Youth is the victim of all wars. This youthful spirit of our friend adds another poignancy to his passing.[15]

As a circuit judge Sawtelle earned a high reputation for his carefully crafted opinions, a number of which were acclaimed nationally as models of clarity and legal insight.[16] An infrequent dissenter, Sawtelle nevertheless employed these opinions to make forward-looking statements of the law. As a former district judge Sawtelle recognized the difficulties of conducting errorless trial proceedings, but not so strongly that he refused to reverse. In a number of cases he showed a willingness to permit recovery by deserving plaintiffs but stopped short when the request for judicial action exceeded acceptable precedent.[17] When Sawtelle died the Ninth Circuit lost an able and hard-working judge. It is impossible to know for certain whether work-related fatigue contributed to Sawtelle's death, but the tragic circumstances of his death spurred the legislative and executive branches to end their shameful neglect of the court's needs.

III.   GARRECHT: ARRIVAL OF A NEW DEALER

The election of Franklin Delano Roosevelt in 1932 transformed the federal judiciary generally and the Ninth Circuit in particular. When Roosevelt took office, the vacancy occasioned by Rudkin's death had yet to be filled and the seat that expired with Gilbert's death had yet to be reauthorized. Within three months of Roosevelt's inauguration, Congress rectified the latter problem. At the time, Republicans held over 90 percent of all federal judgeships. Roosevelt's highly partisan selection process—98.1 percent of his judicial appointees between 1933 and 1941 were Democrats and the rest were independents—significantly diluted the Republican domination of the federal judiciary. Because the district courts contained such a small pool of Democrats, for his appointments to the circuit courts of appeals Roosevelt tended to choose prominent attorneys who had gained experience in the public sector during the Wilson years.[18]

The career of Roosevelt's first appointee to the Ninth Circuit, Francis Arthur Garrecht, fit this pattern well. The president selected Garrecht to fill the seat vacated by Frank Rudkin's death. By succeeding Rudkin, Garrecht extended the long linkage between their careers that had begun when Garrecht was United States attorney in Spokane and Frank Rudkin was district judge. Both possessed "first-rate and studious legal minds," and "the administration of justice . . . was maintained at an exceptionally high level" during their combined service in the eastern district of Washington. The first circuit judge native to the Ninth Circuit, Garrecht was born on September 11, 1870, into a family of devoted Catholics of German descent in Walla Walla, Washington Territory. At the time of his birth, Walla Walla was the Territory's largest settlement, even though it had fewer than 1,400 inhabitants. Despite the deep conservatism of the region and the popularity of Republican values, Garrecht grew up a Democrat and a liberal. A genial and gentle man with a high tolerance for opposing viewpoints, Garrecht had a concern for the weak and a desire to help the deprived and the outcast—attitudes alien to a frontier environment that promoted strength and a belief that the weak deserved to fail. A physically frail and diminutive man, Garrecht was much more the student than the man of action.[19]

Francis Garrecht received his education in schools in Walla Walla and at Whitman College, which also produced Justice William O. Douglas and Judge James A. Fee, the latter of whom served on the federal district court in Oregon and later on the Ninth Circuit. After leaving Whitman College, Garrecht studied law under George T. Thompson and Judge John Sharpstein, "two of the ablest lawyers in Walla Walla." Admitted to the bar of Washington in 1894, he soon gained fame as a brilliant, if unconventional, trial lawyer. Devoid of the showmanship or actor's flair displayed by many notable trial lawyers, Garrecht instead won renown by his lucidity in analyzing legal problems, his untiring industry, and his insight into human nature. He had an unassuming air that belied his strong will.[20] As a state legislator from Walla Walla to the lower house of the Washington legislature from 1911 to 1913, he reaped great praise:

> "Representative Francis A. Garrecht of Walla Walla County is easily a human torchlight of the popular House, and whenever he rises to his feet something coruscating is certain to be demonstrated to the gallery, craning their necks over the edges of the railing in an eager effort to see the curly-haired orator, whose Ingersollian reference to 'the voiceless silence of the dreamless dust' has become a sort of corridor classic."[21]

Garrecht's service in the state legislature attracted the attention of Democrats throughout Washington, and when Woodrow Wilson assumed the presidency in 1913 he appointed Garrecht as United States attorney for the eastern district of Washington. Garrecht moved to Spokane and began his association with Frank Rudkin, then serving as federal district judge there. In his eight years as United States attorney Garrecht built a reputation as a first-rate lawyer. He achieved noteworthy courtroom successes protecting against improper appropriation of water from the Yakima Irrigation Project and resisting claims by the Northern Pacific Railway Company to 64,000 acres of land in the Spokane Indian Reservation. Garrecht's efforts won him the gratitude of Native Americans, particularly the Yakima Nation, which in an elaborate ceremony later elected Garrecht a tribal chief, Chief Khe-ach-nee, "Light of the Morning."[22]

With the election of Warren G. Harding in 1920, Garrecht left the office of United States attorney and returned to private practice. In that capacity Garrecht assisted a number of agricultural organizations, including the Wheat Growers' associations of Washington, Oregon, Idaho, and Montana and the Inland Empire Dairy Producers' Association. Garrecht also served on the State Democratic Committee and as a delegate to the 1932 Democratic National Convention.[23] These legal and political activities marked Garrecht as a fervent New Dealer, one especially concerned with the effects of the Depression on farmers and workers. His appointment to the Ninth Circuit in May, 1933, brought to the court a liberal firebrand whose work would help define the important place of circuit politics in the administration of the court.[24]

During his fourteen years of active service on the court, Garrecht wrote approximately five hundred opinions, including dissents. He was highly sympathetic to the social ideals of the New Deal and only occasionally voted against administrative agencies. His many important opinions for the court included decisions involving the National Labor Relations Board, numerous important patent controversies, the conspiracy case involving Judge Gavin W. Craig of Los Angeles, and the celebrated *Lee Arenas* case, which recognized a Mission Indian's right to a separate allotment of tribal land at Palm Springs.[25] Perhaps more important than these individual contributions was Garrecht's willingness to diverge substantively from Wilbur on issues arising out of the New Deal. As the next two chapters will explore, these disagreements over the formulation of doctrine had a very decided impact on the development of a judicial politics in the Ninth Circuit. The other judge who contributed to this development was Roosevelt's next appointee to the court, William Denman.

IV. DENMAN'S CAMPAIGN FOR A JUDGESHIP

Shortly after Garrecht assumed his new position, Roosevelt nominated William Denman to fill the seat Congress had resurrected. Denman was a remarkable figure in the history of San Francisco and of California. A tireless reformer, Denman attacked social and legal problems with enormous industry and intellect. Born in San Francisco on November 7, 1872, Denman was the second (not the first, as he frequently claimed) of the court's judges to be born in the Ninth Circuit. He received his undergraduate education at the University of California at Berkeley and his law degree from Harvard. Admitted to the California bar in 1898, he commenced the practice of law in San Francisco.[26]

Denman's energy was legendary. He taught at both Hastings College of the Law and the University of California at Berkeley from 1902 to 1906 and chaired a committee to investigate causes of municipal corruption in San Francisco, writing the committee's report between 1908 and 1910. In 1908 he also organized a statewide movement for the nonpartisan election of judges, a reform that became law in 1911. His other state legislative efforts included campaigns for an eight-hour workday for women, increased employers' liability, and the package of progressive reforms known as the "Johnson laws."[27] Denman engaged in the long struggle to free state appellate judges from electioneering, which finally became law with the passage of a constitutional amendment in 1934. During World War I, he helped to draft legislation to create a United States shipping board and then served as its first chairman.[28] He also represented the United States in shipping negotiations with the Balfour World War Mission in 1917. After the war Denman returned to private practice.[29]

Denman never revealed when he first contemplated seeking a position on the circuit court of appeals. As early as 1913 he came to President Wilson's attention as a possible candidate, but a vacancy on the court never materialized. Denman's stint as shipping board chairman brought him into contact with Franklin D. Roosevelt, then assistant secretary of the navy. Roosevelt's campaign for the presidency in 1932 spurred Denman's ambition to leave private practice and reenter public service. His correspondence from this period presents a perspective on the nomination process very different from that of the appointment papers in official archives—a case study, in certain respects, of how federal judges came to be appointed. His letters expose some of the stresses faced by judicial aspirants as they pursued nomination and confirmation and illustrate the ways potential judges sought to overcome traditional concerns and prejudices.[30]

Denman's experiences were surely similar to those of other hopefuls, both those who succeeded in the sometimes Byzantine appointment process and those who did not. Shortly after the Democratic victory, Denman asked Felix Frankfurter, then a law professor at Harvard and a known confidant of the new president, about the possibility of Frankfurter recommending him to Roosevelt as a possible nominee to the Ninth Circuit. "If I weren't a queer fish, I wouldn't be a professor," Frankfurter responded. "One form that my queer-fishiness takes is a psychological inability—it's almost physiological—to take the initiative regarding matters of personnel for political office. Fond as I am of you,

I simply cannot reverse a rooted habit, I won't offend you by calling it a principle, but such it is for me, of volunterring [*sic*] recommendations for appointments to Roosevelt. When he has wanted my opinion on men, he has asked me. . . . You may think me a foolish man and not meant for this world quite, but I think I can count on your imagination and generosity to understand my position. In any event, I prefer to deal quite candidly with you instead of giving you a song and dance." Frankfurter added, "I might say, truthfully, I have no doubt—that it's absurd to assume that my recommendation regarding a California judgeship would really matter."[31]

In spite of Frankfurter's negative reply, Denman pressed his request. Frankfurter himself spurred Denman's campaign by saying in a letter of September 12, 1934, "I have reason to believe that your judicial prospects are promising, and I wish you well." Encouraged by this remark, Denman shared his fears of the coming campaign for the judicial nomination in a letter to Frankfurter on November 6, 1934. He candidly recounted the "excellent professional support" he was receiving from the California bar, but he noted that Senator William G. McAdoo "was most reluctant in giving his and I have always feared he would switch to someone else if there were a contest against me in the White House." On a more practical level, Denman confided that widespread speculation of his impending appointment added stress of a different kind, "since my clientele seems persuaded that I am to receive the appointment and hence for a year and a half have avoided employing me in litigation of any long character. The failure to be appointed would not be a helpful way of advertising for their return."[32]

The midterm election of 1934 presented Denman both with opportunities to press his case and with threats to ward off. Denman sent out numerous telegrams after the election to politicians who might aid his quest. To James A. Farley, the postmaster general, Denman offered "congratulations on the inevitable"; to Nevada Senator Key Pittman, "Congratulations even if it was a certainty"; and to Montana Senator Burton K. Wheeler, "Congratulations. I am sure you will get all your dams." Shortly after the election, Senator Hiram Johnson informed Denman that Senator McAdoo might recommend Judge Albert Lee Stephens of Los Angeles for the Ninth Circuit. Denman quite naturally took this threat seriously. He dashed off a letter to Frankfurter in which he decried a Stephens appointment on the ground that three of the four judges on the court would then have come from the extreme southern end of the Ninth Circuit. But he clearly did not want the Harvard professor to think he was intimidated by the news, for he added, "Of course, such geographical considerations are not of major importance to us, but the Los Angeles 'go-getters', with the Los Angeles Democratic Senator [McAdoo] behind them, can be most effective."[33] Now sixty-two, Denman also feared that his age might prove a liability. In a letter to Senator Hiram Johnson, Denman observed that two Roosevelt nominees had been over sixty, the unofficial cutoff age the Justice Department used for appointments: Garrecht had been sixty-two, and Frank Norcross, sixty-five. He also reported that both Judge Sawtelle, then sixty-five, and Judge Wilbur, sixty-six, had written seventy-two majority opinions in 1933, the highest number of any circuit judges in the United States. Denman's explanation? "It's the climate!"[34]

Johnson responded to Denman's plea by petitioning Attorney General Homer S. Cummings in a letter on November 28, 1934. Although Johnson was not a member of the president's party and therefore could not claim senatorial courtesy, he nevertheless forcefully argued Denman's case. Johnson had known Denman for more than twenty-five years and "saw him tried in the severest test to which a lawyer can be put during the graft prosecution here. . . . Denman stood out then in bold relief as a man of the highest ideals, a lawyer of unblemished character and the finest courage." The senator also parroted Denman's analysis of the age issue and pointed out that each of the last four Ninth Circuit appointees had been older than sixty when nominated. Cummings gave nothing away in his response: "It goes without saying that I think very highly of Mr. Denman, whom I have known for many years," he said, and he candidly admitted past breaches of the sixty-year rule. Nevertheless, the attorney general saw "a certain merit and vitality in the rule in view of the length of contemplated service and the possibility of retirement at the age of seventy. To put it another way, it is a standard to be borne in mind rather than a rule to be strictly followed."[35]

Johnson's enthusiastic recommendation and Cummings's response, which the senator shared with Denman, understandably heartened the San Francisco attorney, who replied with a renewed attack on the age factor. Denman also lobbed another salvo on this issue at Frankfurter, to whom he wrote on the same day: "It would be particularly irritating to have the age limit applied specially in my case, when my physical examination of a month ago gave me a blood pressure of a man of forty, and I did twenty-seven holes of golf yesterday and followed it up with a night's work." A few weeks later, at the funeral for William Sawtelle, Denman stated "that the Judges asked me to stand for the vacancy."

Denman's fears of age, geography, and competition from other aspirants dissipated when President Roosevelt submitted his name to the Senate on December 31, 1934, and the Senate confirmed him on January 29, 1935.[36]

The appointment reinvigorated Denman's reformer impulses. Before long, he had championed the creation of additional Ninth Circuit judgeships and reform of the entire federal judicial system. In testimony before Congress, speeches to bar groups, and letters to the president, Denman worked tirelessly to create an administrative office for the federal courts, to add fifty new district judges and eight new circuit judges nationwide, and to end unnecessary delays in litigation.[37] Denman's zeal for administrative reform, combined with the deeply divergent views among the judges on the legality of the New Deal, gave the internal workings of the Ninth Circuit a much more political imprimatur than it had had in its first four decades. Although Wilbur, Garrecht, and Denman played the paramount roles in this development, the creation of additional Ninth Circuit judgeships brought to the court other jurists who participated in the process.

V. HANEY AND MATHEWS JOIN THE COURT

The appointment of Denman in 1935 signaled the rejuvenation of the Ninth Circuit. Less than two weeks after he took the oath of office, the Senate confirmed Clifton Mathews for the court's fourth authorized judgeship. For the first time in six years, the court was back to full strength. Within six months, Congress created a fifth judgeship for the court, legislation in which Denman took particular pride because he had lobbied strenuously for its passage. The lawyer appointed to this seat, Bert Emory Haney, received his commission on August 24, 1935, and took his oath on September 16, 1935. The paths Haney and Mathews took to reach the federal bench displayed still further the diversity in personal and public service backgrounds that Roosevelt sought from his Ninth Circuit nominees. The experiences of these two judges also exposed caprices in the judicial selection process of a kind different from those encountered by Wilbur, Sawtelle, Garrecht, and Denman.[38]

A native of Georgia, born in Concord on February 12, 1880, Clifton Mathews succeeded to the "Arizona seat" on the Ninth Circuit held by Sawtelle. After studying at Peabody College in Nashville, Tennessee, from 1902 to 1903, Mathews's formal education apparently ended. "He was," stated a colleague, "one of the last of the great self-educated men of this country." Through self-study, Mathews gained admittance to the Louisiana bar in 1904 and practiced there until 1912. He spent a few years in New Mexico, then moved to Bisbee, Arizona, in 1915, where during the 1920s he earned a reputation as one of the state's outstanding lawyers. A highlight for him in this period was working with future Chief Justice Charles Evans Hughes on a brief in the Supreme Court case of *Truax v. Corrigan.* After serving on the Colorado River Commission of Arizona in 1929, Mathews became special assistant to the Arizona attorney general and argued a number of prominent cases for the state between 1929 and 1931. In 1933, President Roosevelt named him United States attorney for the district of Arizona, a post he held until his appointment to the circuit bench in 1935.[39]

The staggering load of pending cases, as much as the nominee's own merits, no doubt occasioned the enthusiastic reception Mathews's appointment received. Not since 1929 had the court enjoyed the service of its full complement of authorized judges, and, even then, Senior Judge Gilbert's failing health curtailed his formerly prodigious output. Faced with a steadily climbing caseload, the court could ill afford to run short-handed. The addition of Denman and Mathews thus brought immediate dividends. In the year during which they first sat, the Ninth Circuit disposed of 326 cases. The following year, their first full year, it dispatched 404. In this two-year period the number of cases pending dropped from 257 to 206. In addition, Mathews earned his colleagues' admiration for the care with which he handled his work. Judge Albert Lee Stephens described Mathews as "just about the best lawyer that I have ever known. . . . He was a man of great intelligence and one who read avidly and never forgot anything." Another colleague added: "The Ninth Circuit has produced no greater lawyer than Judge Mathews. For over twenty-five years, he added great luster to our bench."[40]

Mathews was a tough, highly intelligent jurist who viewed the New Deal suspiciously, despite his affiliation with the Democratic party. His new colleague on the court, Bert Emory Haney, who ascended to the Ninth Circuit five months after Mathews, came from a background that was similar in many ways. Haney's path to the bench differed markedly from Mathews's, however, in several key respects. Haney was born in Lafayette, Oregon, on April 10, 1879. His parents, two pioneers of the Oregon country, raised him in circumstances of relative poverty. Haney worked his way through school, doing various odd jobs at neighboring farms and in the town. With the financial assistance of his uncle, Judge George H. Bingham of Salem, Haney attended Willamette University, where he received his undergraduate degree in 1899. Haney later repaid with interest all the money he had borrowed from his uncle. After teaching briefly to make money to pay for a legal education, he entered the University of Oregon and earned his LL.B. degree in 1903.[41]

Haney immediately pursued a career in public service, beginning work as deputy district attorney in Oregon, a job he held for four years. In 1908 he formed a partnership with George W. Joseph, an association that continued in various forms, with some interruptions for public service, until 1935, when Haney left private practice to join the court. Between 1918 and 1920 Haney was United States attorney for the district of Oregon. During his tenure he argued a number of war-related and Prohibition cases before the Ninth Circuit. After a three-year return to private practice Haney once more entered public service when President Harding appointed him to the United States Shipping Board in 1923. Like Denman, who also served on the board, Haney seemed to court controversy. For instance, during his first three-year term Haney decided that Admiral Leigh Palmer was grossly incompetent, and he therefore battled to remove him from his position as head of the Emergency Fleet Corporation. Although Haney was a Democrat, Coolidge reappointed him to a second term, apparently in the belief that the squabbling would stop. Haney persisted, however, and on August 31, 1925, the president demanded Haney's resignation. In response, Haney pointed out that the public knew his differences with Palmer and that he had believed Coolidge reappointed him in spite of them. Haney did eventually resign from the Shipping Board in early 1926, effective March 1.[42]

The Shipping Board controversies showed Haney's combativeness. Fighting all his life to achieve material success and professional respect, Haney attracted powerful opponents in the years that led up to his nomination to the Ninth Circuit, and they nearly succeeded in derailing the appointment. Throughout the summer of 1935, as Congress considered legislation to authorize a fifth judgeship for the Ninth Circuit, the Justice Department investigated possible nominees. Perhaps because Oregon's last representative on the court, William Gilbert, had died in 1931, attention centered on candidates from that state. Unlike the nomination papers of virtually every other Ninth Circuit judge, Haney's contain numerous letters impressing the political considerations on the decision makers. Patronage played a far greater role in this appointment than in any earlier Ninth Circuit nomination. Opponents of Haney urged his rejection because he had allegedly supported diversion of electricity from Bonneville Dam to powerful corporate interests. The more critical threat to the nomination, however, originated in the Justice Department itself. On July 23, 1935, Attorney General Homer Cummings directed his assistant, Harold M. Stephens, to "check up on [Haney's] record more fully" after he received an endorsement by telephone from Congressman Walter M. Pierce of Oregon.[43]

Stephens immediately made secret inquiries about Haney. What he found disturbed him. Stephens had asked a close friend, attorney Jay H. Stockman of Portland, to investigate Haney, especially in regard to the disbarment of one of Haney's partners, George Joseph. Joseph's disbarment resulted from "what most lawyers in Portland felt was a mean and at least unsportsmanlike attack upon the Oregon Supreme Court and one of its justices." Stockman discovered that Haney "was not in any way involved in the charges." He did, however, learn that leaders of the Oregon bar viewed a Haney appointment as "purely political." These conversations satisfied Stockman that "the Bar would not be pleased with the appointment as a judicial selection." Stockman passed along one unidentified comment, quite possibly made by Wallace McCamant, who was listed as one of the Portland attorneys consulted. The memorandum did not reveal the utterant, stating only that another attorney had said that Haney "was honest but that he had a stubbornness like Hiram Johnson with similar . . . strong likes and dislikes that would handicap him. He is not near the student of the law as many of the others. Not qualified for Judicial work." From another source, Frank E. Holman of the Seattle Bar Association, Stephens learned that "Haney is a lawyer of some considerable personality and forcefulness but not a lawyer of extraordinary ability or learning."[44] In a telling conclusion, Holman added:

> The only further thing I have to contribute to this matter is to say that the Ninth Circuit Court of Appeals has been a distinguished court. Gilbert, Ross, Hunt, Rudkin and Dietrich in the last twenty-five years have upheld the highest standards of the bench. They are now all gone. You might be interested in knowing that we lawyers now look upon the court as a very weak court. Any new appointment in my opinion ought to be made for the purpose of strengthening the personnel of the court as much as possible.[45]

Powerful political influences blunted these objections to Haney's nomination. Numerous Oregon attorneys lauded Haney, and Cummings himself saw "strong arguments for the recognition of Oregon in this matter." Commerce Department officials also urged Haney's nomination. One such official, Chester H. McCall, urged Secretary of Commerce Daniel C. Roper to mention Haney's qualifications to Cummings at a cabinet meeting in March, 1935. Roper apparently followed his assistant's suggestion: in a letter he wrote a few months later he referred to "our previous conversation concerning Mr. Haney" and spoke of Haney's "exceptional qualifications." To ignore two such requests from a fellow cabinet officer would not have been good politics; to ignore a similar entreaty from James A. Farley, the powerful chairman of the Democratic National Committee and later postmaster general, would have been decidedly bad politics.[46] Haney got the job.

President Roosevelt nominated Haney on August 19, 1935, and Congress confirmed him four days later. He took the oath of office on September 16, 1935, and assumed his position on the court. Haney served only eight years, however, dying on September 18, 1943, at the age of sixty-four. In that brief time Haney staunchly supported the New Deal and established himself as a jurist who was sympathetic to the plight of those hit by the Depression. Despite a stubborn streak, Haney was very likable, and his colleagues seemed genuinely to miss him when he died. Although he was not a brilliant jurist, Haney's record on the Ninth Circuit validated Roosevelt's decision to appoint him in the face of belittling remarks made of his candidacy by some members of the Oregon bar. As one of Haney's colleagues on the Ninth Circuit, William Denman, said to Haney just before his death, "No judges are more meticulous in arriving at their own conclusions and giving their own completely prepared contribution to a decision than yourself and Judge Mathews." In a memorial oration, a friend captured Haney's hard road to the bench: "He was willing to pay the price of success. He knew that respect, esteem and an exalted place among his fellowmen could not be purchased save by study, self-denial, undaunted resolution and a fidelity to high purposes. He attained a place on the bench of this court, a well-merited honor, among the highest that can be bestowed, and that comes to but few."[47]

With the addition of Haney, the Ninth Circuit had five sitting members for the first time in its history and joined the Second and Sixth Circuits as the largest circuit courts of appeals in the United States. These five judges—Wilbur, Garrecht, Denman, Mathews, and Haney—traveled different life and career paths to the bench. Virtually the only trait they shared was that none had ever served as federal district judge. As practicing lawyers, each had trial experience. But for the first time since Erskine Ross's elevation to the Ninth Circuit in 1895, the court boasted no one who had risen from the district court ranks.[48] This common trait did not translate into agreement on such issues as deference to trial court proceedings, willingness to scrutinize fact-findings, or judicial philosophy. The New Deal brought into immediate focus the ideological similarities and differences of these new members of the court, as well as the extent to which substantive differences contributed to the need for administrative reform.

NINE

Adjudicating the New Deal

We are stricken by no plague of locusts.
Franklin D. Roosevelt, 1933

The country was well into the Great Depression when the new judges took their seats on the court. The election of Franklin Roosevelt brought a "new deal" to the American people; it also brought a new direction to the Ninth Circuit. With the appointment of Francis Garrecht in 1933, the Democrats held a majority on the court for the first time in its history. More Democrats joined the court in the ensuing four years, until Curtis Wilbur was left as the lone Republican on a seven-member court. Although Democrats dominated, they were not all of the same mind in adjudicating issues raised by FDR's New Deal programs. The judicial battles over the legality of the president's initiatives were as spirited as any the court had seen between Erskine Ross and William Gilbert, and the stakes were as high. The severity of the Depression in the West and the unprecedented array of government programs aimed at the region combined to thrust the Ninth Circuit into the limelight. Just as the philosophical disagreements between Ross and Gilbert had affected the course of natural resource development in the West, so too differences among the 1930s-era judges influenced the region's economic recovery.

In addition to highlighting the court's place in the process of western development, the New Deal era witnessed the evolution of several critical features in the federal court system. First, by the 1930s, role specialization among the country's circuit judges was complete. The judges who took their seats on the appellate bench almost never heard trials as district judges sitting alone. And although district judges still occasionally sat on appellate panels, they did so far less frequently than had been the case

187

in the first four decades of the circuit courts of appeals. Second, the growth in federal law throughout the early twentieth century reached a new high in the 1930s with the promulgation of countless New Deal programs. Unlike some of the key cases in the World War I and Prohibition periods, in which the Ninth Circuit had opportunities to expound on grand constitutional themes, cases arising in the New Deal era tended to present questions of statutory interpretation with broader social effects but lesser legal significance. Once the Supreme Court had decided the constitutionality of a New Deal statute, for instance, the work of the circuit courts of appeals devolved to applying statutory analysis to the given facts. Third, in conjunction with the specialization in judicial roles, this functional change in the Ninth Circuit's work produced a very interesting dynamic: the development of a distinct politics in the court, in which substantive disagreements exposed the administrative shortcomings in fair assignment of judges to cases. By the end of the 1930s the Ninth Circuit was becoming more self-consciously political, as the next chapter will attempt to demonstrate. In this chapter the substantive foundation for that process will be laid in a review of the Ninth Circuit's role in western development in the New Deal era and the changes in the court's work that created the need for administrative reforms.

I. THE DEPRESSION IN THE WEST

"We are stricken by no plague of locusts." When President Franklin D. Roosevelt launched a New Deal for the American people with these words in 1933, he meant that human solutions, not divine intervention, would lead the country out of economic troubles caused by human actions. The task did not promise to be easy. At that time, the Great Depression was three and a half years old and unemployment nationally stood at 24.9 percent. The western states were struck particularly hard. As income declined, so did consumption of products from the sale of which westerners derived their livelihoods. Ranchers suffered when per capita consumption of beef and veal fell by 10 percent between 1936 and 1939. Mining income plummeted, and oil production rose only slightly in the West throughout the 1930s.[1]

The Depression discouraged many potential immigrants from moving to the Far West. Contrary to the images conjured up by writers and artists of Dust Bowl migrants blown westward off their Midwest and Great Plains farms, regional population grew more slowly in the 1930s than in any other decade since the 1840s. The metropolitan communities that blossomed after World War II had been only small towns in the 1930s: Phoenix numbered 65,000 inhabitants in 1940; Tucson, 37,000; Las Vegas, 8,422. Throughout the 1930s Reno, Nevada's largest city, had only 21,000 residents. The population of the great Pacific Coast cities of San Francisco, Los Angeles, Portland, Seattle, and San Diego stayed steady throughout the 1930s. Only two cities in the Ninth Circuit, San Francisco and Los Angeles, were counted among the top twenty-five urban areas in the United States in 1940. At this late date in the country's development, the West contained only 14 percent of the country's population, even though it made up one-half of the nation's land mass.[2]

The economy of the western states had developed quickly from the mid-nineteenth century to the Great Depression, but natural resources still comprised their primary source of wealth. The Ninth Circuit states lagged far behind the rest of the country in industrial might as well as population density. Consequently, when the Depression caused a drop in agricultural and ore prices worldwide, the Far West suffered most severely. The region's farmers and miners could do little to counteract the falling prices for their goods caused by the systemic effects of the Depression. The lack of a dense population severely constrained the ability of state and local governments to raise revenues for relief and work programs. The dire experience of Montana in the 1920s served as an extreme example for her sister Ninth Circuit states in the following decade. As wheat, copper, and timber prices had plummeted in the early 1920s, Montanans had learned that they lacked the population base and economic diversity to extract themselves from an economic downturn as harsh as the Great Depression was to be.[3]

What states such as Montana were unable to do at the state level Roosevelt pledged to try at the national. Roosevelt swept into the White House with a mandate to attack the Depression with federal programs. A combination of economic necessity and political expediency brought the West a higher per capita share of New Deal beneficence than any other region of the country. Nevada garnered the most federal expenditures per capita, at $1,130, with Montana second, at $710. Each Ninth Circuit state surpassed the national average of $224. These programs, which included reclamation projects, agricultural price and support programs, the building of great dams and power plants, and numerous construction projects, resulted in federal expenditure in Ninth Circuit states between 1933 and 1939 of an estimated $7.5 billion.[4]

Just as the New Deal programs transformed the West, so did the Roosevelt administration usher in significant developments for the Ninth Circuit. By the middle of 1935, Roosevelt had named four of the five judges who sat on the court. These judges came to the bench with a wide array of political and judicial philosophies. Some wholly favored the New Deal; others abhorred it. The court's decisions during this period reveal these differences. In some cases, judges antipathetic to the New Deal found in the judicial process ways to subvert Roosevelt's programs, even when these judges constituted a minority on the court as a whole. Fissures on the Ninth Circuit reflected nationwide disagreement among judges and lawyers about the constitutionality of key New Deal programs. Until 1937, by slender majorities the Supreme Court invalidated many crucial recovery laws. These rulings forced Ninth Circuit judges who favored the president's programs to devise creative ways of avoiding Supreme Court precedent. Analyzing these cases sheds light not only on how the Ninth Circuit's judicial process worked in the 1930s but also on how that process affected substantive developments in the West.

Moreover, the addition of two new judgeships in 1937 brought the court's strength up to seven for the first time and presented Roosevelt with an opportunity to pack the Ninth Circuit with jurists sympathetic to his programs. The two Roosevelt chose were Albert Lee Stephens of Los Angeles and William Healy of Boise, Idaho. Born in Indiana on January 25, 1874, Stephens attended public schools before graduating with the LL.B. degree in 1903 from the University of Southern California and taking up the practice of law. In 1906, Stephens began a long career in public service that included stints as justice of the peace in Los Angeles (1906–1910), member of the Civil Service Commission of Los Angeles (1911–1913), Los Angeles city attorney (1913–1919), judge of the California superior court (1920–1932), associate justice of the district court of appeals (1932–1933), and then presiding justice (1933–1935). President Roosevelt appointed Stephens as United States district judge for the southern district of California in 1935, the position from which he was elevated to the Ninth Circuit in 1937.[5]

A lifelong Democrat, Stephens was an early backer of Woodrow Wilson. Legend has it that Stephens played a prominent, if well-concealed, role in the 1916 reelection of Wilson over Charles Evans Hughes. While Hughes was stumping in the Los Angeles area, Stephens contrived to take newsmen on a tour of Hollywood. Hughes went on to Long Beach unaware that Governor Hiram Johnson was staying there. As Chief Judge Richard Chambers told the story at a memorial for

Stephens in 1965, "Somehow the non-sympathetic newspapermen got back to Long Beach [and] the sympathetic newspapermen who might have given Mr. Hughes the good advice to go see the governor never reached there. Thus, the famous snub occurred which supposedly elected Woodrow Wilson."[6]

The second new member to the court was William Healy of Idaho. Born September 10, 1881, in Windham, Iowa, Healy graduated in 1906 with an A.B. degree from the University of Iowa. Two years later he received the LL.B. degree from the Iowa Law School and gained admission to the Idaho bar that same year. After engaging in private practice for many years, Healy served as general counsel for the Farm Credit Administration in Spokane, Washington, from 1934 to 1937. He was prominent in state affairs, serving as a member of the legislature in 1913–1914, as a member of the state board of education and board of regents of the University of Idaho from 1917 to 1920, and as a delegate to the Idaho Constitutional Convention in 1933.[7]

Healy and Stephens joined a group of judges who generally backed the president's programs on appellate review. For Garrecht, Denman, Haney, Stephens, and Healy, the dire economic circumstances of the country affected their analysis of Congress's power to legislate recovery through regulation of commerce and of agency efforts to administer congressional directives. Discussions of the prevailing economic conditions fill their opinions. Wilbur viewed Congress's power much more restrictively even in the midst of crisis, as apparently did Mathews, who routinely voted against the New Dealers' position but rarely wrote to explain why. For these two judges, law had a more static quality: it was to be guided by enduring principles rather than by the exigencies of the moment. These fundamental differences of opinion underlay the court's handling of most of the legal problems emanating from the Depression. Not unlike their Ninth Circuit predecessors, who debated the proper role of the court in adjudicating the diverse issues posed by natural resource development and Prohibition, the New Deal–era judges disagreed on fundamental principles of constitutional law and statutory interpretation.

In both eras, the Ninth Circuit's decisions mattered a great deal, even to people who had only the vaguest notion of the court's existence. The court's rulings on New Deal programs, like those on natural resource controversies a generation earlier, proved that for a vast array of intermediate-level disputes, the circuit court of appeals contributed greatly to regional development. True, not many of these disputes formed the factual basis for decisions of enduring constitutional significance, and the most important of such cases would be superseded on appeal to the Supreme Court. But the Ninth Circuit decided numerous cases that had social and economic importance for the people of the region it served.[8] Cases across the spectrum of New Deal efforts, from agriculture to emergency recovery legislation, labor relations, and public works, confirm the court's important role in the assault on the Great Depression. These cases also highlight how the court itself was changing as an institution.

II. AGRICULTURAL WOES

Highly dependent on activities, such as farming, livestock production, and lumbering, that produced renewable resources, the West suffered severely from the Great Depression. Farm land prices declined precipitously; average per capita income among the agricultural population dropped to below half the non-farm level, which itself had fallen dramatically. Foreclosures escalated. Agricultural prices generally decreased 63 percent between 1929 and 1933, whereas industrial prices dipped by 15 percent.[9]

The New Deal represented the first federal attempt to help farmers who had been victimized by adverse economic circumstances. In his first hundred days, Roosevelt launched the Agricultural Adjustment Administration (AAA) to oversee government efforts designed to boost prices, stabilize production, and reduce crop surpluses. Over the next seven years a number of laws followed to refine these basic principles, including price support and production controls, crop insurance, disaster relief, and a host of other programs created to resettle poor farmers, improve soil conservation efforts, extend farm credit, establish rural electrification, and distribute surplus food. These legislative efforts built on the price-support and production-adjustment schemes of the original Agricultural Adjustment Act of 1933, which set out to raise farm prices and stabilize the agricultural market through government regulation. The theory of the self-correcting marketplace, most New Dealers believed, could not explain the prevailing economic forces. The plight of western and midwestern farmers required some type of government action. The act attempted to redress fundamental market problems principally by regulating the price of certain commodities, restricting production, and authorizing payment to farmers who agreed not to produce certain agricultural products.[10]

Farmers throughout the Ninth Circuit's constituent states eagerly participated in programs administered by the AAA. The AAA carefully monitored the extent of this involvement, and the statistics it gathered highlight the importance of the New Deal agricultural reforms for western farmers. By early 1936, in a bid to shore up prices the AAA had signed 127,001 contracts with Montana farmers to regulate crop production. The numbers of contracts in other Ninth Circuit states testified to the widespread impact of the programs: in Arizona, 5,680 contracts; in California, 25,300; in Idaho, 75,259; in Nevada, 1,388; in Oregon, 31,533; and in Washington, 48,301. In the period from 1932 through 1935, the program appeared to be making strong headway in restoring cash income levels for farmers. Nationwide, agricultural income rose by 66 percent in this four-year period, from $4.377 billion to $7.201 billion. The comparative benefit to the western states was greater still: each Ninth Circuit state except Oregon and Washington far outpaced the national average in farm income growth, and these two states were just below average at 60 and 62.5 percent, respectively.[11]

The AAA worked to control milk production. In California, the milk industry had made a modest recovery by 1935. Income from milk production had risen 11.5 percent in the previous four years, from $65.5 million to $73.0 million. Even this gain was imperiled in early 1935, when the Ninth Circuit considered a challenge to the administration of the AAA milk program in California. Judge Curtis Wilbur's opinion in *Berdie v. Kurtz* set the tone for the struggle among the Ninth Circuit judges over the New Deal's agricultural programs. In *Berdie*, the court ruled that the 1933 Agricultural Adjustment Act did not empower the secretary of agriculture to issue licenses regulating intrastate production, sale, or distribution of milk.[12] Charles Cavanah, a district judge from Idaho who sat on the panel by designation, joined Wilbur's opinion.

Berdie reflected Wilbur's overall disapproval of government regulation and his hostility to the theory that regulations on intrastate activity were acceptable if they had interstate commercial effects. He could not strike down the legislation as an improper restraint on intrastate commerce, however, because the Supreme Court had already sustained regulation of exclusively intrastate activities that burdened interstate commerce. Nor could he invalidate the regulation under the delegation doctrine, which held that delegations of authority by Congress to executive agencies were invalid if they called for the agency to exercise "legislative" power. The explicit nature of the statutory standards blunted such a challenge. Instead, Wilbur interpreted the agency's stat-

utory authority as narrowly as possible, writing that Congress had
delegated authority to the secretary only to regulate interstate commerce
and that therefore this particular regulation was invalid, since it dealt
solely with the Los Angeles milk industry and thus concerned intrastate
commerce.[13]

Wilbur went to some lengths to advance a more overtly free-market
political agenda, a position his colleague Francis Garrecht found completely untenable under the prevailing economic circumstances. In a
sharply worded dissent, Garrecht took the court's senior judge to task
for downplaying the interstate effects of intrastate regulation of the milk
industry. The chain of these consequences began with the decrease in
income among the general population in Los Angeles that had caused a
decline in milk purchases. Between 1929 and 1932, the gross income of
California dairy farmers from milk sales dropped by 35.4 percent. As
milk producers competed for shrinking markets, the resulting price wars
steadily drove dairy farmers out of the milk business. Increasingly desperate, these milk producers shifted to butter and cheese production, a
process that in turn had interstate commercial effects. Over 60 percent
of the butter and 85 percent of the cheese sold in Los Angeles during the
previous four years had been produced outside California. Garrecht thus
saw a direct link between regulation of the local milk price and interstate
commerce in butter and cheese products. Garrecht was a fervent New
Dealer and the first Roosevelt appointee to the Ninth Circuit, but his
position fell victim to the court's procedure of drawing a district judge
to fill out a panel—in this case, a judge persuaded by Wilbur. Nor did
Garrecht have the option of calling for the full court to reverse through
en banc reconsideration. It would be six years before Congress authorized a procedure by which all members of the circuit courts of appeals
could reconsider the decision of one of its panels. Nevertheless, Garrecht's views of Congress's power to regulate intrastate commerce eventually prevailed, not only on his court but in the Supreme Court as well.[14]

A more supportive view among the federal judiciary for Roosevelt's
agriculture program would not develop for another few years. Nine
months after the Ninth Circuit's decision in *Berdie*, the Supreme Court
issued an even more sweeping denunciation of the legality of the Agricultural Adjustment Act. On January 6, 1936, the Court held that the
1933 act exceeded the constitutional authority of Congress to regulate
commerce, and it expressly invalidated a processing tax as an improper
regulation of agricultural production. A week later the Court struck
down the Agricultural Adjustment Act of 1935, which had extensively

modified the 1933 program. Neither decision explicitly addressed the crop-production-control provisions, but the Court's sweeping language on the limits of Congress's power to regulate commerce left the many farmers who had signed contracts in doubt as to their continued legality. The Court's rulings thus sparked widespread discontent in the West. Despite the recognized flaws in the emergency agricultural legislation, farm groups across the country supported the general scheme presented in these Agricultural Adjustment acts.[15]

The period following the *Berdie* decision and the Supreme Court's invalidations of Agricultural Adjustment Act taxing provisions offered a great challenge to the New Dealers on the Ninth Circuit. Subordinate to the Supreme Court, the Ninth Circuit had to express its obeisance to precedent. The Court's AAA rulings must have disenchanted such jurists as Garrecht, who had represented many farmer groups before ascending to the bench. The New Dealers on the Ninth Circuit soon demonstrated that the complexity of the agriculture statutes, the uncertainty among the justices as to the constitutionality of other disputed provisions, and their own intellectual talents in distinguishing away unfavorable rulings combined to yield a more pro-administration jurisprudence than their senior judge would countenance. *Berdie* had demonstrated that despite their numerical edge, the Democratic judges were at times unable to stop the determined opposition of Judge Wilbur to the New Deal. But although the fluidity of the appellate panel process worked to the disadvantage of Garrecht in *Berdie*, it also weakened the doctrinal hold of Wilbur's position.[16]

When the Ninth Circuit next considered an appeal involving the AAA, Wilbur was not on the panel, a factor that surely shaped the tenor, if not the outcome, of the decision. In a test case on constitutional aspects of provisions of the 1935 AAA amendments not at issue in the earlier Supreme Court case, a panel composed of Garrecht, Denman, and Haney heard a fruit shipper's appeal from a permanent injunction granted in favor of the United States against shipments of oranges and grapefruit grown by the shipper in California or Arizona. The case provided an ideal vehicle for deciding the constitutional questions, because the shipper, Edwards Fruit Company, stipulated to the facts and rested its sole argument on the unconstitutionality of these AAA amendments. By going beyond the issues directly presented in the case, moreover, Denman's opinion started the erosion of the rule Wilbur had crafted in *Berdie*.[17]

Pursuant to the 1935 law, the secretary of agriculture had issued orders limiting the amount of citrus fruits each shipper could transmit in interstate or foreign commerce in a given week. By establishing prices, the order sought to restore purchasing power to an equivalent of the prewar period of August, 1909, to July, 1914. The statute also directed the secretary to take into account the effect on consumers if prices escalated too rapidly. Edwards Fruit Company's challenge to the constitutional validity of this statutory authorization raised a question with significant commercial consequences. Of the 50,000 growers of oranges and grapefruits in the United States, 36 percent resided in Arizona and California. Together these citrus fruits ranked in national value behind only apples. In California, the farm value of oranges and grapefruits was three times greater than that of any other fruit crop. As the prices for these fruit products fell, so did California's total farm worth. Population growth had not kept pace with the escalating stock of oranges. From 1930 to 1937, the market supply of oranges increased ten times more rapidly than the United States population. Given that 90 percent of California's oranges, then, moved in interstate or foreign commerce, the secretary's order had far-reaching consequences in the citrus industry.[18]

In assessing the statute under these circumstances, Denman's approach differed significantly from Wilbur's. The two clearly diverged on whether an order affecting *intrastate* activity could be justified as a regulation of *interstate* commerce. The question presented in *Edwards v. United States*—whether Congress could empower the secretary to set prices for goods moving in interstate commerce—was far different from that posed in *Berdie*—whether the secretary could issue orders regulating intrastate milk production, sales, and distribution. *Edwards* seemed squarely within Congress's constitutional power to regulate commerce "among the several States." In an elaborate opinion, Denman took judicial notice that such interstate price controls would influence intrastate production. He then proceeded to show that governmental actions affecting intrastate activities were valid exercises of constitutional authority under the Commerce Clause. As Denman put it in *Edwards*, "The orchards are the springs from which flow the streams of that commerce."[19]

Partly to justify this seemingly unnecessary analysis and partly to apply the Supreme Court precedents that only months before had signaled what appeared to be a change in the Court's perspective, Denman determined that *NLRB v. Jones and Laughlin Steel Corporation*, which the Court had decided in April of 1937, overruled *Carter v. Carter Coal Company*. In *Carter*, the Court had invalidated a statute that attempted to justify intrastate coal production codes as regulations of interstate commerce. In *Jones and Laughlin*, the Court upheld a statute permitting employees not engaged in interstate or foreign commerce to organize for collective bargaining purposes, on the ground that their intrastate actions affected interstate commerce. These opinions seemed irreconcilable, but the *Jones and Laughlin* Court itself merely said that *Carter* was "not controlling here," which Denman interpreted to mean that *Carter* was "not 'determinative' of this question, solely because it is overruled." Although legal scholars have vindicated Denman's reading, Judge Bert Haney was surely correct in his concurrence that Denman need not have gone so far. Haney did agree, however, with Denman's holding that *Jones and Laughlin* sanctioned congressional regulation, under the Commerce Clause, of "merchandise produced within and carried out of the state or that produced and remaining within it."[20]

Discussing his opinion in *Edwards*, Denman later wrote to a friend that one "of the pleasant incidents of a life tenure is that one can put in one page of an opinion citations from Karl Marx, Sutherland, and Van Devanter, and make what at least reads like a logical argument for the constitutional validity of a congressional act." But the *Edwards* decision did more than string together a few seemingly incongruous references, as Denman well knew. The seed planted there sprouted a year later when the court heard a challenge by a walnut marketer to AAA regulation of the walnut industry in California, Oregon, and Washington. Judge William Healy joined a Denman opinion that upheld the AAA regulations. Using *Edwards* as the controlling precedent, in this 1938 case Denman extended his analysis of Congress's power to regulate commerce to include, not only the producer of a commodity, but also the intrastate actions of a marketer. His opinion held that Congress could regulate intrastate commerce if that regulation bore a reasonable relation to the prevention of the economic evil of disparate pricing in the interstate walnut trade. Denman's opinion sanctioned the viability of intrastate regulations if they had some interstate effects; it also expressed deference to fact-findings by the secretary regarding the effect of these intrastate regulations on interstate prices. Clifton Mathews, who along with Curtis Wilbur was outnumbered by the New Dealers on the court, dissented without opinion.[21]

Before the Supreme Court's decision in *Jones and Laughlin*, which Denman's *Edwards* opinion extended to the agricultural recovery program, the Supreme Court's invalidation of the Agricultural Adjustment acts had threatened harsh consequences for some western agricultural producers. Much of the federal farm aid during the New Deal flowed westward from Washington. The fifteen million farmers in the western

half of the country received two-thirds of the agricultural benefits dis-
bursed by the government, with the rest going to the fifteen million
farmers in the East. Between 1933 and 1938, federal agricultural assistance went overwhelmingly to Ninth Circuit states. Six of the seven
Ninth Circuit states ranked among the top eight recipients in total loans
and expenditures per farm capita, and the other, Oregon, was thirteenth
nationally. The farmers in these states benefited the most because they
had lost most at the onset of the Depression: states that suffered the
greatest drop in farm income between 1929 and 1932 were granted the
highest levels of federal benefits.[22]

The Ninth Circuit's handling of cases arising out of these agricultural
programs offered an early warning of the need for court procedural
reforms. As the court gained its sixth and seventh members in 1937, the
disparity in judges' views was sufficiently great that panel composition
could and did significantly affect the outcome of a case. A majority of
two on a panel could theoretically bind the other five members of the court
in the announcement of Ninth Circuit law. As Denman's studied avoidance of Wilbur's *Berdie* opinion revealed, clever judges distinguished
away precedents with which they disagreed. Clearly such a system was
undesirable, but no solution had as yet been devised. And even as the
ideological focus on the court's schisms offers one insight into the development of the Ninth Circuit's politics, sympathy for the New Deal was
not the sole driving force in the establishment of a procedure for the entire
court to consider a case. As cases arising under the National Industrial
Recovery Act demonstrated, even judges sympathetic to the Roosevelt
administration sometimes disagreed sharply among themselves.

III.   JUDICIAL CHASMS OVER
RECOVERY LEGISLATION

Democrats generally viewed the National Industrial Recovery Act
(NIRA) as the legislative centerpiece of Roosevelt's first hundred days.
Like the many New Deal agricultural reform efforts, this program gave
statutory expression to a popular assumption that the market system
had failed. Government action, New Dealers contended, would restore
proper returns for businesses and ensure reasonable wages for workers.
The NIRA accordingly required the establishment of codes of fair competition and minimum wages for workers. Principally through these
two mechanisms, but also through other measures, the Roosevelt administration hoped to achieve several ambitious goals: to put idle plants
back into operation, to boost employment by decreasing working

hours, and to create equitable pricing. The statute attempted to balance the interests of labor, business, and consumers. The Democrats believed that industry and labor would abstain from unfair competition if they were permitted to establish mutually agreeable rules governing competition. This program received an immediate legal challenge, and commentators attacked the plan as "naive advice" to business: "Congress realizes that it has not found the key to recovery, and it abdicates in favor of business. The Act which it has adopted and which has since been put forward, with the fanfare of trumpets, synthetic war psychology, and extravagant advertising, as the National Industrial Recovery Act is a comprehensive blank."[23]

Congress delegated to the private sector the authority to fill in this blank through the establishment of local codes of fair competition, a deputation found unconstitutional by the Supreme Court in the landmark case of *A.L.A. Schechter Poultry Corporation v. United States*. The Court held that, by vesting in nongovernmental entities the authority to establish self-policing codes with the force of law, Congress had violated separation of powers principles. Pacific Northwest lumber interests, who had objected to the codes from the outset, particularly applauded the decision. In Oregon, a large number of independent lumber concerns refused to cooperate with the National Recovery Administration. One Oregonian described the NIRA program as the "'worst misfortune that [had] ever befallen the United States.'"[24] *Schechter Poultry* signaled, not only the Supreme Court's concern about the constitutional underpinnings of a critical Roosevelt program, but also the deep chasm in viewpoint between conservatives, who occupied many leadership positions in business and who composed a majority on the Supreme Court, and New Dealers, both in the administration and on the federal bench.

In the years after *Schechter Poultry*, the Ninth Circuit considered several NIRA cases, albeit none with the far-reaching significance of the appropriately nicknamed "sick chicken case." These cases highlighted the increasing importance of federal statutory analysis in the court's work. In one such case, in which the Ninth Circuit reversed a district court decision that invalidated a contract between a school district and a contractor, Judge Bert Haney's opinion exemplified the subtle power of the appellate court. The school district had received a grant from the United States to build an addition to a school, and in the contract the government had imposed as a condition that the contractor must abide by NIRA regulations. After beginning work on the school addition in January, 1934, but before its completion in February of 1935, the parties agreed to numerous changes in plans that slowed construction. The school district alleged that because of these delays the contractor owed liquidated damages for breach of contract. The contractor in turn asserted that the district owed over $42,000 for nonpayment under the contracts. The district court ruled that the contracts were invalid because they contained an illegal delegation of power from a state governmental entity, a school district, to the United States government. If, for example, the contractor failed to abide by the NIRA codes, the contract empowered the administration to render such a determination and invalidate the contract. The court reasoned that the district had no authority to delegate such power to the national government.[25]

Judge Bert Haney, who wrote also for Francis Garrecht, concluded that Congress could constitutionally condition the granting of money for school additions on compliance with the NIRA codes. That power derived from the legislature's power to spend money for the general welfare. By contrast to the Supreme Court's decision in *Schechter Poultry*, which cast the problem of delegation in a more sterile theoretical light with no apparent consideration of the country's desperate economic situation, and *United States v. Butler*, which appeared to reject such an expansive view of congressional spending power, in his decision Haney placed the constitutional issues in the context of the prevailing difficulties: "At the time of the enactment of the National Industrial Recovery Act, a severe economic emergency was upon us, nationwide in scope. To relieve that emergency the act was passed providing for a program which would promote employment, and thus aid in the relief of the emergency. To that end a large appropriation was made for expenditures in public works. The appropriation was valid." In a separate concurrence, Judge Clifton Mathews exposed just how far afield Haney had gone to assert Congress's power to redress the economic malaise. Mathews believed simply that the contractor had no standing to assert the unconstitutionality of the delegation by the school district under the conditions of the grant, which were the contractual terms between the United States government and the school district. Mathews's theory attracted no other adherents on his court, however, and to the extent that other circuit courts of appeals confronted similar issues, they expressed Haney's view.[26]

The Ninth Circuit's division over the NIRA was symptomatic of the wider rifts in the federal judiciary on the act's validity. The composition of the Ninth Circuit reflected the ideological divisions on the Supreme Court, except that in numbers the Ninth Circuit favored the New Dealers. The positions taken by Curtis Wilbur, the only Republican, reliably comported with those of the uncertain Supreme Court majority that struck down New Deal legislation until 1937.[27] Wilbur's colleagues were all Roosevelt-appointed Democrats, albeit not all reliable New Dealers. Clifton Mathews frequently voted against the Roosevelt administration's position, but he rarely invoked the constitutional obstructions to New Deal legislation favored by Wilbur. The other five judges—Garrecht, Denman, Haney, Stephens, and Healy—supported Roosevelt's program. Occasionally the circumstances of the case drew a dissenting vote, but these five provided a solid New Deal majority on the Ninth Circuit, with Garrecht as the most ardent advocate of national power to redress the prevailing economic difficulties.

Cases arising under the excise tax provision of the NIRA elicited some of the diversity of views found even among the New Deal sympathizers on the Ninth Circuit and presented a different facet of the recovery program: the need to raise money to pay for the New Deal. Section 213 of the NIRA imposed a 5 percent excise tax on company dividends declared after enactment of the NIRA on June 16, 1933. In a series of cases, the Ninth Circuit held that dividends declared *before* the enactment of the NIRA were nevertheless subject to the excise tax. In the first of the series, the court liberally construed the excise tax provision to cover a declaration of dividends made before the NIRA's effective date. Garrecht's opinion, which Haney joined, reasoned that because the declaration of dividends could still be voided by the company, it was not final. Stephens, who had upheld California recovery legislation when he was a state judge, believed that Garrecht had gone too far. He dissented because the "dividends upon which tax is claimed were absolutely and unqualifiedly declared prior to the date of the enactment of the statute." In other circuits that examined this issue, the views of both Garrecht and Stephens resonated, the Seventh siding with the former and the Fifth lining up with the latter.[28]

Garrecht's opinion expressed a preference for furthering the national government's interests in financing the recovery effort over the complaints of the region's businesses, which had to pay the resultant taxes. A generation earlier, the court had sided with companies when sued by the federal government in disputes over natural resources; Garrecht's position, then, perhaps signaled a changed attitude among Ninth Circuit judges regarding assertions of government power. In a similar case handed down in 1939, a completely different panel of the court (Denman, Mathews, and Healy) sustained Garrecht's position. The district court had ruled that the commissioner of internal revenue improperly disallowed a claimed refund because the company's "dividend declared" created a binding debtor-creditor relationship between the company and the stockholder. Citing Garrecht's opinion in the earlier case as authority, the Ninth Circuit reversed. Writing also for Denman over a dissent without opinion by Mathews, Healy found that the company had qualified its payment by declaring that dividends would be paid "whenever in [the judgment of the secretary and treasurer] there are moneys available to pay the same." In a subsequent case, Healy and Denman extended this rule still further. Although the corporation had not only made a firm declaration but had actually paid a dividend, the court nonetheless upheld the application of the excise tax. The company had paid the dividend, in the full amount declared, two weeks after the NIRA's enactment on June 16, 1933. Healy and Denman deemed this fact immaterial because the company still had discretionary authority to revoke the dividend before the act's effective date. In a pattern that was by now becoming familiar, Mathews once again dissented without opinion.[29]

The NIRA excise tax cases demonstrated the willingness of a majority of Ninth Circuit judges seemingly to go beyond the plain meaning of the statute in order to sanction the Roosevelt administration's attempts to collect these revenues. Having these revenue collection measures upheld greatly assisted the administration in its attempts to revive the economy through federal programs. Between 1934 and 1941, nearly 17 percent of the Ninth Circuit's docket consisted of tax matters. Except in the NIRA excise cases, however, the court tended to balance the government's interest in revenue collection with the taxpayer's interest in avoiding payment.[30] Although they were surely an important facet of the court's day-to-day work, these tax cases arguably had much less impact in shaping regional developments than did the labor cases that arose under the National Labor Relations Act.

IV. LABOR CONTROVERSIES

The labor controversies of the 1910s and 1920s in the West involved efforts by miners and industrial workers to organize in order to gain basic collective rights. The most acute labor disputes centered in the large coastal communities of San Francisco, Los Angeles, Seattle, and San Diego. The steadily rising unemployment rate threatened to renew labor unrest in these urban centers. By 1932, 31 percent of the unionized workforce in Los Angeles were unemployed; in San Francisco, 24 percent were out of work. For organized building trades, the figures were even higher: 52 percent in Los Angeles and 62 percent in San Francisco. Statewide, 28 percent—700,000 workers—were jobless. Even those who were employed suffered, as average wages fell by more than 50 percent between August of 1930 and June of 1932. Grievances varied from worker to worker, but solidarity was sufficiently strong that San Francisco was paralyzed when a walkout by longshore workers in 1934 spread into a general strike, an event notable for its widespread rioting and violence. By the 1930s, grave difficulties between labor and management had spread inland, as farm laborers and growers struggled to protect themselves during the economic downturn. During this decade, 140 agricultural labor strikes involving 127,000 workers occurred in California. In 34 of those strikes, at least 1,000 workers walked out. In Oregon a total of seventeen strikes involved 8,000 laborers.[31]

Although workers had long been granted the right to join labor unions, the power of employers severely limited their exercise of this right. The New Deal, especially section 7(a) of the National Industrial Recovery Act, gave new impetus to organized labor. That provision codified workers' rights to organize and to bargain collectively through their own chosen representatives. Although the NIRA sanctioned a new vehicle for the expression of workers' rights, companies were reluctant to implement section 7(a). A number of strikes broke out because employers would not recognize and bargain with unions. Many companies refused to negotiate with any labor representative who did not work at their plant and obstructed efforts to resolve claims that were supported by more than one union group. As J. Warren Madden, the first chairman of the National Labor Relations Board, later wrote with decided understatement, "It was all very frustrating."[32]

Congress responded to the ineffectiveness of NIRA's section 7(a) by enacting the National Labor Relations Act (NLRA) in 1935. The NLRA codified the right of employees to organize unions, to bargain as a group, and to engage in collective action. It defined "unfair labor practices" to include interference with these rights, use of company unions to discourage effective organization, discrimination against employees because of their union activities, and discharge or other discrimination against employees for exercising their rights or filing grievances against their employers. The act also established the National Labor Relations Board (NLRB) and empowered it to order employers to cease and desist from unfair labor practices. Congress vested jurisdiction over appeals from these orders in the circuit courts of appeals, with subsequent review by the Supreme Court on writ of certiorari.[33]

Nine days after the first members of the NLRB took their posts, a pro bono lawyers' group attacked the constitutionality of the NLRA. The board responded by arranging test cases to establish the act's validity in a variety of economic contexts. The initial cases brought by the board immediately raised the specter that the federal courts would strike down the act as unconstitutional. At least one circuit court of appeals was apparently "unwilling to be the first to face the constitutional questions" posed by the NLRA; that court was not, however, the Ninth Circuit.[34] From the perspective of the Roosevelt administration, the Ninth Circuit panel formed to assess the NLRA's constitutionality could not have been worse: it consisted of Wilbur, Mathews, and Garrecht. Wilbur had already expressed his deep-rooted opposition to the New Deal through both constitutional and statutory arguments. Mathews had not written on a pivotal case, but his dissents without opinion spoke loudly enough to give the administration little comfort. Garrecht's was the only vote on this panel likely to uphold the NLRA's constitutionality.

That Wilbur and Mathews appeared repeatedly on the panel in these important cases challenging the constitutionality of New Deal programs may or may not have been coincidental. Under the Ninth Circuit's internal rules, Wilbur as senior judge had the authority "after conference with the Circuit Judges [to] designate and assign the judges who are to hear the causes placed upon the calendars of the court; such designation or assignment may be modified or set aside by a majority of the judges."[35] Until the Supreme Court began to adopt a more permissive view of the constitutionality of New Deal legislation in 1937, Wilbur and Mathews seemed to staff panels in important cases with a regularity that belied randomness. Wilbur's papers shed no light on his decision-making process in this regard, nor do they reveal any dissatisfaction on the part of his fellow judges concerning how cases were assigned. This issue, however, was not one that could be raised easily without a serious breach of judicial etiquette. As the court's disposition of the NLRA test case intimated, Wilbur's colleague Francis Garrecht must have chafed under his senior judge's exercise of this power.

The case, *NLRB v. Mackay Radio and Telegraph Company*, was noteworthy for more than the frustration it may have caused Garrecht. More important, it represented an intellectual crossroads on the Ninth Circuit regarding the acceptance of economic substantive due-process doctrines. Over the previous three decades, the Supreme Court had developed a position that generally limited the power of Congress and the states to enact laws regulating working conditions. The most famous progenitor of this doctrine, the Court's 1905 decision in *Lochner v. New York*, struck down New York's maximum-hours law for bakers as a violation of freedom of contract and due process. Throughout the *Lochner* era, the justices disagreed sharply among themselves over the extent to which statutes regulating business violated substantive due process. Even as late as 1936, a majority of five struck down such laws. Within a year, Justice Owen Roberts seemingly shifted his position to join a new majority of five in upholding a Washington provision that established a minimum wage for women and children workers.[36] The Supreme Court's own uncertainty provided ambiguous guidance for the lower federal courts. The Ninth Circuit's handling of *Mackay Radio* illustrated the disparate views percolating in the lower federal courts, the ability of a single judge to impose his positions on the court, and the need for a process to enable the full court to review panel decisions.

The case arose when employees at a San Francisco telegraph office joined a nationwide strike. The company replaced the strikers with nonstriking employees from other offices. After some of the San Francisco strikers decided to abandon the walkout, management agreed to accept the returnees but refused to unseat any replacements who wished to remain in San Francisco. The company also required eleven strikers to submit new applications for employment and ultimately denied reinstatement to five of them, all of whom had been prominent in the union activities. The rejected employees notified the NLRB, which investigated, brought charges, made findings, and issued a cease-and-desist order. The board then petitioned the Ninth Circuit to enforce the order.[37] The court announced its decision on January 11, 1937, through Judge Wilbur, whose lengthy opinion held the NLRA to be unconstitutional. Mathews concurred separately, and Garrecht dissented. Attempting to breathe new vigor into *Lochner*ism, Wilbur wrote that this exercise of Congress's commerce power unconstitutionally abridged the right of companies to make contracts freely under the Fifth Amendment due process clause. With a reverential bow to *Lochner* and numerous citations to turn-of-the-century cases of the same ilk, Wilbur argued that the right of companies to make contracts unqualifiedly trumped Congress's authority to regulate interstate commerce.[38] Wilbur believed that the *Lochner* era's prohibitions on minimum wage and hours legislation applied equally well to collective bargaining contracts:

> It is argued on behalf of the petitioner that, as the right to bargain collectively is a well-recognized right, Congress can protect that right. That is true, but in so doing Congress is at the threshold of private and personal rights with

which its power to interfere is limited by the Constitution. In that field the right of the individual is superior to the power of Congress, save in exceptional cases. The right of Congress begins only where these inherent and inalienable rights of the individual end. The right to bargain collectively in its essence is the right of a group of persons to select its own agents—an inherent right. When the form of legislation prohibits an individual worker from bargaining for the terms of his own employment, or from selecting his own agent for that purpose, the act destroys instead of protects the right upon which collective bargaining is recognized and sustained; that is, the right to contract by and through any chosen agent, or without any agent at all.[39]

The implications of this reading of substantive due process were clear: "[B]y reason of the Fifth Amendment to the Constitution Congress has no power to compel employers and employees engaged in interstate commerce to negotiate their contracts of employment in a specific way and to prohibit the negotiation in any other way."[40]

Expressing a view he would later repeat, Mathews contended that the specific facts, and not the Constitution, compelled the result Wilbur wanted. He believed it unnecessary to decide the constitutional question, because the board had not provided sufficient evidence to sustain its order. From the NLRB's perspective, this type of reasoning was potentially more destructive to its purposes than was Wilbur's. Once the Supreme Court established the constitutionality of the NLRA, Wilbur would have no choice but to apply precedent. By focusing on the facts and expressing a strong willingness to reverse the board's fact-findings, Mathews more subtly achieved the result both judges apparently sought, without raising issues of obvious merit in a petition for certiorari to the Supreme Court. When the Court reversed the senior judge's opinion in *Mackay Radio*, Wilbur moved closer to Mathews's view.[41]

Garrecht dissented with an eloquence that very likely sprang from a law clerk he employed from 1934 to 1948, Gilbert Cosulich. Cosulich had a penchant for flowery language. In addition to holding a law degree, he was a journalist. He began his legal career as a law clerk to Judge William Sawtelle, whose opinions also show signs of Cosulich's touch. After Sawtelle died, Garrecht hired Cosulich as a clerk, and after Garrecht's death in 1948 Cosulich moved to Hawaii, where he served under Territorial Judge Frank McLaughlin. In 1958 he attempted to make his way back to the Ninth Circuit. At the time, Judge Albert Lee Stephens was strongly considering hiring him, but Judge James A. Fee allegedly told Stephens, "No associate of mine is going to have a ghostwriter," and Stephens reconsidered. Whether Cosulich drafted these opinions without any editing, as he boasted in his 1958 applications for a job as a law clerk, or whether he simply assisted Judge Garrecht and others to improve their prose, his gifts as a writer surely helped the judges for whom he worked to fill the *Federal Reporter* with powerful images.[42]

Almost certainly with Cosulich's assistance in *Mackay Radio*, Garrecht closely tied the prevailing economic circumstances to his interpretation of the appropriate law: "The increase and magnitude of the conflicts between employers and workers are appalling. In many instances much loss and suffering are precipitated upon those in no sense responsible for these difficulties and at times the general welfare of the country becomes involved in the struggle." Garrecht curtly rejected Mathews's objection to the order. The statute provided that the board's fact-findings should be "conclusive"; in his view, the evidence that the company had discharged the five workers for their labor union activities was "convincing." As for Wilbur's opinion, the senior judge had taken Supreme Court doctrine much further than a fair reading of those cases warranted: "[E]ven the authorities relied upon in the main opinion do not go to any such extreme." Garrecht had little patience with Wilbur's attempts to revive economic substantive due process. He argued that the *Lochner*-era cases cited by Wilbur were in themselves limited to a qualified due-process right in relation to the Commerce Clause and that the Supreme Court had silently overruled or modified many of them. He ended with a sharp jab: "The main opinion argues for absolute liability to contract, but the irony of the situation is that under existing economic conditions such freedom as between master and worker is mostly mythical. The only liberty interfered with is the liberty of the strong to oppress the weak."[43]

The *Mackay Radio* decision, the first major case regarding the NLRB to be decided by the Ninth Circuit, exposed deep divisions on the court. The Supreme Court decisively upheld the NLRA's constitutionality, but Wilbur remained undaunted. When the Ninth Circuit reconsidered its decision in *Mackay Radio* through a petition for rehearing brought later that year, the panel lined up exactly as before, only this time Wilbur wrote that a statutory defect prohibited the board from enforcing its order. Wilbur drew a distinction between "reinstatement" as provided in the NLRA and "reemployment," a term used for new or former employees: Congress could order the former, but not the latter. This distinction failed to persuade either Mathews, who again concurred in the result on the ground that the board had lacked evidence to sustain its order, or Garrecht, who again dissented. As Garrecht candidly said of Wilbur's opinion, "This view appears to me to be a strained construction designed to nullify the National Labor Relations Act in an important field of its operations."[44] In light of other circuit court of appeals rulings and the Supreme Court's reversal of Wilbur's opinion the following year, Garrecht's assessment seemed accurate. Long after the Ninth Circuit's role in *Mackay Radio* was forgotten, the vitality of the Supreme Court's treatment continued.[45]

Once the Supreme Court firmly and finally decided the constitutionality of the NLRA and the statutory authority of the NLRB, cases steadily flowed into the board and up to the circuit courts of appeal. The Ninth Circuit itself rendered decisions that involved some of the largest corporations in the West, including Oregon Worsted Company, a textile manufacturer; American Potash and Chemical Corporation, one of the largest borax and potash distributor-producers in the world; Union Pacific Stages, a regional transportation company; M and M Wood Working Company, a lumber company with operations in Oregon and Washington; the Hearst Corporation, the newspaper and media giant; and Pacific Greyhound Lines.[46] In these cases the court began the long process of filling in the administrative and procedural details authorized under the NLRA.

Except for Wilbur and Mathews, the members of the court agreed that the board had power to enforce orders against recalcitrant companies who acted in violation of the NLRA. General agreement did not, however, mean uniformity of view. For two years after *Mackay Radio*, a flood of separate opinions accompanied nearly every ruling, as each judge struggled to understand and articulate principles to guide future adjudication. Although marked by disagreement, these decisions nevertheless fleshed out the legal process by which labor and management could resolve many of their disagreements in a more orderly, less violent manner than they had in the past. Neither union leaders nor corporate officials viewed the NLRB as a panacea, but the board did help to impose a legal imprimatur on labor-management relations. Between 1937 and 1942, when the board was young, the Ninth Circuit granted more than 80 percent of the NLRB's petitions for enforcement and thereby significantly aided the process of transferring worker grievances from the picket lines to government hearing rooms. The number of strikes decreased, and the western labor movement entered a more overtly political phase, in which rival unions vied for worker support.[47]

V.   DAMS AND WATER

Recovery legislation brought immediate aid to westerners, emergency agricultural relief propped up suffering farmers, and national labor laws defused tension between workers and management. The benefits accrued from these laws, though very real, paled somewhat in comparison to the longterm significance of programs launched by the Department of the Interior. The New Deal's greatest impact in the Ninth Circuit states arguably stemmed from the Roosevelt administration's water development policy. In the 1934 budget for the Public Works Administration, for example, Congress allocated more than $103 million, a sum that equaled half the total amount spent on Bureau of Reclamation projects from 1902 to 1933. Whereas before 1933 the annual federal expenditure for reclamation had averaged nearly $9 million, from 1933 to 1940 it exceeded $52 million. These projects used scarce water for a variety of purposes, including consumption as drinking water, erosion and flood control, generation of electricity, irrigation, wildlife conservation and forest development, and recreation. Although the impetus for water control had begun three decades earlier with the enactment of the New-lands Reclamation Act on June 17, 1902, before the New Deal era the federal government launched only a few major projects in the West.[48]

The great water projects of this period—Boulder Dam, Grand Coulee Dam, and the Central Valley project—changed the West and touched the lives of people in most of the Ninth Circuit states. Electricity was but one such benefit. During World War II, reclamation projects accounted for 84 percent of the growth in total electricity production in the eleven states of the Far West. By December, 1944, with more than thirty of its power plants in the West on line, the Bureau of Reclamation claimed to be "'the largest single producer of power in the world.'" Boulder (later renamed Hoover) Dam provided electricity for Los Angeles and other cities in Arizona and Nevada, irrigation water for the Imperial Irrigation District, which covered 500,000 acres, and silt protection for irrigators in southern California, Arizona, and Mexico. By 1940, Bureau of Reclamation projects provided irrigation for approximately six million acres of arid land and directly supported over one million people.[49]

These projects transformed the Far West. Without the efforts of untold numbers of federal officials and private construction workers and the institutional backing of the national government and large corporations they would not have been possible. The great complexity of these undertakings invariably led to legal disputes that required the western federal courts' attention. The Supreme Court's ability to review only a small number of cases left the Ninth Circuit effectively as the court of last resort in controversies both large and small. At each stage in a project, the court adjudicated disputes on a range of issues, balancing the public interest in project completion against the concerns of parties adversely affected by development plans. The first legal questions raised by these federal projects addressed the adequacy of compensation for lands "taken" by the federal government. Such enormous projects as the Grand Coulee Dam in Washington and Shasta Dam in California required the expropriation of thousands of acres. The government designated the largest tracts at the dams' backwaters, which were flooded to create reservoirs. The Grand Coulee Dam, for example, involved the taking of an estimated 18,000 acres of privately owned land that was divided into 600 tracts with 900 different owners. In addition to these privately owned plots, the backwater lands included parts of the Colville Indian Reservation and the Spokane Indian Reservation. These large takings sparked major litigation by a disgruntled land company attempting to extract a higher level of compensation. The company asserted that it should get compensation in the value of the land as a dam site, with water for irrigation and generation of electricity, since private capital could have developed the project. The Ninth Circuit rejected this creative theory. The point of the government's venture was to put relatively valueless land to a more economically productive use. To assess the government a higher cost of compensating because of the theoretical possibility that private enterprise could build a dam and a hydroelectric plant might have threatened other public reclamation projects.[50]

The Ninth Circuit generally upheld the government's position in these condemnation proceedings, but in an important case involving the Central Valley project the Ninth Circuit sided with the landowner. The first task in every takings case of this type was to determine the appropriate date for assessing market value. For the Central Valley project, this normally pedestrian issue became more challenging, because the government did not decide precisely which land to appropriate until after Congress had formally adopted the program by statute. Landowners knew that some but not all of the lands in the area surrounding the proposed site of Shasta Dam would be condemned. Land speculation set off a rise in values, and the Ninth Circuit had to determine whether to credit that increase. The district court ruled that the fair market value of the land had to be assessed as of August 26, 1937, because on that date Congress enacted the Central Valley project legislation. The court reasoned that the taking became publicly known at that time.

The Ninth Circuit reversed. In an opinion by Judge Albert Lee Stephens, the court permitted admission of evidence on the increased value between August of 1937 and December 14, 1938, because no one publicly knew the precise location of the affected land until the latter date.

The value of some land that the government did not expropriate naturally rose. Stephens found no unfairness in the speculation that increased value in the vicinity between August, 1937, and December, 1938, because not all landowners would benefit by being able to sell their land to the government through the taking. Judge Francis Garrecht concurred in part and dissented in part. He believed that permitting the inflated value worked an unfairness "'to the public which is to pay for it.'"[51] The disagreement of the two Roosevelt appointees concerned who was to assume the burden of reimbursing the landowners at the higher rate. Stephens's prevailing position assessed that cost on the taxpayer at large, whereas Garrecht would have deprived the landowner of the rise in value.

Once the court decided takings issues of the Central Valley type, the next array of litigation issues typically arose from project construction. The dams were hazardous to build. During the construction of Boulder Dam, for example, at least fifty workers lost their lives and countless others were injured. The federal courts' jurisdiction over matters of state law between citizens of different states brought one unusual Boulder Dam personal injury suit before the Ninth Circuit. A man was injured when he appeared on site to apply for a construction job. Caught in the rain, he requested and received permission to enter the premises to get dry. An explosion occurred near the boiler where he had strung his wet clothes. He sued for damages but received nothing. The Ninth Circuit upheld the district court's order sustaining demurrers to the complaint because the injured worker had not pleaded a theory under which the law permitted recovery. In addition to construction-related lawsuits involving personal injuries, the court also rendered decisions at the construction phase of project development regarding contracts and performance bonds.[52]

Once the land had been taken and the dams and electricity plants built, legal controversies then arose over the distribution of water rights. The completion of Boulder Dam enabled water from the Colorado River to be used for irrigation in the Imperial and Coachella valleys. Until the completion of the All-American Canal, commercial and agricultural enterprises in these valleys received water at high rates from a canal that crossed from Mexico. In a major suit against the Imperial and Palo Verde irrigation districts, the Coachella Valley County Water District, the Metropolitan Water District of Southern California, the City of Los Angeles, and the City and County of San Diego, an individual sought an injunction to stop the water districts and communities from contracting to apportion the water that California was to receive under the Colorado River compact. Had the court sided with the complainant, the entire water distribution agreement would have been threatened. Sensitive to the implications of this lawsuit, the Ninth Circuit refused to upset the delicate compromise that made the allocation agreement possible. "The instant issue is not one alone affecting an individual citizen or his separate property," District Judge Jeremiah Neterer (sitting by designation) wrote. "The water of the river is a treasure that offers necessity of life to at least several millions of people, and must be apportioned in harmony with the provisions of law, in equality of right and equity for the common good." In this same spirit, the court determined in another case that the United States was an indispensable party and that a suit between a reservoir district and the Idaho watermaster to adjudicate water rights for the American Falls Reservoir project could not be maintained without the participation of the secretary of the interior.[53]

Perhaps the most contentious lawsuit over rights to water in these years involved the City of San Francisco and its water supply. The 1906 fire had first exposed the gross inadequacy of the city's water sources; the problem grew as more people moved to the Bay Area. During the next seven years a struggle ensued between the competing interests of a water-starved growing city and a conservation movement led by the famed John Muir, who believed that the Hetch Hetchy Valley slated for submersion was every bit as spectacular as the Yosemite Valley nearby. In this instance the conservationists lost. In 1913 Congress passed the Raker Act, under which the United States ceded to San Francisco rights to use lands and waters in Yosemite National Park. The statute authorized construction of a dam in the Hetch Hetchy Valley to impound surplus water for generation of electricity and consumer use in San Francisco. Section 6 of the law provided that "the grantee is prohibited from ever selling or letting to any corporation or individual, except a municipality or a municipal water district or irrigation district, the right to sell or sublet the water or the electric energy sold or given to it or him by the said grantee." The Raker Act thus required public ownership of the utility operations, but the city left the distribution of power and water to the Pacific Gas and Electric Company (PG&E).[54]

During the 1930s, the man most responsible for water development projects in the West, Harold Ickes, attempted to enforce the 1913 statute. On August 24, 1935, he issued an opinion which declared that PG&E and the City of San Francisco were in violation of section 6 of the Raker Act. The city responded by informing Ickes that it would continue to dispose of its electricity under its contract with PG&E until a court ordered it to cease and desist. The interior secretary promptly sought a district court order finding that the city had contravened the Raker Act and enjoining any further violation. The court considered whether a contract of July 1, 1925 between the city and PG&E complied with the act. The contract attempted to establish an agency agreement whereby the city would turn over its power to the utility company at a substation thirty-five miles outside San Francisco. In a detailed examination of the history of the project, the Raker Act's language, and Congress's legislative intent, District Judge Michael J. Roche of San Francisco issued an injunction against the city on the ground that the agency agreement failed to comply with the strict terms of the act. He cited seemingly unequivocal statements by the law's author, John E. Raker of California, suggesting that the legislation was intended to require San Francisco to supply its own people with electricity and water before selling any excess to a private corporation. As Judge Roche summarized his findings, "The language of the section makes it clear that no private corporation was to enjoy any profits from the government grant, which was to be enjoyed in its entirety by the consumers." He further concluded that the so-called "agency agreement" was actually a contract for resale, in which the alleged principal, the City of San Francisco, divested itself of control when it received payment for electricity from PG&E. Accordingly, he issued an injunction against the city, but, recognizing the harsh economic consequences of a sudden disruption of operations, he made its effective date six months after the decision was handed down.[55]

A decision of such regional importance was sure to be challenged. The city appealed to the Ninth Circuit, and Wilbur, Mathews, and Denman heard the case. (After submission, for reasons that the record does not clarify, Denman disqualified himself.) For a Roosevelt administration that had by now grown accustomed to losing when Wilbur and Mathews were on the panel together, the Ninth Circuit's reversal must have come as no surprise. The court held that contracts drawn up between the city and PG&E evidenced an "agency" relationship rather than an unlawful sale of power and water by the city. Wilbur's opinion interpreted the 1925 contract between the city and PG&E on its face to create an agency relationship. He saw no disingenuity in the parties' agreement that the city would employ the company as the "temporary" distributor for the city of electrical power in an arrangement that was continued fourteen years after the contract had been signed.[56] Wilbur wrote not a word about the legislative history, an omission for which Justice Hugo Black's opinion for the Supreme Court implicitly took him to task:

> To limit the prohibitions of § 6 of the Act narrowly to sales of power for resale without more, as the City asks, would permit evasion and frustration of the purpose of the lawmakers. Congress clearly intended to require—as a con-

dition of its grant—sale and distribution of Hetch-Hetchy power exclusively by San Francisco and municipal agencies directly to consumers in the belief that consumers would thus be afforded power at cheap rates in competition with private power companies, particularly Pacific Gas & Electric Company. It is not the office of the courts to pass upon the justification for that belief or the efficacy of the measures chosen for putting it into effect. Selection of the emphatically expressed purpose embodied in this Act was the appropriate business of the legislative body.[57]

The Supreme Court reversed the Ninth Circuit decision and upheld the district court injunction. Ickes thus won the legal battle, but the victory proved fleeting. Despite the Court's ruling that San Francisco was violating the 1913 law, the city to this day does not publicly own and manage its water and electricity distribution system.[58]

The denouement of the Hetch Hetchy saga constituted a rare setback for Ickes's New Deal effort to ensure public ownership of electric and water resources generated through government programs. At the Ninth Circuit level, the case again suggested the need for an internal procedure to review panel decisions. Whether the New Dealers on the court would have voted the other way in the Hetch Hetchy litigation is impossible to say, but the composition of the panel formed to hear the case was as unsympathetic to the New Deal as one could get on the Ninth Circuit. Wilbur and Mathews had consistently voted against the government's position in a variety of New Deal contexts. For these two judges to be the sole decision makers for the court (after Denman's recusal) when the New Deal Democrats easily outnumbered them must have been a source of frustration for Garrecht, Haney, Healy, and Stephens. At an entirely different level, the Hetch Hetchy litigation and the many other water-project cases decided by the Ninth Circuit demonstrated the important role of the court in deciding issues with direct effects on the cost, time-liness, and efficiency of these vast endeavors. If Hetch Hetchy serves as an example of the limits of judicial power to enforce court decisions, the other water project cases establish the court's significance in the development process.

At crucial junctures during the 1930s, the Ninth Circuit decided cases that had widespread regional effects. Sometimes these cases involved statutory interpretations that reached far beyond the immediate concerns of the litigants. At other times, the court's adjudication of program administration issues directly touched the lives of westerners. Even though it was riven by internal disagreements over the legality and constitutionality of key New Deal laws and was hampered by its own internal operating procedures, the Ninth Circuit played a substantial part in the government's response to the economic crisis. With a few noteworthy exceptions, the court's decisions upheld agricultural programs upon which thousands of western farmers relied, supported the federal government's efforts to collect taxes from recalcitrant businesses, upheld efforts by the National Labor Relations Board to stop anti-labor actions by companies, and balanced competing interests in the struggle to put scarce water resources to productive use. The personalities and judicial philosophies of the judges contribute to an understanding of the court's decisions in this era, just as the procedural rules of the court help to explain the seeming anomaly of one judge, Curtis Wilbur, being able periodically to thwart the wishes of the Democrats on the court. As the New Deal era came to a close in the late 1930s and the country braced itself for war, the internal operations of the court became the subject of an unprecedented public debate between two of the court's jurists over whether the Ninth Circuit should be divided.

TEN

A Court Too Large?

So while it is inevitable that the northern part of the circuit
will eventually be separated from the southern part, the time
is not yet here.

Judge William Denman, 1937

Splitting the Ninth Circuit is an old idea whose time has not
yet arrived.

Chief Judge Alfred T. Goodwin, 1990

The New Deal transformed the work of the Ninth Circuit. In prior
decades issues of railroad consolidation, Chinese immigration, mining
and natural resource development, and criminal appeals under war-
related and Prohibition statutes had constituted a large segment of the
court's docket. By the late 1930s and early 1940s, appeals raising issues
under Roosevelt's New Deal programs increasingly occupied the attention, not just of the Ninth Circuit, but of every federal circuit court of
appeals. At the same time that the nature of its docket was changing, the
Ninth Circuit as an institution was undergoing revision. The seven new
judges seated by 1937—Wilbur, Garrecht, Denman, Mathews, Haney,
Stephens, and Healy—each undoubtedly brought a new perspective to
the court, but the changes touched on a deeper concern: whether, within
the existing framework of court rules and procedures, a court of seven
members with a wide range of ideological and jurisprudential viewpoints could provide justice across the circuit's massive geographical
jurisdiction.

The issue of the Ninth Circuit's ideal size was a source of controversy
even before the Evarts Act of 1891 had created the circuit courts of
appeals. A year before that law's enactment, San Francisco attorney
Frank M. Stone had urged the Senate Judiciary Committee to reconsider
its configuration of the Ninth Circuit. Such a large circuit, Stone wrote,
"would be more than any one such court of appeals . . . could possibly

attend to without the business running behind, and the calendar becoming clogged, if such circuit judges attended to nothing but the appeals, and sat as a court of appeals." To emphasize his point, he enclosed a large map of the West with the proposed circuit boundaries marked. These concerns, however, had more to do with fears of administrative unwieldiness than with regional variations in the substance of the cases appealed to the court or fears that judges appointed from one part of the Ninth Circuit would be insensitive to the social and economic concerns of litigants in other parts of the circuit.[1]

In the first two decades of the twentieth century, for example, a southern California circuit judge, Erskine Ross, had more often than not succeeded in protecting Pacific Northwest lumber interests over the determined opposition of his Oregon colleague, William Gilbert.[2] But concern over efficient judicial administration persisted and, as the court's first half-century came to a close, sparked a contentious debate among Ninth Circuit judges over dividing the circuit.

I. DOCKET PRESSURES

Individual lawyers had been expressing concern for some time, but concerted debate over the ideal size of the Ninth Circuit did not begin in earnest until the 1930s. At the time, the burden of handling cases arising from the largest geographical land mass under the jurisdiction of any United States court, save the Supreme Court itself, stemmed primarily from the vast travel distances required of judges and litigants. Through 1939, when it ranked behind only the Second Circuit, the Ninth Circuit had stood comfortably amid the other circuits in the number of new cases filed each year, but in fact all the circuit courts of appeals had experienced significant growth in annual docketings. The Ninth Circuit itself reported an increase from 158 appeals filed in 1920 to 363 in 1935. The Eighth Circuit had exceeded the Ninth in total number of filings between 1900 and 1929, but in 1929 Congress divided the Eighth, and by the following year the new Eighth had five judges and the new Tenth had four. In comparison, the Ninth was severely shorthanded, with only three judges.[3]

During the 1920s a number of factors combined to increase the court's workload. One was the economic and population growth of the West. The clerk of the court, Paul O'Brien, reported that part of the court's burgeoning caseload was attributable to a 40 percent increase in immigration into the circuit between 1920 and 1930. From 1900 to 1930, the population in the Ninth Circuit's states grew from 3,204,752 to 10,131,325. The increase in the number of judges was not concomitant. Although the official number of authorized circuit judgeships remained at three in 1900 and 1930 (William Hunt's assignment from the moribund Commerce Court added a fourth seat between 1911 and 1928), the number of district judges in the circuit rose from eleven to twenty-eight.[4]

In addition to the natural growth in population and economic activity and the large number of Prohibition-related cases during this decade, another significant influence on the federal appellate judiciary's work-load came from the Judiciary Act of 1925. The movement to reform the Supreme Court's jurisdiction in the mid-1920s had to overcome many of the old misgivings that had accompanied the creation of the circuit courts of appeals in 1891. In the late 1880s many lawyers believed that litigants had a right to Supreme Court review to vindicate their federal claims. Lawyers initially resisted having the circuit courts of appeals effectively serve as courts of last resort when the Supreme Court denied certiorari, even when the cases raised no important national or consti-tutional issues. By the 1920s, however, distrust of the appellate court system had diminished, thanks to the effectiveness and efficiency of the circuit courts of appeals in handling a large number of cases that until the Evarts Act would have required Supreme Court review.[5]

Unburdened by the bar's previous resistance to conferring greater authority on the appellate tribunals to dispose of cases, Chief Justice Taft and his brethren promoted a bill that aimed to meet the Supreme Court's needs. The central goal of the "Judges' Bill," as it was appropriately nicknamed, was to preserve for Supreme Court review only those cases of national significance. In 1924, nearly one-third of the Court's docket consisted of mandatory appeals from district courts. A smaller but no less important source of work for the Court consisted of cases requiring mandatory review of certain decisions by circuit courts of appeals. From 1916 to 1925 the Supreme Court considered an average of forty such cases each year. The Judges' Bill proposed to end the Court's nondis-cretionary review of these latter cases. Virtually all cases disposed of by a circuit court of appeals would henceforth be reviewed only upon a writ of certiorari by the Supreme Court. In this manner the bill proposed to magnify the importance of the appellate courts' work. It would also increase the number of situations in which these courts would review district court decisions. Because the Supreme Court had more discretion under the 1925 law to decide which cases to hear, the circuit courts of appeals became in practical terms the tribunals of last resort for all but a small percentage of federal cases. The reform enabled the Supreme Court to regulate its caseload with relative ease, but the appellate courts had no such luxury. They became completely captive to the litigation tendencies of their regions; as litigation increased, so too did the dockets of the lower federal courts.[6]

By affecting review of cases from dependencies of the United States, the 1925 act had a significant direct effect on the Ninth Circuit. In the years leading up to the Judges' Bill Congress had enacted a wide array of laws that accorded miscellaneous review in the Supreme Court to cases arising in Hawaii, Alaska, Puerto Rico, the Philippines, the Panama Canal Zone, the Virgin Islands, and the United States Court in China. The 1925 act withdrew these varied avenues of review by the Supreme Court and distributed them to the appropriate circuit courts of appeals. For the Ninth Circuit, this reform involved accession of cases from Hawaii, Alaska, and the China Court.[7] And whereas economic, demographic, and jurisdictional influences theoretically would affect the circuits more or less equally, the Ninth Circuit was in practice hit particularly hard by the increase in cases. The longevity of Gilbert, Ross, and Morrow, which enabled the court to build a fine reputation in its early decades, gave way to the short tenures of judges under whom the court's docket fell increasingly in arrears and its reputation for quality work declined. The failed nomination of Wallace McCamant, the short terms of Frank Dietrich and William Sawtelle (three years each), and the untimely death of Frank Rudkin threw the court into a decade-long disarray from 1925 to 1935.

By the end of 1930, the state of affairs in the Ninth Circuit had reached crisis proportions: Dietrich had died in October, and Gilbert, senior judge of the court, was seriously ill. Shorthanded as it was, the court struggled to dispatch an ever-increasing caseload. The number of cases docketed in the Ninth Circuit totaled 307 in 1930, 327 in 1931, 378 in 1932, and 322 in 1933. In this same period, the number of cases pending at the end of the term grew from 99 in 1930 to 160 by 1933. The shortage of judges became particularly acute in 1934, when at the close of the fiscal year 220 cases were still awaiting decision. The appointment of new judges did not help ease the load until long after the end of 1935, when 257 cases remained undecided. In May of 1932, therefore, the California State Bar passed a resolution urging Congress to create a fourth judgeship on the Ninth Circuit.[8]

Legislation to increase the size of the court was not, however, immediately forthcoming. Congress did enact legislation in 1933 to reauthorize the Ninth Circuit seat that had lapsed with Judge William B. Gilbert's death. The death of Gilbert on April 27, 1931, was followed almost at once by Rudkin's death, on May 3, 1931. Three years later William H. Sawtelle died, leaving Wilbur and Garrecht alone to constitute the court, with two positions remaining to be filled. The senior judge, Wilbur, had only four years' experience; Garrecht, only one. With the number of cases in arrears steadily mounting, President Roosevelt attempted to fill these vacancies, but to no avail. His nomination of Judge Frank H. Norcross, of Carson City, Nevada, was never acted upon by the Senate. The judge who eventually filled this seat, which had once been held by Gilbert, was William Denman, who did not join the court until March of 1935.[9]

As the court limped along with this shortage in judicial personnel, it adopted expedient means of handling cases, the most controversial of which was the "one-judge decision." It is unclear when the court started this practice, but as the number of pending cases mounted, the court informally began to assign a case to a particular judge before oral argument. After the hearing, but before any conference was conducted, that judge prepared a complete and final opinion of the court without knowing what the other two members of the panel thought of the case. In his first year on the court William Denman prepared sixty-five such opinions. As he confessed to the Senate Judiciary Committee during hearings on more judgeships for the court, "I take no pride in them, I pray they are right, for in 90 percent of them we never had a conference. The opinion came back O.K.'d by the other judges, with whom the cases had not been discussed. That has been the practice of the court for six or seven years." The Ninth Circuit's senior judge, Curtis D. Wilbur, believed that the step was necessary if they were to attempt to keep up with the workload.[10]

A wide gulf existed between the Ninth Circuit's elimination of post-argument conferences and the Supreme Court's practice of full conferences on every case it heard. Wilbur maintained that application of the Supreme Court procedure, which was also generally followed in the Tenth Circuit, would cut the output of the Ninth Circuit roughly in half. Denman flatly rejected this view, but his colleague from Washington, Francis Garrecht, was ambivalent. Garrecht agreed with Denman that full conferences would promote better justice, but he also acknowledged the partial validity of Wilbur's contention that the court could not keep abreast of its work if it had a full conference after each case was heard.[11]

It is difficult to gauge the merit of Wilbur's view, given the modern practice of brief, post-argument conferences. The "one-judge decisions" somewhat speeded the handling of cases. The average time between submission of the appeal and the rendering of an opinion between 1926 and 1935 was 123 days, whereas during the first three decades of the court's history the average time of disposition fluctuated between 145 and 168 days. When the court reached its full complement of judges during the New Deal era, the Ninth Circuit judges averaged 70 days to render an opinion. Not only did the addition of more judges speed the actual decision-making process, the court's reversal rate in the Supreme Court also dropped. In 1942, when the court was at its full strength of seven judges, Denman wrote to Bert Haney regarding the difference in reversal rate between the "no conference" period and the "conference" period, which began again after the authorization of two additional judges in 1937. Taking two-year periods before and after, Denman reported that in the former, the court decided 416 cases and was reversed 21 times. In the latter, the court decided 876 cases and was reversed in 26; the reversal rate had dropped from 5 percent to 2.9 percent. This decline could not be attributed to the Supreme Court's general acceptance after 1937 of the constitutionality of the New Deal, since only a small fraction of the reversals involved such issues (3 of 21), with a like ratio in the latter period. Although these statistics did not compel specific conclusions, Denman pointed out that "in several conferences with the justices of the Supreme Court there has been comment upon the improvement in the character of the opinions of this court since we have had seven judges."[12]

II.   "DENMAN'S JUDGESHIPS"

By January, 1935, with two vacancies still remaining, Wilbur and Garrecht undoubtedly could not even begin to envision the seven-member court that would exist by 1937. Perhaps because he was still smarting from the skirmish over the Norcross nomination, Roosevelt had tarried in sending new names to the Senate. He finally nominated William Denman of San Francisco and Clifton Mathews of Phoenix. From the start, Denman worked tirelessly to improve judicial administration and add more judges to the Ninth Circuit. His third day in chambers had barely ended when he began his lobbying effort for more circuit judgeships. Citing the vast growth in docketings, Denman wrote to Roosevelt that four judges "cannot possibly discharge this volume of business.

Already the court is heavily in arrears and by the October term will be 300 cases behind its docketings." He pointedly spelled out the political implications: "The Bar is bitterly resentful, which is not helpful to the Administration. The resentment is justifiable, though, of course, its objective is not."[13]

By the summer of 1935, Roosevelt was able to respond that he was "in the throes of the problem and the bill will be signed in a week." Roosevelt made good on his promise, and Bert E. Haney of Oregon brought the court's strength up to five in September of 1935. Such lobbying success, especially by a new judge, would satisfy most people, but Denman was not yet content. In the face of what he later would describe bluntly as the "defeatist" attitude of Garrecht and Wilbur, Denman continued to push for more judgeships. Having failed to persuade his colleagues that it was in their interest to contribute funds, Denman traveled to Washington at his own expense to pressure Congress and the president.[14]

In March, 1936, Denman began to write Roosevelt with relentless regularity, and Roosevelt approved of his efforts. After one series of letters, Roosevelt replied that Denman should "[k]eep up the good work and keep my material up to date. I am getting all ready for a real speech on the subject. Legislation at this session is, I fear, out of the question but it is a fine objective and a fine platform." Denman employed numerous tactics to get the president's attention. In one letter he appealed to the president's sense of public accountability: once the Roosevelt administration had "adequately staffed the courts," he said, and "given them abundant funds under their own administration, just as with the Congress—you and the Congress can properly call them to account in the performance of their 'coordinate' constitutional function." Denman also raised the party issue, pointing out that 186 district, circuit, and Supreme Court jurists had been appointed since Wilson left office; only 14 of the 159 selected by Republican presidents were Democrats. (Twenty-seven judges had claimed no party affiliation, and Denman was quick to suggest that these "should be checked up by someone.") Denman strongly hinted that the president should lay the blame for the courts' backlogs on the Republican domination of the courts.[15]

Denman did not confine his lobbying to the president. He also wrote to Attorney General Homer Cummings, sending carbon copies to Roosevelt. He persuaded Senior Judge Curtis Wilbur to propound publicly the need for between twelve and fifteen new circuit court judgeships, an increase systemwide of 30 percent. Although Denman knew Wilbur did not expect him to succeed, he was not above trumpeting the senior judge's support in his letters to Roosevelt. He also convinced Garrecht to write a supportive letter to Representative Hatton W. Sumners, who chaired the House Judiciary Committee. And, lest Roosevelt uncharacteristically fear Republican opposition to the administration's quest for an expanded judiciary, Denman took the opportunity of Chief Justice Charles Evans Hughes's proposal for more judges to argue that this freed the president to pursue reform. In this election year, Denman had no doubt that Roosevelt would retain his office. He urged the president to think ahead: "[W]hat must be done in your next term! The need of the litigant for more judges will then be at its peak."[16]

This correspondence subsided briefly while Denman addressed the pile of opinions to be written from his first full term on the court. In letters to Wilbur and Haney at the end of June, 1936, Denman expressed his pleasure in distributing sixty-nine opinions during his first fiscal year, about forty of them during the second six months. To Haney he explained, "The reason I pressed through the number I have written is because I do not want some of the Congressmen to say, when I am lobbying for more judges at the next session, 'this fellow Denman is trying to shunt off to somebody else his own work, because he can't keep up with the procession.'" As soon as Roosevelt triumphed over Alf Landon in the 1936 election, Denman renewed his lobbying, prefacing his congratulatory missive with the curt statement, "The New Deal needs more Federal Judges." The letter surveyed a number of national and international problems before coming to the main point: "Hence, in my congratulations, I repeat it as a credo. More Judges." It is unclear whether Denman's "Dear Franklin" letters had any direct impact on the president. Roosevelt responded at intervals only with a brief note of encouragement. But even if these letters were limited in their effect, despite Denman's clever attempts to get them on the president's desk, the judge's testimony before Congress provided powerful evidence of the need for more judges.[17]

Testifying before a subcommittee of the Senate Judiciary Committee on February 24, 1937, Denman used both quantitative and qualitative arguments to establish the severe need for more Ninth Circuit judges. He noted, not only that the number of appeals to the court had doubled during the past fifteen years, but also that the cases had become increasingly complex. One outcome of the shortage was that southern California and Arizona, which provided 37 percent of the appeals to the Ninth Circuit, could not have a session of the court in Los Angeles.

Denman added that, in part because the state of California alone produced 59 percent of the Ninth Circuit's appeals, the California Bar
Association firmly backed reform efforts. In 1936, according to Denman,
it had passed a resolution calling on Congress to relieve the congestion
by appointing more judges.[18]

The problem had reached alarming proportions. One measure of the
Ninth Circuit's size was the enormous number of federal districts and
territorial supreme courts over which it had appellate jurisdiction. In
1937 the Ninth Circuit heard appeals from twenty-eight federal district
judges and the Hawaii Supreme Court: according to Denman, this was
double the average number of district judges of the other nine circuits and
one-third more than the circuit next in number of districts. In addition,
the court had jurisdiction over appeals from the United States Court for
China. Not only did the court preside over a large number of subordinate
tribunals, the states composing the Ninth Circuit enjoyed the highest rate
of population increase, and this growing population engaged in a vast
array of social and economic activities that bred litigation. The range of
issues requiring adjudication covered the spectrum of western development: agriculture, reclamation, gold dredging, lumber, Native American
issues, Hawaiian feudal law, petroleum, stock raising, irrigation, immigration, shipping, commercial fishing, electrical power, manufacturing
of all kinds, and community property. The number of judges on the court
had not begun to keep pace with the litigation produced by these social
and economic concerns. The near-doubling of the caseload between
1922 and 1937 with the addition of only one judgeship meant that each
jurist had to take on two-thirds more work.[19]

The hearing at which Denman gave this testimony concerned a bill
proposed by Senator Homer T. Bone of Washington to add two judges
to the court. Bone was later to be a key player in the struggle to divide
the circuit, a policy alternative Denman in 1937 believed to be inevitable.
"We need these two additional judges now," he testified. "Before long,
as I will later discuss, you will have to divide the circuit and have still
more judges." By 1941, when a serious proposal to split the circuit had
to be confronted, Denman changed his view. Nevertheless, the Ninth
Circuit's geographical size suggested two competing options: one, to
increase the number of judges on the court; the other, to divide the circuit,
as Congress had done with the Eighth. The latter alternative, however,
invariably required the authorization of more judgeships to ensure that
each of the new circuits would have at least three active judges. The
predominant issue, therefore, was whether administrative need justified

division. Denman did not think so. In 1937, when the threat of division
was low, he estimated the number of appeals from Washington, Oregon,
Montana, Idaho, and Alaska as 111 per year, which he did not deem
significant enough to warrant a split. Such numbers could not be padded
easily by alternate configurations, since a division of California—the
easiest way to balance the caseloads of the two proposed circuits—would
lead inevitably to conflicting interpretations of state law.[20]

Just as quantitative data supported the need for more judges, so too
did qualitative factors. The court sat predominantly in San Francisco,
although once per year it held a session of approximately ten days that
was divided between Seattle and Portland. Addition of two more judges
would enable the court to fix regular panels to sit in Los Angeles, San
Francisco, Portland, and Seattle, with Senior Judge Wilbur "sitting less
frequently than the rest, watching between the two groups to see that there
was no conflict of opinion." The addition would also rid the court of the
"unsatisfactory" situation of needing to use district judges to fill out
panels. The occasional use of district judges had not obviated the problem
of delay, but Denman carefully couched his criticism in administrative
terms. The district judge who sat by designation, he testified, "has to hurry
back to his crowded district. [He] has no library in his temporary chambers. He has no law clerk, nothing but a stenographer. He is not equipped
for that work. Our work as a supreme court is intensive and requires
permanent resident judges always ready for conference."[21]

Denman's testimony signaled a significant change in the practice of the
federal courts. Ever since two district judges had conducted the very first
argument session of the Ninth Circuit, district judges had participated
frequently in circuit court of appeals panels. In the first decade of the
twentieth century, when the court of Gilbert, Ross, and Morrow was at
the height of its powers, the use of district judges to complete appellate
panels ebbed somewhat, but it never ceased. As the caseload of the court
increased after World War I and the original corps of judges began to
retire, district judges again contributed mightily to the Ninth Circuit. By
the early 1930s, when the growth in filings combined with the shortage
of judges to produce a crisis of serious proportions, district judges
assisted Wilbur, Sawtelle (until his death in 1934), and Garrecht between
1931 and 1935. The addition of five new members to the court between
1935 and 1937 then subtly changed the nature of judicial functions.
Whereas in the Ninth Circuit's first two decades, circuit and district
judges routinely performed both trial and appellate duties, by the mid-
1930s they had become more specialized. Circuit judges heard virtually

all appeals in the Ninth Circuit without the assistance of district judges. And whereas Gilbert, Ross, and Morrow had sat frequently as trial judges until the end of 1911, when the old circuit courts were abolished, the circuit judges of the 1930s and 1940s almost never tried cases.[22]

If Denman's effort to secure two additional Ninth Circuit judgeships contributed to the transformation in judicial functions, he did not highlight that fact for Congress. Instead he presented the legislation as being mandated simply by administrative need. Denman approached his lobbying with an uncommon zeal undampened by his colleagues' lack of enthusiasm. Wilbur and Garrecht apparently doubted whether Congress would authorize the additional seats. They must have viewed Denman's lobbying as a waste of time and money. In a letter to Wilbur, Garrecht conceded that "all the judges here (four) agree that the volume of the court's business warrants an increase in the number of judges, but we are not agreed as to the method that we should follow in order to secure results." Denman attributed this position to "a defeatist feeling that they will not get attention and will not get relief." Indeed, Denman held Wilbur partly responsible for the court's urgent need for two more judges. In a typically direct letter to his colleagues on the court, Denman complained that "our Senior not only made no recommendation for relief to the Judicial Conference but actually joined in the Conference report (1934) that all was well with the Circuit Courts of Appeal." Denman's determination to see this reform through reflected a spirit that could easily cause offense but whose aims were generally admirable: "If I fail this time here I shall come on again and again, if necessary, if, as now, I can borrow, or, later have the money for the expense."[23]

Denman did not fail. Congress authorized the appointment of two additional Ninth Circuit judges in April of 1937. In a letter he wrote but did not send, Wilbur gave Denman sole credit for the bill's passage: "I think you realize that none of the judges here believed that Congress would pass legislation at this time for additional judges in this circuit and we all realize that it is wholly due to your efforts that you have gotten so far along with it. As you know, my view did not accord with yours in regard to the presentation of the matter to Congress but that question need not be discussed further at this time." Wilbur may well have decided not to send the letter because a later paragraph chided Denman's "continued absence" as an "embarrassment in regard to some of the cases under submission." With the authorization of two more judges, any backlog caused by Denman's lobbying was quickly dissipated. In two and one-half years, the Ninth Circuit had grown from two sitting judges to seven, becoming for the moment the largest circuit court of appeals.[24]

III. PROPOSALS TO DIVIDE THE NINTH CIRCUIT

The court benefited immediately from the added judgeships, which were assumed by Albert Lee Stephens and William Healy. In 1937, 332 cases were docketed, with 310 decided and 228 pending. Two years later, only 150 cases were pending, even though more were docketed in the meantime. Put another way, the court terminated 363 cases in 1938 and 352 in 1939. The slight drop in filings in 1938 and 1939, with 290 and 347 docketed respectively in those years, contributed to this increased efficiency.[25] A second benefit of the additional judgeships was less quantifiable. The court now was more representative of its geographical area: Francis Garrecht of Spokane, Bert Haney of Portland, and William Healy of Boise came from the northwestern quadrant of the circuit; Curtis Wilbur and William Denman provided the San Francisco perspective; and Clifton Mathews of Phoenix and Albert Lee Stephens of Los Angeles represented the southern tier. Of the non–San Francisco judges, only Healy and Mathews relocated to the court's Bay Area headquarters. With this geographical spread, the court was well positioned to handle hearings in a number of different locations without unduly disrupting the judges' lives.

Despite being well represented on the Ninth Circuit, litigants in the Pacific Northwest nevertheless felt aggrieved. A single annual session was shared between Portland and Seattle, and even that session was far from ideal. In 1938, the Seattle Bar Association formally petitioned Senior Judge Wilbur to assist in expediting completion of the new federal courthouse in Seattle. Such facilities would enable the court to sit there more often (without relying on temporary, inadequate chambers) with the sessions held "in rooms more appropriate, the existing courtrooms being so noisy that counsel and witnesses are heard with difficulty."[26] Completion of the new courthouse was to play an important role in heading off plans to split the Ninth Circuit, a proposal that Oregon United States Attorney Carl Donaugh had advanced in 1937.

Details of Donaugh's proposal are sketchy. Apparently at some point in 1937 he wrote to Attorney General Homer Cummings advocating division of the Ninth Circuit. When an assistant attorney general sent the Ninth Circuit judges a copy of Donaugh's letter, they protested hotly. In an unsigned report that bears all the indicia of Denman's authorship, the court launched a full broadside at the U.S. attorney's proposal, particularly for his failure to notify the judges and his use of erroneous data that inflated the need for a new circuit. This proposal threatened to undo the benefits of the added judgeships. According to the court's statement, each judge in the new Eleventh Circuit would have only 34.4 opinions each year to write, whereas the remaining four in the Ninth Circuit would have 77.5 each.[27]

As proponents of both sides of the issue collected data, devised arguments, and drafted legislation, builders were busy at work on courthouses in Los Angeles and Seattle. Completion of these new facilities in 1938 and 1939, respectively, would arguably have the greatest impact on the future success of proposals to split the circuit. These buildings ultimately enabled the judges to "ride circuit" more effectively in the fashion envisioned in the 1789 Judiciary Act for Supreme Court justices. The Seattle and Los Angeles courthouses would provide the judges with temporary chambers, library support, and courtrooms. Instead of placing the travel burdens and costs on most litigants, the government and its officers would contribute a greater share to the expense and hardship associated with travel to Ninth Circuit hearings. Although some attorneys in the Pacific Northwest were particularly restive in advocating creation of a new circuit, not surprisingly, perhaps, others opposed such efforts because of the attractions of spending a few days in San Francisco at clients' expense.[28]

The strongest effort to divide the court was made in 1940 by Judge Bert E. Haney. Apparently at the behest of some members of the Oregon bar, Haney issued a pamphlet from his chambers in October of 1940 advocating splitting the Ninth Circuit into two: one to consist of California, Nevada, Arizona, and Hawaii; the other to comprise Oregon, Washington, Idaho, Montana, and Alaska. Perhaps to insulate himself from criticism, Haney commissioned the pamphlet from his law clerk, Vernon J. Veron, and published it under the clerk's name.[29] This pamphlet served as the seed for bills proposed in Congress the following year.

Veron offered four reasons for dividing the circuit, each of which was to arouse rancorous debate. He first contended that the Ninth Circuit covered too large an area, one twice the size of the next biggest—the Tenth—and twenty-five times greater than the smallest—the First. The principal difficulty of the circuit's vast size was the travel cost and burden on litigants from the Pacific Northwest, 80 percent of whom had to journey as far as 1,800 miles round trip to argue in San Francisco before the court. Veron derived this fact from an estimate that only one-fifth of the cases that originated in the Pacific Northwest were heard in the annual sitting in Seattle and Portland.[30] The solution seemed obvious: to base a new circuit in Seattle, so litigants would not have far to travel.

Veron next maintained that the present seven-member court was unwieldy, since any two judges could theoretically bind the court to a particular view of the law even though the other five disagreed with it. Such a situation had already arisen in the case of *Lang v. Commissioner*. In *Lang*, a case raising an issue of estate tax determination, the panel of Denman, Mathews, and Healy disagreed with the controlling precedent established by an earlier case that had been decided by a split decision with Haney and Garrecht in the majority and Wilbur in dissent. Because *Lang* required application of this unpopular precedent, Denman's panel certified the question to the Supreme Court, out of a concern that a minority of two could bind the other five members of the court.[31] When the case returned to the Ninth Circuit, Denman explained that the 1891 statute establishing the circuit courts of appeals did not authorize sittings of panels greater than three judges.

> Any other interpretation of the [Evarts Act] would lead to grave difficulties of administration. If, because there are four or six circuit judges in a circuit, a four or six-judge court were deemed created by Congress, then each judge may well have the right and the duty to demand his place in the hearing on each appeal. This would lead to the embarrassment of an evenly divided court. More important still, it would increase so greatly the amount of work of each individual judge that it would cause again the arrearages which the additional judges have been created to remove.[32]

If Denman's fears appear quaint to modern observers accustomed to large *en banc* panels, the concerns of adequately administering the federal courts of appeals as they grow in size nonetheless seem to endure. Administrative concerns that in succeeding decades would become routine trifles seemingly presented fundamental questions to Judge Haney and his law clerk in 1940: "[W]ho should have authority to designate who shall and who shall not sit in any particular case? Who should have authority to determine when any particular judge should sit? Could all judges sit in one case at the same time?"[33]

A third reason for division cited by Veron was that three-judge courts impaired the Ninth Circuit's efficiency. Such courts were authorized in 1910 during the relative infancy of the circuit courts of appeals, when Congress was reluctant to vest full power in the appellate courts to pass on constitutional issues. Accordingly, Congress required a three-judge court, composed of one circuit judge and two district judges, to rule on interlocutory injunctions against enforcement of state statutes by state officers. Decisions made by this panel were appealable directly to the Supreme Court. In subsequent decades Congress expanded the courts' jurisdiction to include injunctions of administrative orders by an agency acting under a state statute, hearings on permanent as well as interlocutory injunctions, and challenges to the constitutionality of congressional legislation.[34]

As the situations calling for three-judge courts multiplied, so did the amount of time spent by judges traveling to hear these suits. Veron calculated that for each three-hour hearing attended by a three-judge court in the far-flung Ninth Circuit, the circuit judge had to travel between three and six days between the hearing site and San Francisco. These cases—an average of four per year—required over sixteen travel days annually. The solution proposed by Veron was, not to restrict the situations in which such courts were needed or to abolish them altogether, as Congress finally decided in 1976 for all cases except those concerning congressional district apportionment, but to split the circuit to decrease the distances traveled by circuit judges from a Seattle headquarters to the hearing site.[35]

Although the three-judge cases must have been an irritant to the circuit judges, the marginal utility of Veron's solution hardly justified dividing the circuit. He thus offered a fourth rationale: the increasing amount of litigation in the states that would compose the contemplated Eleventh Circuit. Unable to show a significant growth in the number of cases originating in the Pacific Northwest, however, Veron clung to the tenuous thesis that the region's people "are more litigious than others." He calculated that the proposed circuit would outrank eight others in per capita litigation. Even if the proposed new circuit's population would be lower than that of every other circuit, Vernon reasoned, "[i]t follows . . . that the per capita litigation displaces total population as a test." In any event, the base level of population and amount of litigation were "sufficient" to justify a split.[36]

Driving the proposal seemed to be disgruntlement among the bar and its clientele over the amount of travel required to litigate appeals in the Ninth Circuit. As the *Seattle Post-Intelligencer* editorialized, "Three members of the present ninth circuit were appointed from the Pacific Northwest and retain residences in its states. It is certainly more reasonable to ask them to establish permanent quarters in Seattle or in Portland than to require lawyers from this region to journey to San Francisco whenever a case is carried into the circuit courts." The Oregon

State Bar Association echoed these concerns, focusing on the "unduly large cost of litigation" for parties involved in Ninth Circuit appeals. At its meeting in October, 1940, the Oregon Bar passed a resolution calling for the division of the Ninth Circuit. The State Bar of Washington and the Board of Governors of the Montana Bar approved similar resolutions, but the Alaska Bar opposed division.[37]

Although the Ninth Circuit judges may have heard of these actions by the various state bars, they apparently did not yet know of Veron's pamphlet or of Haney's role in promoting division. Indeed, in June, 1941, at the Ninth Circuit Conference—the statutory venue for advising Congress on the ways and means of "improving the administration of justice" in each circuit—Haney had not said a word about splitting the circuit. Instead, he had circulated his pamphlet to lawyers and newspapers in the Pacific Northwest without sharing it with his colleagues. As Denman later complained, "Here is our friend sitting with us all these days, never telling us what is going on, and we find this situation." If Haney suffered any angst in deciding whether to distribute Veron's pamphlet among his colleagues, he apparently had none in sending it to Senator Homer T. Bone of Washington, who translated its policy directives into legislation.[38]

On July 28, 1941, Bone proposed a bill to divide the Ninth Circuit. The new Ninth Circuit would consist of the federal districts in California, Nevada, Hawaii, and Arizona. The new Eleventh Circuit would comprise the districts of Alaska, Idaho, Montana, Oregon, and Washington. The bill authorized the Ninth Circuit to sit in San Francisco and Los Angeles and the Eleventh Circuit to hear cases in Portland and Seattle. The bill assigned the existing Ninth Circuit judges to these respective circuits based on their current residency. Accordingly, Garrecht, Haney, and Healy would sit on the new Eleventh Circuit, and Wilbur, Denman, Mathews, and Stephens would remain Ninth Circuit judges. A similar bill was proposed in the House of Representatives by Warren Magnuson, also of Washington.[39]

IV. JUDICIAL OPPOSITION TO DIVISION

With the introduction of these bills, the debate over splitting the circuit left the realm of theory and entered a more overtly political phase. The *San Francisco Recorder* joined the discussion by observing that the number of cases docketed in the proposed new Ninth Circuit was double that of the proposed Eleventh Circuit. According to the newspaper, the three Eleventh Circuit judges would be responsible for approximately twenty-one opinions each, whereas the Ninth Circuit jurists would have to write fifty opinions each to keep the court current.[40] If the Bone bill passed, the new Ninth Circuit would experience a crunch like the one that had required authorization of more judges during the 1930s.

On August 12, 1941, the court issued an announcement that it hoped would derail the momentum building toward division. The judges published a new internal operating rule requiring an additional sitting in Seattle and Portland. Henceforth the court would conduct sittings in September and in March or April in those cities. The court thus hoped to remove "the most powerful argument" for dividing the circuit, the expense of traveling from the Pacific Northwest to San Francisco for hearings. It could no longer be accused of giving insufficient attention to the needs of that region's litigants. Significantly, every judge signed this internal operating rule amendment except Haney, who decried it as a rank political ploy: "Believing it to be apparent that the Court was being induced to officially enter the field of politics, I did not attend the meeting in San Francisco, and declined to sign the order mentioned."[41]

A week later, on August 20, 1941, Denman issued a lengthy pamphlet attacking Haney's proposal to split the circuit. With the attention to detail and analysis of relevant statistics for which he had undoubtedly become renowned on Capitol Hill, Denman proceeded to rebut the arguments in Veron's pamphlet point by point, exposing the "errors and omissions of fact which must have had a compelling influence on the members of the bar and the newspapers to whom they were given."[42] Denman began his dissertation by elucidating those features of the Ninth Circuit's administration of justice that made it different from other circuits:

> Unique among the circuits, (1) we have practically abolished terms of court by making the last day of the term the day before the beginning of the next; (2) the court sits in fifty of the fifty-two weeks of the year—the seven judges arranging their vacations so that this is possible. . . . (3) Unlike in some of the understaffed circuits, [it] is the fact that practically every case decided on the merits is upon written opinion, thus making certain for litigants the disciplined reasoning of its judges. . . . With the seven judges we now have the necessary judicial energy (4) to study our briefs before hearing; (5) to grant freely extended time to counsel for argument; (6) to give a true conference between bench and counsel in the course of the presentation of the appeal; (7) thereafter to have, before decision, a conference (and often conferences) in chambers of three fully prepared judges; (8) to assign the case for opinion

writing only after reaching a decision based upon such consideration; and (9) for the careful study by the other two judges of the final form of the opinion before it is handed down.[43]

From a high of 257 cases pending in 1935, the Ninth Circuit had steadily reduced its arrearage to 150 in 1939, two years after Stephens and Healy joined the court. By the end of the fiscal year, in June of 1941, the court had decided all but fourteen cases, and by the end of July only five were left. Having addressed its longstanding backlog of cases, the court could no longer be accused of being inefficient.[44]

With this preface, Denman began to dissect Veron's arguments. He observed that the principal concern articulated by advocates of the split—travel burdens—was no longer relevant. Adoption of the new rule meant that henceforth all Pacific Northwest litigants could argue their appeals in Portland or Seattle. Haney's complaint that this rule was a "political ploy" suggested that perhaps unarticulated intangibles, such as the Pacific Northwest's historic disdain of California domination, might be operating. Local bias was difficult to combat or rebut, and no one in this era was unseemly enough to suggest that prejudice justified reform. Haney's position on this issue was somewhat curious. It might be expected that he would approve the new rule both as a concession to the bars of the Northwest and as personally advantageous, but instead he opposed holding additional sittings outside San Francisco. He wrote that the value of such sessions was "too disproportionate to the cost in money and drain on the strength of the Judges."[45] He thus opposed excessive travel for both litigants *and* judges without proposing any alternative to division.

In the other judges' minds, the alleged need for a new circuit was based on decreasing litigants' travel burdens. Once that problem had been redressed, the question remained whether a division could be justified as an administrative matter. Caseload statistics and comparisons to other circuits became the focal point of the debate. Denman alleged that filings in the proposed Eleventh Circuit had actually decreased during the preceding three years. Dividing the last twelve years into four segments, Denman contended that the average number of appeals filed in these states had declined from 117 in 1930–1932 to 90 in the 1939–1941 period. Based on the last triennium, the Pacific Northwest Circuit's caseload would be minuscule, only 78 percent of the "greatly overstaffed" First Circuit, which ranked last among the circuits. Indeed, the "admitted excess of judge power [in the First Circuit] has led to repeated proposals to transfer to it two of the states of the adjoining" Second Circuit.[46]

Veron also had attempted to justify creation of a new circuit by contending that the number of cases generated in the region was equivalent to the average number filed during the entire Ninth Circuit's first two decades. This kind of appeal to history struck Denman as somewhat foolish. Not only did it ignore basic developments in transportation and communication that increased judicial efficiency, it also failed to acknowledge the tremendous amount of trial work that had been done by Ninth Circuit judges in the old circuit courts. According to Denman, the court's minutes from 1905 recorded that William Morrow had presided over 628 trials in circuit court and heard the appeals of another 122 cases in the circuit court of appeals.[47] By omitting mention of this double function, Veron greatly underestimated the judicial work of the circuit judges during the first two decades under the Evarts Act.

As a corollary to this caseload argument, Veron had calculated, by dividing the 250 working days each year by the 100 average cases likely to be heard in the new Eleventh Circuit, that each judge would have two and one-half days to consider a case and write an opinion on it. Denman made short work of this argument by noting that full judicial work would be required on fewer than 100 cases. Veron's analysis erred by anticipating that every case docketed mandated a full hearing and written opinion. Of these 100 cases, over 25 percent were disposed of by stipulation or dismissed without needing any expenditure of judicial effort. The proposed Eleventh Circuit would therefore actually have approximately 71 cases that required a hearing and an opinion. Denman did not even mention that the time necessary to dispose of a case was significantly less than two and one-half days when the judge was not responsible for writing the opinion. He also ridiculed the proposal by observing that if an eleventh circuit could be justified on the basis of 71 cases per year, the United States ought to have thirty-three circuit courts of appeals rather than just the ten in existence. Such a ratio of workload to personnel would require doubling the size of the judiciary. "At the risk of mauling the obvious," Denman added sardonically, "it may be remarked that such an addition of judicial power would cost $20,000 per judge or for 50 about $1 million per annum."[48]

If the caseload generated in the new circuit failed to justify division, there still remained the issue of the vast geographical area covered by the Ninth Circuit. Including the territories of Alaska and Hawaii, the Ninth Circuit embraced an area of 1,372,461 square miles. The next largest circuit, the Tenth, was only 41 percent as large. "All this seems irrelevant," Denman commented, "once we consider that with the sessions now provided in Portland and Seattle no litigant need travel any farther to have his case heard" in the proposed Eleventh Circuit "than he does in the present [N]inth."[49] By adjusting its internal rules to accommodate litigants' travel burdens, therefore, all the Ninth Circuit judges except Haney hoped to avert a division of the circuit.

The only arguments that remained arose from the alleged administrative difficulties encountered in the large circuit. In a typically drawn three-judge appellate panel, if two judges agreed on the law and the third dissented, the decision of two judges would bind four other judges who had not sat on the appeal and who might disagree with the panel majority. This problem, Denman suggested, did not arise in the Court of Appeal of Great Britain, where panels of two or three heard appeals. That court had twenty-five judges eligible to hear appeals, and Denman knew of no complaints about British justice arising from a pair of judges binding the entire Court of Appeal. Moreover, in his six years as circuit judge Denman could remember only one case in 1,200 in which a majority of the Ninth Circuit judges had formally complained about a decision by a two-member panel majority. In a sense, the San Francisco judge was being disingenuous in denying the existence of the problem that Veron had raised. If the New Deal cases were any guide, a majority on the Ninth Circuit had seemingly suffered in collective silence as the court's two most conservative judges—Wilbur and Mathews—were often able to hamstring the president's recovery program. Of course, one solution to this problem, which Congress had authorized and the court employed, was to certify the question to the Supreme Court.[50]

Another alternative, not discussed by Denman and Haney at the time, emerged in December, 1941, when the Supreme Court sanctioned *en banc* panels for circuit courts of appeals, thereby enabling all members of the court to sit in review of a case. In *Textile Mills Securities Corporation v. Commissioner*, the Supreme Court upheld the Third Circuit's use of an amendment to its internal rules by providing the option of *en banc* sittings in certain contexts. In *Lang v. Commissioner*, the Ninth Circuit had read the Judicial Code as precluding this option. The Supreme Court's decision to side with the Third Circuit's statutory interpretation by authorizing *en banc* sittings of the circuit courts of appeals would in time prove to be a major innovation in the federal court system. It enabled Congress to add circuit judgeships without fear that pockets of powerful minorities could bind majority members of the court through deviant panel decisions. When the Ninth Circuit heard its first appeal *en banc* in 1942, the judges of the court had little reason to know that this experiment would provide a source of stability and continuity in the circuit for more than three decades and that, as the numbers of judges grew greater still in the late 1970s, the procedures adopted for a limited *en banc* would themselves supply ammunition to both sides in the on-going debates over dividing the circuit.[51]

The Supreme Court's ratification of *en banc* hearings would directly address the Haney-Veron concern over intracircuit conflicts of opinion. The Ninth Circuit's adoption of the rule requiring an extra Northwest sitting had already ostensibly mitigated the issue of the burdens of travel. But the release of Denman's rebuttal pamphlet aroused media attention, bringing the debate between Haney and his San Francisco colleague to public view. On August 29, 1941, "Denman Criticizes Judge Haney" ran as a headline in the *San Francisco Chronicle*. The paper cited a letter Denman wrote to Senator Frederick Van Nuys, the chairman of the Senate Judiciary Committee, attacking the Haney-Veron analysis. A war of words ensued. The press surely placed the dispute in a more personally antagonistic light than the correspondence between Denman and Haney reveals. Nevertheless, the *Chronicle* reported that long-time court watchers "here do not recall a time" when one of the judges "took such a strong stand against a colleague as has Judge Denman." In his long legal career Denman rarely, if ever, backed down from a fight, and this controversy was no exception. Haney could be equally stubborn. Despite the adverse publicity in local newspapers, the two jurists continued to battle over the preservation of the existing Ninth Circuit.[52]

Meanwhile, the editorial positions of newspapers around the circuit suggested conflicting regional viewpoints. The *San Francisco Chronicle* wrote that Denman "took up the cudgel" against Haney's proposal. The *Portland Oregonian* quoted Haney as advocating a new Pacific Northwest circuit "'despite the illusory statements of my colleague, Judge William Denman, San Francisco.'" The *Seattle Post-Intelligencer* merely noted that the judges' disagreement over the proposal "was accentuated in Portland yesterday." All three newspapers, however, reported the statements issued by both chambers. Denman accused Haney of making "substantial errors" and being "misinformed" in his pamphlet advocating a new circuit. Haney was certainly entitled to advocate the "destruction of the historic Ninth Circuit," Denman conceded, but the Oregon judge should not be applauded for publishing erroneous statistics.[53]

The row escalated when the California State Bar held its annual meeting at Yosemite National Park in September of 1941. The Bar considered a resolution to disapprove the Bone and Magnuson bills "as legislation destructive of the service now rendered by the United States Court of Appeals for the Ninth Circuit, and creating an unnecessary Eleventh Circuit at an unwarranted cost to federal taxpayers." Denman and Haney received invitations to debate the issue at the meeting, but Haney politely declined. He was sitting in Portland beginning September 15 and feared that he would be unable to get to Yosemite in time. Haney did respond, however, to Denman's pamphlet in a letter to the State Bar. Denman's charge of statistical inaccuracy, particularly the allegation that Veron had overestimated the caseload in the Northwest, had stung. Haney contended that the numbers differed because Veron had analyzed a ten-year average given by the clerk of the Ninth Circuit, whereas Denman had broken down a twelve-year period into four three-year chunks. For reasons that no one seemed able to explain, the most recent three-year period showed a marked decrease in the caseload originating in the Pacific Northwestern states. Haney accused Denman of minimizing that region's litigation by emphasizing this statistically anomalous period when the ten-year average was 100.8 cases per year. This figure comported with the annual average in the twelve-year period chosen by Denman, which was 100.4 cases per year.[54]

Denman was present at the California State Bar Association meeting and spoke immediately after Haney's letter was read. He began with a trenchant point: "[T]his is not merely one judge disagreeing with another judge as to the destruction of the Circuit. It is six judges of the Circuit disagreeing with another judge. The other five will express their views before the Senate and the House Committees, that is if this bill ever comes up for consideration." Nor was Denman persuaded that the new rule requiring an additional sitting in the Northwest was a "political question," as Haney had asserted. To Denman, this rule demonstrated the court's accountability to Congress and the public for passage of the two-judge legislation in 1937. That assistance merited action by the court to improve service to litigants. Such an internal reform by the court should not be considered "politics," Denman continued, "unless you take politics in the broadest sense of the term and include the sometimes exceptional performance of the promises you give to legislators when they grant you legislation."[55]

Denman also adroitly handled Haney's contention that the new circuit would *hear* one hundred cases per year. Regardless of whether the average was ninety or one hundred docketings per year, a large number required no judicial action. Denman repeated the point he made in his pamphlet that approximately 25 percent of all docketings were dismissed or settled by stipulation without requiring any judicial action. The delegates to the California State Bar meeting were undoubtedly predisposed to resist division, but Denman's arguments did help to solidify this sentiment. A motion carried that the bar opposed the Bone and Magnuson bills. In language highly reminiscent of Denman's August pamphlet, the resolution proclaimed the unfair effects of division on the southern states remaining in the Ninth Circuit. The court "will be required either to accumulate heavy arrearages," it concluded, "or decide its cases without giving its litigants the full appellate process."[56]

The debates over splitting the Ninth Circuit publicly signaled for the first time the court's awareness of its own politics. The disagreements between Ross and Gilbert over natural resource cases earlier in the century had seemed almost as if they were occurring in an academic setting by contrast with the highly visible quarrel between Denman and Haney over dividing the Ninth Circuit. By the early 1940s, the judges' conceptions of the court had changed, as institutionally it had been subjected to numerous influences through its first half-century. No longer was the court a somewhat monastic institution in which virtually every decision about court administration was kept private. The Denman-Haney debates announced that the judges knew they were accountable to the public in dispatching their work in a timely and just manner.

Conclusion

The 1941 Judicial Conference expressed its disapproval of the Bone-Magnuson bills to split the Ninth Circuit and Congress took no further action, but the dispute would not die. Denman might well have thought that the proponents of splitting the circuit had lost their only champion on the court when Bert Haney died in 1943. Appointed to fill the vacancy, however, was Homer Truett Bone himself.

For the next five decades, proposals to split the Ninth Circuit arose periodically. In the early 1970s, Judge Ben. C. Duniway advocated dividing the circuit along lines similar to the Bone-Magnuson plan of the early 1940s, an idea sanctioned by the Hruska Commission on Revision of the Federal Court Appellate System, but the proposal lacked sufficient support. When, in 1978, the number of Ninth Circuit judgeships swelled from thirteen to twenty-three, discussion of splitting the circuit was revived. After the Fifth Circuit judges rejected the option of "limited" *en banc* panels composed of fewer than the total number of judges and then concluded that a "full" *en banc* was too unwieldy, they unanimously petitioned Congress to divide their circuit. Alone among the courts of appeals, the Ninth Circuit adopted a "limited" *en banc* procedure, wherein ten active judges drawn by lot joined the chief judge in a court to review the original three-member panel decision. During the early 1980s, a bill to split the Ninth Circuit received little support, but Senator Slade Gorton's proposal of the late 1980s and early 1990s was described by one scholar as "the most credible effort yet, as eight senators have joined as cosponsors."[1]

Consideration of the idea to divide the Ninth Circuit offers an opportunity to reflect on the court's role in its first fifty years, a common heritage for new Ninth and Twelfth Circuits should such legislation succeed. The judges who staffed the court until the 1930s were themselves pioneers who had made the long transcontinental trek or transoceanic voyage to the West. Appointed in the 1890s, the earliest judges were products of the Civil War era who had traveled westward from both sides of the Mason-Dixon line in search of greater opportunities. Even in the New Deal era, as the court expanded in size from three to seven judges, only three, Garrecht, Denman, and Haney, were native to the region. The individual experiences of the court's judges surely affected their approaches to judging—from the ex-Confederate soldier Ross's suspicion of exercises of national power to Garrecht's fervent support of New Deal recovery programs, forged in his earlier representation of farmer associations.

As the circuit courts of appeals established their proficiency in handling important matters, Congress enlarged their jurisdiction and broadened the Supreme Court's discretion to review cases, thus heightening still further the significance of the intermediate federal tribunals. The Ninth Circuit's evolving docket helps to document that transformation. The court's earliest cases established its regional importance in such matters as railroad development, Chinese immigration, and natural resource extraction. To this regional imprimatur the court added its constitutional voice in questions of law enforcement arising out of World War I–related and Prohibition-era appeals. By the days of the New Deal, this conjunction of roles had flowered completely, with the court considering both the constitutionality and the statutory application of a range of government programs.

In its first fifty years the court's work mirrored the prevailing concerns of the West. Despite the broad diversity of the vast region within the court's jurisdiction, many issues that arose in one section also affected others, often crossing the boundaries contemplated by a division of the circuit. The railroad and Chinese-exclusion issues of the 1890s, for example, touched California, Oregon, and Washington. The mining controversies of the early twentieth century stretched from Alaska to Arizona, taking in California, Nevada, Idaho, and Montana as well. Certainly lumber issues were concentrated in the Pacific Northwest, but the timber-cutters of northern California were no less interested in the court's decisions. The onset of World War I and Prohibition raised national concerns, but western states—especially Arizona, the northern district of California, and the western district of Washington—witnessed their most zealous enforcement. Labor controversies involving the Industrial Workers of the World erupted throughout the circuit, from Washington and Montana to California and Arizona. Finally, the New Deal era also demonstrated how key western issues transcended alternative circuit boundaries, from the common agricultural needs of farmers in Washington and California to the great water reclamation projects that transformed peoples' lives in nearly every Ninth Circuit state.

Along with these developments, the court itself was mirroring significant changes in the federal system. In its earliest years, a flexibility of roles marked the court, with circuit and district judges frequently sharing trial and appellate responsibilities. This flexibility essentially prevented any single judge or small group of judges from imposing a particular jurisprudential viewpoint on the rest of the court. The Chinese exclusion cases illustrate this phenomenon. Even though McKenna and Morrow had established their deep support for restrictions on Chinese immigrants, for example, they were unable to control the course of the court's doctrine, which provided occasional openings for the Chinese. Similarly, early in the twentieth century, as Ross and Gilbert began to disagree on numerous issues associated with natural resource development, the case reports reveal that they frequently sat on panels together, with the third judge drawn from the other circuit judges of the court or from district judges around the circuit. The existing records of the court do not disclose how panels were assigned, but the fact that Ross and Gilbert dissented from each other several hundred times in just a few decades suggests that they purposely limited their work as trial judges to concentrate on their appellate roles so that each might blunt the influence of the other in the establishment of Ninth Circuit precedent.

Consequently, what had begun as a rather fluid process of assigning judges to circuit court of appeals panels rigidified in the early twentieth century in the course of struggles over the substance of the court's work. But since the disputes were between only two of the judges, no significant administrative reform seemed called for, especially since the two so often sat together on appellate panels. By the 1920s, Ross and Gilbert were clearly aged warriors, in the judicial sense, but they had established an important administrative precedent for circuit judges to specialize as appellate judges. Their successors on the Ninth Circuit followed this lead, although the short tenures of most of them left the court in sufficient disarray that district judges frequently assisted by serving on appellate panels.

By the mid-1930s, Denman's energetic reform efforts had produced a court with seven circuit judges, more than ample for the Ninth Circuit's workload, and the need for district judges to serve on appellate panels ebbed. With the available pool from which to draw such panels effectively limited to seven, and with a deep ideological chasm between the court's most conservative member, Wilbur, and Garrecht, its most liberal, attention focused anew on administrative matters. As the assigning judge, Senior Judge Wilbur appeared to exercise his authority by often placing himself and Mathews, the most conservative of the Roosevelt appointees, on the panel together in the most politically charged cases. Thus, the Ninth Circuit was in the somewhat curious position of having a majority of judges who were deeply sympathetic to the New Deal often unable, because they were seldom assigned to such cases, to stop the conservative minority from thwarting the administration's program. In the course of the Haney-Denman debates over splitting the circuit, only one case was highlighted as an example of two judges subverting the will of the other five, but even a casual reader of the court's decisions in the New Deal era can find any number of examples in which Wilbur and Mathews agreed on the outcomes of cases in a manner flatly inconsistent with how a majority of the court's judges would have decided the case.

The debates over splitting the circuit thus helped to define the political sense of the Ninth Circuit as one in which substantive disagreements over cases had to be accommodated in a nonpartisan process of assigning judges to panels and of creating a mechanism to override the panel's decision if a majority of the judges desired to do so. Administrative evenhandedness thus became a major priority when heretofore the court had put very little emphasis on administration. The idea that a court would require a "fair" and "evenhanded" means of administration may hardly seem revolutionary, yet it is noteworthy that the Ninth Circuit existed for nearly fifty years before pressure built up for such a reform.

This growing politicization of the court occurred simultaneously, and arguably not coincidentally, with the growth in the court's power. At their inception, the circuit courts of appeals were a major experiment by Congress, which refused to vest in these intermediate tribunals jurisdiction over the most important cases. For the first few decades, the Ninth Circuit's work consisted primarily of Chinese immigration appeals, continuing issues associated with railroad land grants, and property disputes related to public lands over such issues as mining, timber, and oil extraction. These cases offered the court few opportunities to propound principles of lasting constitutional significance. But the competence evidenced by the circuit courts of appeals in these early decades encouraged Congress to shift an ever-growing range of cases to them through amendments to the Supreme Court's jurisdiction. Instead of providing for appeals of cases directly from district courts to the Supreme Court, Congress eventually routed almost all cases through the circuit courts of appeals and gave the Supreme Court discretionary jurisdiction to review their decisions.

Because of the nature of its work and the peculiarities of the region it served, the Ninth Circuit well illustrated the growing federalization of the law. From its earliest years, the court had been deciding such federal law cases of genuine regional significance as the Chinese-exclusion and *Stanford* cases. True, the Chinese cases arose out of the federal government's authority over immigration, but it is important to recognize that at the time the restrictive laws were perceived as necessary to protect domestic labor; that was the lens through which the Ninth Circuit judges saw their work. The vast public lands in the Ninth Circuit, and the congressional acts that regulated them, provided a major source of cases for the court in the late nineteenth and early twentieth centuries. Because of the way extractive enterprises arose in the West, federal involvement in economic development was common and expected, as was the place of the federal courts in dispute resolution. Similarly, when war- and Prohibition-related issues came to dominate the court's docket in the late 1910s and 1920s, the incursion of federal action into local affairs became quite prominent. Thus, the federalization of law and the increasing importance of federal courts to development were established, at least in the West, long before the New Deal.

This increasing federalization of the law placed a central emphasis on the court's handling of its administration. As the range of issues subject to the Supreme Court's discretionary review increased, so too did the importance of the circuit courts of appeals. By the time Wilbur and Garrecht were clashing over the interpretation and application of federal statutes to westerners during the New Deal era, the stakes had become high. Inherent limitations on the Supreme Court's workload prevented it from reviewing all but the most noteworthy cases emanating from the lower federal courts, and it was unlikely to review cases involving issues of statutory interpretation unless a conflict developed among the courts of appeals. Therefore the substantive disagreements between the circuit judges had significant consequences for westerners, because the Ninth Circuit had become functionally the court of last resort in all but a small percentage of the cases it heard.

Until the construction in the 1930s and 1940s of courthouses through-out the West facilitated greater "circuit riding" by the judges, the court's San Francisco headquarters remained the focal point of the Ninth Circuit. Even in succeeding decades, when most of the court's judges kept their chambers outside the Bay Area, the building at Seventh and Mission served as the nerve center for the country's largest federal appellate court. Massive damage to the court's headquarters in the 1989 Loma Prieta earthquake, however, gave rise to numerous proposals, several of which were sensitive to the issues of division and administration. One recom-mendation was that the courthouse be repaired and a tower be built to rise out of the middle area that had long been used as a sorting room for the Post Office. A judge suggested that this addition be called the Bone Tower.[2] Only those who knew the story of Homer Bone's attempt to split the circuit caught the irony of the idea. The suggestion was more than ironic, however; it also reflected the importance of recognizing regional influences that had contributed to the court's history.

Tower or no, the issues surrounding repair of the San Francisco courthouse fueled speculation that the court's headquarters would be moved to the Los Angeles area. Some southern judges pressed for this option, and one judge believed that such a transfer would eventually lead to the splitting of the circuit.[3] In this view, San Francisco's position in the approximate center of the circuit perhaps looms large for preserving the original boundaries of the court. Nor is it just a question of geog-raphy. Historically San Francisco has served as a gateway for arriving immigrants and a meeting point for commerce throughout the West. It has also been a symbolic balancing point between the attitudes of the northern and the southern tiers of the circuit.

No court could effectively exercise its power from the Arctic Circle to the tropics without developing some sensitivity to the historical concerns and traditions of a multitude of groups in between. The con-tinuing conflict over the boundaries of the Ninth Circuit reflects the need to understand the respective legal and economic interests of the states in the circuit. In its first fifty years, the circuit court of appeals for the Ninth Circuit evolved institutionally as the changing circumstances of regional development produced issues for the court to resolve and opportunities for it to place an enduring mark on the West.

Ninth Circuit Statistical Study

During research on this book, I conducted a statistical study on the Ninth Circuit's docket. The data came from two sources: the official docket books of the court, and the annual reports of the attorney general. In the notes, information on case filings from the Attorney General Reports is indicated. The docket book study attempted to code and classify information about the nature of the Ninth Circuit's caseload. I went through every fifth case docketed in the court from 1891 through roughly 1942, when I reached No. 10,000. This sample of 2,000, I believed, would be statistically representative of the court's docket.

From the clerk's docket book I coded the parties, noting, for example, whether the party was an individual, a corporation (and, if so, whether it seemed readily identifiable by name, e.g., Alaska Gold Mining Company), the United States, some other governmental entity or a res (such as a ship in admiralty cases). I inserted the dates of docketing, argument and submission, and decision rendered, to gauge the length of the appellate process. The docket sheets described the procedural type of action and the disposition, so I included that data too. Beginning in the 1930s, the clerk began to note the subject matter of the appeal in the docket book. These notations were very general, such as "Bankruptcy." I included the categories by type (and coded them) for the years they were available.

The purpose of the study was to obtain what I hoped would be information useful in the writing of this book. I am not a statistician, and I did not intend this study to be a major component of my work on the court's history. This caveat made, others may find the data of interest. Accordingly, I have deposited the study with the Ninth Circuit library to make it available to the court and researchers.

Notes

The notes that follow include every source I found useful in writing this book; they exclude additional sources I examined but found unhelpful. Sources for each point or issue of interest are clustered at that point in the discussion. My aim in adopting this format was to provide the most accessible form of reference for researchers. To avoid cluttering the text with numerous note references, I consolidated the notes, placing in sequence the sources upon which I relied for the information in that paragraph. This may force the researcher to look up an extra source or two to find out more about an issue I mentioned only in passing, but it should prove less jarring for the many readers who have no interest in further research.

I have used asterisks to indicate sources I quote directly, when the source of the quotation is not obvious from the cited reference. Materials marked with an asterisk are given in the order in which they are quoted in the text, the only exception being multiple quotations from the same page of a source.

INTRODUCTION

1. Act of Mar. 3, 1891, ch. 517, 26 Stat. 826; *San Francisco Chronicle*, June 17, 1891, at *12, col. 3.

2. *San Francisco Chronicle*, June 17, 1891, at *12, col. 3. *See* R. Solomon, *History of the Seventh Circuit, 1891–1941*, at 24–25 (1981).

3. 1 Minutes of the United States Circuit Court of Appeals for the Ninth Circuit *1–2, *5 (June 16, 1891) (hereinafter Ninth Circuit Minutes). Field also announced the appointment of the court's first clerk, Frank D. Monckton, as well as sureties of the court, who were Monckton, as principal, and Thomas B. Hayer, Joseph Nash, and John C. Franks (*id.* at 2). According to his biographer, Field wrote 620 opinions for the Supreme Court and 57 for the circuit court and circuit court of appeals in his more than thirty years on the bench; the latter figure comes

to fewer than two per year (C. Swisher, *Stephen J. Field: Craftsman of the Law* 445 [1930; reprint 1969]). Act of Mar. 3, 1891, ch. 517, § 1, 26 Stat. 826, 826. The statute provided that "one or more district judges within the circuit shall be competent to sit in the court according to such order or provision among the district judges as either by general or particular assignment shall be designated by the court" (*id.* § 3, 26 Stat. at 827).

4. *San Francisco Chronicle*, June 17, 1891, at *12, cols. 3–4. The following week, on June 22, 1891, Field, Sawyer, and Deady convened to agree on the new court's rules. The Evarts Act provided that each court "shall have power to establish all rules and regulations for the conduct of the business of the court within its jurisdiction as conferred by law" (Act of Mar. 3, 1891, § 2, 26 Stat. at 827). The judges decreed that the Ninth Circuit's term would be held annually in San Francisco beginning on the first Monday of October of each year, but the term was regarded as a continuing one and the court could, upon notice to parties, be held at any time during the year. The court also announced that it would meet at San Francisco on the first Monday in January, April, and July of each year and that a calendar of cases pending should be made by the clerk to be called for hearing on those days. Finally, the court directed that when it was necessary to summon district judges to constitute a quorum of the circuit court of appeals, those judges would be enlisted by seniority. The court also directed the appointment of a marshal, a crier, and a messenger. *See id.* at 6–7.

5. It is true that the act also defined "circuits" consisting of state groupings, but the circuit courts were tribunals with the same territorial jurisdiction as the district courts. Act of Sept. 24, 1789, ch. 20, 1 Stat. 73; Act of Mar. 3, 1875, § 1, 18 Stat. 470.

6. Act of Mar. 3, 1891, ch. 517, 26 Stat. 826; Act of July 3, 1890, ch. 656, § 16, 26 Stat. 215, 217; Act of Feb. 22, 1889, ch. 180, § 23, 25 Stat. 676, 683; Act of June 20, 1910, ch. 310, § 31, 36 Stat. 557, 576; Act of Mar. 3, 1911, ch. 231, §§ 116, 133, 36 Stat. 1087, 1131–34; Organic Act of Guam, Pub. L. 81-630, § 23, 64 Stat. 384, 390 (1950); Act of Mar. 24, 1976, Pub. L. 94-241, § 401, 90 Stat. 263, 266. Little has been written about the United States Court for China, and even less about the Ninth Circuit's review of its decisions. Because the issues the Ninth Circuit reviewed from this extraterritorial court fall outside the themes developed in this book, an examination of this fascinating facet of the court's jurisprudence must be left for another day. For an introduction to the China court, see Lobingier, "A Quarter Century of Our Extraterritorial Court," 20 Geo. L.J. 427 (1932); Loring, "American Extraterritoriality in China," 10 Minn. L. Rev. 407 (1926); Note, "The United States Court for China," 49 Harv. L. Rev. 793 (1936).

7. *See*, e.g., 1 B. Ackerman, *We the People: Foundations* 105 (1991); W. Murphy, J. Fleming, and W. Harris, *American Constitutional Interpretation* 402–4 (1986); R. McCloskey, *The American Supreme Court* 145–69 (1960); Corwin, "The Passing of Dual Federalism," 36 Va. L. Rev. 1, 17 (1950).

1. ORIGINS AND EARLY YEARS

1. U.S. Const. art. III, *§ 1. *See* Act of Sept. 24, 1789, ch. 20, 1 Stat. 73. Massachusetts and Virginia were divided into two districts each to cover addi-

tional territory that eventually became Maine and Kentucky, respectively. Rhode Island and North Carolina were not included in the 1789 Judiciary Act. Circuit courts also had original jurisdiction over certain other civil and criminal actions (*id.* §§ 2, 4, 9, 11, 1 Stat. at 73–79).

2. Act of Mar. 3, 1911, ch. 231, § 301, 36 Stat. 1087, 1169. In practice, circuit and district courts had original jurisdiction over different types of actions. Over time, however, Congress vested overlapping original jurisdiction in these courts. *See generally* B. Curtis, *Jurisdiction, Practice, and Peculiar Jurisprudence of the Courts of the United States* (2d rev. ed. 1896).

3. *See* 2 M. Marcus, ed., *The Documentary History of the Supreme Court of the United States, 1789–1800: The Justices on Circuit, 1790–1794* (1988); 3 M. Marcus, ed., *The Documentary History of the Supreme Court of the United States, 1789–1800: The Justices on Circuit, 1795–1800* (1990). Act of Feb. 13, 1801, 2 Stat. 89 (1801). By this time Congress had already abandoned the two-justice requirement for circuit duty and had provided instead for one justice and one district judge to sit as the circuit court (Act of Mar. 2, 1793, ch. 22, 1 Stat. 333; Act of Feb. 13, 1801, §§ 6–7, 2 Stat. 89, 90).

4. Act of Mar. 8, 1802, ch. 8, 2 Stat. 132; Act of Apr. 29, 1802, ch. 31, §§ 1, 4, 2 Stat. 156, 157. *See* G. Haskins and H. Johnson, *Foundations of Power: John Marshall, 1801–15*, 2 The Oliver Wendell Holmes Devise, *History of the Supreme Court of the United States* 163–80 (1981). The Adams-appointed circuit judges themselves declined to challenge the 1802 annulment of their stations. A justice of the peace named William Marbury, appointed under a comparable act, did bring suit, and the anti-Federalists anticipated that a Supreme Court decision holding that statute unconstitutional would provide grounds for impeachment of the Supreme Court justices. For a highly readable account of this interesting episode by a later Supreme Court justice, *see* Burton, "The Cornerstone of Constitutional Law: The Extraordinary Case of *Marbury v. Madison*," 36 A.B.A. J. 805 (1950). The avoidance by the justices of circuit-riding occurred over time. Professor Charles Fairman writes of the "imperfect compliance" by the justices of circuit duty (C. Fairman, *Reconstruction and Reunion, 1864–88: Part Two*, 7 The Oliver Wendell Holmes Devise, *History of the Supreme Court of the United States* 372 [1987]). Edwin Surrency reports that "by the end of the Civil War it must have been the exception for a justice to preside in the circuit court" (E. Surrency, *History of the Federal Courts* 32 [1987]). From an early date, justices apparently did not regularly attend circuit court in all the states of their respective circuits (*see id.* at 30–31). The 1802 Act, however, provided that a district judge could hold circuit court in the absence of a justice (Act of Apr. 29, 1802, ch. 31, § 4, 2 Stat. 156, 158). Over the years, Congress gradually loosened the attendance requirement of justices at circuit court (*see* Act of Mar. 10, 1838, ch. 33, 5 Stat. 215, requiring the justice to attend at least one term annually in the newly reorganized Seventh Circuit; Act of June 17, 1844, ch. 96, § 2, 5 Stat. 676, 676, extending this rule to all other circuits; Act of Apr. 10, 1869, ch. 22, § 4, 16 Stat. 44, 45, requiring attendance at one term every two years). *See generally* K. Turner, "The Judiciary Act of 1801" (Univ. of Wisconsin diss. 1961).

5. Hill, "The Federal Judicial System," 12 A.B.A. Rep. 289, *302 (1889). Act of Mar. 2, 1855, ch. 142, 10 Stat. 631. Congress had earlier provided for

district courts in California by the Act of Sept. 28, 1850, 9 Stat. 521. By this time Congress had also established nine numbered circuits (Act of Mar. 3, 1837, ch. 34, 5 Stat. 176). C. Fritz, *Federal Justice in California: The Court of Ogden Hoffman, 1851–1891*, at 30–33 (1991).

6. For brief biographical material on Judge McAllister, see J. Gordan, *Authorized by No Law: The San Francisco Committee of Vigilance of 1856 and the United States Circuit Court for the District of California* 5–7 (1987); 6 D. Malone, ed., *Dictionary of American Biography* 546–47 (1933); *Who Was Who in America: Historical Volume, 1607–1896*, at 342 (1963); Watson, "The San Francisco McAllisters," 11 Cal. Hist. Soc. Q. 124 (1932); "Matthew Hall McAllister," 30 Fed. Cas. 1383 (1897).

7. For more on the nature of the circuit court docket during McAllister's tenure, see J. Gordan, *supra* note 6; 1 *McAllister's Reports of Cases Argued and Determined in the Circuit Court of the United States for the District of California* (1859). *San Francisco Daily Herald*, Feb. 23, 1855, at 1, col. 3; *id.*, Mar. 10, 1855, at 1, col. 1; *id.*, Mar. 18, 1855, at 1, col. 1. C. Swisher, *Stephen J. Field: Craftsman of the Law* 114–16 (1930; reprint 1969).

8. The most celebrated of these cases, *The Prize Cases*, was a five-to-four decision upholding the legality of the North's blockade of the South (*The Prize Cases*, 67 U.S. 635 [1863]). This decision was handed down on March 10, 1863. The week before, Congress had created the tenth justiceship (Act of Mar. 3, 1863, ch. 100, 12 Stat. 794). For more on the history of the *Prize Cases*, see C. Swisher, *The Taney Period*, 5 The Oliver Wendell Holmes Devise, *History of the Supreme Court of the United States* 877–900 (1974).

9. S. Field, *Personal Reminiscences of Early Days in California* *115 (1893; reprint 1968). Act of March 3, 1863, ch. 100, §§ 1, 2, 12 Stat. 794. C. Fritz, *supra* note 5, at 34–35. There is some evidence that the tenth justiceship was intended to be a more exalted circuit judge position (*see* E. Surrency, *supra* note 4, at 46, noting that the statute authorizing the tenth justiceship provided for payment of $1,000 "for his travelling expenses for each year in which he may actually attend a session of the supreme court of the United States" [quoting Act of Mar. 3, 1863, ch. 100, § 5, 12 Stat. 794, 795]; and newspapers cited in *supra* note 7). After Field was sworn in as associate justice in Sacramento, he proceeded to San Francisco to hold circuit court (C. Swisher, *supra* note 7, at 118–19). For more on Field generally and on the development of his jurisprudence, see McCurdy, "Stephen J. Field and the American Judicial Tradition," in *The Fields and the Law* 5–18 (1986).

10. Act of July 23, 1866, ch. 210, 14 Stat. 209. Act of Mar. 3, 1863, ch. 100, 12 Stat. 794. Administratively, Nevada's federal courts were closely linked to those of California and Oregon (*see* Act of Feb. 27, 1865, ch. 64, § 7, 13 Stat. 440, 440–41). The 1801 Act authorized three circuit judges for each circuit except the Sixth (*see* Act of Feb. 13, 1801, 2 Stat. 89). Act of Apr. 10, 1869, § 4, ch. 22, 16 Stat. 44, 45. *See also* 6 Op. Atty. Gen. 271 (1854), advocating the system Congress enacted in 1869.

11. Historians of the federal courts have struggled to learn precisely how often justices rode circuit, but with little success (*see*, e.g., Surrency, "Federal District Court Judges and the History of Their Courts," 40 F.R.D. 139, 144

[1967]; C. Swisher, *supra* note 7, at 121, noting that Field rented rooms in Washington each fall "when he returned from the long trip to the Pacific Coast, where he spent some months holding court"). But in 1870 Field established a home in Washington, and it is likely that his trips to California thereafter became less frequent (*see id.*, at 121).

12. *See* 17 Sen. Exec. J. 335 (1870), available at National Archives, Washington, D.C. For an interesting discussion of the appointment process leading up to Sawyer's nomination, see C. Fritz, *supra* note 5, at 42–47. For general biographical information on Sawyer, see O. Shuck, *Bench and Bar in California* 66 (1889); 8 D. Malone, ed., *Dictionary of American Biography* 395–96 (1935); L. Sawyer, *Way Sketches* 13–16 (1926).

13. L. Sawyer, *supra* note 12, at *14, *120. *See also* C. Fritz, *supra* note 5, at 42; 8 D. Malone, ed., *supra* note 12, at 395–96.

14. Act of Apr. 9, 1866, ch. 31, 14 Stat. 27; Act of May 31, 1870, ch. 114, 16 Stat. 140; Act of Feb. 28, 1871, ch. 99, 16 Stat. 433; Act of Mar. 1, 1875, ch. 114, 18 Stat. 335.

15. *See* Act of Mar. 3, 1863, ch. 81, § 5, 12 Stat. 755, 756; *see also* Act of May 11, 1866, ch. 80, §§ 3–4, 14 Stat. 46, 46. The Act of Feb. 5, 1867, ch. 27, 14 Stat. 385, authorized habeas corpus removals when the defendant was in the actual custody of state officials under state process. Act of Mar. 3, 1875, ch. 137, 18 Stat. 470. Until this time, a person had to assert most federal rights through state courts and appeal to the Supreme Court for the full vindication of federal rights in a federal tribunal (C. Wright, *The Law of Federal Courts* 209, 219–20 [4th ed. 1983]). On the floor debate, *see*, e.g., 2 Cong. Rec. 4301–4 (1874). *See generally* F. Frankfurter and J. Landis, *The Business of the Supreme Court* 61–64, *64 (1928).

16. On the South's economic state after the Civil War in comparison to the rest of the country's, see E. Foner, *Reconstruction: America's Unfinished Revolution, 1863–1877*, at 392 (1988). F. Frankfurter and J. Landis, *supra* note 15, at 57–60. Population during the period from 1860 to 1890 doubled, from 31,443,321 to 62,947,714. 1 U.S. Bureau of the Census, *Historical Statistics of the United States* 8 (1975).

17. McCrary, "Needs of the Federal Judiciary," 13 Cent. L.J. 167, 168 (1881); Hill, *supra* note 5, at 304. Hill did not state which four years he analyzed.

18. F. Frankfurter and J. Landis, *supra* note 15, at 91–93. One expression of these states' concerns was articulated by Samuel Moulton of Illinois in the House of Representatives (*see* 15 Cong. Rec. App. 286–87 [1884]; *see also* 22 Cong. Rec. App. 249 [1891], Alabama Representative William Oates urging a restriction in federal jurisdiction so that more suits then filed in federal courts would be heard by state courts).

19. A short note cannot do this story justice. While riding circuit, Field had ordered a Mr. and Mrs. Terry to jail for contempt of court in a highly contentious divorce proceeding involving the late William Sharon, who had been one of the richest men in the West. Mrs. Terry, the former Sarah Hill, claimed to have been married to Sharon. When the circuit court per Field and Sawyer rejected her various contentions, she and her new husband settled on a violent revenge. After being released from jail, Mr. and Mrs. Terry encountered Field at a train station

not far from Fresno. Mr. Terry allegedly assaulted the justice, and in the ensuing scuffle, U.S. Marshal David Neagle shot Terry dead. *See* C. Swisher, *supra* note 7, at 321–61; R. Kroninger, *Sarah and the Senator* (1964).

20. *See* C. Fritz, *supra* note 5, at 39–48; C. Fritz, "A Nineteenth Century 'Habeas Corpus Mill': The Chinese Before the Federal Courts in California," 32 Am. J. Leg. Hist. 347, 348–51 (1988). On the circuit-riding situation in the Eighth and Ninth Circuits, see 1890 Att'y Gen. Ann. Rep. xviii.

21. 2 U.S. Bureau of the Census, *supra* note 16, at 1083. F. Frankfurter and J. Landis, *supra* note 15, at 88–89.

22. 1885 Att'y Gen. Ann. Rep. 37–39. Garland excluded bankruptcy appeals from this blueprint (*id*. Act of Mar. 3, 1887, ch. 359, 24 Stat. 505). By this act district courts were given concurrent jurisdiction with the court of claims in cases raising claims against the United States where the amount in controversy did not exceed $1,000, and the circuit courts were given concurrent jurisdiction if the claim was greater than $1,000 but less than $10,000. The effect of this act was large. In the years 1887 to 1892, the attorney general reported that 922 cases were brought under it in the district and circuit courts, 22 of which went on to the Supreme Court (*see* 1892 Att'y Gen. Ann. Rep. 10–11).

23. 21 Cong. Rec. 3402–3, 3049 (1890). *See* Budd, "The United States Circuit Courts of Appeals," 9 L. Q. Rev. 51, 56 (1893).

24. 21 Cong. Rec. 8133 (1890). *See* F. Frankfurter and J. Landis, *supra* note 15, at 99–100. *See* 21 Cong. Rec. 10218 (1890). The issues Congress made appealable directly from district or circuit courts to the Supreme Court under this proposal included questions involving the Constitution, jurisdiction, criminal matters involving the death penalty, prize cases, and constitutional challenges to state laws (*id*.). The bill made justices "competent" to sit as circuit judges but did not require such service (*id*.). This provision is embodied in the Act of Mar. 3, 1891, ch. 517, § 3, 26 Stat. 826, 827.

25. Act of Mar. 3, 1891, ch. 517, 26 Stat. 826. 1898 Att'y Gen. Ann. Rep. v. 1897 Att'y Gen. Ann. Rep. *xv.

26. Deady died on March 24, 1893; Field, April 9, 1899. For more on Deady, see M. Clark, ed., *Pharisee Among Philistines: The Diary of Judge Matthew Deady, 1871–1892* (1975).

27. A number of letters in the appointment file of William B. Gilbert express this sentiment. The question was, Which person from the two states would receive President Harrison's nomination? (See File of William B. Gilbert, Department of Justice Appointment Files, Ninth Circuit, 1855–1901, Tray 1, RG 60, National Archives, Washington, D.C. [hereinafter Gilbert Appointment File]).

28. One biographer asserts that anti-Catholicism was the key reason for McKenna's electoral defeats (T. Campbell, *Four Score Forgotten Men* 304 [1950]). This appears to have been McKenna's own perception, which another biographer does not believe to have been well founded (McDevitt, "Joseph McKenna" 41–42 [Ph.D. diss. Catholic University of America, 1946]. 6 D. Malone, *supra* note 6, at 87–88; "Joseph McKenna," 30 Fed. Cas. 1384 (1897); O. Shuck, *History of the Bench and Bar of California* 653 (1901).

29. O. Shuck, *supra* note 28, at 654. *See San Francisco Examiner*, Dec. 4, 1897, at 1, col. 6; McDevitt, *supra* note 28, at 80. Several decisions that McKenna wrote or joined evidenced his impartiality with respect to the railroad: *see*, e.g., *Southern Pac. Co. v. Lafferty*, 57 F. 536 (9th Cir. 1893); *Southern Pac. Co. v. City of Oakland*, 58 F. 50 (9th Cir. 1893). *See* 6 D. Malone, *supra* note 6, at 88.

30. For biographical sketches of Gilbert, see "In Memoriam: Hon. William B. Gilbert," 52 F.2d xxxi (1931); "William B. Gilbert," 30 Fed. Cas. 1374 (1897); *Judges of the United States* 182 (2d ed. 1983).

31. For the letters in this episode, see Gilbert Appointment File, especially *Wallace McCamant to Attorney General W. H. Miller, Jan. 29, 1892; Zera Snow to Senator J. N. Dolph, Jan. 30, 1892. On Gilbert's confirmation, see 28 Sen. Exec. J. 188 (1892), available at National Archives, Washington, D.C.

32. For more on the McCamant episode, see *infra* Chapter Six.

33. *See generally* "In Memoriam," *supra* note 30, at xxxi. Eighth Circuit Judge Walter H. Sanborn received his commission on March 17, 1892, thus giving him a day's seniority over Gilbert. Sanborn served until his death on May 10, 1928. On Sanborn, see Senate Judiciary Committee, "Legislative History of the United States Circuit Courts of Appeals and the Judges Who Served During the Period 1801 Through May 1972," 92d Cong., 2d Sess. 156 (1972).

34. *San Francisco Chronicle*, Apr. 28, 1931, at 16, col. 5.

35. Erskine M. Ross to Hon. Claude T. Reno, Jan. 9, 1923, Ross Scrapbook, deposited at Los Angeles County Law Library (hereinafter Ross Scrapbook). The boys from V.M.I. were pressed into service at the battle of Newmarket on May 15, 1864, and were proud to become "the only battalion of boys who ever fought and won a battle" (Wm. A. Thom, Jr., "Battle of Newmarket: A Fight Unique in the History of War," typescript in Ross Scrapbook).

36. For a sketch of Ross and his role in the founding of Glendale, see J. Sherer, *History of Glendale and Vicinity* 305–6 (1922).

37. *Ross to Reno, Jan. 9, 1923, Ross Scrapbook. *Los Angeles Daily Herald*, July 15, 1886, Ross Scrapbook. On these theories, see G. Cosgrave, *Early California Justice: The History of the United States District Court for the Southern District of California, 1849–1944*, at 67–68 (1948).

38. During Cleveland's presidency Field's influence clearly waned (*see* C. Swisher, *supra* note 7, at 316–17). G. Cosgrave, *supra* note 37, at 68. *Francis G. Newlands to Stephen J. Field, Dec. 10, 1886, James de Barth Shorb Papers, SHO Box 81(41), Huntington Library, San Marino, California (hereinafter Shorb Papers). Francis G. Newlands to James de Barth Shorb, Dec. 12, 1886, Shorb Papers, SHO Box 81(65), quoting Field's telegram. *Newlands to Shorb, Dec. 15, 1886, Shorb Papers, SHO Box 81(66).

39. *Daily Herald*, undated clipping, Ross Scrapbook. *In re Grand Jury*, 62 F. 834 (S.D. Cal. 1894). *Chum Shang Yuen*, 57 F. 588 (S.D. Cal. 1893). *See infra* Chapter Three.

40. Act of Feb. 18, 1895, ch. 94, 28 Stat. 665. By retaining original jurisdiction in the old circuit courts in the 1891 Evarts Act but not authorizing any new judges to hear such cases, Congress preserved the system of circuit and

district judges serving as trial judges in circuit courts. Instead of hearing circuit court trials in panels as the system from 1789 contemplated, however, as a practical matter single judges held circuit court between 1891 and the abolition of these tribunals in the 1911 Judicial Code. The movement toward single-judge circuit courts evolved over time (*see* E. Surrency, *supra* note 4, at 43–47). *Bradley v. Fallbrook Irrigation Dist.*, 68 F. 948 (C.C.S.D. Cal. 1895). *See infra* Chapter Five. *United States v. Stanford*, 69 F. 25 (C.C.N.D. Cal. 1895). *See infra* Chapter Two.

41. C. Swisher, *supra* note 7, at 444–45. *San Francisco Call*, Dec. 21, 1896, at 1, col. 4. McDevitt, *supra* note 28, at 90–91.

42. *San Francisco Call*, Feb. 27, 1897, at 3, col. 1.

43. Quoted in *San Francisco Call*, June 7, 1897, at *4, col. 5.

44. C. Swisher, *Stephen J. Field: Craftsman of the Law* 444 (1930; reprint 1969). According to Swisher, the justice "never forgave" President Cleveland for appointing Melville Fuller as chief justice in 1888 instead of elevating him (*id.* at 319).

45. *San Francisco Call*, June 7, 1897, at 4, col. 5. Macdonald, "Erskine Mayo Ross: Courageous Jurist and Generous Benefactor," 33 A.B.A. J. 1172, 1244 (1947). In the second instance, President Taft selected his former Sixth Circuit colleague, Horace Harmon Lurton.

46. Petitions to the Honorable Eugene Hale and to the Honorable William P. Frye, File of Joseph McKenna, Department of Justice Appointment Files, U.S. Supreme Court, RG 60, National Archives, Washington, D.C.

47. McDevitt, *supra* note 28, at 90.

48. *San Francisco Call*, Dec. 3, 1897, at 1, col. 4. For an expression of McKenna's chances for confirmation, see *San Francisco Call*, Nov. 25, 1897, at 1, col. 4.

49. Gilbert's opposition may also have derived from McKenna's clever maneuvering in 1892 to gain seniority. For reasons that the Senate records do not make clear, the Senate deferred Gilbert's confirmation until March 18, 1892, the day after McKenna's, thus giving the Californian seniority (*see* 28 Sen. Exec. J., *supra* note 31, at 188). Scuttlebutt at the federal courthouse was that the two judges had been at loggerheads ever since McKenna had attempted to impose his own man as clerk of the northern district. Through his connections in Congress, McKenna had succeeded in getting a law passed, as a rider to an appropriation bill, that gave him patronage over this position; the same law accorded Gilbert similar power in the district of Oregon. It is difficult to know how far to credit such expressions of animus. *San Francisco Call*, Dec. 4, 1897, at 2, col. 3.

50. *San Francisco Call*, Dec. 4. 1897, at 2, col. 1.

51. *See*, e.g., *San Francisco Call*, Dec. 4, 1897, at 6, col. 2. On the delay, see *San Francisco Call*, Dec. 5, 1897, at 1, col. 7; *id.* Dec. 5, 1897, at 6, col. 2; *id.* Dec. 6, 1897, at 3, col. 1; *id.* Dec. 7, 1897, at 5, col. 1. *San Francisco Call*, Dec. 7, 1897, at *6, col. 1. *San Francisco Call*, Jan. 22, 1898, at *3, col. 3. On his confirmation, see 32 Sen. Exec. J. 509 (1898), available at National Archives, Washington, D.C.

52. *Historical and Contemporary Review of Bench and Bar in California* 119 (1926); O. Shuck, *supra* note 28, at 655.

53. O. Shuck, *supra* note 28, at 656.

54. *United States v. Cassidy*, 67 F. 698, 702 (N.D. Cal. 1895). The charge measures eighty-two pages in the Federal Reporter and was thought to be exceeded by only one other charge in a known jurisdiction, that of Lord Chief Justice Cockburn in the *Tichborne* case. "William W. Morrow," 10 Calif. L. Rev. 1, 4 (1921). This charge is compiled in a book-length printed manuscript, *The Tichborne Trial* (1874).

55. "William W. Morrow," *supra* note 53, at *6. O. Shuck, *supra* note 12, at 656. *See infra* Chapter Six.

56. From 1900 to their respective dates of retirement, Gilbert wrote 1,172 opinions, an average of just over 39 per year; Ross produced 637 opinions, an average of 24.5 per year; and Morrow was responsible for 405 opinions, an average of 14.46 per year (E. Evans, "A Work Sheet of Judicial Labor of Appellate Federal Courts," 1943 Wis. L. Rev. 313, 321). These figures do not include the countless additional cases upon which they sat as *nisi prius* judges in circuit court before 1912. Morrow's statistics come out less favorably in part because he retired in 1923 and has six years of what we now call senior status service factored into his yearly average. Moreover, for all three judges, arguably their most productive years were the 1890s, before Evans began his count. Nor did he factor in the large number of trials handled by these judges in the circuit courts until their abolition in 1911. Judge William Hunt, who served on the court beginning in 1911, produced 545 opinions in his 17 years of service, an average of 32.05 per year (*id.* at 321).

2. RAILROADS, ROBBER BARONS, AND THE SAVING OF STANFORD UNIVERSITY

1. Act of July 1, 1862, ch. 120, §§ 1–9, 12 Stat. 489, 489–94.

2. *Id.* § 9, 12 Stat. at *494. Congress also provided that the Leavenworth, Pawnee, and Western Railroad of Kansas should construct a rail and telegraph line from the Kansas River to link up with the Union Pacific's line. *See id.* § 9, 12 Stat. at 493–94.

3. L. Mercer, *Railroads and Land Grant Policy* 33, 78 (1982). Act of July 1, 1862, ch. 120, § 5, 12 Stat. 489, 492. 1894 Att'y Gen. Ann. Rep. xxviii. For the Southern Pacific Railroad Company, the discovery of oil on granted lands was to increase the value of the land grant dramatically. The litigation involving these lands occupied much attention by the court. *See infra* Chapter Five.

4. Act of July 1, 1862, ch. 120, § 5, 12 Stat. *489, *492–93. Two years later, Congress amended this provision to authorize the security interest to be a second mortgage, thus enabling the companies to sell their first-mortgage bonds to raise much-needed capital (*see* Act of July 2, 1864, ch. 216, § 10, 13 Stat. 356, 360).

5. On their nicknames, see G. Clark, *Leland Stanford* 188–89 (1931). On the Central Pacific's progress, see P. Chiu, *Chinese Labor in California 1850–1880*, at 44–45 (1963); O. Lewis, *The Big Four* 97 (1938).

6. H. Cummings and C. McFarland, *Federal Justice* 274 (1937). 13 Op. Att'y Gen. 360, 363, 368 (1870). Act of Mar. 3, 1871, ch. 116, § 9, 16 Stat. 521, 525.

7. R. Pattison, *Extracts from the Report of the U.S. Pacific Railway Commission* *2, *16 (1888). *In Re Pac. Ry. Comm'n*, 32 F. 241, 249–59 (C.C.N.D. Cal. 1887). Circuit Judge Lorenzo Sawyer concurred (*id.* at 259, Sawyer, J., concurring). On Field's close friendship with Stanford and the Big Four, see C. Swisher, *Stephen J. Field: Craftsman of the Law* 265 (1930; reprint 1969).

8. H. Cummings and C. McFarland, *supra* note 6, at 290–91. An enterprising lawyer from St. Louis, Daniel H. Solomon, wrote to the Justice Department with relentless regularity to press a theory of recovery: that the government could sue the Central Pacific stockholders for the underlying debt of the corporation. Solomon dropped tidbits of his theory at regular intervals in a bid to represent the United States in a suit against the Stanford estate for a 10 percent contingency fee. The Justice Department teased enough information about Solomon's theory from him that it eventually declined his requests and hired another special counsel instead, Lewis D. McKisick. The numerous letters from Solomon are available at the National Archives. Department of Justice Central Files, Year Files: 1892, File 7622: Assorted Letters, Boxes 631 and 632, RG 60, National Archives, Washington, D.C. (hereinafter Justice Department Records).

9. *See* 1 W. Cook, *A Treatise on Stock and Stockholders* §§ 212–19 (3d ed. 1894, outlining general rules); 2 W. Cook, *id.* § 938 (detailing California provisions); *see also* Hohfeld, "Nature of Stockholders' Individual Liability for Corporation Debts," 9 Colum. L. Rev. 285 (1909); H. Henn, *Handbook of the Law of Corporations* 96 n.4 (2d ed. 1970, noting that California's rule of unlimited liability on a proportionate basis was not repealed until 1928).

10. Cal. Const. art. IV, § 36 (1864).

11. O. Lewis, *supra* note 5, at 184–91; 26 Cong. Rec. 5950 (1894).

12. 26 Cong. Rec. *5949, *5896, *5950 (1894). Richard Olney to George F. Hoar, June 8, 1894, Richard Olney Papers, Volume 16, Reel 6, Folios *2687–89, Library of Congress, Washington, D.C.

13. According to one reporter, Olney did "not believe" that bringing a suit would be successful (*San Francisco Call*, June 10, 1894, at 1, col. 1). *San Francisco Call*, June 6, 1894, at *6, col. 2. *San Francisco Call*, June 9, 1894, at *6, col. 2.

14. *San Francisco Call*, June 9, 1894, at 6, cols. 2–3.

15. 26 Cong. Rec. *8620 (1894); *see also San Francisco Call*, Aug. 14, 1894, at 1, col. 4. *United States v. Stanford*, 69 F. 25, 34 (C.C.N.D. Cal. 1895).

16. *See Stanford*, 69 F. at 34. *San Francisco Call*, June 8, 1894, at 1, col. 1.

17. *San Francisco Call*, Mar. 6, 1895, at 12, col. 1; *see also San Francisco Call*, Mar. 16, 1895, at 14, col. 3. O. Shuck, *Bench and Bar in California: History, Anecdotes, Reminiscences* 482–83 (1889). The circuit and district courts retained their confusing bifurcated original jurisdiction at this time. Circuit courts had jurisdiction when the United States was a plaintiff or petitioner. *See* B. Curtis, *Jurisdiction, Practice, and Peculiar Jurisprudence of the Courts of the United States* 116–21 (2d rev. ed. 1896).

18. *San Francisco Call*, Mar. 16, 1895, at 14, col. 3. Parts of the complaint in the *Stanford* case are excerpted in the *Call* on Mar. 16, 1895, at 14, col. 3. For more on Garber, see C. Taylor, *Bench and Bar of California, 1937–38*, at

353 (1938). *San Francisco Call,* June 6, 1895, at *14, col. 1. *Stanford,* 69 F. at 34–35; *see also San Francisco Call,* May 7, 1895, at 9, col. 3.

19. *San Francisco Call,* June 4, 1895, at *7, col. 6. "'Judge McKenna is a little sensitive on this particular matter,' said a prominent attorney yesterday. 'He is afraid that should his decision be in favor of the Stanford estate some one might say that his friendship outweighed his judgment'" (*id.*). Note, "The Decision in the Case of the United States Against Stanford," 29 Am. L. Rev. 617, *617 (1895). This was the first of two law review notes on the *Stanford* decisions published in Volume 29 of the American Law Review.

According to the Minutes of the United States Circuit Court for the Northern District of California, McKenna was slated to hear matters in the circuit court throughout May and June, 1895 (*see* 27 Minutes of the U.S. Circuit Court for the Northern District of California for May 6, 1895, to Feb. 17, 1897, available on microfilm at the U.S. District Court for the Northern District of California, San Francisco). His announcement stated that the case would be continued two days later (*id.* at 29). That day and the next, McKenna apparently sat in both the circuit court and the circuit court of appeals (*see id.* at 29–37).

20. Unfortunately, neither the minutes of the circuit court nor the minutes of the circuit court of appeals shed much light on why Ross was assigned to hear the *Stanford* case. On the same day, June 3, 1891, that he recused himself, McKenna sat with Erskine Ross and District Judge Thomas P. Hawley in the circuit court of appeals. The same panel also sat the next day. On June 5, 1891, when the *Stanford* case resumed with Ross on the bench, William Gilbert had taken Ross's place on the circuit court of appeals panel with McKenna and Hawley (*see* 1 Minutes of the United States Circuit Court of Appeals for the Ninth Circuit at 451–54 [hereinafter Ninth Circuit Minutes]). Gilbert apparently was not present in San Francisco for the June sitting (*see id.* at 451), and McKenna may have summoned him from Oregon to substitute for Ross so that the latter could hear the demurrer motion in the circuit court.

The Evarts Act prohibited a judge or justice from sitting on the appeal of a cause heard by that jurist in the district or circuit court (Act of Mar. 3, 1891, ch. 517, § 3, 26 Stat. 816, 827).

21. During the first two sessions of the court after its formation in June, 1891, district judges conducted the court's business. In October of 1891, District Judge Erskine Ross made his way to San Francisco from Los Angeles and District Judge Thomas Hawley of Nevada heard the first oral arguments in the court's history (*see* 1 Ninth Circuit Minutes 28 [Oct. 5, 1891]; *see also* 1 Ninth Circuit Minutes at 41–44 [Dec. 28, 1891–Jan. 4, 1892, describing January, 1892, session of the court]). Justice Stephen J. Field apparently served as presiding judge of the court pending appointment of the judge to fill the vacancy created by Lorenzo Sawyer's death and the new seat authorized under the Evarts Act (*see* 1 Ninth Circuit Minutes at 26, 41–42; *see also* Chapter One).

As succeeding chapters will illustrate, district judges played an important role in the Ninth Circuit's history. Quantifying this contribution has not been an aim of this study, but after reading many cases, the conclusion is inescapable that the circuit court of appeals was never static in its panel composition, even after abolition of the circuit courts at the end of 1911 largely freed circuit judges of trial responsibilities.

22. *See San Francisco Call*, June 6, 1895, at 14, cols. 2–3. Note, 29 Am. L. Rev., *supra* note 19, at *617.

23. *San Francisco Call*, June 7, 1895, at *16, col. 1. The government asserted, without proving, that Stanford held one-quarter of the Central Pacific's stock. Mrs. Stanford's lawyers neither rebutted nor agreed with this contention (*see Stanford*, 69 F. at 34–35). Note, 29 Am. L. Rev., *supra* note 19, at *618.

24. Note, 29 Am. L. Rev., *supra* note 19, at *618; *San Francisco Call*, June 30, 1895, at *18, col. 2. The lay press was not particularly surprised by Judge Ross's decision: "No one was very much astonished yesterday when it was announced that the demurrer to the Government's complaint against the Stanford estate had been sustained by the United States Circuit Court" (*id.* at 24, col. 1). Note, 29 Am. L. Rev., *supra* note 19, at *617.

25. *Stanford*, 69 F. at *44; *id.* at *39.

26. Mrs. Leland Stanford to Judge E. M. Ross, June, 1895, quoted in G. Nagel, *Iron Will: The Life and Letters of Jane Stanford* *86 (rev. ed. 1985). L. D. McKisick to Attorney General Judson Harmon, July 1, 1895, Letter No. *18,560, Justice Department Records.

27. *San Francisco Call*, Oct. 8, 1895, at *14, col. 1. The August issue of the *American Law Review* does not provide the author's name. *See* Note, 29 Am. L. Rev., *supra* note 19, at 617. Thompson was, however, one of the journal's editors, and the *Call*, *supra*, believed Thompson to have been responsible for this commentary. Note, 29 Am. L. Rev., *supra* note 19, at *623.

28. *See supra* note 9 and accompanying text. *French v. Teschemaker*, 24 Cal. 518, 560 (1864). Note, 29 Am. L. Rev., *supra* note 19, at *625; *id.* at *627; *see also* Cal. Civil Code § 322 (Deering 1915, detailing legislative history of shareholder liability provision). Note, 29 Am. L. Rev., *supra* note 19, at *626.

29. Under the United States Supreme Court's decision in *Burgess v. Seligman*, 107 U.S. 20, 33–34 (1883), Ross was not obliged to follow *French v. Teschemaker*. Ordinarily, federal courts would hold themselves bound to follow decisions of state courts in the interpretation of their own constitutions and statutes when such rulings had fixed property rights. In this instance, however, the Central Pacific had contracted with Congress *before* the California Supreme Court had rendered *French*. The rule in this situation was different, as Justice Bradley explained in *Burgess*: "So when contracts and transactions have been entered into, and rights have accrued under a particular state of decisions, *or when there has been no decision*, of the State tribunals, the Federal courts properly claim the right to adopt their own interpretation of the law applicable to the case, *although a different interpretation may be adopted by the State courts after such rights have accrued*" (107 U.S. at 33–34, emphasis added).

30. Note, 29 Am. L. Rev., *supra* note 19, at 626–27. *See* T. Freyer, *Harmony and Dissonance: The Swift and Erie Cases in American Federalism* 94 (1981). In his highly detailed treatment of this period, Professor Charles Fairman describes these developments (C. Fairman, *Reconstruction and Reunion, 1864–88: Part One*, 6 The Oliver Wendell Holmes Devise, *History of the Supreme Court of the United States* 918–1206 [1971]). *See also* Benedict, "Laissez-Faire and

Liberty: A Re-Evaluation of the Meaning and Origins of Laissez-Faire Constitutionalism," 3 Law and Hist. Rev. 293 (1985).

31. "It is to be regretted that Judge Ross does not point out any respect in which this statute is so indefinite as not to be understood and enforced" (Note, 29 Am. L. Rev., *supra* note 19, at 633).

32. *Stanford*, 69 F. at *45–46. Note, 29 Am. L. Rev., *supra* note 19, at *633.

33. Note, 29 Am. L. Rev., *supra* note 19, at 634–35. For Ross's perception, see *Stanford*, 69 F. at 47.

34. David S. Jordan to Attorney General Judson Harmon, July 2, 1895, Letter No. *10112, Justice Department Records. The Supreme Court rendered its decision on March 2, 1896 (*United States v. Stanford*, 161 U.S. 412 [1896]). Mrs. Stanford herself contributed to the speed of this process by personally lobbying President Cleveland and Attorney General Olney in the spring of 1895 to advance the suit as quickly as possible. To conserve money, she traveled for free by hooking her private railroad car to trains moving in her direction; she then used the car as a private hotel during her stay in Washington. Out of an initial budget of $500, she returned with $300 (E. Mirrielees, *Stanford: The Story of a University* 89–90 [1959]). For the correspondence from this trip, see G. Nagel, *supra* note 26, at 81–83. Including dismissals, the appellate process between September, 1891, and September, 1896, took an average of 264 days; omitting dismissals, the average was 279 days (*see infra*, Appendix). The Supreme Court still had a backlog in 1896 of 383 cases (*see* 1897 Att'y Gen. Ann. Rep. xi).

35. Hawley, a former chief justice of Nevada and federal district judge from that state between 1890 and 1907, often sat by designation in the circuit court of appeals (*San Francisco Call*, Sept. 17, 1895, at 1, col. 2). *San Francisco Call*, Sept. 18, 1895, at *7, col. 4. *See* Argument of L. D. McKisick, *United States v. Stanford*, No. 246, United States Circuit Court of Appeals for the Ninth Circuit, Records of the Ninth Circuit, on deposit at University of California, Hastings College of the Law Library (hereinafter McKisick Argument). This printed oral argument also served as McKisick's brief (*id.* at 142–65).

36. McKisick Argument, *supra* note 35, at 171. *San Francisco Call*, Sept. 18, 1895, at *7, col. 4.

37. Note, "Liability of the Stockholders of the Central Pacific Railroad Company," 29 Am. L. Rev. 926, *926 (1895). Brief of Respondent and Appellee, at *8, *United States v. Stanford*, No. 246, United States Circuit Court of Appeals for the Ninth Circuit, Records of the Ninth Circuit, on deposit at University of California, Hastings College of the Law Library (hereinafter Respondent Brief). *See also id.* at 17. *San Francisco Call*, Sept. 19, 1895, at 5, col. 1.

38. *San Francisco Call*, Sept. 20, 1895, at *9, col. 1. *San Francisco Call*, Sept. 21, 1895, at *11, col. 4.

39. But even Thompson claimed to think that the appellate court would affirm, in spite of his arguments to the contrary. In a subsequent issue, the American Law Review reported that Judge Ross's decision "was, as we predicted, affirmed by the United States Court of Appeals for the Ninth Circuit" (Note, 29 Am. L. Rev., *supra* note 19, at 926). This "prediction" is difficult to distill from its earlier analysis, although the journal did predict that even though the stockholders would be found liable, the law would not be enforced (*see* Note, 29 Am.

L. Rev., *supra* note 19, at 624). *United States v. Stanford*, 70 F. 346 (9th Cir. 1895); for newspaper commentary of the decision, *see San Francisco Call*, Oct. 13, 1895, at 7, col. 2.

40. *Stanford*, 70 F. at *359–60; *see also id.* at 363. *See infra* Chapter Five.

41. Note, 29 Am. L. Rev., *supra* note 19, at *926; *id.* at *936.

42. *See* Act of July 1, 1862, ch. 120, 12 Stat. 489, 489–91 (naming the "corporators" and fixing the organizational details). Congress did precisely that two years after it created the Union Pacific (*see* Act of July 2, 1864, ch. 216, 13 Stat. 356).

43. Act of July 1, 1862, § 18, 12 Stat. at *497.

44. *San Francisco Call*, Oct. 13, 1895, at 7, cols. 2–3. L. D. McKisick to Holmes Conrad, Dec. 10, 1895, Letter No. *18,562, Justice Department Records.

45. *McKisick to Conrad, Dec. 10, 1895, *supra*, note 44.

46. Choate was one of the most distinguished lawyers of the late nineteenth century. He argued before the Supreme Court in such cases as the *Neagle* case and the income tax cases (*see generally* 2 A. Johnson and D. Malone, eds., *Dictionary of American Biography* 83–86 [1957]). The Supreme Court opinion does not contain an abstract of the argument (*United States v. Stanford*, 161 U.S. 412 [1896]). *San Francisco Call*, Jan. 29, 1896, at *2, col. 1.

47. *Stanford*, 161 U.S. at 434; *id.* at 426–27; *id.* at *430.

48. *San Francisco Call*, Mar. 3, 1896, at *2, col. 1. The university also eventually received a $1 million legacy from Thomas Stanford, Leland's brother (*id.* at 2, col. 3). Despite the anticipation of speedy distribution of the estate's assets, the probate proceedings did not wind up until December 28, 1898 (*San Francisco Call*, Dec. 29, 1898, at 12, col. 4).

49. *Stephen J. Field to Mrs. Leland Stanford, Mar. 3, 1896, Mrs. Jane Stanford Papers, Green Library, Stanford University, Stanford, California (hereinafter Stanford Papers). C. Swisher, *supra* note 7, at *245. Swisher has also reported that "letters showing [Field's] close personal relationship with Stanford, Huntington, and others, have been carefully destroyed" (*id.* at 265). H. Cummings and C. McFarland, *supra* note 6, at *292.

50. *Henry S. Foote to Mrs. Leland Stanford, Mar. 8, 1896, Stanford Papers. The rest of the letter was equally obsequious:

> You will stand as you deserve to be the great central heroic figure in all future time, the grief stricken widow and mother, forgetful of her own griefs, smothering her own sorrow, and laboring in season and out of season, with tear dimmed eyes and soft and tender heart, in the same spirit that our great martyrs in religion and patriotism have shed glorious light on the pages of History—
> My Dear Madam to contemplate your character, your sufferings, your noble virtue, your true bravery, and your womanly tenderness, is to bring tears to the eyes and soft feelings to the heart, of even the sternest of men. I trust that Almighty God may reward you in this world for your stay here, as I feel confident he will when you go to join those who . . . doubtless now look down on you from the home of the blessed with love and admiration.
>
> I am your true friend, Henry S. Foote.

(Ellipses here indicate illegible writing.)

51. Only three times has the case been cited since, and then to support descriptive propositions (*see Oregon and Cal. R.R. Co. v. United States*, 238 U.S. 393, 416 [1915], citing *Stanford* to support the proposition that national purposes induced the federal grants to the transcontinental railroads; *Southern Pac. R.R. Co. v. United States*, 183 U.S. 519, 527 [1902], citing *Stanford* to establish that Congress can confer on state-created corporations franchises of a nature similar to those for federally created corporations; *Central Pac. R.R. Co. v. California*, 162 U.S. 91, 161–62 [1896] [Harlan, J., dissenting], citing *Stanford* to support the argument that Congress selected the Central Pacific to build the transcontinental road to accomplish national aims).

52. *San Francisco Call*, Mar. 3, 1896, at *2, col. 1. Maguire's fears about altering California's unlimited liability for shareholders proved to be unfounded. In law review articles pregnant with irony, Stanford Professor Wesley Hohfeld wrote a little over a decade later that California's rule continued in force. In reaching this conclusion Hohfeld never once cited the *Stanford* decisions (Hohfeld, *supra* note 10).

53. This figure of 2 percent does not include dismissals (*see infra*, Appendix).

54. D. Myrick, *Refinancing and Rebuilding the Central Pacific Railroad, 1899–1910*, at 37 (1961).

3. TESTING TOLERANCE

1. A few Chinese apparently had come to the United States before 1848, most of them settling on the East Coast. *See* J. Chen, *The Chinese of America* 3–5 (1980). Department of the Interior Census Office, *Statistics of the Population of the United States: Tenth Census* 3, 379 (1883) (hereinafter *Tenth Census*).

2. A. Saxton, *The Indispensable Enemy* 17, 51–54 (1971). G. Barth, *Bitter Strength* 1–4 (1964). A recent work that questions the sojourner thesis but acknowledges the difficulty of disproving it is S. Chan, *This Bitter-Sweet Soil* xx, 4–5 (1986).

3. P. Chiu, *Chinese Labor in California, 1850–1880*, at 44–46 (1963); *see supra* Chapter Two. Fong, "Sojourners and Settlers: The Chinese Experience in Arizona," 21 J. Ariz. Hist. 227, 233 (1980). Chan argues that the Chinese who worked in agriculture did so out of necessity rather than inclination. *See* S. Chan, *supra* note 2, at 79.

4. The tally of Chinese in California, Oregon, Nevada, Arizona, Idaho, Montana, and Washington—the states or territories that became the Ninth Circuit in 1891—was 100,018 (*Tenth Census, supra* note 1, at 3; Chan, "The Chinese in Nevada: An Historical Survey, 1856–1970," 25 Nev. Hist. Soc. Q. 266, 267 [1982]). *See also* Carter, "Social Demography of the Chinese in Nevada: 1870–1880," 18 Nev. Hist. Soc. Q. 73, 73 (1975). P. Chiu, *supra* note 3, at 63. Even early analysts of the problem argued persuasively that immigrants did not significantly displace white workers (*see* Hourwich, "The Economic Aspects of Immigration," 26 Pol. Sci. Q. 615 [1911]).

5. 4 T. Hittell, *History of California* 99 (1898).

6. *See* McClain, "The Chinese Struggle for Civil Rights in Nineteenth Century America: The First Phase, 1850–1870," 72 Calif. L. Rev. 529, 539–40

(1984) (describing discriminatory taxes) (hereinafter McClain, "The Chinese Struggle"); W. Courtney, "San Francisco's Anti-Chinese Ordinances, 1850–1900," at 4–5 (Univ. of San Francisco diss. 1956, describing the discriminatory bonding law for alien passengers who landed in California). Jones, "The Legislative History of Exclusion Legislation," 34 Annals of Am. Acad. Pol. and Soc. Sci. 131, 134 (1909); R. Heizer and A. Almquist, *The Other Californians* 166 (1971). Wunder, "Law and the Chinese on the Southwest Frontier, 1850s-1902," 2 W. Legal Hist. 139, 141 (1989).

7. The Chinese exclusion movement was not confined to the West politically, but attracted adherents throughout the United States (*see* S. Miller, *The Unwelcome Immigrant* 191–204 [1969]). Treaty Concerning Immigration, Nov. 17, 1880, United States–China, *art. I, 22 Stat. 826. Jones, *supra* note 6, at 134. President Harrison's administration concluded this treaty with the Chinese government, and it was ratified during the first year of Chester A. Arthur's presidency (*see* 22 Stat. at 826, giving signature and ratification dates).

8. *See* Act of May 6, 1882, ch. 126, §§ 1, 4, 14, 22 Stat. 58, 59, 61. *Id.,* 22 Stat. at *58. *See generally* Cohen, "The Social and Economic Consequences of Exclusionary Immigration Laws," 2 Nat. Law. Guild Q. 171, 171 (1939).

9. *See* Jones, *supra* note 6, at 135. Act of July 5, 1884, ch. 220, § 15, 23 Stat. 115, 118. R. Heizer and A. Almquist, *supra* note 6, at 156. The 1886 petition purported to explain to the national government the "Chinese evil" posed to California by the "great Mongolian hive, with its 450,000,000 . . . hungry and adventurous inhabitants" (*see* S. Misc. Doc. No. 107, 49th Cong., 1st Sess. 1 [1886]). Nor were such sentiments confined to the Far West. That same year an armed vigilante group attacked Chinese in Rock Springs, Wyoming, and drove them out of town like cattle. *See generally* J. Chen, *supra* note 1, at 151–52.

10. Act of Sept. 13, 1888, ch. 1015, 25 Stat. 476; *see also* Act of Oct. 1, 1888, ch. 1064, 25 Stat. 504. Earlier presidents had feared that, without a sanctioning treaty, the Chinese government would retaliate against Americans in China for passage of such legislation. *See* Jones, *supra* note 6, at 133.

11. Act of Sept. 13, 1888, ch. 1015, §§ 2, 5, 25 Stat. 476, 476–77. Act of May 5, 1892, ch. 60, § 6, 27 Stat. 25, 25–26. Thomas J. Geary, a Representative to Congress from San Francisco, served from December 9, 1890, to March 3, 1895, and thereupon resumed the practice of law. As a legislator, he created work for the Ninth Circuit as author of the 1892 Chinese Exclusion Act; as a lawyer, he was tried for contempt of court for actions arising out of his practice after he moved to Nome, Alaska, in 1900 (*see infra* this chapter and Chapter Four; *Biographical Directory of the United States Congress: 1774–1989,* at 1050 [Bicentennial ed. 1989]). The 1884 act had required these certificates (*see* Act of July 5, 1884, ch. 220, § 6, 23 Stat. 115, 116). For a discussion of cases arising under this provision, see *infra* text at note 27.

12. Act of Nov. 3, 1893, ch. 14, 28 Stat. 7. Treaty Concerning Immigration, Mar. 17, 1894, United States–China, 28 Stat. 1210, T.S. No. 51. The exclusion principle exerted sufficient appeal that in 1902 Congress extended it indefinitely (Act of Apr. 22, 1902, ch. 641, 32 Stat. 176). This 1902 legislation also extended the law to island territories of the United States and prohibited the immigration of Chinese from such territorial possessions to the continental United States or

from islands to other islands not of the same status. This law was particularly relevant to the Ninth Circuit, which had jurisdiction over Alaska and Hawaii. The steady hammer of these exclusion laws had the desired effect of halting the Chinese influx. By early in this century, with the "problems" of Chinese immigration exhausted, attention began to focus on Japanese immigration. The president acted before Congress did: by executive order, President Theodore Roosevelt excluded from the continental United States any Japanese holding passports that did not specifically entitle them to enter the United States (*see* 1 Am. J. Int'l. L. 449, 450 [1907]). These initial exclusionary laws were followed in 1917 by a comprehensive immigration restriction law that sought to exclude from the United States various classes of immigrants, including Japanese and Asians generally (*see* Act of Feb. 5, 1917, ch. 29, 39 Stat. 875). An additional act passed on October 16, 1918, extended the class of excluded aliens to include persons connected with generally subversive organizations (*see* Act of Oct. 16, 1918, ch. 186, 40 Stat. 1012). These laws merely presaged a general restriction, enacted on May 19, 1921, on the number of immigrants allowed into the United States based on national origins (*see* Act of May 19, 1921, ch. 5, 42 Stat. 5). Three years later, Congress enacted the comprehensive Immigration Act of 1924, which superseded the 1921 law (*see* Act of May 26, 1924, ch. 190, 43 Stat. 158).

13. See *Chae Chan Ping v. United States* (*The Chinese Exclusion Case*), 130 U.S. 581 (1889). The case involved a challenge to Congress's 1888 annulment of laborer reentry certificates. In a unanimous decision written by Justice Stephen Field, the Court affirmed the order denying entry.

14. *San Francisco Examiner*, n.d., *quoted in* 29 Am. L. Rev. 585, 586 (1895).

15. See *People v. Naglee*, 1 Cal. 232 (1850). The court upheld this provision as a valid tax that did not interfere with interstate commerce (*id.* at 242). *See generally* Sandmeyer, "California Anti-Chinese Legislation and the Federal Courts: A Study in Federal Relations," 5 Pac. Hist. Rev. 189, 190 (1936). The California legislature itself repealed the miners' tax the following year, 1851 (*see* J. Chen, *supra* note 1, at 48).

16. Treaty Concerning Friendship, July 3, 1844, United States-China, 8 Stat. 592; Treaty, July 28, 1868, United States–China, art. V, 16 Stat. 739, 740; *id.* art. VI, 16 Stat. at *740. The Chinese guarantees were similar (*id.*). On the holding of Judges Lorenzo Sawyer and Ogden Hoffman that national treaties and statutes preempted certain discriminatory state laws, see *In re Tiburcio Parrott*, 1 F. 481, 514 (C.C.D. Cal. 1880, opinion of Sawyer, J.). Civil Rights Act of 1870, ch. 114, §§ 16–17, 16 Stat. 140, 144. More than a century later, the Supreme Court interpreted a successor statute in a way that sparked a sharp dissent over its reading of the 1870 law's legislative history. See *Runyon v. McCrary*, 427 U.S. 160 (1976). In his dissent, Justice White argued that Congress directed § 16 of the Civil Rights Act of 1870 to the plight of the Chinese in California (*see id.* at 1929, White, J., dissenting). An excellent scholarly treatment of the period agrees with Justice White's analysis (*see* McClain, "The Chinese Struggle," *supra* note 6, at 530–31).

17. *Ho Ah Kow v. Nunan*, 12 Fed. Cas. 252 (C.C.D. Cal. 1879). For the text of this ordinance, see W. Courtney, "San Francisco's Anti-Chinese Ordinances, 1850–1900," at 62–63 (Univ. of San Francisco diss. 1956). Judge Lorenzo

Sawyer was equally hard on a San Francisco ordinance that attempted forcibly to remove the Chinese from the city to South San Francisco, ruling it unconstitutional in 1890 (*In re Lee Sing*, 43 F. 359 [C.C.N.D. Cal. 1890]).

18. *Yick Wo v. Hopkins*, 118 U.S. 356, 361, 374 (1886). While riding circuit, Justice Field had held one of these ordinances invalid four years earlier (*In re Quong Woo*, 13 F. 229 [C.C.D. Cal. 1882]; W. Courtney, *supra* note 17, at 69–70). Another discriminatory law, passed in 1880 by the state of California, forbade aliens who were ineligible to become electors from catching fish for commercial purposes in any waters of the state (*see generally* Sandmeyer, *supra*, at 206). Judge Sawyer struck this statute down, as violating both the Burlingame Treaty and the Fourteenth Amendment (*see In re Ah Chong*, 2 F. 733, 737 [C.C.D. Cal. 1880]).

19. Justice Field, before his own metamorphosis on the Chinese question (*see infra* note 22 and accompanying text), assailed as "absurd" interpretations of the 1882 act that might cause its repeal (*see In re Ah Tie*, 13 F. 291, 294 [C.C.D. Cal. 1882]).

20. Fritz, "A Nineteenth Century 'Habeas Corpus Mill': The Chinese Before the Federal Courts in California," 32 Am. J. Legal Hist. 347, 348 (1988). Between October 1, 1888, and December 1, 1890, Hoffman discharged 533 Chinese by habeas corpus petitions (*id.* at 350 n.8.)

21. *In re Low Yam Chow*, 13 F. 605, *615 (C.C.D. Cal. 1882, opinion of Hoffman, J.). Fritz, *supra* note 20, at 355–56.

22. Field's position virtually urged repudiation of the treaty with China (*see*, e.g., *In re Cheen* [*sic*] *Heong*, 21 F. 791, 793 [C.C.D. Cal. 1884]; *Chew Heong v. United States*, 112 U.S. 536, 537 [1884, Field, J., dissenting]). Treaty Concerning Immigration, Nov. 17, 1880, United States–China, art. II, 22 Stat. 826, *827. Fritz, *supra* note 20, at 356–57.

23. *See*, e.g., *In re Ho King*, 14 F. 724, 727 (D.C. Or. 1883). *See also* Mooney, "Matthew Deady and the Federal Judicial Response to Racism in the Early West," 63 Or. L. Rev. 561 (1984). Fritz points out, for example, that in unpublished exclusion act cases Deady discharged at least 150 Chinese on habeas writs in an eight-year period (1885–1893), whereas Hoffman granted writs to 533 Chinese in the two-year period between October 1, 1888, and December 1, 1890 (Fritz, *supra* note 20, at 350 n.8). On Deady's numbers, see Mooney, *supra*, at 629 n.266.

24. The *Eleventh Census* reported that the total number of Chinese residents in Oregon had grown from 3,330 in 1870, to 9,510 in 1880, to 9,540 in 1890. The respective figures for Portland (Multnomah County) were 508, 1,983, and 5,184. In San Francisco County alone, the comparative increase went from 12,022, to 21,745, to 25,833. Indeed, the outlying counties (Alameda, Marin, Sacramento, San Mateo, Santa Clara, and Santa Cruz) that also fell within the northern district accounted for more Chinese residents than the entire state of Oregon (*see* Department of the Interior Census Office, *Compendium of the Eleventh Census: 1890, Part 1: Population* 516, 521 [1892]). On Hoffman, see Fritz, *supra* note 20, at 360.

25. On these personal characteristics, see L. Sawyer, *Way Sketches* 16 (1926); O. Shuck, *Bench and Bar in California* 74 (1889). On Hoffman, see O. Shuck, *id.*, at 322–23; C. Fritz, *Federal Justice in California: The Court of Ogden*

Hoffman, 1851–1891, at 38 (1991). On Deady, see Mooney, *supra* note 23, at 629.

26. An aspirant for the presidency, Field may have taken a more populist stance for political reasons. If so, the change had little effect. Swisher notes that after Field switched his position "he was by this time so widely disliked and distrusted in California that the trend of a few opinions on the Chinese problem was of no avail in bringing him popularity" (C. Swisher, *Stephen J. Field: Craftsman of the Law* 236 [1930; reprint 1969]).

27. Act of Apr. 29, 1802, § 5, 2 Stat. 156, 158 (providing that "judgment shall be rendered in conformity to the opinion of the judge of the supreme court presiding in such circuit court"). Act of June 1, 1872, ch. 255, § 1, 17 Stat. 196, 196. *In re Cheen [sic] Heong*, 21 F. 791, 793–94 (C.C.D. Cal. 1884), *rev'd*, 112 U.S. 536 (1884). *Id.* at 797–800 (C.C.D. Cal. 1884, Sawyer, J., dissenting). Sabin was an Ohioan who moved to Nevada after serving in the Union Army throughout the Civil War. He was a federal district judge in Nevada between 1882 and 1890 (*see* 30 Fed. Cas. 1392 [1897]). *Chew Heong v. United States*, 112 U.S. 536 (1884). Field, of course, dissented, and Bradley joined him. *See generally* Fritz, *supra* note 20, at 363–66.

28. *See San Francisco Alta California*, Oct. 3, 1888, at 5, col. 2; *San Francisco Chronicle*, Oct. 3, 1888, at 1, col. 6. *In re Chae Chan Ping*, 36 F. 431, 437 (C.C.N.D. Cal. 1888), *aff'd*, 130 U.S. 581, 611 (1889). *San Francisco Alta California*, Oct. 3, 1888, at 8, col. 4.

29. The jurisprudence of the Ninth Circuit was no less important to the Chinese than the earlier circuit and district court decisions, yet very little scholarship examines the period that followed creation of the circuit courts of appeals in 1891. *See, e.g.*, Fritz, *supra* note 20; Mooney, *supra* note 23; McClain, "The Chinese Struggle," *supra* note 6. Fritz, for example, contends that the "efforts of the Chinese to use the federal courts to ameliorate the effects of exclusion were ultimately a losing battle, especially after the deaths of both Hoffman and Sawyer in 1891" (Fritz, *supra*, at 371). On the later period, see L. Salyer, "Guarding the 'White Man's Frontier': Courts, Politics, and the Regulation of Immigration, 1891–1924" (Univ. of California at Berkeley, diss. 1989). In the relevant chapters addressing judicial enforcement, Salyer focuses primarily on the district court's work (*id.* at 150–206).

30. 19 Cong. Rec. *7398 (1888). 19 Cong. Rec. App. *447 (1888). *Id.* at 448–50. *Id.* at *452.

31. H.R. Rep. No. 2915, 51st Cong., 1st Sess. *5 (1890). Morrow submitted this report on August 5, 1890. *See also id.* at 7.

32. 19 Cong. Rec. *7749 (1888). *Id.* at *7752. *Id.* at *7753.

33. *Id.* at *7751–52. M. McDevitt, "Joseph McKenna" 66 (Catholic University of America diss. 1946).

34. John W. Foster to Attorney General, Feb. 21, 1893, Letter No. 2020, File No. 980, Department of Justice Central File, Year Files: 1895, RG 60, Box No. 46, National Archives, Washington, D.C. (hereinafter File No. 980 Records). Tsui Kwo Yin to W. D. Gresham, Mar. 25, 1893, Letter No. 3114, File No. 980 Records. *Fong Yue Ting v. United States*, 149 U.S. 698 (1893). George J. Denis to Attorney General, Sept. 8, 1893, Letter No. *9462, File No. 980 Records.

35. Attorney General Olney to United States Attorney Denis, Sept. 2, 1893, *reprinted in United States v. Chum Shang Yuen*, 57 F. 588, *589 (S.D. Cal. 1893).

36. *See id.* at 589–91; *San Francisco Chronicle*, Sept. 6, 1893, in Scrapbook of Erskine M. Ross, deposited at Los Angeles County Law Library (hereinafter Ross Scrapbook).

37. Erskine M. Ross to President Cleveland, Sept. 26, 1893, Letter No. *1884, File No. 980 Records. *Ross to Olney, Oct. 6, 1893, *reprinted in San Francisco Chronicle*, Oct. 7, 1893, Ross Scrapbook. *Evening Express Company*, unidentified clipping, Ross Scrapbook.

38. *Statement of Marshal George E. Gard, quoted in unidentified newspaper clipping, Ross Scrapbook. *Unidentified newspaper clipping, Ross Scrapbook. The only contrary indication to the assessment in the text is an undocumented, unexplained, and incomplete sentence by Jack Chen: "Erskine Ross, who at the height of the Los Angeles anti-Chinese riot single-handedly stopped a raging mob in its tracks, saving many Chinese and their property" (J. Chen, *supra* note 1, at 158). *Undated editorial statements by *San Francisco Call*, *Riverside Enterprise*, and *San Francisco Chronicle*, in Ross Scrapbook. *Unidentified newspaper clipping, Ross Scrapbook.

39. In his analysis of state supreme courts, Wunder analyzes results in cases involving the Chinese and concludes that in cases decided before the Chinese exclusion acts the supreme courts tended to favor Chinese litigants, whereas after their passage these same Pacific Northwest Supreme Courts tended to go against the Chinese (*see* Wunder, "The Chinese and the Courts in the Pacific Northwest: Justice Denied?" 52 Pac. Hist. Rev. 191 [1983]). The numbers he presents are as follows: in civil cases, four in favor of the Chinese before 1883, three against; in criminal cases, nine in favor, six against. By contrast, in the period 1883 to 1902, these supreme courts decided twelve cases in favor of the Chinese and seventeen against in civil cases, and in criminal cases eight in favor and nineteen against (*id.* at 209). This study is subject to criticism on several counts. First, it relies on a very small sample. No firm conclusion that the Pacific Northwest supreme courts either favored or disapproved Chinese litigants can obtain when of the five courts studied, each heard only one case in the period before 1883, except Washington and Oregon, and those states split evenly in ruling for and against Chinese litigants (*see id.*). Moreover, Wunder does not attempt to determine whether the cases might have come out the way they did on the basis of the law rather than on racial grounds. It thus becomes difficult to accept his conclusion that there was a marked shift in judicial temperament with respect to the Chinese following passage of the Chinese exclusion acts. Wunder is certainly on firmer ground when he quotes passages from decisions that have clear racially biased overtones. One of his examples is particularly striking: "Juries should be loath to convict a Chinaman of murder in the first degree upon Chinese testimony; not wholly on account of a tender regard for the life of the accused, but also from a respect and reverence for truth and justice" (*Oregon v. Ching Ling*, 16 Ore. 419, 425 [1888], *quoted by* Wunder, *supra* at 204–5).

These subjective indications of discrimination were not in evidence in the federal cases decided by the Ninth Circuit during the 1890s and early 1900s. The federal judges, although they more often than not ruled against Chinese litigants, did not memorialize their animus toward the Chinese in the pages of the Federal Reporter. Nevertheless, as discussed in later parts of this chapter, occasional glimpses of racism appear as possible explanations for the results in particularly difficult cases.

40. The retention of top-flight attorneys partly contributed to what Chinese litigation successes they had. Rarely did the American legal system catch the Chinese unawares (*see* McClain, "The Chinese Struggle," *supra* note 7, at 541 n.58). In the 1880s, the early period of Chinese exclusion, Matthew Hall McAllister's son Hall, one of the best lawyers in the country, frequently represented Chinese. A sample of McAllister's representations include: *In re Tiburcio Parrott*, 1 F. 481 (C.C.D. Cal. 1880); *Yick Wo v. Hopkins*, 118 U.S. 356 (1886). During the 1880s and 1890s, Thomas Riordan, another prominent San Francisco attorney, argued numerous cases on behalf of Chinese litigants (*see* C. Fritz, *supra* note 25, at 238–40). In addition to *Chew Heong* (see *supra* note 27 and accompanying text), Riordan represented the Chinese litigants in the landmark case of *United States v. Wong Kim Ark*, 169 U.S. 649 (1898). During the Olney-Ross episode, for instance, Riordan urged the United States attorneys in Los Angeles and San Francisco to dismiss charges against Chinese who had not registered under the Geary Act's grace period (*see* J. Hubley Ashton to Attorney General, Sept. 15, 1893, Letter No. 9547, File No. 980 Records).

41. *See* Act of May 6, 1882, ch. 126, § 6, 22 Stat. 58, 60, *as amended by* Act of July 5, 1884, ch. 220, § 6, 23 Stat. 115, 116. At that time the law did not specify exempt classes, such as merchants and tourists (John W. Foster to Attorney General, Sept. 14, 1891, Letter No. 8839, File No. 980 Records). *See* Acting Secretary of the Treasury (name unidentifiable) to Attorney General, Dec. 27, 1893, Letter No. 13250, File No. 980 Records; *see also* Acting Secretary of the Treasury (name unidentifiable) to Attorney General, Oct. 7, 1892, Letter No. 10296, File 980 Records (describing interdepartmental difference of opinion). 20 Op. Atty. Gen. 693, *694 (1894).

42. *United States v. Mock Chew*, 54 F. 490, 492 (9th Cir. 1893).

43. The Ninth Circuit was similarly strict a decade later when it considered an entry question in a criminal prosecution for aiding and abetting the landing of Chinese laborers. The court, per Gilbert, with Ross and Morrow, rejected the argument that the 1892 Exclusion Act had expired prior to the indictment (*Sims v. United States*, 121 F. 515 [9th Cir. 1903]).

44. In stark contrast to the merchant cases were reviews of orders involving manual laborers. These cases establish few interesting principles, but they do reveal the court's attitude over time in affirming the restrictive intent of Congress (*see, e.g., Lee Joe Yen v. United States*, 148 F. 682 [9th Cir. 1906]; *Law Chin Woon v. United States*, 147 F. 227 [9th Cir. 1906]; *Low Foon Yin v. United States Immigration Comm'r*, 145 F. 791 [9th Cir. 1906]; *Lee Won Jeong v. United States*, 145 F. 512 [9th Cir. 1906]; *Mar Sing v. United States*, 137 F. 875 [9th Cir. 1905]; *Cheung Him Nin v. United States*, 133 F. 391 [9th Cir. 1904]; *Chew Hing v. United States*, 133 F. 227 [9th Cir. 1904]; *Yee Yuen v. United States*, 133 F. 222 [9th Cir. 1904]; *Mok Chung v. United States*, 133 F. 166 [9th Cir. 1904]; *Chain Chio Fong v. United States*, 133 F. 154 [9th Cir. 1904]; *Lee Yue v. United States*, 133 F. 45 [9th Cir. 1904]; *Fong Mey Yuk v. United States*,

113 F. 898 [9th Cir. 1902]; *In re Lee Gon Yung*, 111 F. 998 [C.C.N.D. Cal. 1901, per Morrow, J.]; *United States v. Chun Hoy*, 111 F. 899 [9th Cir. 1901]; *United States v. Lee Seick*, 100 F. 398 [9th Cir. 1900, per curiam]).

45. *United States v. Gee Lee*, 50 F. 271, 273 (9th Cir. 1892). In so ruling, the court construed the district court's judgment of an appeal from the commissioner of a United States court under the 1888 act to be "final," for purposes of § 6 of the Evarts Act (*see* Act of Sept. 13, 1888, ch. 1015, § 13, 25 Stat. 476, 479; Act of Mar. 3, 1891, ch. 517, § 6, 26 Stat. 826, 828).

46. *Lee Kan v. United States*, 62 F. 914 (9th Cir. 1894). The appeal was from the Northern District of California. The reported decision at 62 F. 914 provides neither the name of the district judge nor the docket number of the appeal. I am grateful to the National Archives, San Bruno Regional Branch, for confirming that Morrow wrote the district court opinion. 62 F. at *918. In dicta suggesting that his anti-Chinese views were targeted at laborers, McKenna wrote: "The interpretation of the government makes the law forbid him to stay as a merchant and do business as he formally did, and to what end? That he may be deported? No one desires it. That he may be compelled to register as a laborer? A useless compulsion" (*id.*).

47. 62 F. at 918. Assistant Secretary of the Treasury C. S. Hamlin to San Francisco Collector of Customs, May 17, 1894, Letter No. 5607, File No. 5306, Department of Justice Central Files, Year Files: 1894, RG 60, Box 769, National Archives, Washington, D.C. This result is a reasonable inference from U.S. Attorney Garter's telegram to Olney, dated the day after the Ninth Circuit rendered its decision: "Will consent to mandate in Chinese cases as directed. No cases pending of Chinese merchants coming to the country for the first time since passage of the McCreary Act. Copy of opinion circuit court of appeals forwarded" (Garter to Attorney General, May 22, 1894, Letter No. 5811, File No. 980 Records).

48. *Lew Jim v. United States*, 66 F. 953, 954 (9th Cir. 1895). *Lai Moy v. United States*, 66 F. 955, *957 (9th Cir. 1895).

49. *Wong Fong v. United States*, 77 F. 168 (9th Cir. 1896). Act of Nov. 3, 1893, ch. 14, 28 Stat. 7. 77 F. at 169–70.

50. *Ow Yang Dean v. United States*, 145 F. 801, 803–5 (9th Cir. 1906). Act of Nov. 3, 1893, ch. 14, § 2, 28 Stat. 7, 8. For McKenna's stricter interpretation, *see Lai Moy*, 66 F. at 956–57. The court was not always so generous. In *Cheung Pang v. United States*, 133 F. 392 (9th Cir. 1904), the court affirmed the deportation order of a Chinese person who had entered under a merchant's certificate. The court per Morrow ruled that his initial entry certificate was insufficient because it did not give an estimated value to his business (*id.* at 393).

51. U.S. Const. amend. XIV, *§ 1. Act of May 6, 1882, ch. 126, § 14, 22 Stat. 58, 61; Act of May 5, 1892, ch. 60, § 1, 27 Stat. 25, 25. Woodworth, "Citizenship of Chinamen," in *History of the Bench and Bar in California* 1099, 1099–1100 (O. Shuck ed. 1901). George Collins, a San Francisco attorney, offered to represent the United States as a special counsel in urging the international law theory on the courts (*see* George D. Collins to Secretary of Treasury, June 19, 1895, Unnumbered letter, File 10613, Department of Justice Central

Files, Year Files: 1895, RG 60, Box No. 857, National Archives, Washington, D.C.; Collins to Attorney General, Mar. 6, 1897, Letter No. 12219, File 10613, *id.*). Collins eventually assisted the solicitor general in his brief (*United States v. Wong Kim Ark*, 169 U.S. 649 [1898]). In his lengthy treatment of the citizenship issue, James H. Kettner discusses these theories of citizenship but does not explore the relation of the Chinese to the question (J. Kettner, *The Development of American Citizenship, 1608–1870* [1978]).

52. *United States v. Wong Kim Ark*, 169 U.S. 649, 697 (1898). *In re Look Tin Sing*, 21 F. 905, 909–10 (C.C.D. Cal. 1884). *Gee Fook Sing v. United States*, 49 F. 146, 148 (9th Cir. 1892). A companion case was *Lem Hing Dun v. United States*, 49 F. 148 (9th Cir. 1892, holding that reversal was unwarranted where the only error is a possible dispute of fact).

53. *Gee Fook Sing*, 49 F. at 148. *Lew Moy v. United States*, 164 F. 322, *324 (9th Cir. 1908). *Lee Sing Far v. United States*, 94 F. 834, *836 (9th Cir. 1899); *see also Woey Ho v. United States*, 109 F. 888, 890 (9th Cir. 1901, duty of subordinate federal court to exercise "very wide discretion" to determine credibility of witnesses).

54. E.g., *Ow Yang Dean*, 145 F. at 801; *see supra* notes 44–50 and accompanying text.

55. Fritz, *supra* note 20, at 371–72. Fritz makes much the same point about Sawyer (*id.*).

56. *United States v. Chu Chee*, 93 F. 797, 798, 805 (9th Cir. 1899). Act of Sept. 13, 1888, ch. 1015, § 2, 25 Stat. 476, 476.

57. *United States v. Ah Sou*, 138 F. 775 (9th Cir. 1905). *United States v. Ah Sou*, 132 F. 878, 879 (D. Wash. 1904). *Ow Yang Dean* was another rare reversal. *See supra* note 50 and accompanying text. 138 F. at *778. 132 F. at *879.

58. 1 United States Department of Commerce Bureau of the Census, *Historical Statistics of the United States* 107–8 (1975). Act of Dec. 17, 1943, Pub. L. 78–199, ch. 344, 57 Stat. 600.

4. INTRIGUE AT ANVIL CREEK

1. Carlson, "The Discovery of Gold at Nome, Alaska," in *Alaska and Its History* 353–54, 356 (M. Sherwood ed. 1967). *See Tornanses v. Melsing*, 106 F. 775 (9th Cir. 1901); *Anderson v. Comptois*, 108 F. 985 (9th Cir. 1901).

2. *See generally* Morrow, "The Spoilers," 4 Calif. L. Rev. 89, 92–95 (1916). *San Francisco Call*, Sept. 14, 1899, at 2, col. 4. Carlson, *supra*, note 1, at 364; *Tornanses v. Melsing*, 106 F. 775, 780 (9th Cir. 1901). The notice of location in effect told anyone interested that the ground in question had already been claimed. According to one turn-of-the-century authority on mining law, the essential steps for a notice of location were: (1) a notice posted at the site or obvious from actual possession; and (2) the marking of the boundaries on the ground (G. Costigan, *Handbook on American Mining Law* 247 [1908]). Act of May 10, 1872, ch. 152, § 1, 17 Stat. 91, 91. Lindeberg's citizenship declaration was not effective under the laws of the United States because it should have been made before a court of record, and the commissioner's court was not a court of record for that purpose (*see* Morrow, *supra*, at 95).

3. W. Hunt, *North of 53°* 98 (1974); Carlson, *supra* note 1, at 364-68; Morrow, *supra* note 2, at 96. After initially staking the area incorrectly by claiming the amount permissible for lode or quartz mines, the original locators returned to stake the legal limit of twenty acres per placer claim (Carlson, *supra*, at 365 n.42). Of the three "lucky Swedes," Brynteson located five claims for himself and six for others; Lindeberg, eight for himself and eleven for others; and Lindblom, thirty for himself and thirty for others (*id.* at 374–75). The legal authority for these filings by power of attorney was sanctioned in the Act of June 6, 1900, ch. 786, § 16, 31 Stat. 321, 328.

4. The laws of the United States made applicable to Alaska were clear on the point that aliens could hold mining claims. The Act of May 17, 1884, ch. 53, § 7, 23 Stat. 24, 25–26, provided that the general laws of Oregon were to apply as the laws of Alaska, and the general laws of Oregon in turn provided that an alien could acquire and hold land as if he were a native citizen of Oregon or the United States (*see* 3 Lord's Or. Laws §§ 7172–73 [1910], tracing earlier laws). In addition, the Act of Congress on Mar. 2, 1897, ch. 363, § 2, 29 Stat. 618, 618, specifically exempted alien miners and their claims from its general prohibition on aliens holding ownership of lands in territories. Under the laws of the United States made applicable at the time, therefore, the action of the jump-stakers was without any authority. (W. Hunt, *supra* note 3, at 98–99.)

5. Carlson, *supra* note 1, at 374, 377; Morrow, *supra* note 2, at 95–97. Hence the styling of the case, *Tornanses v. Melsing*, which became the first of the important Ninth Circuit cases arising out of this episode.

6. With apologies to William W. Morrow (Morrow, *supra* note 2, at 100: "Fortunately, the chase of the wild goose in this case turned out to be a financial success").

7. W. Hunt, *Distant Justice* 104–5 (1987); Morrow, *supra* note 2, at 100.

8. Naske, "The Shaky Beginnings of Alaska's Judicial System," 1 W. Legal Hist. 163, *199 (1988). 33 Cong. Rec. 3307 (1900). Naske, *supra*, at 202. 33 Cong. Rec. 3739–40 (1900). *Manuel v. Wulff*, 152 U.S. 505 (1894). 33 Cong. Rec. 3926–30 (1900).

9. W. Hunt, *supra* note 7, at 107. 33 Cong. Rec. *3929 (1900). Act of June 6, 1900, ch. 786, § 4, 31 Stat. 321, 322–23.

10. U.S. Const., art. I, *§ 3. E. Surrency, *History of the Federal Courts* 350–51 (1987).

11. United States Census Office, *Twelfth Census of the United States: Part I, Population* xix (1901). E. Gruening, *The State of Alaska* *103 (1954). C. Naske and H. Slotnick, *Alaska: A History of the 49th State* 80 (2d ed. 1987). If either Noyes or McKenzie left any account of their version of the events in Nome during their residencies there, historians have failed thus far to find them. Two scholars of Alaskan history who have studied this episode in depth conclude that the judge and the receiver were engaged in a conspiracy (*see* W. Hunt, *supra* note 7, at 104; Naske, *supra* note 8, at 198–210).

12. *See Tornanses*, 106 F. at 777. Since Nome did not have a natural port, many vessels stayed as far as a mile offshore and a skiff or other small boat came out from shore to disembark passengers. Whether Noyes stayed on the boat as part of the conspiracy that was about to unfold or whether there was some other

reason for not joining the other passengers in disembarking on July 19 is still a mystery. Act of June 6, 1900, ch. 786, § 4, 31 Stat. 321, 323. *In re Noyes*, 121 F. 209, *213 (9th Cir. 1902). McKenzie also "advised" them to transfer a one-fourth interest in the business of the firm to Joseph K. Wood, the United States attorney, and to make Wood a silent partner in their law firm. If the lawyers agreed to these terms, McKenzie would see to it that Hume would become Wood's deputy. (*id.*). The cases in which the firm had a contingent interest were: *Rodgers v. Kjellman* (Claim No. 2 below Discovery on Anvil Creek); *Comptois v. Anderson* (Claim No. 3 above Discovery); *Melsing v. Tornanses* (Claim No. 10 above Discovery); and *Webster v. Nakkeli* (Claim on Nakkeli Gulch, a tributary to Anvil Creek). Similar action was undertaken in a new suit, *Chipps v. Lindeberg*, which involved the Discovery Claim on Anvil Creek (*id.* at 214).

13. G. Costigan, *supra* note 2, at 520.

14. *In re Noyes*, 121 F. at 214.

15. *In re Noyes*, 121 F. at 215; Morrow, *supra* note 2, at 104–5.

16. *In re Noyes*, 121 F. at *216. Metson gave this testimony at the contempt hearing, which the press covered in lurid detail. *See San Francisco Call*, Oct. 24, 1901, at 5, col. 4. McKenzie did relinquish some of these items six weeks later on the advice of counsel (121 F. at 216).

17. *In re Noyes*, 121 F. at 215. When these revelations became public at the contempt trial of McKenzie, they naturally caused an uproar (*see San Francisco Call*, Nov. 13, 1900, at 4, col. 5; *id.*, Nov. 14, 1900, at 3, col. 3).

18. The firm of Hubbard, Beeman and Hume had instituted four lawsuits. One was an ordinary ejectment action, which did not plead a single allegation in equity that would entitle the plaintiffs to a receivership appointment. Another suit requested an injunction and the appointment of a receiver but was based on an unverified bill of complaint. All of the complaints alleged on their face that plaintiffs were United States citizens but that the defendants/original locators were aliens and not entitled to own a mining claim (*see Tornanses*, 106 F. at 778–80). The author of the court's opinion in *Tornanses*, Erskine Ross, thoroughly understood the necessary elements for appointment of a receiver. In an earlier decision for the circuit court, Ross had explained that a receiver was warranted when two competing parties claimed the same land and statutory law required certain work to be done on the land, for instance, for mining claims on public land. The appointment of a receiver was justified in such an instance to perform the necessary work while preserving the property's value for the prevailing party. *Nevada Sierra Oil Co. v. Home Oil Co.*, 98 F. 673, 674 (C.C.S.D. Cal. 1899, cited by G. Costigan, *Handbook on American Mining Law* 520 n.39 [1908]).

19. *See In re Noyes*, 121 F. at 210, 219; Morrow, *supra* note 2, at 109; *San Francisco Call*, Jan. 17, 1901, at 7, col. 5.

20. *Tornanses*, 106 F. at 782–83. The procedural posture of the case is not entirely clear. Although the "right to take an appeal is an absolute right," wrote one turn-of-the-century authority on federal jurisdiction, "it has been held by the Supreme Court—for reasons which are not fully explained, and which I must say I do not myself fully understand—that an appeal must be allowed by a judge"

(B. Curtis, *Jurisdiction, Practice, and Peculiar Jurisdiction of the Courts of the United States* 99 [H. Merwin ed. 1896]).

21. *In re Noyes*, 121 F. at 216; Morrow, *supra* note 2, at 108–9. *Tornanses*, 106 F. at *783.

22. *In re Noyes*, 121 F. at *216–17. It is unclear whose testimony the court is quoting on the first point. Transcript of Proceedings and Testimony at *529, *In re Noyes*, Nos. 701, 702, 703, and 704, Records of U.S. Court of Appeals for the Ninth Circuit, available at University of California, Hastings College of the Law, San Francisco (hereinafter Transcript). *San Francisco Call*, Oct. 22, 1901, at 3, col. 4.

23. *See* W. Hunt, *supra* note 3, at 125; *San Francisco Call*, Feb. 12, 1901, at 1, col. 5.

24. Transcript, *supra* note 22, at *547. *In re Noyes*, 121 F. at *219 (quoting Arthur H. Noyes to Major John J. Van Orsdale, Sept. 15, 1900); *see also id.* at 218.

25. *See Tornanses*, 106 F. at 783; *In re Noyes*, 121 F. at 220–21. It is unclear when the marshals arrived, but they must have reached Nome only shortly before they arrested McKenzie.

26. Morrow, *supra* note 2, at 109.

27. *San Francisco Call*, Oct. 28, 1900, at *23, col. 2 (quoting the *Nome Chronicle*). *In re Noyes*, 121 F. at *221.

28. *San Francisco Call*, Nov. 9, 1900, at 12, col. 3. Although the functions of the commissioner date from the Judiciary Act of 1789, 1 Stat. 91, the title did not enter the lexicon of the federal courts until the Act of Mar. 1, 1817, 3 Stat. 350. Heacock himself acted under the authority of the Commissioners Act of 1896, 29 Stat. 140, 184. For a general background on these officers of the court, *see United States v. Maresca*, 266 F. 713, 719–21 (S.D.N.Y. 1920, per Hough, J., describing history of commissioners); E. Surrency, *History of the Federal Courts* 361–68 (1987).

29. *San Francisco Call*, Nov. 11, 1900, at *31, col. 5; *see also id.*, Nov. 8, 1900, at 12, col. 3. There is no record of why Morrow received this assignment, but presumably Judge Gilbert, as senior judge, had such assigning authority.

30. *Tornanses*, 106 F. at *783. On McKenzie's political influence, *see* Naske, *supra* note 8, at 199–208; on the miners' view, *see* W. Hunt, *supra* note 3, at 125; *San Francisco Call*, Oct. 28, 1900, at 23, col. 2.

31. The case was styled *Tornanses v. Melsing*, for one of the suits in which McKenzie had been appointed receiver (106 F. at 775, 784, *785–86). In a later appeal involving a Montana mine, Gilbert would uphold a similar appointment of a receiver, over Judge Ross's vigorous dissent (*see Heinze v. Butte and Boston Consol. Mining Co.*, 126 F. 1 [9th Cir. 1903]). For more on this case *see infra* pp. 79–97. *Tornanses*, 106 F. at *786.

32. Act of Mar. 3, 1891, ch. 517, § 11, 36 Stat. 826, *829. *In re Claasen*, 140 U.S. 200 (1891). This case is discussed at some length in Foster, "Recent Decisions Under the Evarts Act," 1 Yale L.J. 95 (1891). *Tornanses*, 106 F. at 787, *aff'd, In re McKenzie*, 180 U.S. 536, 550 (1901).

33. *Tornanses*, 106 F. at *789, 790. *In re McKenzie*, 180 U.S. 536, 551 (1901).

34. *San Francisco Call*, May 25, 1901, at 16, col. 2; W. Hunt, *supra* note 7, at 114–15; W. Hunt, *supra* note 3, at 132 (describing a docket "jammed with hundreds of claim disputes that Noyes has never got around to hearing"). *Compare San Francisco Call*, May 26, 1901, at *27, col. 5, *with* W. Hunt, *supra* note 7, at *114. McKenzie's first bid for a pardon failed, apparently when the Justice Department learned that he still had not returned all the gold he had stolen. After more of the loot had surfaced, Attorney General Philander C. Knox recommended the pardon (*see* Morrow, *supra* note 2, at 110; 1901 Att'y Gen. Ann. Rep. 294). *San Francisco Call*, May 25, 1901, at 16, col. 2. In September, after Noyes left Nome, Attorney General Knox sent Judge James Wickersham of Alaska Division No. 3 to handle the huge backlog of cases remaining in Division No. 2.

35. W. Hunt, *supra* note 7, at 115. For a report of the first day of the hearing, see *San Francisco Call*, Oct. 18, 1901, at 14, col. 3.

36. *In re Noyes*, 121 F. at 211, *212, *213, 221–22. For instance, shortly after they arrived at Nome two of the original locators of the nearby Topkuk Mine approached Noyes and complained of certain trespasses. The judge referred these gentlemen to his private secretary with the observation that the secretary was about to resign and enter the practice of law. Whether Noyes received a kickback is unclear, but his aide insisted on a one-half interest in their mine and promised to secure it for them within twenty-four hours. When the locators balked at this exorbitant demand, Noyes appointed a man named Cameron to act as receiver of the mining property. Like McKenzie, Cameron operated the mine extensively and extracted somewhere between $100,000 and $200,000 worth of gold dust, on expenses of less than $35,000. Although the long rendition of these facts bore no direct relation to the contempt charge in the Anvil Creek Gilbert justified his explication because they "throw light upon the transaction, to show the animus of Judge Noyes in those cases, and to aid the court to interpret the nature of his conduct in the matters upon which contempt is charged" (*In re Noyes*, 121 F. at 223).

37. *In re Noyes*, 121 F. at 225 (sentencing Noyes to a fine of $1,000); *id.* at 232 (Ross, J., concurring, arguing that Noyes should be sentenced to eighteen months' imprisonment); *id.* at 332–33 (Morrow, J., concurring, agreeing with Judge Gilbert that because Noyes held a judicial position his sentence should be a fine of $1,000). It seems unlikely that Gilbert, Ross, and Morrow would actively lobby Congress after being attacked. Gilbert and Ross were distinctly unpolitical; Morrow might have engaged in *sub rosa* communications with political friends in Washington, but I have been unable to uncover any such records.

38. *In re Noyes*, 121 F. at 226.

39. *In re Noyes*, 121 F. at *227 (quoting testimony of Marshal George H. Burnham). *Id.* at 228.

40. *In re Noyes*, 121 F. at 231. Noyes did not appeal. *See* W. Hunt, *supra* note 3, at 127. In addition to the two principal cases of *Tornanses v. Melsing* and *In re Noyes*, the court decided other claims involving Anvil Creek. These included: *Anderson v. Comptois*, 109 F. 971 (9th Cir. 1901); *Lindeberg v. Chipps*, 108 F. 988 (9th Cir. 1901); *Lindeberg v. Requa*, 108 F. 988 (9th Cir. 1901). *See also Kjellman v. Rodgers*, 109 F. 1061 (9th Cir. 1901).

41. R. Beach, *The Spoilers* (1905); *The Spoilers* (1930, with Gary Cooper); *The Spoilers* (1942, with John Wayne, Marlene Dietrich, and Randolph Scott); *The Spoilers* (1955, with Anne Baxter). W. Hunt, *supra* note 7, at 122.

42. E. Harrison, *Nome and Seward Peninsula* 69 (1905); C. Hulley, *Alaska: Past and Present* 269 (1958); D. Estes, ed., *Our Northern Domain* 89 (D. Estes ed. 1910); Helms and Mangusso, "The Nome Gold Conspiracy," 73 Pac. Northwest Q. 10, 12 (1982). C. Naske, *An Interpretive History of Alaskan Statehood* 18 (1973). *San Francisco Call*, Nov. 6, 1900, at 14, col. 6.

43. *See infra*, Appendix. In this 1900–1910 period, at least 12 percent of the court's docket consisted of cases involving mining companies, and approximately 17 percent of the court's cases overall originated in Alaska.

44. *See*, e.g., *Engelstad v. Dufresne*, 116 F. 582 (9th Cir. 1902); *Walton v. Wild Goose Mining and Trading Co.*, 123 F. 209 (9th Cir. 1903); *McKay v. Neussler*, 148 F. 86 (9th Cir. 1906).

45. *See*, e.g., *Charlton v. Kelly*, 156 F. 433 (9th Cir. 1907, Nome ejectment action). On miners' confidence, *see*, e.g., *Lange v. Robinson*, 148 F. 799 (9th Cir. 1906, reversing and remanding for new trial); *Smith v. Cascaden*, 148 F. 792, 795 (9th Cir. 1906, Ross, J., dissenting).

46. W. Hunt, *supra* note 3, at *126; *see also id.* at 134. Typically, contempt sentences ran from three to six months, except where defendants were withholding money, documents, or testimony from the court, in which case they were held until they cooperated with the court. *See*, e.g., *In re Debs*, 158 U.S. 564, 573 (1895); *Pepke v. Cronan*, 155 U.S. 100, 101 (1894); *Anderson v. Comptois*, 109 F. 971, 976 (9th Cir. 1901); *In re Reese*, 98 F. 984, 985 (C.C.D. Kan. 1900). *In re Noyes*, 121 F. at *232 (Ross, J., concurring). Because Noyes was a territorial district judge, he was subject to removal at the discretion of the president. *See* E. Surrency, *supra* note 10, at 350.

47. 35 Cong. Rec. *1324 (1902). *San Francisco Call*, Nov. 6, 1900, at *14, col. 6 (quoting statement attributed to Noyes).

48. *President's Secretary to Attorney General P. C. Knox, Feb. 6, 1902, Letter No. *4475, File No. 10,000–1900, RG 60, Department of Justice General Records, National Archives, Washington, D.C. E. S. Pillsbury to Attorney General P. C. Knox, Feb. 6, 1902, Letter No. 2358, File 10,000-1900 Records. For the record, Noyes was removed from office on February 24, 1902 (W. Hunt, *supra* note 7, at 120).

5. THE JUDICIAL FAULTLINE

1. Denman, "What the Seven Circuit Judges of the Circuit Court of Appeals for the Ninth Circuit Have Created for the Service of Their Litigants," at 5 (1941), Papers of William Denman, Bancroft Library, University of California at Berkeley. The Supreme Court's discretionary jurisdiction meant that only a handful of Ninth Circuit decisions were superseded by decisions of the Court. On public land history, *see generally* P. Gates, *History of Public Land Law Development* (1968); Public Land Law Review Commission, *One Third of the Nation's Land* 23 (1970). The most obvious exception to the generalization in the text about the role of the federal courts in the development of natural resource

law was water. Aside from the signal importance of Supreme Court decisions, the state courts have undertaken the primary responsibility of charting the course of water law development. An admittedly crude indicator is the vast differential in numbers of important state water law cases versus those in the lower federal courts. In his treatise on western water law, for example, Wells A. Hutchins cites 41 Ninth Circuit cases spanning more than eighty years of water law development. By contrast, he cites over 2,000 state court cases. *See* 3 W. Hutchins, *Water Rights Laws in the Nineteen Western States* 656–725 (1977). Certainly some of these 41 cases established important principles of water law, but the *comparative* importance of the western state courts over the Ninth Circuit warrants an omission of these federal cases from a discussion of the judicial battles over natural resources. For an interesting treatment of the role of the courts in California's history of water development, see D. Pisani, *From Family Farm to Agribusiness* (1984).

2. *Bradley v. Fallbrook Irrig. Dist.*, 68 F. 948, 966 (C.C.S.D. Cal. 1895), *rev'd*, 164 U.S. 112 (1896).

3. Act of Feb. 13, 1925, ch. 229, 43 Stat. 936. Even then, this extension of jurisdiction to the circuit courts of appeals contained important exceptions for antitrust and interstate commerce laws, writs of error by the United States in criminal cases, suits to enjoin state statutes or state administrative action, and suits to enjoin Interstate Commerce Commission orders (*id.* § 1, 43 Stat. at 938 [amending Judicial Code § 238]). *See generally* F. Frankfurter and J. Landis, *The Business of the Supreme Court* 262–63 (1928). On the Supreme Court's action, see *Fallbrook Irrig. Dist. v. Bradley*, 164 U.S. 112 (1896). If the large number of newspaper clippings in his scrapbook are an adequate guide, Ross took much pride in his decision in the case. One such article stated: "A careful reading of the full text of Judge Ross' decision brings the comforting assurance that, in these times of enormous aggregation of capital, there is at least one tribunal that holds individual rights are inalienable, and cannot, in justice, be sacrificed even in the interests of an entire community, unless the fact of a direct benefit therefrom be established" (Unidentified newspaper clipping, Scrapbook of Erskine M. Ross, deposited at Los Angeles County Law Library).

4. The legal historian Arnold Paul's delineation of "laissez-faire conservatism" and "traditional conservatism" as prevailing judicial philosophies in the 1880s and 1890s arguably provides little guidance for understanding Gilbert and Ross. "Laissez-faire conservatism," explained Paul, drew "heavily on the anti-paternalism doctrines of Herbert Spencer and dedicated [itself] to the utmost freedom for economic initiative and the utmost restriction upon legislative interference." "Traditional conservatism," by contrast, assigned "the protection of private property to a high status in the hierarchy of values, [but] was especially concerned with the problems of maintaining an ordered society in a world where the forces of popular democracy might become unmanageable" (A. Paul, *Conservative Crisis and the Rule of Law: Attitudes of Bar and Bench, 1887–1895*, at 4–5 [1960]). Ross's opinions displayed his belief in the traditional conservative veneration of private property, but they were less concerned with the challenge of popular democracy to maintaining order. Gilbert's philosophy also appeared to accept aspects of both laissez-faire and traditional conservatism, inasmuch as

he favored economic initiative but did not view legislative incursions into this realm disparagingly and saw maintaining social order as a key goal but not to the extent of hallowing private property. Benedict's article on laissez-faire constitutionalism is somewhat more helpful in creating a framework for understanding the thinking of Ross and Gilbert, but its emphasis on *constitutional* decision making diminishes its usefulness in the Ninth Circuit context, because so few issues the court considered in this era involved the Constitution. The bulk of its work was much more commercial- and property-oriented (*see* Benedict, "Laissez-Faire and Liberty: A Re-Evaluation of the Meaning and Origins of Laissez-Faire Constitutionalism," 3 Law and Hist. Rev. 293 [1985]).

5. Act of Aug. 1, 1912, ch. 269, 37 Stat. 242, *243. *Sutherland v. Purdy*, 234 F. 600, 601 (9th Cir. 1916). 234 F. at *604 (Gilbert, J., dissenting).

6. *Eadie v. Chambers*, 172 F. 73, 75 (9th Cir. 1909), *rev'd sub nom.*, *Waskey v. Chambers*, 224 U.S. 564 (1912). *Id.* at *80–81 (Ross, J., dissenting).

7. *Alaska Treadwell Gold Mining Co. v. Alaska Gastineau Mining Co.*, 214 F. 718, *727 (9th Cir. 1914), *cert. denied*, 238 U.S. 614 (1915), *modified*, 221 F. 1019 (1915).

8. *Id.* at *727; *id.* at *731 (Gilbert, J., dissenting). For another case that illustrates the difference in approach taken by Gilbert and Ross to contract disputes, see *Turner v. Wells*, 238 F. 766 (9th Cir. 1917). In this case Gilbert (with Morrow) upheld a district court judgment for defendants under a grubstake contract that provided that in exchange for supplies the miner would locate prospective mines to be held by the contracting parties. The suit alleged conspiracy to defraud the plaintiff of rights under the contract by filing claims only in the defendant's name. The court affirmed judgment for the defendant on the ground that the evidence was insufficient "to establish any interest of the appellant in the mining claims in controversy" (238 F. at 770). Judge Ross dissented without opinion.

9. *Smith v. Cascaden*, 148 F. 792, *794 (9th Cir. 1906). *See* 148 F. at 797–98 (Ross, J., dissenting). *See also Sturtevant v. Vogel*, 167 F. 448, 453–56 (9th Cir. 1909, Ross, J., dissenting).

10. *Ralph v. Cole*, 249 F. 81, 97 (9th Cir. 1918, Gilbert, J., dissenting), *rev'd*, 248 U.S. 553 (1918). *Compare Consolidated Mut. Oil Co. v. United States*, 245 F. 521, 531 (9th Cir. 1917, Gilbert, J., dissenting) *with Heinze v. Butte and Boston Consol. Mining Co.*, 126 F. 1, 28–29 (9th Cir. 1903, Ross, J., dissenting), *cert. denied*, 195 U.S. 631 (1904). By the Judicial Code of 1911, Congress abolished the circuit courts, leaving district courts as the principal courts of original jurisdiction (Act of Mar. 3, 1911, ch. 231, § 289, 36 Stat. 1087, 1167). *See supra* Chapter One.

11. *See generally* Naske, "The Shaky Beginnings of Alaska's Judicial System," 1 W. Legal Hist. 163 (1988); Coates, "Controlling the Periphery: The Territorial Administration of the Yukon and Alaska, 1867–1959," 78 Pac. Nw. Q. 145 (1987); Baumgartner, "Organization and Administration of Justice in Alaska," 20 A.B.A. J. 23 (1934).

12. *See generally* T. Navin, *Copper Mining and Management* 117–24 (1978); R. Paul, *California Gold: The Beginning of Mining in the Far West* (1947). In Alaska, this movement toward consolidation was in its incipient stages during

the Nome affair and the subsequent gold rush near Fairbanks. Opportunities for individual enrichment were still plentiful, and the Ninth Circuit decided numerous cases in this development. *See supra* Chapter Four. In Arizona, the consolidation occurred in a much less litigious environment; the Ninth Circuit's effect, therefore, was considerably smaller there. The copper companies in Bisbee, for example, agreed not to cannibalize each other (*see* T. Navin, *supra*, at 232). Nevertheless, a few cases did arise (*see*, e.g., *Smith v. Hovland*, 11 F.2d 9 [9th Cir. 1926]; *Martin v. Development Co. of Am.*, 240 F. 42 [9th Cir. 1917]). *See* M. Malone, *The Battle for Butte* (1981); S. McNelis, *Copper King at War: The Biography of F. Augustus Heinze* (1968); C. Glasscock, *The War of the Copper Kings* (1935).

13. *See* M. Malone, *supra* note 12, at 46–51, 134–35. On the origins of the Anaconda and the precursor to Rogers's bid for control of the Montana copper industry, see Toole, "The Anaconda Copper Mining Company: A Price War and a Copper Corner," 41 Pac. Nw. Q. 312 (1950). Anaconda originally incorporated in 1891 as the Anaconda Mining Company. In 1895 it reincorporated as the Anaconda Copper Mining Company, a name it held until 1955, when it became the Anaconda Company (*id.* at 45–46).

14. According to one historian of mining, Heinze developed a sophisticated knowledge of the intricate vein system in the Butte district. He discovered who owned various properties and plotted the likely geographical direction for mineral veins. By purchasing tiny slivers of property adjacent to a rich mine, Heinze could then sue to tie up a competitor's investment: "Heinze found ample scope for predatory litigation, and by means of a few well-selected purchases of claims he started lawsuits that undermined the ownership of some of the richest properties" (T. Rickard, *A History of American Mining* 362 [1932]). *See also* S. McNelis, *supra* note 12, at 17. M. Malone, *supra* note 12, at 142–43. *See*, e.g., *Forrester v. Boston and Mont. Consol. Copper and Silver Mining Co.*, 21 Mont. 544, 564 (1898); *MacGinniss v. Boston and Mont. Consol. Copper and Silver Mining Co.*, 119 F. 96, 101 (9th Cir. 1902).

15. *Morse v. Montana Ore-Purchasing Co.*, 105 F. 337, 348 (C.C.D. Mont. 1900). Knowles, district judge since 1890, had been a territorial judge in Montana as early as Andrew Johnson's administration. This Harvard-educated jurist clearly understood the political machinations of the Butte mining camps. For more on Knowles, see *Judges of the United States* 277–78 (Bicentennial ed. 1983). Malone describes William Clancy, a Montana state judge, as a pliant loyalist of Heinze's who routinely upheld the young copper mogul's interests irrespective of the issue (M. Malone, *supra* note 12, at 143–44).

16. *Heinze v. Butte and Boston Consolidated Mining Co.*, 126 F. 1, *11 (9th Cir. 1903), *cert. denied*, 195 U.S. 631 (1904).

17. 126 F. at 27–29 (Ross, J., dissenting).

18. M. Malone and R. Roeder, *Montana: A History of Two Centuries* 158–59 (1976); Richter, "The Amalgamated Copper Company: A Closed Chapter in Corporation Finance," 30 Q. J. Econ. 387, 388–90 (1916).

19. *See* M. Malone, *supra* note 12, at 173–77; S. McNelis, *supra* note 12, at 76–83. *Heinze v. Butte and Boston Consolidated Mining Co.*, 129 F. 274 (9th Cir. 1904), *cert. denied*, 194 U.S. 632 (1904). As Malone observed, "It is

interesting to note that the [Montana] supreme court, perhaps reflecting the anti-trust sentiment of the state, frequently sustained the rulings of Heinze's Butte judges" (M. Malone, *supra*, at 182). For an interesting account of these negotiations, see B. Forbes, *Men Who Are Making the West* 244–47 (1923); M. Malone, *supra*, at 187.

20. See Johnson, "Electrical Power, Copper, and John D. Ryan," 38 Montana 24 (1988); B. Forbes, *supra* note 19, at 229–30. *Geddes v. Anaconda Copper Mining Co.*, 245 F. 225, 226–31 (9th Cir. 1917), *rev'd*, 254 U.S. 590 (1921). *See id.* at 227 (citing *Wilder Mfg. Co. v. Corn Prods. Ref. Co.*, 236 U.S. 165 (1915)).

21. 245 F. at *226. 245 F. at 243 (opinion of Gilbert, J.). Wolverton, an Oregon federal district judge from 1905 until his death on September 21, 1926, often sat on the circuit court of appeals. Gilbert was not swayed by Ross's contention that the bid auction was a sham because it involved only one company, the Anaconda (*id.*).

22. *See* M. Malone, *supra* note 12, at 203; on Heinze's use of lawyers, see S. McNelis, *supra* note 12, at 52.

23. M. Malone, *supra* note 12, at 42–43; T. Navin, *supra* note 12, at 30–32, 203–4; Toole and Butcher, "Timber Depredations on the Montana Public Domain, 1885–1918," 7 J. of the West 351, 353–60 (1968). Act of June 3, 1878, ch. 150, 20 Stat. *88. For interesting background material on early efforts to protect public timber from depredation, see P. Gates, *supra* note 1, at 531–61.

24. *United States v. Bitter Root Dev. Co.*, 133 F. 274 (9th Cir. 1904), *aff'd*, 200 U.S. 451 (1906). On the federal government's timid prosecutorial efforts to this time, see M. Malone, *supra* note 12, at 227 n.24. 133 F. at *278; *see also id.* at 276–77. Daly had died in 1900, before the bill was brought; the government therefore named his wife, Margaret P. Daly, as executrix on the bill.

25. *United States v. Clark*, 129 F. 241, 244 (C.C.D. Mont. 1904). *United States v. Clark*, 138 F. 294, *303 (9th Cir. 1904), *aff'd*, 200 U.S. 601 (1906). 138 F. at 303 (Gilbert, J., dissenting). Malone criticized the Supreme Court's affirmance in *Clark* in very uncharitable terms, saying that Justice Holmes "reasoned incredibly in his majority opinion that Clark had not been aware of the tricks his subordinates played upon Uncle Sam through fraudulently acquired homesteads" (M. Malone, *supra* note 12, at 44). *See United States v. Clark*, 200 U.S. 601 (1906).

26. McKinney, "A. B. Hammond, West Coast Lumberman," 28 J. Forest Hist. 196, *197 (1984). For the district court opinion, see *United States v. Hammond*, 226 F. 849 (N.D. Cal. 1914). *Hammond v. United States*, 246 F. 40, 41 (9th Cir. 1917).

27. 246 F. at *45. *Id.* at 50–51 (citing *White v. United States*, 202 F. 501 [5th Cir. 1913]). 246 F. at *54 (Gilbert, J., dissenting). Toole and Butcher, *supra* note 23, at 359.

28. As two historians of the Montana timber depredations have written, "In literally dozens of cases, the government won in the lower courts, only to lose on appeal" (Toole and Butcher, *supra* note 23, at 359).

29. *United States v. Van Winkle*, 113 F. 903, 904–5 (9th Cir. 1902). *United States v. Coughanour*, 133 F. 224 (9th Cir. 1904); *Anderson v. United States*, 152 F. 87 (9th Cir. 1907). 1909 Att'y Gen. Ann. Rep. 11, 242–43. Indeed, a

ranking of the top five districts in terms of dollars recovered through such depredation suits shows only one (northern California, $10,989.19) in the Ninth Circuit. The others in the top five were Colorado ($15,332.50), southern Florida ($12,661.00), western Louisiana ($8,991.73), and Wyoming ($8,509.47) (*id.* at 243). 1910 Att'y Gen. Ann. Rep. 403. This rate of recovery—a little over 2 percent—was exceeded slightly the following year, when the government recovered $148,130.66 (approximately 5 percent) on suits requesting $2,800,182.44 (*see* 1911 Att'y Gen. Ann. Rep. 345).

30. E.g., *Multnomah Mining, Milling and Dev. Co. v. United States*, 211 F. 100 (9th Cir. 1914); *Frick v. United States*, 255 F. 612 (9th Cir. 1919); *Washington Sec. Co. v. United States*, 194 F. 59 (9th Cir. 1912), *aff'd*, 234 U.S. 76 (1914). For the land fraud suits, *see*, e.g., *United States v. Jones*, 242 F. 609 (9th Cir. 1917); *McClure v. United States*, 187 F. 265 (9th Cir. 1911); *McLeod v. United States*, 187 F. 261 (9th Cir. 1911); *Jones v. United States*, 179 F. 584 (9th Cir. 1910). This last case brought to light an elaborate conspiracy to defraud the government of public lands through abuse of the homestead provisions that involved, among others, a United States senator from Oregon and the United States commissioner of the General Land Office.

31. The original statute of 1862 provided that the grant to the railroad company would be of "every alternate section of public land, designated by odd numbers, to the amount of five alternate sections per mile on each side of said railroad, on the line thereof, and within the limits of ten miles on each side of said road, . . . *Provided*, That all mineral lands shall be excepted from the operation of this act" (Act of July 1, 1862, ch. 120, § 3, 12 Stat. 489, 492). Two years later, Congress increased the subsidy to ten alternate sections and twenty miles. It also amended the "mineral land" prohibition so that it "shall not be construed to include coal and iron land" (Act of July 2, 1864, ch. 216, § 4, 13 Stat. 356, 358). *See also* Act of July 27, 1866, ch. 278, § 3, 14 Stat. 292, 294. For an interesting examination of these problems from the perspective of Standard Oil Company of California, which lobbied hard to free these lands for exploration and drilling, see G. White, *Formative Years in the Far West: A History of Standard Oil Company of California and Predecessors Through 1919*, at 433–59 (1962). For more on the land-grant subsidy, see *supra* Chapter Two. J. Bates, *The Origins of Teapot Dome* 166–67 (1963); H. Cummings and C. McFarland, *Federal Justice* 398 (1937).

32. *Roberts v. Southern Pac. Co.*, 186 F. 934, 942–46 (C.C.S.D. Cal. 1911), *aff'd*, 219 F. 1022 (9th Cir. 1915). H. Cummings and C. McFarland, *supra* note 31, at 401. *See Burke v. Southern Pac. R.R. Co.*, 234 U.S. 669, 672, 710–11 (1914). Under § 239 of the 1911 Judicial Code, Congress authorized the circuit courts of appeals to "certify to the Supreme Court of the United States any questions or propositions of law concerning which it desires the instruction of that court for its proper decision." The Supreme Court could decide just those questions or request the whole record and render judgment on the case "as if it had been brought there for review by writ of error or appeal." In both instances the Court's decision was binding on the circuit court of appeals (Act of Mar. 3, 1911, ch. 231, § 239, 36 Stat. 1087, 1157). *See generally* J. Hopkins, *The Judicial Code* 204 (1911).

33. 234 U.S. at 692. *See* 1912 Att'y Gen. Ann. Rep. 40. Conforming its pleadings to Ross's decision, the government filed this suit claiming fraud prior to the Supreme Court's ruling (*United States v. Southern Pac. Co.*, 225 F. 197 [S.D. Cal. 1915]). The trial court decision in the consolidated case apparently was not published (*see Southern Pac. Co. v. United States*, 249 F. 785 [9th Cir. 1918, reversing]; 1915 Att'y Gen. Ann. Rep. 37 [reporting victory at district court level]).

34. *Consolidated Mut. Oil Co. v. United States*, 245 F. 521 (9th Cir. 1917). 245 F. at *526 (quoting the executive order). Act of June 25, 1910, ch. 421, 36 Stat. 847.

35. 245 F. at *527. Ross retained in his scrapbook a warm letter from Taft written on November 21, 1921, a few months after Taft became chief justice of the United States. In the letter, Taft recalled that "we became friends now thirty years ago" and expressed his delight that Ross was "still making [himself] the Rock of Gibraltar out in the Ninth Circuit" (William H. Taft to Erskine M. Ross, Nov. 21, 1921, Scrapbook of Erskine M. Ross, deposited at Los Angeles County Law Library). Considering how few letters Ross placed in his scrapbook, the three he kept from Taft—one even dating from 1901, when Taft was serving as civil governor of the Philippines—suggest the depth of his respect for this friend (*see* Scrapbook of Erskine M. Ross, deposited at Los Angeles County Law Library). In the third letter, Taft wrote seeking permission to propose Ross for membership in the American Bar Association (Taft to Ross, Mar. 30, 1914, in *id.*).

36. 245 F. at *531 (Gilbert, J., dissenting). *See, e.g., Heinze v. Butte and Boston Consol. Mining Co.*, 126 F. 1 (9th Cir. 1903), *cert. denied*, 195 U.S. 631 (1904). 245 F. at *532 (Gilbert, J., dissenting). In some exasperation, Gilbert remarked of his colleagues, "Perhaps the members of this court would not have appointed a receiver upon the showing made, but this is not the question here. The question is whether the court below manifestly abused the discretion which was lodged in it" (*id.*).

37. J. Bates, *supra* note 31, at *171; *Southern Pac. Co. v. United States*, 249 F. 785 (9th Cir. 1918); *rev'd*, 251 U.S. 1 (1949).

38. 249 F. at 804–5.

39. *See* 249 F. at 804–5 (Gilbert, J., dissenting). *But see, e.g., Mesa Verde Constr. Co. v. Northern Cal. Dist. Council of Laborers*, 895 F. 516, 520 (9th Cir. 1990, Noonan, J., dissenting without opinion).

40. *United States v. Southern Pac. Co.*, 260 F. 511, 512, *513 (S.D. Cal. 1919). *L. D. McKisick to Holmes Conrad, Dec. 10, 1895, Letter No. 18,562, Justice Department Records.

41. *See* 249 F. at 805. *United States v. Southern Pac. Co.*, 251 U.S. 1 (1919). As Palmer explained in his 1920 Report, "[I]t seemed clear that an appeal would have been not only wasteful of time and money, but it might well be deemed frivolous" (1920 Att'y Gen. Ann. Rep. 112). McKeage, "The Naval Petroleum Reserves: A Modern Perspective," 28 J. of the West 52, *55 (1989). *See infra* Chapter Seven.

42. This happened in at least four major cases: *Morrison v. United States*, 212 F. 29 (9th Cir. 1914), *rev'd*, 240 U.S. 192 (1916); *Consolidated Mut. Oil Co.*

v. United States, 245 F. 521 (9th Cir. 1917); *Hammond v. United States*, 246 F. 40 (9th Cir. 1917); and *Southern Pac. Co. v. United States*, 249 F. 785 (9th Cir. 1918).

43. *Mountain Copper Co. v. United States*, 142 F. 625 (9th Cir. 1906), *appeal dismissed*, 212 U.S. 587 (1908). For the facts of this case, see 142 F. at 625–29.

44. 142 F. at *629. This approach did not anticipate the Supreme Court's treatment of a related issue in a decision handed down the following year. In *Georgia v. Tennessee Copper Co.*, 206 U.S. 230 (1907), a case brought under the Court's original jurisdiction, the Court issued an injunction requiring abatement of noxious fumes after allowing the copper company reasonable time to complete pollutant-decreasing structures under construction. The Court found that the injury sustained by Georgia was not less when it sued in its capacity as an individual landowner than it was when it sued in its role as quasi-sovereign (*id.* at 237). In *Mountain Copper*, Ross had taken the opposite approach (142 F. at 640). 142 F. at *638.

45. *Woodruff v. North Bloomfield Gravel Mining Co.*, 18 F. 753 (C.C.D. Cal. 1884). For an interesting commentary on Sawyer's decision in historical context, see D. Smith, *Mining America* 69–73 (1987). 18 F. at 809. 142 F. at *644, *647 (Hawley, J., dissenting).

46. *McCarthy v. Bunker Hill and Sullivan Mining and Concentrating Co.*, 164 F. 927 (9th Cir. 1908), *cert. denied*, 212 U.S. 583 (1909). *McCarthy v. Bunker Hill and Sullivan Mining and Concentrating Co.*, 147 F. 981, 985 (C.C.D. Idaho 1906), *aff'd as modified*, 164 F. 927 (9th Cir. 1908), *cert. denied*, 212 U.S. 583 (1909).

47. 160 F. at *940. *See supra* notes 2–3 and accompanying text.

48. *See* 164 F. at 936.

49. *Bliss v. Washoe Copper Co.*, 186 F. 789, *825 (9th Cir. 1911), *cert. dismissed*, 231 U.S. 764 (1913). On Ross's landownings, most of which he earned as a legal fee before becoming a judge, see G. Cosgrave, *Early California Justice* 71 (1948); J. Sherer, *History of Glendale and Vicinity* 305–6 (1922).

50. Comment, "Mining and Water Law: Pollution of Water by Mining Operations: Injunction," 1 Calif. L. Rev. 545, 545 (1913). *Arizona Copper Co. v. Gillespie*, 230 U.S. 46, *56 (1913). The court added: "The wrong and injury, whether it results from pollution of a stream or otherwise, is not condoned because of the importance of the operations conducted by the defendant to either the public or the wrongdoer, and for that wrong, there must be a remedy" (*id.*).

51. *See generally* S. Hays, *Conservation and the Gospel of Efficiency: The Progressive Conservation Movement, 1890–1920* (1959); E. Richardson, *The Politics of Conservation: Crusades and Controversies, 1897–1913* (1962); B. Hibbard, *A History of the Public Land Policies* 472–75 (1924; reprint 1965).

52. *Cameron v. United States*, 250 F. 943 (9th Cir. 1918), *aff'd*, 252 U.S. 450 (1920). *See generally* Comment, "Mining Law: Jurisdiction of Land Department to Declare Mining Claims Invalid," 9 Calif. L. Rev. 433, 434 (1921). *Cameron v. United States*, 252 U.S. 450 (1920).

53. *See, e.g., American Smelting and Refining Co. v. Godfrey*, 158 F. 225, 130, 235 (9th Cir. 1907, upholding an injunction for nuisance and distinguishing

the Ninth Circuit's decision in *Mountain Copper* based on value of the damaged property); *Thropp v. Harpers Ferry Paper Co.*, 142 F. 690 (4th Cir. 1902, upholding an injunction for pollution that interfered with a downstream landowner's reasonable use of the stream).

6. REPLACING THE VANGUARD

1. Its last new member, William W. Morrow, joined the court in 1897. The only circuit to approach this longevity record was the Fifth Circuit, which gained a new member in 1899. (*see* Committee on the Judiciary, "Legislative History of the United States Circuit Courts of Appeals and the Judges Who Served During the Period 1801 Through May 1972," Senate Comm. on Judiciary, 92d Cong., 2d Sess. [1972, charts on each circuit; hereinafter Senate Judiciary Committee, "Legislative History"]).

2. Fortunately, the building emerged relatively undamaged from these disasters, although enough latent damage apparently occurred to render the courthouse uninhabitable after the 1989 Loma Prieta earthquake. For more on the history of this building, see Farneth, "'A Post Office That's a Palace': U.S. Court of Appeals and Post Office Building," 1 West. Legal Hist. 57 (1988).

3. 1897 Rep. Att'y Gen. at 3; *id.* for 1913, at 75. A review of the court's docket books for these years reveals that the clerk officially recorded 72 appeals in 1897, rather than 71 as the attorney general reported (*see* Ninth Circuit Statistical Study, Comparison Table of Docket Books and Attorney General Reports, on file with the Ninth Circuit Library, San Francisco, California).

4. Act of Mar. 3, 1911, ch. 231, § 289, 36 Stat. 1087, 1167. For more on the 1930s reforms that created more Ninth Circuit judgeships, *see infra* pp. 221–227.

5. Act of June 18, 1910, ch. 309, 36 Stat. 539, 539–40. Heretofore, the circuit courts reviewed ICC orders (*id.*).

6. Act of June 18, 1910, 36 Stat. at 541. In President Taft's nomination message to the Senate, he nominated Hunt for the Ninth Circuit and designated him to serve for three years in the Commerce Court (*see* 42 J. of Senate Exec. Proceedings 55 (1942), available at National Archives, Washington, D.C.). This nomination message appears to conflict with the statutory language, for the statute vests such assigning power in the chief justice. The Commerce Court never had a great deal of support among bench and bar, and it had been created by narrow majorities in both the House and the Senate (*see generally* F. Frankfurter and J. Landis, *The Business of the Supreme Court* 153–74 [1928]). Senate Judiciary Committee, "Legislative History," at 27; *see also* Act of Oct. 22, 1913, ch. 32, 38 Stat. 208, 219 (reauthorizing assignment under Act of June 18, 1910, ch. 309, § 1, 36 Stat. 539, 540).

7. *See generally* File of William H. Hunt, Department of Justice Appointment Files, Ninth Circuit, 1855–1901, Tray 2, RG 60, National Archives, Washington, D.C. *Judges of the United States* 240–41 (2d ed. 1983).

8. *William H. Hunt to Erskine M. Ross, July 7, 1915, Scrapbook of Erskine M. Ross, deposited at the Los Angeles County Law Library (hereinafter Ross Scrapbook). The only other judges whose correspondence Ross memori-

alized in this way were Chief Justice William Howard Taft and Justice James C. McReynolds. Except for incidental references in newspaper clippings, a reader of Ross's scrapbook would not know that he served for nearly thirty years with William B. Gilbert and William W. Morrow.

9. Act of Mar. 3, 1911, ch. 231, § 260, 36 Stat. 1087, 1161.

10. *See* Senator Thomas J. Walsh to Attorney General James C. McReynolds, May 29, 1913, File of Hon. William Kent, House of Representatives, Re: Federal Judgeships in California, Apr. 12, 1913, Judges, Ninth Circuit Court of Appeals, A–H, Department of Justice Records, RG 60, National Archives, Washington, D.C. (hereinafter Kent File). William Kent to Woodrow Wilson, Apr. 9, 1913, Kent File. President Franklin D. Roosevelt appointed Denman in 1935. *See infra* Chapter Eight. For the source of the rumors, see Walsh to McReynolds, May 29, 1913, Kent File. *See also* Macdonald, "Erskine Mayo Ross: Courageous Jurist and Generous Benefactor," 33 A.B.A. J. 1172, 1173 (1947). Unidentified newspaper clipping, Ross Scrapbook.

11. *See* G. Cosgrave, *Early California Justice: The History of the United States District Court for the Southern District of California, 1849–1944*, at 71 (1948). When Ross became physically disabled is unknown. 57 Cong. Rec. *380–81 (1919). Act of Feb. 25, 1919, ch. 29, § 6, 40 Stat. 1156, *1157, *1158.

12. *See San Francisco Examiner*, Jan. 8, 1919, at 1, col. 2. On Morrow's friendship with Johnson, *see* Hiram Johnson to Sons, Mar. 26, 1922, Hiram Johnson Papers, Bancroft Library, University of California at Berkeley (hereinafter Johnson Papers). On the marriage of his daughter to Colonel Roosevelt, *see San Francisco Examiner*, Dec. 28, 1927, at 1, col. 3. *San Francisco Examiner*, Apr. 26, 1920, at *2, col. 5. *San Francisco Examiner*, May 26, 1920, at 1, col. 4. Gilbert and Ross did not share Morrow's view of what statements a judge was permitted to make in public. Both were scrupulous in avoiding public discussions of partisan politics. In this area Morrow departed sharply from the standards set by his longtime predecessor as district judge in northern California, Ogden Hoffman (*see* C. Fritz, *Federal Justice in California: The Court of Ogden Hoffman, 1851–1891*, at 38 [1991]).

13. *San Francisco Examiner*, Oct. 5, 1921, at 13, col. 13. *San Francisco Examiner*, Oct. 7, 1921, at 8, col. 3. *San Francisco Chronicle*, Oct. 6, 1921, at *7, col. 2. *San Francisco Examiner*, Oct. 10, 1921, at *3, col. 4.

14. Act of Feb. 25, 1919, § 6, 40 Stat. 1156, 1157. *San Francisco Chronicle*, Jan. 6, 1923, at *5, col. 1. A LEXIS search reveals that Morrow sat on the panel of ninety-nine appeals in published cases and wrote thirty-four opinions, including one dissent, during this period (*San Francisco Examiner*, Dec. 28, 1927, at 1, col. 3). *McDonough v. United States*, 299 F. 30 (9th Cir. 1924). *McDonough v. United States*, 1 F.2d 147, *149 (9th Cir. 1924). His wife, Margaret, died in 1926 after sixty-one years of marriage, and in 1928 Morrow surprised the community by wedding his nurse, Julia Neill, aged fifty-one. Morrow was then eighty-four. What the *San Francisco Chronicle* had written in 1921 seemed equally true seven years later: "Unlike the high candle-power lamp which burns brightly, fiercely, then suddenly goes out, his life may be likened to the wax taper sheltered from the wind, never flickering nor flaring up, but burning slowly and steadily until finally consumed." Morrow's candle finally expired on July 14,

1929 (*San Francisco Chronicle*, Oct. 6, 1921, at 7, col. 2). On his death *see San Francisco Chronicle*, July 25, 1929, at 13, col. 6; July 26, 1929, at 17, col. 8; July 26, 1929, at 28, col. 1.

15. "In Memoriam: Hon. Frank H. Rudkin," 52 F.2d xxiii (Sept. 14, 1931). Snippets of information on Rudkin appear in C. Sheldon, *A Century of Judging: A Political History of the Washington Supreme Court* (1988). Senator Miles Poindexter to Attorney General Harry M. Daugherty, Jan. 4, 1923, File of Frank H. Rudkin, Judges, Ninth Circuit Court of Appeals, N–Z, Department of Justice General Records, RG 60, National Archives, Washington, D.C. (hereinafter Rudkin Appointment File). Senator Wesley L. Jones to Attorney General H. M. Daugherty, Dec. 30, 1922, Rudkin Appointment File. *Charles S. Albert to Colonel Guy D. Goff, Assistant to Attorney General, Nov. 17, 1921, Rudkin Appointment File.

16. "In Memoriam," 52 F.2d at *xxix, xxx.

17. *See*, e.g., *Carney v. United States*, 295 F. 606 (9th Cir. 1924); *Rossi v. United States*, 49 F.2d 1 (9th Cir. 1931).

18. *See* newspaper clippings in Ross Scrapbook. *Gilbert to Denman, Jan. 3, 1925, William Denman Papers, Bancroft Library, University of California, Berkeley.

19. William W. Morrow to Attorney General Harlan F. Stone, Jan. 3, 1925, File of Erskine M. Ross, Confidential Regarding His Retirement, Judges, Ninth Circuit Court of Appeals, N–Z, Department of Justice General Records, RG 60, National Archives, Washington, D.C. (hereinafter Ross Retirement File).

20. *Oscar Lawler to William W. Morrow, Jan. 9, 1925, Ross Retirement File. *Harlan F. Stone to Frank F. Flint, Jan. 30, 1925, Ross Retirement File.

21. Erskine M. Ross to President Calvin Coolidge, Mar. 16, 1925, Ross Retirement File. By this time Ross had heard rumors that Coolidge was considering removing him under the "incapacitated judge" provision of the 1919 act. The last paragraph of this letter to the president suggests that it was fear of such "highly reprehensible" treatment that induced him to resign. He said, "No suggestion that my retirement was desired was ever made to me by any one," which, if true, would cast great doubt on the execution of the Morrow-Gilbert plan.

22. *President Calvin Coolidge to Erskine Mayo Ross, Apr. 1, 1925, Ross Retirement File.

23. President Coolidge's letter to Ross left open the possibility that the retiring judge might serve in senior status capacity (Coolidge to Ross, Mar. 30, 1925, Ross Retirement File). Given that President Coolidge wrote two letters to Ross and invited the judge to share the other, more personal message with the press, this letter of March 30 was very likely a form letter. Senior Judge Gilbert apparently never called on Ross to serve as a senior status judge (*see San Francisco Chronicle*, Apr. 3, 1925, at 24, col. 7).

24. *William H. Hunt to Erskine M. Ross, Mar. 19, 1925, Ross Scrapbook. For more on the public reaction to Ross's retirement, see unidentified newspaper clippings, Ross Scrapbook. *See San Francisco Chronicle*, Dec. 11, 1928, at 17, col. 3; *San Francisco Examiner*, Dec. 11, 1928, at 18, col. 1; *San Francisco Examiner*, Dec. 13, 1928, at 7, col. 6.

25. William J. Donovan, "Memorandum for the Attorney General," April 25, 1925, at *3, Circuit Judge—Ninth Circuit General File, Judges, Ninth Circuit Court of Appeals, A–H, Department of Justice General Records, RG 60, National Archives, Washington, D.C. (hereinafter Donovan Memorandum). Donovan makes no direct statement, but his view can be inferred from his remark, "There are no other endorsements of Mr. Mackintosh" (Donovan Memorandum, at 4). He made a similar remark about McEnery's file (*id.*).

26. Donovan, "Memorandum," *supra* note 25, at *5, *6.

27. Donovan, "Memorandum," *supra* note 25, at *8, *Appendix. In its official records, the Senate Judiciary Committee incorrectly listed Dietrich's date of birth as January 23, 1865 (*see* Senate Judiciary Committee, "Legislative History," at 174).

28. See Papers of Wallace McCamant, Special Collections, University of Oregon Library, Eugene, Oregon (hereinafter McCamant Papers).

29. George H. Ellis to Wallace McCamant, July 22, 1920, McCamant Papers. *See*, e.g., Wallace McCamant to Governor Calvin Coolidge, Sept. 7, 1920; *McCamant to Coolidge, Nov. 5, 1920; McCamant to Coolidge, Nov. 13, 1920; McCamant to Coolidge, Nov. 17, 1923 (referring to a letter from Coolidge of Nov. 12, 1923), McCamant Papers. *Attorney General Harry M. Daugherty to Wallace McCamant, Dec. 8, 1923, McCamant Papers. When Daugherty proposed that McCamant serve as assistant attorney general as a stepping-stone to a judgeship, McCamant at first expressed his reluctant acceptance; he retracted a few days later, but feared that he was irrevocably damaging his judicial prospects (McCamant to Daugherty, Dec. 15, 1923; McCamant to Daugherty, Dec. 17, 1923). Daugherty laid these fears to rest, assuring McCamant that his refusal to accept an unwanted position "will not make any difference, for I would be glad to recommend you, with the President's consent, whether two additional judges are provided for the Ninth Circuit or there is a vacancy elsewhere in the meantime" (Daugherty to McCamant, Dec. 22, 1923, McCamant Papers).

30. *John Marshall, Assistant Attorney General, Memorandum for the Attorney General, May 25, 1925, File of Wallace McCamant, Confidential, Judges, Ninth Circuit Court of Appeals, I–M, Department of Justice General Records, RG 60, National Archives.

31. U.S. Const. art. II, § 2. 41 Op. Att'y Gen. 463, 370 (1960); 33 Op. Att'y Gen. 20 (1921).

32. *See* McCamant to Charles W. Nibley, Oct. 23, 1923, McCamant Papers. In this letter McCamant explained the source of his conflict with Senator Hiram Johnson and requested Nibley's aid in talking to Senators Smoot and King about supporting McCamant's confirmation "in case the appointment should come to me." On March 23, 1925, McCamant wrote to Senator Robert N. Stanfield of Oregon, asking to be kept apprised of the "probable action of the Senate in case my name is sent in by the President" (McCamant to Senator Robert N. Stanfield, Mar. 23, 1925, McCamant Papers). "Nomination of Wallace McCamant," Hearings Before the Senate Comm. on the Judiciary, 69th Cong., 1st Sess. 1 (1926; hereinafter McCamant Hearing). *See* 67 Cong. Rec. 1503 (1926); *New York Times*, Jan. 6, 1926, at 11, col. 4.

33. *New York Times*, Jan. 13, 1926, at 14, col. 5. Clapper, "Portrait of a Federal Judge," 46 *The New Republic*, March 17, 1926, at 96. Johnson himself believed that this vote would guarantee McCamant's confirmation: "I had Mc-Camant beaten very much to my surprise at the close of the executive session last Tuesday. The occasion was one where I got started on the right foot and quite outdid myself. After three hours the representatives of the administration found the only way in which they could prevent defeat was to refer the matter again to the judiciary committee, and by a vote of 43 to 33, against my protest, this was done. In the time now afforded them, those in power will whip into line the recalcitrant senators, and undoubtedly, McCamant will be confirmed" (Hiram Johnson to Sons, Jan. 16, 1926, Johnson Papers).

34. *New York Times*, Jan. 19, 1926, at 18, col. 1. Appearances by judicial candidates were not the norm during this period, and there is some documentary support for the view that McCamant could easily have chosen not to attend the hearing; *see* William H. Hunt to McCamant, Jan. 13, 1926, McCamant Papers: "It may be that you will think it wise to go to Washington." In this letter, Hunt again displayed his collegiality to his colleagues on the court. He added, "If you do, you must not let any feeling of duty to the Court interfere for I will sit with pleasure at any time that you might be sitting if here. I do not want you to be unjustly dealt with and if I can do anything to serve you, be assured it will be done with earnest attention and loyalty" (*id.*)

35. *See generally* McCamant Hearing. Most of the material available from the National Archives relating to the committee's proceedings was printed in this hearing. Because of the readier availability of the printed hearing, citations have been made from it rather than from the original documents. Other cited materials may be found in the National Archives: File of Wallace McCamant, Nomination Papers of Ninth Circuit Judges, RG 46, National Archives, Washington D.C. (hereinafter McCamant Nomination File). *See* Senator Hiram Johnson to Senator A. B. Cummins, Chairman, Committee on the Judiciary, Dec. 10, 1925, McCamant Nomination File. McCamant Hearing, at 35–36, *37.

36. *See* McCamant Hearing, at 43–45. For the record, if McCamant delivered his speech as it was written, the objectionable reference was as follows: "By his recent appointment of a mountebank to the Federal Supreme Court Woodrow Wilson has demonstrated his utter unfitness to dispense judicial patronage" (Wallace McCamant, "The Republican Party and History," Lincoln Day Speech, 1916, at 12, McCamant Papers).

37. McCamant Hearing, at *48.

38. J. Abels, *In the Time of Silent Cal* 20–21 (1969); W. White, *A Puritan in Babylon* 177–217 (1938). McCamant had been a delegate to the Republican state conventions in 1892, 1894, 1896, 1898, and 1900. He had also been a delegate to the 1896 and 1900 Republican national conventions (*History of the Bench and Bar in Oregon* 176 [1910]). McCamant Hearing, at *48.

39. McCamant quoted the prior statute as providing: "Every such delegate to a national convention to nominate candidates for President and Vice President shall subscribe an oath— . . . that he will as such officer and delegate to the best of his judgment and ability faithfully carry out the wishes of his political party,

as expressed by its voters at the time of his election." This law had been repealed in 1919. McCamant Hearing, at 48–49, *50.

40. *See* McCamant Hearing, at *51. This response showed some disingenuity. In his private correspondence McCamant left traces that he wanted both to oppose Johnson and to avoid a direct confrontation with allies of the California senator. His original platform contained the statement: "I am an admirer of Charles E. Hughes. For this and other reasons I am unwilling to vote for Hiram Johnson" (McCamant to C. E. Ingalls, Apr. 5, 1920, McCamant Papers). McCamant excised the offending reference when a friendly journalist wrote to him: "In reference to the Johnson matter,—I feel just as strongly about him as you do and he is the only candidate whom I am fighting in my paper. I detest him thoroly [*sic*]. Nevertheless, I think you are not only justified in failing to mention him, but I think you owe it to your friends to do nothing that might defeat your election. It is not probable tha[t] any candidate will be elected on the first ballot. Therefore, I would change your statement as I have indicated" (Ingalls to McCamant, Apr. 7, 1920, McCamant Papers).

41. McCamant Hearing, at *51, *56, *57, 59. McCamant was so certain that the 1920 campaign episode would become an issue in his confirmation that he started contacting potential affiants soon after he assumed his judicial post under the recess appointment (*see*, e.g., McCamant to Hon. A. L. Leavitt, June 24, 1925, McCamant Papers).

42. McCamant Hearing, at 61.

43. McCamant Hearing, at 62.

44. That plank stated: "That when an Act, passed under the police power of the State, is held unconstitutional under the State Constitution, by the courts, the people, after an ample interval for deliberation, shall have an opportunity to vote on the question whether they desire the Act to become law, notwithstanding such decision" (R. Diamond, ed., *Congressional Quarterly's Guide to U.S. Elections* 47 [1975]).

45. McCamant Hearing, at *62–63. Johnson took no small satisfaction in the accomplishment. As he later wrote to his sons, "Yesterday, McCamant appeared to poor advantage, and I had the satisfaction, at least, of showing him up before the Senate Judiciary Committee" (Hiram Johnson to Sons, Jan. 30, 1926, Johnson Papers).

46. McCamant Hearing, at 77.

47. The hearing does not give the date of the telegrams (*see* McCamant Hearing, at 77), but the National Archives records reveal that Gilbert sent his telegram on January 14 and Hunt and Morrow transmitted theirs on January 15, 1926 (McCamant Nomination File). *See generally* Evans, "A Work Sheet of Judicial Labor of Appellate Federal Courts," 1943 Wis. L. Rev. 313, 321. *Campbell v. United States*, 12 F.2d 873 (9th Cir. 1926). In this case, McCamant wrote also for Gilbert in affirming the conviction of the defendant for fraud. On appeal the defendant contended that the district judge had made one-sided instructions favoring the government. McCamant wrote that the evidence was so overwhelming as to warrant conviction in spite of the error. In dissent, Rudkin contended that the "constitutional guaranty [of a fair and impartial trial by jury]

is not satisfied by a partisan, one-sided charge to the jury" (*Campbell*, 12 F.2d at 878 [Rudkin, J., dissenting]). McCamant Hearing, at 77.

48. *See New York Times*, Feb. 12, 1926, at 6, col. 2; *id.*, Feb. 17, 1926, at 5, col. 2. Coolidge even invited McCamant to lunch with him at the White House a few days after the hearing. Clapper, *supra* note 33, at 98. In a poll taken a few days before the vote the Senators who indicated their opposition to McCamant included Chairman Cummins and Senator Borah, Republicans, and Neely, Walsh, Reed, Overman, Ashurst, and Caraway, Democrats. In favor of McCamant were Senators Deneen, Goff, and Ernst, Republicans (*San Francisco Recorder*, Mar. 12, 1926, at 1, col. 7). The official committee vote of ten to four was reported in the *San Francisco Recorder*, Mar. 17, 1926, at 1, col. 5, 67 Cong. Rec. 5796 (1926). *See* Senate Resolution, March 17, 1926, Wallace McCamant File, Appointment Papers, Judges, Ninth Circuit Court of Appeals, I–M, Department of Justice General Records, RG 60, National Archives (hereinafter McCamant Appointment File). *San Francisco Recorder*, Mar. 18, 1926, at 1, col. 6. *Hiram Johnson to Hiram Johnson, Jr., Mar. 14, 1926, Johnson Papers. *Senator Robert N. Stanfield to McCamant, Mar. 17, 1926, McCamant Papers.

49. Wallace McCamant to Calvin Coolidge, Apr. 19, 1926, McCamant Appointment File. Calvin Coolidge to Wallace McCamant, Apr. 24, 1926, McCamant Appointment File. The information on the recess appointments derives from a number of sources. For all appointments made up through May 1972, see Senate Judiciary Committee, "Legislative History." This document contains charts of each circuit and notes when a judge received a recess appointment. For recess-appointed judges after this date, see Congressional Research Service, "Recess Appointments by President Ford: Aug. 9, 1974–Jan. 20, 1977" (1984); Congressional Research Service, "Recess Appointments by President Carter: Jan. 20, 1977–Jan. 20, 1981" (1984); Congressional Research Service, "Recess Appointments by President Reagan: Jan. 20, 1981–July 5, 1984 (1984); Congressional Research Service, "Recess Appointments by President Reagan: Oct. 12, 1984–Sept. 8, 1985 (1985; President Reagan made no recess appointments between July 5 and October 12, 1984); Congressional Research Service, "Recess Appointments Made by President Reagan" (1988); Congressional Research Service, "Recess Appointments by President Bush" (1991). *See generally* Congressional Research Service, "Recess Appointments: Legal Overview" (1987).

50. 1924 Att'y Gen. Ann. Rep. 115; 1925 Att'y Gen. Ann. Rep. 133. Gilbert's average is given from 1926 to 1930. Evans places the average at 37.20 but counts 1929 as a year Hunt served, which is inaccurate. *See* Evans, *supra* note 47, at 324. Hunt took senior status on January 31, 1928, and left the court completely on November 30, 1928, to resume the practice of law. He died February 4, 1949, at the ripe age of ninety-one.

51. The evidence for this view is not entirely firm. It is based on snippets from some newspaper articles, most particularly one in the *San Francisco Chronicle*, Dec. 27, 1926, at 10, col. 4. In this article the paper noted that Coolidge had also refused to push for a bill that would have provided additional judges for the Northern and Southern Districts of California (*id.*).

52. *Attorney General to Calvin Coolidge, Dec. 22, 1926, File of Frank S. Dietrich, Judges, Ninth Circuit Court of Appeals, A–H, Department of Justice General Records, RG 60, National Archives, Washington, D.C. (hereinafter Dietrich Appointment File). *Senator Frank Gooding to President Calvin Coolidge, Apr. 1, 1926, Dietrich Appointment File. See also Edward J. Cannon to Attorney General William E. Mitchell, Apr. 22, 1930, Dietrich Appointment File.

53. Dietrich was confirmed on January 3, 1927, and took the oath of office two weeks later, on January 18, 1927. On Dietrich's background, see generally *Judges of the United States* 131 (2d ed. 1983); 33 *National Cyclopedia of American Biography* 195–96 (1947); "In Memoriam: Hon. Frank Sigel Dietrich," 42 F.2d xi (Nov. 5, 1930). E.g., *Nixon v. United States*, 36 F.2d 316, 317–18 (9th Cir. 1929, reversing a conviction for possessing liquor on ground of unreasonable search); *American Surety Co. v. Jackson*, 24 F.2d 768, 771 (9th Cir. 1928) (Dietrich, J., dissenting, arguing that the trial court had correctly dismissed action brought by surety against the receiver of a bank). For details of his death, see *San Francisco Chronicle*, Oct. 3, 1930, at 7, col. 1. Evans, *supra* note 47, at 324.

7. WAR, LIQUOR, AND THE QUEST FOR ORDER

1. *San Francisco Examiner*, July 25, 1916, at *1, col. 8; for the first reports of the bombing, *see id.* July 23, 1916, at 1–10. *See* C. Gentry, *Frameup: The Incredible Case of Tom Mooney and Warren Billings* 11–30 (1967); R. Knight, *Industrial Relations in the San Francisco Bay Area, 1900–1918*, at 309–13 (1960).

2. *San Francisco Examiner*, July 27, 1916, at *2, col. 5. *See also* San Francisco Chamber of Commerce, *Law and Order in San Francisco: A Beginning* 20–27 (1916), describing speeches and reactions. The full story of the Preparedness Parade bombing and the trial of the chief suspect, Tom Mooney, are well told in R. Frost, *The Mooney Case* (1968).

3. *San Francisco Examiner*, Mar. 30, 1917, at *3, col. 1. *San Francisco Chronicle*, Apr. 8, 1917, at *34, col. 2.

4. The court's records do not reveal why Morrow sat on so few panels and wrote even fewer opinions for the court in war-related cases.

5. *New York Times*, June 28, 1917, at *1, col. 6 (giving enlistment numbers); *New York Times*, Apr. 29, 1917, at 1, col. 6. Bartholomae, "A Conscientious Objector: Oregon, 1918," 71 Or. Hist. Q. 213, 214 (1970). Act of May 18, 1917, ch. 15, § 2, 40 Stat. 76, *78. These age limits represented a compromise between the War Department, which sought men between the ages of nineteen and twenty-five; the House, which favored a range of twenty-one to forty; and the Senate, which proposed twenty-one to twenty-seven. The failure to raise an adequate number of soldiers and sailors caused Congress on August 31, 1918, to adjust the criteria to all men between eighteen and forty-five (Act of Aug. 31, 1918, ch. 166, 40 Stat. 955). *See generally* Tryon, "The Draft in World War I," 54 Current Hist. 339, 343, 368 (1968).

6. *Phelan v. United States*, 249 F. 43 (9th Cir. 1918). *See*, e.g., *Pass v. United States*, 256 F. 731 (9th Cir. 1919); *Pass v. United States*, 256 F. 735 (9th Cir. 1919); *Napore v. Rowe*, 256 F. 832 (9th Cir. 1919).

7. *See*, e.g., *Hardwick v. United States*, 257 F. 505 (9th Cir. 1919); *Whiteside v. United States*, 257 F. 509 (9th Cir. 1919). Act of Aug. 31, 1918, ch. 166. 40 Stat. 955. *Gordnier v. United States*, 261 F. 910, 912 (9th Cir. 1920).

8. Act of May 18, 1917, ch. 15, §§ 12–*13, 40 Stat. 76, 82–83. For more on prostitution in the city, see "Warnings to Girls from San Francisco," 34 Survey 39 (1915). One contemporary report noted that "only three large cities in the United States . . . still countenance this curious, barbaric survival: New Orleans, Cincinnati and San Francisco" (Dosch, "Extinguishing the Red-Light," 37 Sunset 38, 38 [1916]).

9. Issues arising under the bawdy house provision apparently occupied very little of other circuits' attention (*see Hunter v. United States*, 272 F. 235 [4th Cir. 1921]; *Gray v. United States*, 266 F. 355 [3d Cir. 1920]; *Thaler v. United States*, 261 F. 746 [6th Cir. 1919]; *Pollard v. United States*, 261 F. 336 [5th Cir. 1919]). The constitutional challenge was raised in *Pappens v. United States*, 252 F. 55, *57 (9th Cir. 1918, quoting U.S. Const., art. I, § 8).

10. *Blanc v. United States*, 258 F. 921, 922 (9th Cir. 1919). *Brown v. United States*, 260 F. 752, 754 (9th Cir. 1919). *Anzine v. United States*, 260 F. 827, 829 (9th Cir. 1919). *Goublin v. United States*, 261 F. 5, 6 (9th Cir. 1919). *Nakano v. United States*, 262 F. 761, 762 (9th Cir. 1920). *Anzine v. United States*, 260 F. 827, *829 (9th Cir. 1919). *Nakano v. United States*, 262 F. 761, *761 (9th Cir. 1920). The court also permitted evidence from the physician of the City Board of Health, who testified that all of the women arrested on the premises had venereal diseases (*id.* at 762).

11. *Goublin v. United States*, 261 F. 5 (9th Cir. 1919) (*id.* at 11–12, Ross, J., dissenting; referring to *DeFour v. United States*, 260 F. 596, 599 [9th Cir. 1919]).

12. H. Scheiber, *The Wilson Administration and Civil Liberties, 1917–1921*, at 19 (1960); Scheiber cites J. O'Brian, *National Security and Individual Freedom* 49–50 (1955); O'Brian in turn provides no citation for this information. Lawrence, "Eclipse of Liberty: Civil Liberties in the United States During the First World War," 21 Wayne L. Rev. 33, 38 (1974); H. Cummings and C. McFarland, *Federal Justice* 413–31 (1937); "America Infested with German Spies," 55 Lit. Dig. 9 (1917); Ohlinger, "German Propaganda in the United States," 117 Atlantic Monthly 535 (1916). *See generally* C. Child, *The German-Americans in Politics 1914–1917*, 154–79 (1939).

13. Act of June 15, 1917, ch. 30, § 3, 40 Stat. 217, *219.

14. Scheiber first collated these statistics (*see* H. Scheiber, *supra* note 12, at 42–43, 61–63, reporting statistics compiled from 1918–1921 Rep. Att'y Gen.). Interestingly, two of these U.S. attorneys, Francis A. Garrecht of eastern Washington and Bert E. Haney of Oregon, later served on the Ninth Circuit. For the record, the number of cases brought in Garrecht's district was much smaller than that for the western district of Washington: in 1918, three cases were prosecuted in the eastern district and twenty-two in the western district; the following year, the respective numbers were fourteen and twenty-four; and in 1920, eight cases

were brought in the western district and none in the eastern district. The corresponding numbers for Oregon were eleven prosecutions in 1918 and twenty-three in 1919 (*id.*).

15. *Schenck v. United States*, 249 U.S. 47, *52 (1919). For the description of the reaction as "hysterical," *see* Oliver Wendell Holmes, Jr., to Harold Lasky, March 16, 1919, in 1 *Holmes-Lasky Letters* 190 (M. Howe ed. 1953). H. Scheiber, *supra* note 12, at *43.

16. *Equi v. United States*, 261 F. 53, 55 (9th Cir. 1919, applying *Schenck*, 249 U.S. at 47), *cert. denied*, 251 U.S. 560 (1920). *Schulze v. United States*, 259 F. 189, 190 (9th Cir. 1919). *Rhuberg v. United States*, 255 F. 865, *866 (9th Cir. 1919). *Albers v. United States*, 263 F. 27 (9th Cir. 1920), *rev'd*, 256 U.S. 706 (1921). In a comprehensive examination of the origins of modern First Amendment doctrine, David M. Rabban analyzes many lower federal court decisions that protected and punished wartime expression. His exposition of these cases suggests that courts did not achieve consistent results in adjudicating prosecutions for speech-related offenses. To isolate only the Ninth Circuit decisions he cites, the court rendered decisions that both punished and supported such speech (*see* Rabban, "The Emergence of Modern First Amendment Doctrine," 50 U. Chi. L. Rev. 1205, 1233 and n.139, 1241 and n.193, and n.198 [1983]). Even allowing for doctrinal development and adaptation to evolving Supreme Court precedent, a possible explanation for these discrepant results is that the court treated different speakers differently. As the cases discussed *infra* in the text indicate, the court adopted a more lenient posture generally—with the harsh exceptions well noted—toward I.W.W. speakers than toward German-Americans, European aliens of Germanic descent, and other anti-war activists (*Sandberg v. United States*, 257 F. 643, 648 [9th Cir. 1919]). For example, the court affirmed the convictions of Frank P. Howenstine and Idell Kennedy for a conspiracy to persuade draftable men to refuse duty. The pair allegedly attempted to persuade prospective draftees to go to an oculist and optician (Howenstine) who would fit them with eyeglasses that would so impair their vision that they would be rejected for duty and discharged from service. In affirming their convictions, the court rejected a claim that government agents had entrapped Kennedy, holding that it was "entirely proper for witnesses in the employment of the government to approach the defendants to obtain further evidence of the unlawful scheme in which they were believed to be engaged" (*Howenstine v. United States*, 263 F. 1, 5 [9th Cir. 1920]).

17. *United States v. Motion Picture Film "The Spirit of '76,"* 252 F. 946, *946–47, *948 (S.D. Cal. 1917).

18. *Goldstein v. United States*, 258 F. 908, *910, *911 (9th Cir. 1919).

19. *Stephens v. United States*, 261 F. 590, 590–91 (9th Cir. 1919).

20. *Id.* at *592. In another case involving dissemination of *The Finished Mystery*, Judge Gilbert framed the issue as "not whether the publication contained expressions only of opinion, and not statements of fact, but it is whether the natural and probable tendency and effect of the words quoted therefrom are such as are calculated to produce the result condemned by the statute" (*Shaffer v. United States*, 255 F. 886, 887 [9th Cir. 1919], *cert. denied*, 251 U.S. 552 [1919]). *See also Hamm v. United States*, 261 F. 907 (9th Cir. 1920); *Sonnenberg*

v. United States, 264 F. 327 (9th Cir. 1920). On the modern reaction, see H. Kalven, *A Worthy Tradition* 131 (1988, commenting on the mildness of a similar pamphlet at issue in *Schenck*).

21. *Shilter v. United States*, 257 F. 724, 725–26 (9th Cir. 1919). *Mead v. United States*, 257 F. 639, *642 (9th Cir. 1919); *see also Magon v. United States*, 260 F. 811, 813 (9th Cir. 1919).

22. *See generally* H. Kalven, *supra* note 20, at 138; Rabban, *supra* note 16, at 1353 (observing that application of the modern *Brandenburg* test "would arguably have overturned convictions in all of the cases in which the Supreme Court, using different standards, upheld convictions for subversive advocacy").

23. *Von Bank v. United States*, 253 F. 641, *641–42, *643 (8th Cir. 1918). Other Eighth Circuit reversals of Espionage Act convictions include: *Grubl v. United States*, 264 F. 44 (8th Cir. 1920); *Stokes v. United States*, 264 F. 18 (8th Cir. 1920); *Granzow v. United States*, 261 F. 172 (8th Cir. 1919); *Stenzel v. United States*, 261 F. 161 (8th Cir. 1919); *Harshfield v. United States*, 260 F. 659 (8th Cir. 1919). For the Sixth Circuit, *see, e.g., Mamaux v. United States*, 264 F. 816 (6th Cir. 1920); *Wimmer v. United States*, 264 F. 11 (6th Cir. 1920); *Lockhart v. United States*, 264 F. 14 (6th Cir. 1920); *Shoborg v. United States*, 264 F. 1 (6th Cir. 1920).

24. E.g., *Schaefer v. United States*, 251 U.S. 466, 480–81 (1920). *Schenck v. United States*, 249 U.S. 47 (1919). *See generally* Rabban, *supra* note 16, at 1303–5 (discussing Supreme Court majority opinions during the 1920s). *See, e.g., Whitney v. California*, 274 U.S. 357 (1927); *Gitlow v. New York*, 268 U.S. 652 (1925). Rudkin, for example, wrote the *Equi* decision upholding the constitutionality of the Espionage Act against a First Amendment challenge (*see* 261 F. at 53). On the backgrounds of Morrow, Ross, and Gilbert, see *supra* Chapter One; on Hunt's, see *supra* Chapter Six.

25. *See generally* W. Preston, *Aliens and Dissenters: Federal Suppression of Radicals, 1903–1933*, at 88–89 (1963). One of the first Espionage Act cases decided by the Ninth Circuit, however, upheld the conviction of an I.W.W. speaker who told a public audience that she was not fighting for the red, white, and blue of the American flag, but, rather, for the "red banner that stood for the blood of the Industrial Workers" (*Equi v. United States*, 261 F. 53, 54 [9th Cir. 1919], *cert. denied*, 251 U.S. 560 [1920]). In this case the Ninth Circuit upheld the constitutionality of the statute against a First Amendment challenge. *See id.* at 57; *see also supra* note 16 and accompanying text.

26. W. Preston, *supra* note 25, at *43. Tyler reports that the nickname may have derived from a Chinese restaurant owner in Canada, "who responded to criticism [for catering to I.W.W. members] by saying, 'I likee Eye Wobbly Wobbly'" (R. Tyler, *Rebels of the Woods: The I.W.W. in the Pacific Northwest* 1 [1967]). On the free speech fights, which arose primarily in state courts, *see generally* M. Dubofsky, *We Shall Be All* 173–97 (1969); 4 P. Foner, *History of the Labor Movement in the United States* 172–213 (1965); W. Preston, *supra*, at 35–62; P. Brissenden, *The I.W.W.: A Study of American Syndicalism* 260–61 (1919, describing jailings by local officials). The Ninth Circuit did not to my knowledge become involved in I.W.W. speech-related issues before the World War I period (H. Peterson and G. Fite, *Opponents of War, 1917–1918*, at *49,

49–52, 56–57 [1957]). H. DeWitt, *Images of Ethnic and Radical Violence in California Politics, 1917–1930*, at 18 (1975).

27. *See* W. Preston, *supra* note 25, at 120–21. H. Cummings and C. Mc-Farland, *supra* note 12, at 420–21. On these trials generally, see Taft, "The Federal Trials of the IWW," 3 Lab. Hist. 57, 77–78 (1962).

28. The published Ninth Circuit opinion does not give the district judge's name (*Anderson v. United States*, 269 F. 65, 65 [9th Cir. 1920], *cert. denied*, 255 U.S. 576 [1921]), but Taft reports that Rudkin tried the case (*see* Taft, *supra* note 27, at 78). It is unclear why Rudkin, at that time a Washington federal district judge, should sit on a trial in the northern district of California, except insofar as it comported with the practice of the circuit's judges holding court outside their districts. "Ol' Rags an' Bottles," The Nation, Jan. 25, 1919, at *115. DeWitt writes that "it was obvious the federal government did not have a strong case" (H. DeWitt, *supra* note 26, at 41). R. Tyler, *supra* note 26, at *126. *Anderson*, 269 F. at 80.

29. *See Collins v. United States*, 253 F. 609 (9th Cir. 1918); *Foster v. United States*, 253 F. 481, *482 (9th Cir. 1918). *See also* H. Peterson and G. Fite, *supra* note 26, at 170–71 (discussing *Collins* and *Foster*).

30. *Kumpula v. United States*, 261 F. 49, *50, *51, *52–53 (9th Cir. 1919). *See Shidler v. United States*, 257 F. 620, 621 (9th Cir. 1919). It is true that the statements in *Shidler* and the I.W.W. cases are dissimilar. Nevertheless, what made the difference in Hunt's approach striking was that he made no effort to base the procedural standard in the I.W.W. case on this factual distinction. In an interesting Prohibition case involving a Wobbly, Hunt seemingly departed from this more protective view of defendant's rights (*see Maki v. United States*, 12 F.2d 668 [9th Cir. 1926]). In this case the court upheld the conviction of an Idaho worker for nuisance and unlawful possession of whiskey. The trial judge admitted into evidence against the defendant a torn bit of newspaper found in his possession from *Industrialist*, the Finnish daily organ of industrial unionism in the United States. Part of the headline of the torn newspaper read, "I.W.W." Hunt's opinion for the court on appeal held that the admission of this evidence could not have been prejudicial because the newspaper contained no translation (*id.* at 669). This reasoning seemed dubious, because the evidence was geared as much to influence the jury against the defendant as it was for any probative purpose. If the court correctly determined that the newspaper had no bearing on the jury's sympathies, it should perhaps also have stricken the evidence as irrelevant to the question of the defendant's guilt on the whiskey and nuisance charges.

31. Act of Feb. 5, 1917, ch. 29, *§ 19, 39 Stat. 874, 889. R. Tyler, *supra* note 26, at 141–42.

32. W. Preston, *supra* note 25, at *157. *See* "In the Matter of the Application of Carl Holm for a Writ of Habeas Corpus," File No. 196663, Box No. 2891, Straight Numerical Files, Department of Justice General Records, RG 60, National Archives, Washington, D.C. (hereinafter Holm File). *See also* W. Preston, *supra*, at 185–86; R. Tyler, *supra* note 26, at 143.

33. Holm File, at *4. W. Preston, *supra* note 25, at 188–90. *United States v. Ault*, 263 F. 800 (W.D. Wash. 1920); *United States v. Listman*, 263 F. 798

(W.D. Wash. 1920); *United States v. Strong*, 263 F. 789 (W.D. Wash. 1920). In *Rowan v. United States*, 18 F.2d 246, 247 (9th Cir. 1927), the Justice Department prosecuted James Rowan, a naturalized United States citizen originally from Great Britain. This suit was one of the last cases in the department deportation campaign against foreign-born Wobblies. The government claimed that Rowan had fraudulently gained citizenship by falsely swearing allegiance to the United States Constitution in 1907. The district court agreed, on the ground that in 1917 Rowan had been convicted under the Espionage Act. Speaking through Hunt, the Ninth Circuit rejected this analysis and held that Rowan's actions in 1917 did not call into question his loyalty to the United States when he received his naturalization papers in 1907 (*id.* at 248).

34. H. Scheiber, *supra* note 12, at *52. R. Murray, *Red Scare* 111 (1955). R. Tyler, *supra* note 26, at *185.

35. *See generally* 4 P. Foner, *supra* note 26; P. Taft, *Organized Labor in American History* 290–98 (1964). *See supra* note 29 and accompanying text.

36. Historians now believe that the middle class was the bulwark of the Prohibition movement (*see* J. Blocker, *Retreat from Reform: The Prohibition Movement in the United States, 1890–1913*, at 240–41 [1976]; N. Clark, *The Dry Years: Prohibition and Social Change in Washington* 121–23 [1965]; J. Gusfield, *Symbolic Crusade: Status Politics and the American Temperance Movement* 117–19 [1963]). Anecdotally, women apparently backed Prohibition much more enthusiastically than men until the mid-1920s, when evidently even they fell off the wagon (*see* Smalley, "What Prohibition Did to Arizona," 36 Sunset 26, 26 [1916]; Kyvig, "Women Against Prohibition," 28 Am. Q. 465, 465 [1976]). On state distinctions, see Burt, "The Dry West," 83 Scribners 142, 146–47 (1928).

37. Act of Nov. 21, 1918, ch. 212, 40 Stat. 1045, 1046. U.S. Const. amend. XVIII, § 1 (1919, repealed 1933). Act of Oct. 28, 1919, ch. 85, 41 Stat. 305.

38. J. Blocker, *supra* note 36, at 237–38. Burt, *supra* note 36, at *146–47. For an interesting discussion of these conflicting tensions, *see* Drescher, "Organized Labor and the Eighteenth Amendment," 8 Lab. Hist. 280, 281, 290 (1967); *see also* "Labor and Prohibition," Lit. Digest, Mar. 25, 1922, at 14. "Labor Sentiment on Liquor," Lit. Digest, June 23, 1923, at *32. Indeed, Nevada repealed its state legislation as early as February 22, 1923. *See generally* Smith, "Prohibition in Nevada," 19 Nev. Hist. Soc. Q. 227, 242 (1976).

39. Brown, "Will the Eighteenth Amendment Overwhelm the Federal Courts?" 91 Cent. L.J. 321, 321 (1920).

40. Shelton, "Congested Federal Court Dockets," 94 Cent. L.J. 127, 128 (1922). The court heard 3 criminal appeals in these two years, 2 in 1892 and 1 in 1893, out of a total of 147 appeals (*see* 1892 Att'y Gen. Ann. Rep. 3; 1893 Att'y Gen. Ann. Rep. 3). 1908 Att'y Gen. Ann. Rep. 97; 1909 Att'y Gen. Ann. Rep. 240; 1910 Att'y Gen. Ann. Rep. 191; 1911 Att'y Gen. Ann. Rep. 187; 1912 Att'y Gen. Ann. Rep. 201. In 1925, the court docketed 134 criminal and 225 civil appeals (1925 Att'y Gen. Ann. Rep. 133).

41. *Page v. United States*, 278 F. 41 (9th Cir.), *cert. denied*, 258 U.S. 627 (1922). *Heitman v. United States*, 5 F.2d 887, *889 (9th Cir. 1925, Gilbert, J., dissenting).

42. *Bell v. United States,* 9 F.2d 820, *822 (9th Cir. 1925, Gilbert, J., dissenting); *see also Temperani v. United States,* 299 F. 365, 368 (9th Cir. 1924, Gilbert, J., dissenting).

43. The judges' divergent approaches to criminal matters comported with their differing judicial philosophies, as was explored in more detail in Chapter Five. Gilbert tended to ground his dissents in disputes with the majority on the facts and his deferential approach to trial court rulings (*see,* e.g., *Lindgren v. United States,* 260 F. 772, 777–78 [9th Cir. 1919, Gilbert, J., dissenting, arguing that evidence was sufficient to sustain conviction]; *Dwinnell v. United States,* 186 F. 754, 760 [9th Cir. 1911, Gilbert, J., dissenting, contending that the trial judge did not commit reversible error by admitting certain evidence]; *Owens v. United States,* 130 F. 279, 285 [9th Cir. 1904, Gilbert, J., dissenting, admitting that part of the jury instruction was erroneous but disputing the majority's conclusion that reversal was warranted]). Ross wrote the majority opinion in each of those cases, reversing for some trial error. When Ross dissented, the disagreements centered on his inability to persuade a majority of the panel of his strict interpretation of language, statutes, and precedent (*see,* e.g., *Duehay v. Thompson,* 223 F. 305, 308 [9th Cir. 1915, Ross, J., dissenting, construing the statute strictly to dispute grant of parole based on amount of time served on concurrent sentences]; *Houston v. United States,* 217 F. 852, 860 [9th Cir. 1914, Ross, J., dissenting, urging reversal based on a Supreme Court precedent that seemed to require proof of an overt act to sustain a conspiracy charge]; *Griggs v. United States,* 158 F. 572, 578 [9th Cir. 1908, Ross, J., dissenting, maintaining that erroneous jury instructions compelled reversal]).

44. *Raine v. United States,* 299 F. 407, *412 (9th Cir.), *cert. denied,* 266 U.S. 611 (1924, Ross, J., dissenting). Ross's position on this issue may not have stemmed from the same libertarian source that animated Frank Rudkin's thinking (*see infra* note 47 and accompanying text). A strict constructionist of legislative enactments, Ross may have upheld these warrant requirements simply because the statute said as much. Ross may also have taken this position because of the clear violations of such searches to the sanctity of property, another value he held dear (*see supra* Chapter Five). *Raine,* 299 F. at *415 (Ross, J., dissenting). Gilbert won on this point because Rudkin concurred on narrow evidentiary grounds. Rudkin found evidence that had been legally gathered sufficient to affirm the conviction and felt it unnecessary to reach the constitutional question upon which Gilbert and Ross disagreed (*see id.* at 412 [Rudkin, J., concurring]).

45. *Forni v. United States,* 3 F.2d 354, *357 (9th Cir. 1925, Ross, J., dissenting).

46. "In Memoriam: Frank H. Rudkin," 52 F.2d xxiii, xxiv (1931, statement of Committee of the Bar). *Simpson v. United States,* 289 F. 188, *191 (9th Cir., Rudkin, J., dissenting), *cert. denied,* 203 U.S. 707 (1923). District Judge Charles Wolverton joined Gilbert's opinion.

47. *See,* e.g., *Terry v. United States,* 7 F.2d 28 (9th Cir. 1925, prejudicial jury instructions). Ross also dissented vigorously when Gilbert persuaded another member of the court to permit what Ross considered prejudicial jury instructions (*see,* e.g., *Brolaski v. United States,* 279 F. 1, 7 [9th Cir. 1922, Ross, J., dissenting]; *Pincolini v. United States,* 295 F. 468, 473 [9th Cir. 1924, Ross, J.,

dissenting]). *Carney v. United States*, 295 F. 606, *609 (9th Cir. 1924, Gilbert, J., dissenting, quoting district court). From the cursory reversal by Hunt, joined by Rudkin, Gilbert appeared to have lost his court. Gilbert's reads very much like a majority opinion, and the succinctness of the majority in its reversal suggests that Gilbert's opinion had lost support for a majority of the court. A very similar opinion is *Rossi v. United States*, 49 F.2d 1 (9th Cir. 1931). In *Rossi*, Judges Rudkin and Sawtelle voted to reverse a conviction of conspiracy by a large number of municipal officers of Wallace, Idaho, in violation of the National Prohibition Act. Judge Curtis D. Wilbur wrote a dissent nine times longer than the two-page majority opinion. In comparing these two opinions, one is left with the perception that the dissenters lost their court and published their former majority opinions as dissents with only the barest of cosmetic changes. *Brooks v. United States*, 8 F.2d 593, *594 (9th Cir. 1925). *Traversi v. United States*, 288 F. 375, *376 (9th Cir. 1923).

48. *Olmstead v. United States*, 19 F.2d 842 (9th Cir. 1927), *aff'd*, 277 U.S. 438 (1928). N. Clark, *supra* note 36, at 162–69.

49. *Olmstead*, 19 F.2d at 846–47.

50. *Brown v. United States*, 4 F.2d 246 (9th Cir. 1925). The court's earlier opinions had demonstrated some sympathy for defendants' rights (*see supra* notes 45–48 and accompanying text). Ross, however, who had been largely responsible for this attitude, had retired two years earlier (Edward J. Cannon to William E. Mitchell, Apr. 22, 1930, File of Frank S. Dietrich, Judges, Ninth Circuit Court of Appeals A–H, Box No. 364, Department of Justice General Records, RG 60, National Archives, Washington, D.C.). Of the ninety-one defendants indicted, some were not apprehended, others were acquitted, and still others pleaded guilty. Twenty-one were convicted, nine of whom filed the writ of error at issue on appeal (*Olmstead*, 19 F.2d at 843).

51. 19 F.2d at 846. Wigmore counseled that the witness need not necessarily have produced the writing, but that "no hard-and-fast rules can be laid down for invariable application" of the "legitimate use of written aids" (3 J. Wigmore, *A Treatise on the Anglo-American System of Evidence* 101 [3d ed. 1940]). The extensive literature on the constitutionality of wiretapping includes: E. Lapidus, *Eavesdropping on Trial* (1974); Halperin, "National Security and Civil Liberties," 21 For. Pol. 125 (1976); Donner, "Electronic Surveillance: The National Security Game," 2 Civ. Liberties Rev. 15 (1975). 19 F.2d at *847. The last quotation quotes *Firth Sterling Steel Co. v. Bethlehem Steel Co.*, 199 F. 353, 355 (E.D. Pa. 1912).

52. 19 F.2d at *848, *849 (Rudkin, J., dissenting, quoting *Ex Parte Jackson*, 96 U.S. 727, 733 [1878]). In *Jackson*, however, the court did uphold a federal statute prohibiting the dissemination of abortion literature through the mails (96 U.S. at 736–37). 19 F.2d at *850 (Rudkin, J., dissenting). Clark argues that the strength of Judge Rudkin's dissent gave Olmstead's attorneys ample reason to petition the Supreme Court for a review of the case (N. Clark, *supra* note 36, at 175).

53. *Olmstead v. United States*, 277 U.S. 438, *464, *466 (1928).

54. *Id.* at *469–70 (Holmes, J., dissenting). *Id.* at *473, *479 (Brandeis, J., dissenting).

55. *Id.* at *485 (Brandeis, J., dissenting). *See,* e.g., *Orsatti v.United States,* 3 F.2d 778 (9th Cir.), *cert. denied,* 268 U.S. 694 (1925); *Rossi v. United States,* 49 F.2d 1 (9th Cir. 1931). The court handled one case involving Regal Drug Store at 1110 Market Street (*Regal Drug Corp. v. Wardell,* 273 F. 182 [9th Cir. 1921]).

56. *See* Smalley, *supra* note 36, at 26–27; "What One Year of Prohibition Did to Business in Seattle," 62 Current Opinion 443, 443–44 (1917). D. Kyvig, *Repealing National Prohibition* 178, 182 (1979). *See generally* J. Kobler, *Ardent Spirits: The Rise and Fall of Prohibition* (1973).

57. Merz, "At the Bottom of the Oil Story," Century, May 24, 1924, at 87. *See* J. Bates, *The Origins of Teapot Dome* 236 (1963).

58. *See Southern Pac. Co. v. United States,* 249 F. 785 (9th Cir. 1918), *rev'd,* 251 U.S. 1 (1919). *See supra* Chapter Five. Walsh, "What the Oil Inquiry Developed," Outlook, May 21, 1924, at 97.

59. Exec. Order No. 3474 (May 31, 1921). *See Pan American Petroleum and Transp. Co. v. United States,* 273 U.S. 456, 487–89 (1927). J. Bates, *supra* note 57, at 237. *See also* Act of June 4, 1920, ch. 228, 41 Stat. 812, 813; Act of Feb. 25, 1920, ch. 85, 41 Stat. 437.

60. One such bureaucrat, Harry A. Slattery, was convinced that Secretary Fall was pursuing a course that, if not illegal, at least conflicted with the stated conservation goals of Congress.: *see* B. Noggle, *Teapot Dome: Oil and Politics in the 1920s* 1–42, 51 (1962). Noggle paints a fascinating portrait of Slattery's efforts behind the scenes to encourage the investigations of Senators Robert LaFollette and Thomas J. Walsh. Jt. Res. of Feb. 8, 1924, ch. 16, 43 Stat. 5, *6. The Supreme Court reported Coolidge's approval (*Pan American,* 273 U.S. at 491).

61. According to Noggle, there is no evidence of any wrongdoing by Daugherty, but he was nevertheless ostracized within the Republican Party and resigned in ignominy (B. Noggle, *supra* note 60, at 118–29). *United States v. Pan-American Petroleum Co.,* 6 F.2d 43, 55, 88–89 (S.D. Cal. 1925), *aff'd in part, rev'd in part,* 9 F.2d 761 (9th Cir. 1926), *aff'd,* 273 U.S. 456 (1927). *United States v. Mammoth Oil Co.,* 5 F.2d 330, 343–54 (D. Wyo. 1925), *rev'd,* 14 F.2d 705 (9th Cir. 1926), *aff'd,* 275 U.S. 13 (1927).

62. *Pan American Petroleum Co. v. United States,* 9 F.2d 761, 770, *771, 772–73 (9th Cir. 1926), *aff'd,* 273 U.S. 456 (1927).

63. *United States v. Mammoth Oil Co.,* 14 F.2d 705, *716, 731, 733 (8th Cir. 1926), *aff'd,* 275 U.S. 13 (1927). *Pan American Petroleum,* 273 U.S. at 510. *See Mammoth Oil Co. v. United States,* 275 U.S. 13 (1927). Although some historians have revised the traditional view that Fall acted corruptly, Gilbert's analysis of the record Roberts generated is persuasive. *But see* B. Noggle, *supra* note 60, at 213 (suggesting that if Fall had wanted to take a bribe the properties were worthy of a much greater one); Gardner, "Teapot Dome: Civil Legal Cases that Closed the Scandal," 28 J. of the West 46, 51 (1989, arguing that Albert B. Fall "was not the black-hearted individual that historians have heretofore portrayed"). Fall was convicted in a criminal proceeding that was affirmed in 1931 and which the Supreme Court refused to review (*Fall v. United States,* 49 F.2d 506 [D.C. Cir.], *cert. denied,* 283 U.S. 867 [1931]). Interestingly, Edward Doheny was acquitted of conspiring to bribe Fall. *See generally* F. Busch, *Enemies*

of the State 123–56 (1954). For more on Doheny's background, see B. Forbes, *Men Who Are Making the West* 97–119 (1923).

64. *See generally* B. Noggle, *supra* note 60, at 148. *See infra* Chapter Eight. McKeage, "The Naval Petroleum Reserves: A Modern Perspective," 28 J. of the West 52, 52 (1989); *see also* Hagland, "The Naval Reserve Leases," 20 Geo. L.J. 293 (1932); G. Nash, *United States Oil Policy, 1890–1964* (1968).

65. In his article on the First Amendment's modern doctrinal origins, David Rabban places much greater emphasis on decisions by District Judges Learned Hand of New York and George M. Bourquin of Montana. *See* D. Rabban, *supra* note 16, at 1235–40. The Ninth Circuit did not consistently apply the type of protective reasoning advanced by Judge Bourquin (*see supra* notes 50–52 and accompanying text). *See generally* E. Lapidus, *supra* note 51, at 16–20 (describing the "erosion" of the *Olmstead* rule permitting warrantless searches by wiretaps).

8. DIFFERENT PATHS TO THE BENCH

1. Between Gilbert's death on April 27, 1931, and Rudkin's death on May 3, 1931, the court did not meet. When it convened on May 4, 1931, Senior Judge Curtis Wilbur observed that Rudkin had succeeded Gilbert as senior judge after Gilbert's death. Rudkin thus had the shortest term as senior or chief judge—six days—in the history of the court (33 Minutes of the United States Court of Appeals for the Ninth Circuit 282 [May 4, 1931]).

2. Scholarship on the appointment process prior to the 1950s is scanty. Professor Kermit Hall has written extensively about the nineteenth-century selection process (*see*, e.g., K. Hall, *The Politics of Justice: Lower Federal Judicial Selection and the Second Party System 1829–61* [1979]; Hall, "The Children of the Cabins: The Lower Federal Judiciary, Modernization, and Political Culture, 1789–1899," 75 Nw. U.L. Rev. 423 [1980]; Hall, "Mere Party and the Magic Mirror: California's First Lower Federal Judicial Appointments," 32 Hastings L.J. 819 [1981]). Judge Evan A. Evans wrote an interesting survey of the politics of appointment from the Cleveland through the second Roosevelt administration (Evans, "Political Influences in the Selection of Federal Judges," 1948 Wis. L. Rev. 330). Evans's article focuses heavily on the partisan impulses of the administration in power, however, and not on the internal administration procedures for selecting judges. On the present system, from the 1950s onward, scholarly treatments of the appointment process are more plentiful: *see*, e.g., H. Chase, *Federal Judges: The Appointing Process* (1972); Goldman, "Judicial Appointments to the United States Courts of Appeals," 1967 Wis. L. Rev. 186; Scott, "The Selection of Federal Judges," 24 Wash. and Lee L. Rev. 205 (1967). The mechanics of judicial appointment in the half-century covered by this study are thus neglected in the scholarly literature on the federal courts. Analysis of the Ninth Circuit judges appointed by Roosevelt provides an opportunity to explore the role of such key considerations as age, geography, political activity, prior judicial experience, and patronage, in the selection process for federal appellate court judges. At the same time, the personal stresses and experiences encountered by judicial candidates more readily appear.

3. Act of Oct. 22, 1913, ch. 32, 38 Stat. 208, 219. Act of Mar. 1, 1929, ch. 413, 45 Stat. 1414. Act of Mar. 1, 1929, ch. 413, § 1, *§ 2, 45 Stat. 1414; see S. Rep. No. 1486, 70th Cong., 2d Sess. 1 (1929).

4. H.R. Rep. No. 782, 70th Cong., 1st Sess. (1928). S. Rep. No. 1486, 70th Cong., 2d Sess. 1–2 (1929). U.S. Department of Commerce, Bureau of the Census, 2 *Historical Statistics of the United States* 1083 (1975). In 1920, 158 appeals were docketed in the Ninth Circuit, compared to 339 in 1929 (*see* 1920 Att'y Gen. Ann. Rep. 199; 1929 Att'y Gen. Ann. Rep. 89). The court's docket books show 339 appeals filed in the court in 1929, rather than the 338 listed by the attorney general (*see infra*, Appendix).

5. *San Francisco Chronicle*, Mar. 2, 1929, at 1, col. 5. *See San Francisco Chronicle*, Jan. 15, 1929, at 9, col. 2. The press's reasoning about Californians proved to be false, for Hoover appointed Curtis Wilbur's brother Ray as secretary of the interior (*San Francisco Chronicle*, Mar. 3, 1929, at 22, col. 3). *San Francisco Chronicle*, Mar. 21, 1929, at 1, col. 4. *See San Francisco Chronicle*, Mar. 19, 1929, at 5, col. 1; *id.*, May 3, 1929, at 1, col. 5. *See* File of Curtis D. Wilbur, Nomination Papers of Ninth Circuit Judges, RG 46, National Archives, Washington, D.C.

6. For a fascinating look at Wilbur's background and early childhood, see *The Memoirs of Ray Lyman Wilbur, 1875–1949*, especially chapters 1 and 2 (E. Robinson and P. Edwards, eds., 1960). His brother, Ray Lyman Wilbur, was not only a prominent doctor and secretary of the interior but also a president of Stanford University. Curtis married Ella T. Chilson on November 9, 1893, but she died only three years later. On January 13, 1898, he married Olive Doolittle, with whom he had four children (*Dictionary of American Biography*, Supp. 5 at 746 [1977]).

7. For additional biographical information on Wilbur, *see Judges of the United States* 532 (2d ed. 1983).

8. For a brief description of the Washington Treaty, see C. Colombos, *The International Law of the Sea* 492–93 (6th ed. 1967). *See generally Dictionary of American Biography*, *supra* note 6, at 746.

9. His length of service was certainly a record up to May of 1972, when the Senate Judiciary Committee issued its committee print (*see* Committee on the Judiciary, "Legislative History of the United States Circuit Courts of Appeals and the Judges Who Served During the Period 1801 Through May 1972," Senate Comm. on Judiciary, 92d Cong., 2d Sess. [1972, charts on each circuit]) (hereinafter Senate Judiciary Committee, "Legislative History"). *San Francisco Chronicle*, Apr. 28, 1931, at *16, col. 5.

10. Wilbur expressed his great respect for Gilbert in his address to commemorate Gilbert's service on the court: "We should recognize frankly that it is impossible to appraise the value of his work, for the result of his keen intellect, his industry and his sense of justice and fair dealing manifested in a rapidly growing section of the country during its entire formative period must have pervaded the community in ways and with results that cannot be known" ("In Memoriam: Hon. William B. Gilbert," 52 F.2d xxxi, xxxii [1931, statement of Senior Circuit Judge Curtis D. Wilbur]). On the Judicial Conference of Senior Judges, *see generally* F. Frankfurter and J. Landis, *The Business of the Supreme*

Court 217–54 (1928); P. Fish, *The Politics of Federal Judicial Administration* 40–90 (1973).

11. He retired on his seventy-eighth birthday, May 10, 1945, but continued to hear appeals as a senior status judge until his death on September 8, 1954.

12. Of Hoover's judicial appointees, 85.7 percent were Republican; of Taft's, 82.2 percent. With one exception, all of the other presidents in this period, including Franklin Roosevelt, appointed members of their own party to over 90 percent of the available posts; Benjamin Harrison appointed 87.9 percent (*see* Evans, "Political Influences in the Selection of Federal Judges," 1948 Wis. L. Rev. 330, 334). "As a practitioner he was noted for the care and thoroughness with which he examined all matters and the fairness with which he conducted, both in and out of court, all matters intrusted to his charge" ("In Memoriam: Honorable Wm. H. Sawtelle," 79 F.2d xi, xi [Dec. 17, 1935, statement of Honorable Samuel L. Pattee]).

13. He received his commission on January 29, 1931, and took his oath on February 6, 1931. *See generally* File of William H. Sawtelle, Nomination Papers of Ninth Circuit Judges, RG 46, National Archives, Washington, D.C. (hereinafter Sawtelle Circuit Judgeship Nomination File). M. C. Atchison to Senator George W. Norris, Jan. 12, 1931, Sawtelle Circuit Judgeship Nomination File. Charles H. Richeson to Senator George W. Norris, Feb. 2, 1931, Sawtelle Circuit Judgeship Nomination File. For more on Sawtelle's appointment to the district court, see "Memorandum for the President Concerning William H. Sawtelle, Tucson, Arizona, whose Nomination to be United States District Judge for the District of Arizona is Recommended," July 24, 1913, File of William H. Sawtelle, Judges, Ninth Circuit Court of Appeals, Department of Justice General Records, RG 60, National Archives, Washington, D.C.

14. Doctors initially diagnosed the cause of death as a heart attack, but later decided that he died when he struck the back of his head at the bottom of the staircase (*San Francisco Chronicle*, Dec. 18, 1934, at 4, col. 1). Evans, "A Work Sheet of Judicial Labor of Appellate Federal Courts," 1943 Wis. L. Rev. 313, 321. Evans placed the average much lower because he counted 1930 and 1935, years in which Sawtelle was not on the court. The fifteen opinions Evans cites from 1935 may have been released by the other judges after Sawtelle's death (*see id.*). 1929 Att'y Gen. Ann. Rep. 89; 1930 Att'y Gen. Ann. Rep. 105; 1932 Att'y Gen. Ann. Rep. 145. 79 F.2d at *xiv (statement of Curtis D. Wilbur).

15. 79 F.2d at xv (statement of Francis A. Garrecht). 79 F.2d at *xvi (statement of William Denman).

16. A number of his opinions were cited by American Law Reports (ALR) (*see*, e.g., *Ocean Accident and Guar. Corp. v. Rubin*, 73 F.2d 157 [9th Cir. 1934], cited by 96 A.L.R. 412; *Madden v. LaCofske*, 72 F.2d 602 [9th Cir. 1934], cited by 95 A.L.R. 370; *Fidelity and Deposit Co. v. Lindholm*, 66 F.2d 56 [9th Cir. 1933], cited by 89 A.L.R. 279; *California Prune and Apricot Growers Ass'n v. Catz Am. Co.*, 60 F.2d 788 [9th Cir. 1932], cited by 85 A.L.R. 1117; *Yoshizawa v. Hewitt*, 52 F.2d 411 [9th Cir. 1931], cited by 79 A.L.R. 317).

17. *See*, e.g., *Donahue v. United States*, 56 F.2d 94, 97 (9th Cir. 1932, Sawtelle, J., dissenting; search and seizure case); *Darrow v. United States*, 61 F.2d 124 (9th Cir. 1932; war risk insurance case). *Compare Ocean Accident and*

Guar. Corp. v. Rubin, 73 F.2d 157 (9th Cir. 1934; permitting recovery on an insurance contract) and *Fidelity and Deposit Co. v. Lindholm*, 66 F.2d 56 (9th Cir. 1933; permitting action at common law to avoid the statute of limitations) *with Howes v. United States Fidelity and Guar. Co.*, 73 F.2d 611 (9th Cir. 1934; denying recovery for failure to comply with a condition precedent under an accident policy).

18. Act of June 16, 1933, ch. 102, 48 Stat. 310. Evans, *supra* note 12, at 335–36. In his 90 percent figure, Evans does not break down the tallies for the district courts and the circuit courts of appeals, but even assuming that most of the Democratic judges were on the district court, Roosevelt nevertheless still had a very small group from which to elevate (*see id.* at 336). Of the seven judges Roosevelt appointed to the Ninth Circuit, only Albert Lee Stephens was promoted from the district bench, and he had been appointed to that seat by Roosevelt himself.

19. "In Memory of Honorable Francis Arthur Garrecht," 169 F.2d li, lii–iii, *lv (Aug. 31, 1948, statement of Benjamin H. Kizer).

20. *See* "Francis A. Garrecht: Senior Circuit Judge: Ninth Circuit," 33 A.B.A. J. 239, *239 (1947). Four years later, Garrecht married Miss Frances T. Lyons, also from Walla Walla; the marriage was to last forty-seven years (169 F.2d at liv).

21. "Francis A. Garrecht," *supra* note 20, at 240 (quoting press dispatch).

22. *United States v. West Side Irrigating Co.*, 230 F. 284 (E.D. Wash. 1916, per Rudkin, J.), *aff'd*, 246 F. 212 (9th Cir. 1917), *appeal dismissed per stipulation*, 260 U.S. 756 (1922). *Northern Pac. Ry. Co. v. Wismer*, 230 F. 591 (9th Cir. 1916), *aff'd*, 246 U.S. 283 (1918). "Francis A. Garrecht," *supra* note 20, at 240.

23. *See* "Francis A. Garrecht," *supra* note 20, at 240–41.

24. Roosevelt nominated Garrecht on May 3, 1933, and the Senate confirmed him on May 16, 1933. He assumed his post on May 22, 1933. *See generally San Francisco Chronicle*, May 5, 1933, at 10, col. 6; *see also* Senate Judiciary Committee, "Legislative History," at 23–28. File of Francis A. Garrecht, Nomination Papers of Ninth Circuit Judges, RG 46, National Archives, Washington, D.C. Francis A. Garrecht Personnel File, Federal Records Center, National Archives, St. Louis, Missouri (hereinafter Garrecht Personnel File).

25. *See*, e.g., *NLRB v. Montgomery and Ward Co.*, 133 F.2d 676 (9th Cir. 1943); *NLRB v. Union Pacific Stages, Inc.*, 99 F.2d 153 (9th Cir. 1938); *Phillips v. Baker*, 121 F.2d 752 (9th Cir. 1941); *Gillons v. Shell Oil Co.*, 86 F.2d 600 (9th Cir. 1936); *Craig v. United States*, 81 F.2d 816 (9th Cir. 1936); *United States v. Arenas*, 158 F.2d 730 (9th Cir. 1946). *San Francisco Recorder*, Aug. 12, 1948, at 1, col. 5. Garrecht became senior judge of the Ninth Circuit upon Wilbur's retirement on May 11, 1945, and his service on the court ended with his death by heart attack on August 11, 1948, at the age of seventy-seven. For details of his death, see *San Francisco Chronicle*, Aug. 12, 1948, at 7, col. 1; *see also San Francisco Recorder*, Aug. 12, 1948, at 1, cols. 3–4.

26. Act of June 16, 1933, ch. 102, 48 Stat. 310–11. The statute provided: "That the President is authorized, by and with the advice and consent of the Senate, to appoint a circuit judge to fill the vacancy in the United States Circuit

Court of Appeals for the Ninth Judicial Circuit occasioned by the death of Honorable William B. Gilbert. A vacancy [sic] occurring at any time in the office of circuit judge referred to in this section is authorized to be filled." Biographical sketches of Denman are plentiful. See C. Taylor, Bench and Bar of California, 1937–38, at 146–47 (1937); C. Taylor, Bench and Bar of California 64 (Centennial ed. 1949); 3 Who Was Who in America, 1951–1960, at 221 (1963); "In Memoriam: Honorable William Denman," 262 F.2d 7 (Mar. 30, 1959); Biographical Sketch, William Denman Papers, Bancroft Library, University of California, Berkeley (hereinafter Denman Papers); Biographical Sketch, William Denman Personnel File, Federal Records Center, National Archives, St. Louis, Missouri (hereinafter Denman Personnel File). Garrecht was the first Ninth Circuit judge to be born in the circuit. On Denman's claims, see, e.g., Denman to Hiram Johnson, Nov. 28, 1934, Denman Papers. As a private practitioner, Denman's first celebrated case was in admiralty, involving the unseaworthiness of the steamer Rio de Janeiro, which was lost just inside the Golden Gate in 1901 because her Chinese crew failed to understand the orders of her American officers. As the story was told after his death, Denman matched wits against the celebrated Hall McAllister, one of the greatest lawyers in California history, with Denman winning the case for the claimants (see "In Memoriam, Honorable William Denman," 262 F.2d at 8 [statement of William R. Wallace]). But if Denman opposed a Hall McAllister, it was probably the son of Cutler McAllister, who was the great Hall's brother and the son of Judge Matthew Hall McAllister, the first circuit judge in California (see Watson, "The San Francisco McAllisters," 11 Calif. Hist. Soc. Q. 124, 126 [1932]). In any event, Denman had a very successful career at the admiralty bar and a lifelong interest in maritime issues.

27. See generally C. W. Taylor, Bench and Bar of California, 1937–38, at 146. These laws included attempts to eliminate corruption among California political bosses, to diminish the political power of the Southern Pacific Railroad, to remove legislative control from internal county affairs, and to augment environmental conservation measures (see H. Melendy and B. Gilbert, The Governors of California: Peter H. Burnett to Edmund G. Brown 308–12 [1965]).

28. No stranger to controversy, Denman was considered "honest but insignificant" as shipping board chairman (San Francisco Examiner, June 26, 1917, unnumbered editorial page). An incident that foreshadowed the many public controversies that followed Denman throughout his career involved a brouhaha of colossal proportions between Denman and Major General George W. Goethals over responsibility for constructing a merchant fleet to overcome the growing German submarine menace. Goethals advocated building steel ships, Denman proposed wooden vessels; the press lambasted the chairman publicly for not deferring to the general (see id.), but President Wilson eventually sided with Denman. The conflict apparently consumed a fair amount of the president's attention. On July 24, 1917, for example, he wrote to Denman three times regarding the affair (see Correspondence with Woodrow Wilson, Denman Papers).

29. In 1934, Denman claimed that this service severely impinged on his later legal practice: "Up to that time [when he became Shipping Board chairman] I had

had the cream of the admiralty practice here and had a record of winning somewhere around eighty percent of my cases. Since that time no American shipowner has brought me a pice [sic] of litigation. What admiralty litigation I have had on the vessel owner's side has been bootlegged to me by the insurers of the hull. No doubt what I had to do on the Shipping Board with reference to cutting the charter rate on United States ships to less than one-half the going freight helped make permanent the owners' blacklisting" (William Denman to Felix Frankfurter, Nov. 6, 1934, Denman Papers).

30. When Denman and Roosevelt met is not clear. The first letters between Denman and Roosevelt in the Denman Papers date from World War I (see Denman Papers, Bancroft Library). They may have met through Denman's wife, Leslie Van Ness Denman, who knew Roosevelt well enough to send him a letter urging the nomination of Denman to the Ninth Circuit (Leslie Van Ness Denman to Franklin D. Roosevelt, Aug. 20, 1933, Denman Personnel File).

31. Denman's request of Frankfurter may have been oral, since the Denman Papers contain no letter predating Frankfurter's response. An earlier letter indicated a meeting between Denman and Frankfurter in late 1932 or early 1933 (Felix Frankfurter to William Denman, Jan. 13, 1933, Denman Papers). *Felix Frankfurter to William Denman, Feb. 7, 1933, Denman Papers. According to the editor of Frankfurter's correspondence with Roosevelt, the Harvard law professor rarely ventured an "uninvited suggestion" to the president regarding an appointment prospect, but if Roosevelt solicited his views, Frankfurter was more than willing to push people he respected (see Roosevelt and Frankfurter: Their Correspondence, 1929–1945, at 8 [M. Freedman ed. 1967]).

32. *Frankfurter to Denman, Sept. 12, 1934, Denman Papers. *Denman to Frankfurter, Nov. 6, 1934, Denman Papers.

33. *Denman to Hon. James A. Farley, Nov. 7, 1934; *Denman to Senator Key Pittman, Nov. 7, 1934; and *Denman to Senator Burton K. Wheeler, Nov. 7, 1934, Denman Papers. In this count Denman included Sawtelle from Arizona (who would be dead in little over a month), Wilbur as being from Los Angeles because he had practiced law there for thirteen years, even though he presently sat in San Francisco, and Stephens, who was a district judge in Los Angeles. *Denman to Frankfurter, Nov. 10, 1934, Denman Papers.

34. The Senate did not confirm Norcross after his nomination in September, 1933. In a later letter Denman misstated Frank Dietrich's age at appointment as seventy; he had been sixty-three (see Denman to Hiram Johnson, Nov. 30, 1934, Denman Papers). *Denman to Hiram Johnson, Nov. 28, 1934, Denman Papers.

35. Under the convention of senatorial courtesy, senators of the party in power have a predominant—some would say preeminent—say in the appointment of federal officials in that state. How this tradition has fared with circuit judge appointees, whose positions cover more than one state, is unclear. In any event, as a Republican, Johnson had no standing to push, other than through persuasion, Denman's appointment with the Democratic administration. On senatorial courtesy, see generally J. Harris, The Advice and Consent of the Senate 215–37 (1953). *Hiram Johnson to Honorable Homer S. Cummings, Nov. 28, 1934, Denman Papers. *Homer Cummings to Senator Hiram W. Johnson, Dec. 4, 1934, attached to Johnson to Denman, Dec. 10, 1934, Denman Papers.

36. Denman to Johnson, Nov. 30, 1934, Denman Papers. *William Denman to Felix Frankfurter, Nov. 30, 1934, Denman Papers. Frankfurter responded: "At least Hiram J. is forthright and powerful in his views of support. That's a fine letter of his" (Frankfurter to Denman, Dec. 6, 1934, Denman Papers). *Denman to Johnson, Dec. 19, 1934, Denman Papers. He took the oath of office March 11, 1935. For official documents, see Denman Personnel File. *See also* Johnson to Denman, Jan. 1935, announcing that his name had come to the Senate for appointment; Denman to Roosevelt, Jan. 18, 1935, Denman Papers, expressing gratitude for the appointment.

37. After Garrecht died in 1948, Denman continued to push for reform as chief judge of the Ninth Circuit until his retirement in 1957. A "passionate advocate of good government, in all its branches," Denman worked with uncommon drive to improve the operation of government. Somehow he also made time in twenty-four years of judicial service to produce 846 opinions for the court, 44 concurrences, and 77 dissents. Whether it was the climate or his own dedication, Denman clearly proved that it would have been folly to hold his age against him. Nor did he mellow with advanced age. When, in 1957, members of Congress considered passing a law to terminate a chief judge's tenure at age seventy, the pugnacious eighty-four-year-old jurist agreed with the aim of the so-called "Denman Bill" so that he could do more judicial work—he had written fifty-seven opinions the previous year. "In Memoriam: Honorable William Denman," 262 F.2d at 10 (statement of William R. Wallace). Congress changed the designation of "senior judge" to "chief judge" in 1948 (Act of June 25, 1948, ch. 646, § 45, 62 Stat. 869, 871). "In Memoriam: Honorable William Denman," 262 F.2d at 9, 11. Denman to Hon. Emanuel Celler, Chairman, House Judiciary Committee, May 3, 1957, Denman Papers. But for all his fighting spirit, this seemingly rather cold, hard man could not bear the loss of his beloved wife, Leslie Van Ness Denman, who died on February 9, 1959, after a long illness. The childless, eighty-six-year-old jurist took his own life on March 9, 1959. In an intriguing letter written two decades later, Denman's former secretary, Ione McGee, responded to a request by Judge James M. Carter for any historical anecdotes about her former boss:

> Judge Denman was not a warm man, and he earned the most devoted of enemies, but he had a social conscience, an abstract one, perhaps, which may have been the most useful kind in a man of his position. When he attempted a kind exchange with building employees, or with some of the unfortunates that used to stumble into our offices before the days of high security, he scared the living daylights out of them just because of the kind of face he had. He knew this. He made vague expressions of regret about it.
>
> I could wish there were tenderer memories of him around. But then in time to come there will be no memories at all, but only such data as goes into the records you and your colleagues are now compiling. These will tell of a man's place in the world, but are not designed to tell very much about the nature of a man.
>
> Ione McGee to Judge James Carter, Aug. 29, 1979, Historical File,
> U.S. Circuit Court of Appeals for the Ninth Circuit Library, San Francisco.

38. The Senate confirmed Mathews on March 20, 1935, and he was sworn in on April 18, 1935 (*see San Francisco Chronicle*, Apr. 23, 1935, at 28, col. 3). Mathews took the seat of Judge William H. Sawtelle, who died December 17, 1934. Denman assumed the seat of Judge Gilbert, who died in 1931 and whose

position was reauthorized by act of Congress in 1933 but held vacant until the appointment of Denman two years later (Act of Aug. 2, 1935, ch. 425, 49 Stat. 508). For a detailed account, *see infra* Chapter Ten. Senate Judiciary Committee, "Legislative History," at 174.

39. Biographical information on Mathews derives from the following: *Judges of the United States, supra* note 7, at 319; 4 *Who Was Who in America, 1961–1968,* at 619 (1968); "Memorial Proceedings: Honorable Clifton Mathews," 312 F.2d 5 (Oct. 10, 1962). Only the *Judges of the United States* gives information of Mathews receiving a formal degree—a B.A. from the University of Nashville in 1904. The other sources state that he left Peabody without a degree. "Memorial Proceedings," *supra,* at *13 (statement of Chief Judge Richard H. Chambers). *Truax v. Corrigan,* 257 U.S. 312 (1921). In this case, the Supreme Court by a five-to-four margin held an Arizona statute invalid. Mathews successfully argued that a state statute that deprived a business from enjoining picketers violated the business's Fourteenth Amendment right to the equal protection of the laws (*id.* at 315, 339). See "Memorial Proceedings," 312 F.2d at 7 (statement of George Reed Carlock). Hiram Johnson later wrote of Mathews that "he did more than any one man" to accomplish the Boulder/ Hoover Dam Project (Hiram Johnson to Hiram W. Johnson, Jr., May 5, 1940, Hiram Johnson Papers, Bancroft Library, University of California, Berkeley).

40. *San Francisco Chronicle,* Mar. 14, 1935, at 9, col. 3. 1935 Att'y Gen. Ann. Rep. 181; 1936 Att'y Gen. Ann. Rep. 161; 1937 Att'y Gen. Ann. Rep. 173. This great figure of the bar and bench died the same day as the great literary figure Karen Christence Dinesen (Baroness Blixen-Finecke), better known by her pen name of Isak Dinesen (*see San Francisco Chronicle,* Sept. 8, 1962, at 1, col. 3). *San Francisco Chronicle,* Sept. 8, 1962, at *17, col. 4 (quoting Judge Albert Lee Stephens). *Id.* at *17, col. 3 (quoting Chief Judge Richard H. Chambers).

41. "In Memory of Honorable Bert Emory Haney," 142 F.2d XV, XVI (April 26, 1944, statement of Hall S. Lusk).

42. For the initial controversy *see San Francisco Examiner,* Sept. 1, 1925, at 9, col. 1. For the resignation of Haney *see San Francisco Chronicle,* Feb. 24, 1926, at 12, col. 8.

43. Given his role in nominating Coolidge for the vice presidency in 1920, Wallace McCamant's nomination in 1925 also seemingly fell into the category of patronage. Yet the internal Justice Department memorandum on McCamant scrupulously avoided mentioning this fact, and the recommendation letters lauded McCamant's high qualifications for the job (*see supra* Chapter Six). See, e.g., telegrams by Henrietta B. Martin, President, Good Government Congress, Inc., Personnel File of Bert E. Haney, Federal Records Center, National Archives, St. Louis, Missouri (hereinafter Haney Personnel File). *H. Cummings, "Memorandum for Judge Stephens," July 23, 1935, Department of Justice, Haney Personnel File.

44. Haney's firm was named Joseph, Haney and Veach. *Harold M. Stephens, "Memorandum for the Files," July 21, 1935, Department of Justice, Haney Personnel File. *Jay H. Stockman to Harold M. Stephens, July 28, 1935, Haney Personnel File. In the previous paragraph, Stockman wrote that he had

spoken with McCamant, George Neuner, Nicholas Jaureguy, and "several others." *Stephens, *supra*.

45. Stephens, "Memorandum for the Files," *supra* note 42.

46. *H. Cummings, "Memorandum for Judge Stephens," *supra* note 43. *See generally* Haney Personnel File. Memorandum from Chester H. McCall to Secretary Roper, Mar. 8, 1935, Haney Personnel File. The earlier "suggestion" urged Haney's appointment to the district court; the later one specifically mentioned the Ninth Circuit. *See* *Daniel C. Roper, Secretary of Commerce, to Attorney General Homer Cummings, June 27, 1935, Haney Personnel File. *See* James A. Farley to Homer S. Cummings, Nov. 24, 1933, Haney Personnel File.

47. William Denman to Bert Emory Haney, Sept. 28, 1942, Denman Special File, Curtis D. Wilbur Papers, U.S. Court of Appeals for the Ninth Circuit, San Francisco. "In Memory of Honorable Bert Emory Haney," 142 F.2d at XX (statement of Colonel A. E. Clark).

48. Ever since this period, the Ninth Circuit has always had at least one jurist who was elevated from the district court.

9. ADJUDICATING THE NEW DEAL

1. *See* U.S. Department of Commerce Bureau of the Census, *Historical Statistics of the United States* 135 (1975); Keyserling, "The New Deal and Its Current Significance in Re National Economic and Social Policy," 59 Wash. L. Rev. 795, 797 (1984). Nationwide, per capita income between 1929–33 and 1947–49 decreased by 28 percent. In California it fell by 29 percent; in Idaho, 39 percent; in Nevada, 28 percent; in Oregon, 31 percent; and in Washington, 33 percent (E. Pomeroy, *The Pacific Slope: A History of California, Oregon, Washington, Idaho, Utah, and Nevada* 293 n.1 [1965]). G. Nash, *The American West Transformed: The Impact of the Second World War* 6 (1985).

2. *See* J. Gregory, *American Exodus: The Dust Bowl Migration and Okie Culture in California* 11 (1989). 2 U.S. Department of Commerce Bureau of the Census, *Sixteenth Census of the United States: 1940, Population* 382, 629, 651, 657, 759, 1041 (1943); G. Nash, *supra* note 1, at 9–10.

3. *See generally* M. Malone and R. Roeder, *Montana: A History of Two Centuries* 216–18 (1976).

4. Arizona received $597; California, $266; Idaho, $399; Oregon, $355; Washington, $373. Figures for Hawaii and Alaska are unavailable (*see* Arrington, "The New Deal in the West: A Preliminary Statistical Inquiry," 38 Pac. Hist. Rev. 311, 311–16 [1969]).

5. For a biographical sketch of Stephens, see C. Taylor, *Bench and Bar of California* 24 (1938).

6. "In Honor of Albert Lee Stephens, Sr.," 345 F.2d 3, 18 (1965, statement of Judge Richard H. Chambers).

7. C. Taylor, *Eminent Judges and Lawyers of the Northwest, 1843–1955*, at 34 (1954); 4 *Who Was Who in America, 1961–1968*, at 423 (1968). *See also* William Healy Personnel File, Federal Records Center, National Archives, St. Louis, Missouri.

8. To the extent that they discuss such matters, the histories of other circuit courts of appeals also suggest a heavy regional imprimatur on their work (*see* J. Morris, *Federal Justice and the Second Circuit* [1987]; R. Solomon, *History of the Seventh Circuit* [1981]; T. Fetter, *History of the Eighth Circuit* [1977]).

9. Kirkendall, "The New Deal and Agriculture," in 1 *The New Deal* 83–86 (J. Braeman, R. Bremner, and D. Brody eds. 1975); E. Hoyt, *The Tempering Years* 219–38 (1963). Breimyer, "Agricultural Philosophies and Policies in the New Deal," 68 Minn. L. Rev. 333, 341 (1983). R. Lowitt, *The New Deal and the West* 8–64 (1984).

10. *See generally* Feder, "Farm Debt Adjustments During the Depression— the Other Side of the Coin," 35 Agric. Hist. 78, 78 (1961). Agricultural Adjustment Act of 1933, ch. 25, 48 Stat. 31. For an excellent overview of New Deal agricultural programs, see Rasmussen, "New Deal Agricultural Policies After Fifty Years," 68 Minn. L. Rev. 353 (1983). *See* Agricultural Adjustment Act of 1933, ch. 25, 48 Stat. 31; Tobacco Control Act, ch. 866, 48 Stat. 1275 (1934); Potato Control Act of 1935, ch. 641, tit. II, 49 Stat. 750, 782; Agricultural Marketing Agreement Act of 1937, ch. 296, 50 Stat. 246; Sugar Act of 1937, ch. 898, 50 Stat. 903; Agricultural Adjustment Act of 1938, ch. 30, 52 Stat. 31; Federal Crop Insurance Act, ch. 30, tit. V, 52 Stat. 31, 72 (1938); Act of April 13, 1934, ch. 121, 48 Stat. 589; Act of Feb. 11, 1937, ch. 10, 50 Stat. 19 (establishing the Disaster Loan Corporation); Bankhead-Jones Farm Tenant Act, ch. 517, 50 Stat. 522 (1937); Soil Conservation and Domestic Allotment Act, ch. 104, 49 Stat. 1148 (1936); Agricultural Adjustment Act of 1938, ch. 30, tit. I, 52 Stat. 31; Emergency Farm Mortgage Act of 1933, ch. 25, tit. II, 48 Stat. 31; Farm Credit Act of 1933, ch. 98, 48 Stat. 257; Federal Farm Mortgage Corporation Act, ch. 7, 48 Stat. 344 (1934); Farm Credit Act of 1935, ch. 164, 49 Stat. 313; Farm Credit Act of 1937, ch. 704, 50 Stat. 703; and Rural Electrification Act of 1936, ch. 432, 49 Stat. 1363. *See generally* Breimyer, *supra* note 9, at 342–46.

11. These statistics have been gathered from the *State Summary Series* prepared for each state and available in the National Archives Printed Government Documents section (United States Department of Agriculture Agricultural Adjustment Administration Division of Information, "Changes in the Agricultural Situation in Arizona, 1932–1935," *State Summary Series: Arizona #2*, at 1, 3, 5 [1936, income rose 200 percent]; *id., California #2*, at 4, 7 [1936, 140 percent]; *id., Idaho #2*, at 5, 6 [1936, 80 percent]; *id., Montana #3*, at 3, 5 [1937, 102 percent]; *id., Nevada #3*, at 3, 5 [1937, 100 percent]; *id., Oregon #3*, at 3, 5 [1937, 60 percent]; *id., Washington #3*, at 3, 5 [1937, 62.5 percent]).

12. *See State Summary Series: California #2, supra* note 11, at 2. *Berdie v. Kurtz*, 75 F.2d 898, 904 (9th Cir. 1935).

13. *See Berdie*, 75 F.2d at 905. *Stafford v. Wallace*, 258 U.S. 495 (1922, upholding regulation of stockyards).

14. 75 F.2d at 906 (Garrecht, J., dissenting). Arguably the furthest extension of this position in this era was the Supreme Court's validation of regulations on intrastate production of agricultural commodities not intended for sale (*Wickard v. Filburn*, 317 U.S. 111 [1942]).

15. *United States v. Butler*, 297 U.S. 1, 61–68 (1936). *Rickert Rice Mills v. Fontenot*, 297 U.S. 110, 113 (1936, striking down Agricultural Adjustment Act amendments, 49 Stat. 750 [1935]). *See* Murphy, "The New Deal Agricultural Program and the Constitution," 29 Agric. Hist. 160, 162 (1955).

16. On the statutory complexity, see Oehmann, "The Agricultural Adjustment Act of 1938," 26 Geo. L. Rev. 680, 680 (1938).

17. *Edwards v. United States*, 91 F.2d 767 (9th Cir. 1937). This case involved provisions of the 1935 amendments different from those held invalid in *Rickert Rice Mills v. Fontenot*, 297 U.S. 110 (1936).

18. 91 F.2d at 772–73 (discussing Agricultural Adjustment Act Amendments, 49 Stat. 750 [1935]). *Id.* at 774–77.

19. *U.S. Const. art. I, § 8, cl. 3. *91 F.2d at *779. *Compare Berdie v. Kurtz*, 75 F.2d 898, 904 (9th Cir. 1935): "Unless the court can say that as a matter of fact the business transactions . . . are a part of interstate commerce the Secretary of Agriculture has no authority to deal with the subject no matter how interrelated the interstate and intrastate commerce may be."

20. 91 F.2d at 781–82. *NLRB v. Jones and Laughlin Steel Corp.*, 301 U.S. 1, 38–39, *41 (1937); *Carter v. Carter Coal Co.*, 298 U.S. 238, 310 (1936). 91 F.2d at *782. E.g., Stern, "The Commerce Clause and the National Economy, 1933–1946," 59 Harv. L. Rev. 645, 679–81 (1946). Judge Haney concurred separately because he did not believe it was necessary to reach this issue. *See* 91 F.2d at 789–90 (Haney, J., concurring). Garrecht joined Denman's opinion without comment. 91 F.2d at *783. Denman also disposed of the fruit company's Fifth Amendment due process and delegation doctrine challenges. In both situations Denman found valid exercises of power by Congress, with the imposition of standards sufficiently fair to establish rationality for due process purposes and sufficiently precise to pass delegation scrutiny (*see* 91 F.2d at 784–87 and n.8). Denman reached back in time to cite *Fallbrook Irrigation Dist. v. Bradley*, 164 U.S. 112, 178 (1896), for the proposition that the imposition of conditions by the legislature did not constitute improper delegations of legislative authority (*see* 91 F.2d at 789). The Supreme Court's decision in the *Fallbrook* case had reversed a decision by his predecessor on the court, Erskine Ross. Even though *Berdie v. Kurtz* raised similar Commerce Clause and delegation doctrine challenges, Denman neither cited nor discussed that case, indicating perhaps a desire subtly to shift the court's direction in its Commerce Clause jurisprudence.

21. *William Denman to G. Stanleigh Arnold, July 27, 1937, William Denman Papers, Bancroft Library, Berkeley, California. *See also* 91 F.2d at 784. *Wallace v. Hudson-Duncan Co.*, 98 F.2d 985, 993 (9th Cir. 1938). *Id.* at 994 (Mathews, J., dissenting). The Second Circuit's position seemed to accord with the view expressed by Denman for the Ninth Circuit (*see*, e.g., *United States v. Adler's Creamery*, 107 F.2d 987 [2d Cir. 1939]).

22. For agricultural producers, the Ninth Circuit held that the unconstitutionality of the AAA also rendered void contracts drawn pursuant to it and forced a bankrupt farmer to repay the government $2,019 that had been paid under the AAA (*see Gridley v. Rogers*, 83 F.2d 817, 818 [9th Cir. 1936, per curiam]). The court also permitted a different agricultural producer to keep the windfall of a price hike that had included a tax held invalid by the Supreme Court. When the

United States sought to recover the tax, the Ninth Circuit—over a dissent by Healy—permitted the company to keep a $2,284.68 windfall because the tax had been enacted pursuant to an unconstitutional statute. (*See United States v. Hagan and Cushing Co.*, 115 F.2d 849 [9th Cir. 1940]). Arrington, "Western Agriculture and the New Deal," 44 Agric. Hist. 337, 348 (1970). Nevada ranked first with $3,257 per farm capita; Arizona, third with $970; Montana, fourth with $895; California, sixth with $693; Washington, seventh with $692; and Idaho, eighth with $672. Oregonians received $602 in per farm capita. By contrast, the lowest totals were in West Virginia ($72), Virginia ($92), and Pennsylvania ($98) (Arrington, "Western Agriculture," *supra*, at 346). These totals included reclamation expenditures, but even without such aid all the Ninth Circuit states ranked in the top twenty, with all but Washington making the top thirteen. Wyoming and North Dakota ranked second and fifth, respectively (*id*.). *Id*. at 350–51. According to Arrington, the "relationship here is strongly positive"—about 0.82 (*id*.). *See generally* M. Malone and R. Roeder, *Montana: A History of Two Centuries* 229 (1976); Malone, "The New Deal in Idaho," 38 Pac. Hist. Rev. 293, 298–99 (1969); Arrington, "The Sagebrush Resurrection: New Deal Expenditures in the Western States, 1933–1939," 52 Pac. Hist. Rev. 1, 12–13 (1983).

23. National Industrial Recovery Act (NIRA), ch. 90, 48 Stat. 195 (1933). *See generally* Gifford, "The New Deal Regulatory Model: A History of Criticisms and Refinements," 68 Minn. L. Rev. 299, 300–1 (1983). *See* NIRA, § 7, 48 Stat. at 198–99. *See generally* Note, "The Codes Under the Recovery Act," 8 St. John's L. Rev. 400, 406–7 (1934). Weiner, "The New Deal and the Corporation," 19 U. Chi. L. Rev. 724, 725 (1952). *United States v. A.L.A. Schechter Poultry Corp.*, 8 F. Supp. 136 (E.D.N.Y. 1934), *aff'd in part and rev'd in part*, 76 F.2d 617 (2d Cir. 1935). Isaacs and Taeusch, "The NIRA in the Book and in Business," 47 Harv. L. Rev. 458, *459, *464 (1934).

24. *A.L.A. Schechter Poultry Corp. v. United States*, 295 U.S. 495, 541–51 (1935). Burton, "The New Deal in Oregon," in 2 *The New Deal* *360 (J. Braeman, R. Bremner, and D. Brody eds. 1975, quoting C. C. Cook, "the conservative owner and editor of the influential *Crow's Pacific Coast Lumber Digest*"); *see also* Dembo, "The Pacific Northwest Lumber Industry During the Great Depression," 24 J. of the West 51, 55 (1985).

25. After *Schechter Poultry*, the Ninth Circuit did not decide a case involving the NIRA until 1937 (*School Dist. No. 37 v. Isackson*, 92 F.2d 768, 770–71 [9th Cir. 1937]).

26. U.S. Const. art. I, § 8, cl. 1 provides: "The Congress shall have Power To lay and collect Taxes, Duties, Imposts and Excises, to pay the Debts and provide for the common Defense and general Welfare of the United States . . ." *School Dist. No. 37*, 92 F.2d at *771, 771–72. On *Schechter*, see 295 U.S. at 531–37. On *Butler*, see 297 U.S. at 64. *See also* L. Tribe, *American Constitutional Law* 321–22 (2d ed. 1988). 92 F.2d at 772 (Mathews, J., concurring). *See, e.g.*, *Greenwood County v. Duke Power Co.*, 81 F.2d 986, 994 (4th Cir. 1936); *Kansas Gas and Elec. Co. v. City of Independence*, 79 F.2d 32, 43–44 (10th Cir. 1935).

27. *See generally* Currie, "The Constitution in the Supreme Court: The New Deal, 1931–1940," 54 U. Chi. L. Rev. 504 (1987); Galloway, "The Court That

Challenged the New Deal (1930–1936)," 24 Santa Clara L. Rev. 65 (1984); Rankin, "The Supreme Court, the Depression and the New Deal: 1930–1941," 40 Neb. L. Rev. 35 (1960).

28. NIRA, § 213, 48 Stat. at 206. *United States v. Southwestern Portland Cement Co.*, 97 F.2d 413, 415 (9th Cir. 1938). 97 F.2d at *416 (Stephens, J., dissenting). *In re Lasswell*, 1 Cal. App. 2d 183 (Cal. Ct. App. 1934). *See*, e.g., *United States v. Murine Co.*, 90 F.2d 549 (7th Cir. 1937); *United States v. Southwestern R.R. Co.*, 92 F.2d 897 (5th Cir. 1937).

29. *Maloney v. Western Cooperage Co.*, 103 F.2d 992, *994 (9th Cir. 1939). *United States v. Baldy*, 108 F.2d 591, 592 (9th Cir. 1939).

30. *See also Carter v. Farmer Underwriters Ass'n*, 115 F.2d 302, 304 (9th Cir. 1940, upholding enforcement of NIRA Stock Tax provisions). Between 1933 and 1939, federal government spending nearly doubled, from $4.6 billion to $8.8 billion. This was the largest peacetime increase in expenditure over a six-year period in United States history (*see* 2 U.S. Department of Commerce Bureau of the Census, *supra* note 1, at 1104–5). On the NIRA's ineffectiveness generally, see B. Bellush, *The Failure of the NRA* (1975). *See infra*, Appendix. Some evidence for this conclusion about balance is that the court's affirmance rate in tax cases varied little depending on whether the United States was appellant or appellee; in both situations, the court affirmed nearly 80 percent of the time.

31. P. Taft, *Labor Politics American Style: The California State Federation of Labor* 87, 91–99 (1968). J. Auerbach, *Labor and Liberty: The La Follette Committee and the New Deal* 177 (1966).

32. *See generally* Madden, "The Origin and Early History of the National Labor Relations Board," 29 Geo. Wash. L. Rev. 234, 235, *237 (1960, citing *American Steel Foundries v. Tri-City Council*, 257 U.S. 184, 209 [1921] [hereinafter Madden, "The Origin and Early History"]). NIRA, § 7(a)(1), 48 Stat. at 198.

33. National Labor Relations Act (NLRA), ch. 372, §§ 8, 10(e), 49 Stat. 449, 452, 454 (1935).

34. For an interesting description of this litigation strategy and the constitutional attack on the NLRB by a group of lawyers acting pro bono, see the article written by the first chairman of the NLRB, J. Warren Madden (Madden, "The Origin and Early History," at 242–47). *See also* Madden, "Origin and Early Years of the National Labor Relations Act," 18 Hastings L.J. 571 (1967). *See* Madden, "The Origin and Early History," at *244 (discussing but not naming the court that delayed its decision until other courts had rendered a ruling).

35. William Denman, "What the Seven Circuit Judges of the Circuit Court of Appeals for the Ninth Circuit Have Created for the Service of Their Litigants," at 20 (Aug. 20, 1941), Denman Papers. I am uncertain when this rule became part of the Ninth Circuit's operating procedures.

36. *NLRB v. Mackay Radio and Tel. Co.*, 87 F.2d 611 (9th Cir. 1937), *rev'd*, 304 U.S. 333 (1938). *Lochner v. New York*, 198 U.S. 45, 57–61 (1905). Sometimes the Court upheld the law, as it did in *Muller v. Oregon*, 208 U.S. 412 (1908). But decisions favoring such laws were infrequent (*see generally* L. Tribe, *supra* note 26, at 574). E.g., *Morehead v. New York ex rel. Tipaldo*, 298 U.S. 587, 611 (1936; "the State is without power by any form of legislation to

prohibit, change or nullify contracts between employers and adult women workers as to the amount of wages to be paid."). *West Coast Hotel Co. v. Parrish*, 300 U.S. 379, 398 (1937).

37. The Supreme Court opinion relates the facts much better than the Ninth Circuit's decision (*see NLRB v. Mackay Radio and Tel. Co.*, 304 U.S. 333, 337–41 [1938]).

38. *See* 87 F.2d at 616 ("'The right to purchase or to sell labor is part of the liberty protected by [the fourteenth amendment],'" quoting *Lochner v. New York*, 198 U.S. 45, 53 [1905]). One of the cases often cited by Wilbur was *Adair v. United States*, 208 U.S. 161 (1908), in which the Court invalidated a congressional statute that prohibited a carrier in interstate commerce from discharging an employee solely because of that person's membership in a labor organization. The Court reasoned that such a law abridged a company's liberty and property rights under the Fifth Amendment due process clause (*id.* at 180). 87 F.2d at 615–19.

39. 87 F. 2d at 624.

40. 87 F. 2d at *627. Despite the board's arguments to the contrary, Wilbur downplayed the significance of *Texas and New Orleans R.R. Co. v. Brotherhood of Ry. and S.S. Clerks*, 281 U.S. 548 (1930), which appeared to move away from earlier *Lochner*-era decisions so as to render them less authoritative (*see* 87 F.2d at 619).

41. *See Mackay Radio*, 87 F.2d at 631 (Mathews, J., concurring). In the first *Mackay Radio* decision, Wilbur appeared ready to concede the fact-findings by the Board and strained to find legal reasons to deny the board's order (*compare Mackay Radio*, 87 F.2d at 627 *with NLRB v. Mackay Radio and Tel. Co.*, 92 F.2d 761, 765 [9th Cir. 1937, finding on rehearing that the statute prohibited the board from making its order after the Supreme Court had upheld the constitutionality of the NLRA]). In a later case, Mathews and Wilbur reversed a board order on the ground of insufficient proof (*see M and M Wood Working Co. v. NLRB*, 101 F.2d 938 [9th Cir. 1939]).

42. *See* Memorandum of Judge James M. Carter to Judge Richard H. Chambers, "Circuit History," Oct. 26, 1979, Files of United States Court of Appeals for the Ninth Circuit, San Francisco.

43. *Mackay Radio*, 87 F.2d at *632, *633, *634, 634–39, *649–50 (Garrecht, J., dissenting).

44. Prior to its decision in *Mackay Radio*, the court had issued a short per curiam opinion denying a request for an injunction pending appeal (*see Carlisle Lumber Co. v. Hope*, 83 F.2d 92 [9th Cir. 1936, per curiam]). It had also rendered a short memorandum decision in the same case six months later (*see Carlisle Lumber Co. v. Hope*, 85 F.2d 1010 [9th Cir. 1936, per curiam]). *NLRB v. Mackay Radio and Tel. Co.*, 92 F.2d 761 (9th Cir. 1937). On the Supreme Court's rulings affirming the NLRA's constitutionality, *see*, e.g., *NLRB v. Jones and Laughlin Corp.*, 301 U.S. 1 (1937, manufacturing and production operations); *NLRB v. Fruehauf Trailer Co.*, 301 U.S. 49 (1937, manufacturer of commercial trailers); *NLRB v. Friedman-Harry Marks Clothing Co.*, 301 U.S. 58 (1937, manufacturer of garments); *Associated Press v. NLRB*, 301 U.S. 103 (1937, news service); and *Washington, Virginia and Maryland Coach Co. v.*

NLRB, 301 U.S. 142 (1937, interstate bus line). 92 F.2d at *764–65. 92 F.2d at 765 (Mathews, J., dissenting); *id.* at 765, *767 (Garrecht, J., dissenting).

45. *NLRB v. Mackay Radio and Tel. Co.*, 304 U.S. 333 (1938). Interestingly, the Court "granted certiorari because of an asserted conflict of decision" (*id.*) at 336. Three other circuits had affirmed the statutory authority of the NLRB to issue such orders (*Black Diamond S.S. Corp. v. NLRB*, 94 F.2d 875 [2d Cir. 1938]; *NLRB v. Bell Oil and Gas Co.*, 91 F.2d 509 [5th Cir. 1937]; *Jeffery-DeWitt Insulator Co. v. NLRB*, 91 F.2d 134 [4th Cir. 1937]). The court also pointed out the internal conflict among Ninth Circuit decisions (333 U.S. at 336 n.3, citing *NLRB v. Carlisle Lumber Co.*, 94 F.2d 138 [9th Cir. 1937, opinion by Haney joined by Stephens over Wilbur's dissent that enforced the board's order]). In *Mackay Radio*, the Supreme Court recognized the right of businesses to hire permanent replacement workers during strikes (304 U.S. at 346). Decades later, scholars continued to criticize this doctrine, but courts took little heed (*see* Sales, "Replacing *Mackay*: Strikebreaking Acts and Other Assaults on the Permanent Replacement Doctrine," 36 Rutgers L.J. 801 [1984]; Janes, "The Illusion of Permanency for *Mackay* Doctrine Replacement Workers," 54 Texas L. Rev. 126, 126 [1975]).

46. *See NLRB v. Oregon Worsted Co.*, 96 F.2d 193 (9th Cir. 1938); *NLRB v. American Potash and Chem. Corp.*, 98 F.2d 488 (9th Cir. 1938); *NLRB v. Union Pac. Stages*, 99 F.2d 153 (9th Cir. 1938); *M and M Wood Working Co. v. NLRB*, 101 F.2d 938 (9th Cir. 1938); *NLRB v. Hearst Corp.*, 102 F.2d 658 (9th Cir. 1939); *NLRB v. Pacific Greyhound Lines*, 106 F.2d 867 (9th Cir. 1939).

47. See cases cited in previous note. P. Taft, *supra* note 31, at 103–26. In 1937, when the Supreme Court upheld the NLRA's constitutionality, the number of strikes nationwide had totaled 4,720 and had involved almost two million workers, levels that exceeded the strike-torn year of 1934 (F. Dulles, *Labor in America* 279 [1966 ed.]). The Ninth Circuit granted NLRB petitions for enforcement approximately 82 percent of the time in this period. Other results included dismissals, rejections, and modifications of orders (*see infra*, Appendix).

48. R. Lowitt, *supra* note 9, at 81. Swain, "The Bureau of Reclamation and the New Deal, 1933–1940," 61 Pac. Nw. Q. 137, 142 (1970). Act of June 17, 1902, ch. 1093, 32 Stat. 388.

49. Swain, *supra* note 48, at *146. The story of how Boulder Dam became Hoover Dam recalled the politics that had played a large part in the history of the Ninth Circuit. Judge Curtis Wilbur's brother, Ray Lyman Wilbur, when he was secretary of the interior had renamed the dam after President Hoover. Roosevelt's interior secretary, Harold Ickes, insisted that Ray Wilbur had no right to change the name. (Apparently Hiram Johnson had resented the change to Hoover Dam and lobbied with Ickes.) Congress restored the name Hoover Dam in 1947 after Ickes had left office (*see* Swain, *supra* note 48, at 138 n.6). Ray Wilbur's comment on Ickes's attempt to undo his nomenclature was direct: "Pettiness is paltry enough without being applied to anything as huge as the Hoover Dam" (R. Wilbur, *The Memoirs of Ray Lyman Wilbur* 462, E. Robinson and P. Edwards eds. [1960]). R. Lowitt, *supra* note 9, at 84 and 94.

50. *See Continental Land Co. v. United States,* 88 F.2d 104, 106–8 (9th Cir.), *cert. denied,* 302 U.S. 715 (1937). In another case involving the Grand Coulee Dam, the court rejected a claim of error in the assessment of the value of a landowner's property. He had claimed a value of $100,000, and the Ninth Circuit affirmed a jury award of $3,000 (*Brett v. United States,* 86 F.2d 305 [9th Cir. 1936], *cert. denied,* 201 U.S. 682 [1937]). For more on the general history of the Grand Coulee Dam, see R. Lowitt, *supra* note 9, at 164–70.

51. *Miller v. United States,* 125 F.2d 75, 80–81 (9th Cir. 1942). For a general historical overview of the project, see Lee, "California Water Politics: Depression Genesis of the Central Valley Project, 1933–1934," 24 J. of the West 63 (1985). *Id.* at *82 (Garrecht, J., dissenting, quoting *Searl v. School Dist. No. 2,* 133 U.S. 553, 561 [1890]).

52. R. Lowitt, *supra* note 9, at 82. Another historian puts the death toll at 110 (*see* Lear, "Boulder Dam: A Crossroads in Natural Resource Policy," 24 J. of the West 82, 87 [1985]). *King v. Six Companies,* 63 F.2d 302, 303 (9th Cir. 1933). The court reasoned that the complaint was insufficient, on the grounds that the plaintiff was either an invitee or a licensee (*see,* e.g., *Nev-Cal Elec. Sec. Co. v. Imperial Irrigation Dist.,* 85 F.2d 886 [9th Cir. 1936]; *United States v. John K. and Catherine S. Mullen Benev. Corp.,* 63 F.2d 48 [1933]).

53. *See generally* Warshall, "The Great Colorado River War," 23 Am. West 42 (1986). The compact apportions use of Colorado River waters between Colorado, New Mexico, Utah, Wyoming, Arizona, California, and Nevada, with some water unapportioned. Under the compact, the California State Legislature had to limit its use of the river to 4,400,000 acre-feet per year of the water apportioned to the lower basin states (California, Nevada, and Arizona) (*see Greeson v. Imperial Irrigation Dist.,* 59 F.2d 529, 531, *533 [9th Cir. 1932]). The Boulder Canyon Project Act is at 43 U.S.C. §§ 617–617t (1988). *American Falls Reservoir Dist. No. 2 v. Crandall,* 82 F.2d 973 (9th Cir. 1936).

54. For an interesting discussion of the historical background and survey of the literature, see Clements, "Politics and the Park: San Francisco's Fight for Hetch Hetchy, 1908–1913," 48 Pac. Hist. Rev. 185 (1979). Act of Dec. 19, 1913, ch. 4, § 6, 38 Stat. 242, *245.

55. *United States v. City and County of San Francisco,* 23 F. Supp. 40, 44–45, *45, 53 (N.D. Cal. 1938).

56. *City and County of San Francisco v. United States,* 106 F.2d 569, 575 (9th Cir. 1939).

57. *United States v. City and County of San Francisco,* 310 U.S. 16, *26 (1940).

58. 310 U.S. at 26. *See generally* R. Lowitt, *supra* note 9, at 192–93. On Ickes, *see* 1 H. Ickes, *Secret Diary: The First Thousand Days* 357 (1953); H. Ickes, *Secret Diary: The Inside Struggle* 124–25, 422, 426–27 (1954).

10.   A COURT TOO LARGE?

1. Frank M. Stone to Senator George F. Edmunds, Folio on *S.194, Folder 2, Senate Judiciary Committee Papers, SEN 51A-F16, S.1 to S.1445, Box 60, RG

46, Records of the U.S. Senate, 51st Cong., National Archives, Washington, D.C. Almost exactly a century later, Senator Slade Gorton of Washington on May 9, 1989, introduced a bill to divide the Ninth Circuit and to create a Twelfth Circuit to be composed of Washington, Oregon, Idaho, Montana, Alaska, Hawaii, Guam, and the Northern Mariana Islands. The new Ninth Circuit would comprise California, Nevada, and Arizona. Gorton purported to justify the measure on a number of grounds, which included the vast size of the Ninth Circuit, the alleged frequency of intracircuit conflicting opinions, the heavily weighted geographical representation of California judges on Ninth Circuit panels, the asserted importance of regional concerns in federal appellate litigation, and the increasingly important role played by staff in the judicial process. At the hearings on Gorton's bill, Chief Judge Alfred T. Goodwin and former Chief Judge James R. Browning testified in the strongest terms against splitting the circuit. On each of the points propounded by Senator Gorton, they attempted to demonstrate either that the purported problem did not exist or that it was being addressed in a creative way which presented a possible model for other federal courts of appeals as they grew in numbers of judges (S.948, 101st Cong., 1st Sess.). *See* "Ninth Circuit Court of Appeals Reorganization Act of 1989," Hearing on S.948 Before the Subcomm. on Courts and Administrative Practice of the Senate Comm. on the Judiciary, 101st Cong., 2nd Sess, 19–25 (1990) (hereinafter 1990 Hearings). Gorton also suggested that the American Bar Association had taken no official position and that the costs of such a split would be minimal (*id.* at 26). On Goodwin's testimony, see *id.* at 307–19. As Goodwin succinctly summarized in a colloquy on the issue with Oregon Senator Mark Hatfield, "The problem is not structure, but workload" (Goodwin, "Splitting the Ninth Circuit—No Answer to Caseload Growth," 1990 Oreg. St. Bar Bull. 10, 11, *reprinted in* 1990 Hearings, at 352–53). For an extensive treatment of the many issues associated with dividing the Ninth Circuit, see A. Hellman, ed., *Restructuring Justice* (1990).

2. *See supra* Chapter Five.

3. In 1895, the Ninth Circuit ranked sixth; in 1905, third; in 1915, third; and in 1925, third (1895 Att'y Gen. Ann. Rep. 39; 1905 Att'y Gen. Ann. Rep. 109; 1915 Att'y Gen. Ann. Rep. 84; 1925 Att'y Gen. Ann. Rep. 133). *See infra,* Appendix. *See also* 1920 Att'y Gen. Ann. Rep. 199; 1935 Att'y Gen. Ann. Rep. 181. Act of Feb. 28, 1929, ch. 363, Sec. 2, § 118, 45 Stat. 1346, 1347; S. Rep. No. 57, 73d Cong., 1st Sess. 1 (1933). For the background to this reform, see T. Fetter, *A History of the United States Court of Appeals for the Eighth Circuit* 43–46 (1977). At this time four judges—Gilbert, Rudkin, Dietrich, and Wilbur— sat on the court, but the statute authorizing Wilbur's seat also provided for the elimination of Gilbert's upon the latter's death, resignation, or retirement (Act of Mar. 1, 1929, ch. 413, § 2, 45 Stat. 1414).

4. *San Francisco Chronicle,* Mar. 11, 1935, at 11, col. 5. S. Rep. No. 57, 73d Cong., 1st Sess. 1 (1933). The figure of twenty-eight must have included district judges on senior status and those in Alaska and Hawaii.

5. F. Frankfurter and J. Landis, *The Business of the Supreme Court* 258 (1928).

6. Of the total of 353 cases docketed for the Supreme Court, 102 were from district courts. As a source of work, such cases were eclipsed only by the 119 from the highest state courts (Frankfurter and Landis, "The Supreme Court Under the Judiciary Act of 1925," 42 Harv. L. Rev. 1 [1928]). Parties could appeal directly from a district court decision to the Supreme Court if the case involved the "construction or application of the Constitution of the United States"; "the constitutionality of any law of the United States, or the validity or construction of any treaty made under its authority"; prize causes; the jurisdiction of the district court as a federal court; and cases in which a state constitution or law was "claimed to be in contravention of the Constitution of the United States" (*see* Act of Mar. 3, 1911, § 238, 36 Stat. 1087, 1157; hereinafter Judicial Code). The list of cases in which parties had a right of two appeals was long, from civil suits by United States officers to suits for damages by citizens whose federal constitutional rights were violated. For a list, see F. Frankfurter and J. Landis, *supra* note 5, at 261–62. The principal exception involved cases in which a court held a state statute in conflict with "the Constitution, treaties, or laws of the United States" (Act of Feb. 13, 1925, ch. 229, Sec. 1, § 240, 43 Stat. 936, 938–39). The exceptions for cases directly appealable from district courts to the Supreme Court were: (1) antitrust and interstate commerce suits; (2) writs of error by the United States in criminal cases; (3) injunctions against the enforcement of state statutes or action by state administrative officers; (4) suits to enjoin orders of the Interstate Commerce Commission (*see id.* sec. 1, § 238, 43 Stat. at 938). Chief Justice Taft did not see the increased workload of the lower federal appellate courts as a problem (*see* Taft, "The Jurisdiction of the Supreme Court Under the Act of February 13, 1925," 35 Yale L.J. 1, 10 [1925, "ventur[ing] to doubt" fears that the circuit courts of appeal would be unable to keep abreast of their work because of the increased burdens created by the 1925 act]). For more on the expanded jurisdiction of the circuit courts of appeals, *see* Manton, "Organization and Work of the U.S. Circuit Court of Appeals," 12 A.B.A. J. 41 (1926).

7. Act of Feb. 13, 1925, ch. 229, sec. 1, § 128, 43 Stat. 936, 936. In 1905 Congress had given the Supreme Court appellate jurisdiction in cases involving more than $5,000 from the Supreme Court of Hawaii (Act of Mar. 3, 1905, ch. 1465, § 3, 33 Stat. 1035). In 1909 Congress vested jurisdiction in the Court over appeals from the District of Hawaii in all cases where direct appeal would lie from district courts to the Supreme Court (Act of Mar. 3, 1909, ch. 269, § 1, 35 Stat. 838, 839). The Ninth Circuit had appellate jurisdiction over all other cases (*see* Judicial Code § 128). The Act of July 9, 1921, ch. 42, § 313, 42 Stat. 108, 119–20, reenacted the provisions regarding appellate jurisdiction of the Supreme Court and of the circuit courts of appeals over the District of Hawaii.

These provisions were substantially repeated for Alaska (*see* Act of Mar. 3, 1899, ch. 429, § 202, 30 Stat. 1253, 1307; Act of June 6, 1900, ch. 786, § 504, 31 Stat. 321, 414). Section 505 of the 1900 act declared Ninth Circuit decisions in those cases reviewed to be final unless they were certified to the Supreme Court (*Alaska Pacific Fisheries v. Alaska*, 249 U.S. 53 [1919]). Nor was there direct review in capital cases (*Itow v. United States*, 233 U.S. 581 [1914]).

The Ninth Circuit had appellate jurisdiction over all cases in the United States Court for China by the Act of June 30, 1906, ch. 3934, § 3, 34 Stat. 814, 815. Judicial Code § 131 reenacted this provision. The Supreme Court could review by certiorari or through certification. The 1925 act thus did not increase the Ninth Circuit's work regarding the China Court.

8. See infra, Appendix. 1930 Att'y Gen. Ann. Rep. 105; 1931 Att'y Gen. Ann. Rep. 139; 1932 Att'y Gen. Ann. Rep. 145; 1933 Att'y Gen. Ann. Rep. 137; 1934 Att'y Gen. Ann. Rep. 169; 1936 Att'y Gen. Ann. Rep. 161; see also San Francisco Chronicle, Oct. 7, 1930, at 13, col. 7. State Bar of California, Proceedings of the Fifth Annual Meeting 91 (1932); San Francisco Chronicle, May 20, 1933, at 15, col. 8 (reporting on similar action by California State Bar Board of Governors).

9. Act of June 16, 1933, ch. 102, 48 Stat. 310, 311. The legislative history made clear the compelling need for these judgeships, which William Denman and Clifton Mathews ultimately filled (see S. Rep. No. 57, 73d Cong., 1st Sess. 1–2 [1933]). For press reactions to Congress's reauthorization of the seat held by Gilbert, see San Francisco Chronicle, June 6, 1933, at 14, col. 7; San Francisco Chronicle, June 23, 1933, at 8, col. 4. The Senate did not act on Judge Norcross's nomination because an investigation was conducted—inspired by Senator William G. McAdoo—of receiverships that Judge Norcross had granted in Carson City, particularly of the Owl Drug Company. As the Chronicle described it, Senator McAdoo's law partner, Colonel William H. Neblett, "attempted to pillory" Judge Norcross. Rather than face what would have been a bloody battle, Judge Norcross asked that his name be withdrawn (see San Francisco Chronicle, Jan. 4, 1935, at 28, col. 1).

10. "Appointment of Two Additional Circuit Judges for the Ninth Judicial Circuit," Hearings on S.1550 before a Subcomm. of the Senate Comm. on the Judiciary, 75th Cong., 1st Sess. *13 (Feb. 24, 1937) (hereinafter February 1937 Hearing).

11. See id. at 13–14, 15 (quoting letter).

12. The present practice is for the judges to meet for an hour or two after the oral arguments in each set of cases to discuss them briefly. No one seems to have suggested during the course of these hearings why this procedure would have been unworkable. At most it would simply have delayed matters by half a day. At root, however, may be the phenomenon Denman later described, wherein the other two judges on the panel simply did not prepare the cases at all, leaving to the judge who had been assigned the opinion the lion's share of the work on how the case would be decided.

The figures on handling time do not include dismissals, which typically shortened the process. Interestingly, as the judges became more efficient the clerk's office became less so. The time between docketing and submission increased from 152 days on average between 1926 and 1935 to 201 between 1936 and 1941 (see infra, Appendix). *William Denman to Bert Emory Haney, Sept. 28, 1942, Haney File, Curtis D. Wilbur Papers, U.S. Court of Appeals for the Ninth Circuit, San Francisco (hereinafter Wilbur Papers). Denman did not provide the numbers for the latter period.

13. *Denman to Roosevelt, Mar. 14, 1935, William Denman Papers, Bancroft Library.

14. *Roosevelt to Denman, July 25, 1935, Denman Papers. Act of Aug. 2, 1935, ch. 425, § 1, 49 Stat. 508, 508. Denman to Associates, June 15, 1937, Denman Special File, Wilbur Papers.

15. *Roosevelt to Denman, Mar. 21, 1936, Denman Papers. *Denman to Roosevelt, Mar. 16, 1936. The appeal to party loyalty was somewhat disingenuous, given that Denman's official political affiliation was Independent (*see* Committee on the Judiciary, "Legislative History of the United States Circuit Courts of Appeals and the Judges Who Served During the Period 1801 through May 1972," at 174 [1972]). I have been unable to confirm through any other source Denman's political affiliation.

16. *See*, e.g., Denman to Roosevelt, Mar. 19, 1936; Denman to Cummings, Mar. 19, 1936, Denman Papers. Denman to Roosevelt, Mar. 20, 1936. Francis A. Garrecht to Hatton W. Sumners, Mar. 30, 1937, Denman Papers, Bancroft Library. *Denman to Roosevelt, May 8, 1936, Denman Papers.

17. *Denman to Haney, June 30, 1936; *see also* Denman to Wilbur, June 30, 1936, Denman Papers. Although he wrote to Roosevelt in the interim, those letters were on the topics of reform of the administration of federal courts and the establishment of an Administrative Office of the Courts (*see* Denman to Roosevelt, Sept. 5, 1936, Denman Papers). *Denman to Roosevelt, Nov. 7, 1936, Denman Papers. On one occasion, Denman sent a letter through Mrs. Roosevelt (Denman to Roosevelt, Dec. 21, 1938, Denman Papers). On another, he went through Roosevelt's secretary, Marguerite Le Hand. Denman to Roosevelt, Mar. 16, 1936, Denman Papers.

18. February 1937 Hearing, at 8–9. This resolution does not appear to have been reproduced in the relevant California State Bar proceedings for this year (*see* State Bar of California, *Proceedings of the Ninth Annual Meeting* [1936]).

19. Denman's description of the situation in other circuits was slightly exaggerated. The Fifth Circuit had twenty-four district judges; the Second Circuit, twenty-three. Denman also must have counted judges in Alaska, Hawaii, and China (*compare* 88 F.2d v–x [1937] *with* February 1937 Hearing, at 9). The United States Court for China would be abolished in 1943 when the United States relinquished its extraterritorial rights in China (Treaty Respecting the Relinquishment of Extraterritorial Rights in China and the Regulation of Related Matters, Jan. 11, 1943, United States–China, 57 Stat. 767, T.S. No. 984). For state population statistics, see 1 U.S. Department of Commerce Bureau of the Census, *Historical Statistics of the United States* 24–37 (Bicentennial ed. 1975). February 1937 Hearing, at 10.

20. February 1937 Hearing, at *12, 17. When in 1941 Haney strongly challenged Denman, he reversed his position and strengthened his argument by dramatically reducing the reported caseload. At that time he reported fewer than 100 cases from those sources, and he brought that number down to under 70 by injecting the high number of dismissals of cases.

21. February 1937 Hearing, at *17, *18.

22. A newspaper article in 1946 reported that for "the first time in a generation, a United States Circuit Judge has stepped down from his high bench to preside over litigation in the lower Federal District Court in San Francisco," when Judge William Healy volunteered to help the overburdened district court for northern California in January, 1946 (see *San Francisco Chronicle*, Jan. 8, 1946, at 11, col. 2).

23. February 1937 Hearing, at *14 (quoting Garrecht's letter and stating Denman's criticism of it). *Denman to Associates, Mar. 29, 1937, Denman Papers. Wilbur, however, did respond to House Judiciary Committee Chairman Hatton W. Sumners's request for his views with a lengthy, if somewhat incoherent, endorsement of the bill to add two judges to the court (see Hatton W. Sumners to Curtis D. Wilbur, Mar. 29, 1937; Wilbur to Sumners, Mar. 30, 1937, Reorganization of Courts File, Wilbur Papers). Clifton Mathews also endorsed the bill (see Clifton Mathews to Sumners, Mar. 30, 1937, Reorganization of Courts File, Wilbur Papers).

24. Act of Apr. 14, 1937, ch. 80, 50 Stat. 64. *Wilbur to Denman, Apr. 1, 1937, Denman Special File, Wilbur Papers (marked "Not sent"). The Bar Association of San Francisco also lauded Denman's efforts (Bar Association of San Francisco, "Judge Denman's Contribution to the Reorganization of the Lower Federal Courts and Its Relation to the Court Enlargement Bill of 1937" [1939, address of William R. Wallace], Denman Papers, Bancroft Library). *San Francisco Chronicle*, Apr. 9, 1937, at 3, col. 3. The Second Circuit was next largest, with six judges.

25. See 1937 Att'y Gen. Ann. Rep. 173; 1938 Att'y Gen. Ann. Rep. 217; 1939 Att'y Gen. Ann. Rep. 199.

26. Walter A. McClure, President of the Seattle Bar Association, to Curtis D. Wilbur, Sept. 15, 1938, Reorganization of Courts File, Wilbur Papers.

27. I have been unable to locate Donaugh's correspondence with Attorney General Homer Cummings in which he makes this proposal. The National Archives houses these documents, but the filing system yielded no obvious leads and a few furtive stabs in sundry folders produced nothing. *See* "Statement Concerning the Frustration of the Purpose of Attorney General Cummings and the Congress to Create a 'Current' Court of Appeals for the Ninth Circuit in Giving It Seven Judges, in the Proposal of District Attorney Donaugh to Divide the Circuit . . . ," at 1–2, 7, December 3, 1937, Denman Special File, Wilbur Papers (hereinafter 1937 Court Statement); *see also* "Memorandum from Denman, C.J., to Associates of the Ninth Circuit Bench," undated, Denman Special File, Wilbur Papers (discussing Donaugh proposal). A one-term United States senator from Washington, Lewis B. Schwellenbach, also explored the possibility of dividing the Ninth Circuit in 1937 (*see* William Denman to Senator L. B. Schwellenbach, Dec. 17, 1937, Division of Circuit File, Wilbur Papers). From this date Denman dutifully collected data of the appeals from the proposed Eleventh Circuit (see memoranda in Division of Circuit File, Wilbur Papers).

28. Confidential interview. Obviously even these buildings and those erected thereafter have not completely freed litigants from traveling to court. But they have lessened the burdens to litigants overall. By way of comparison, to celebrate

the court's centennial, in 1991 the court held sessions in San Francisco, Pasadena, Phoenix, San Diego, Reno, Portland, Seattle, Boise, Anchorage, Helena, and Honolulu.

29. Veron, "Proposal to Divide the Ninth Judicial Circuit and to Create an Eleventh Judicial Circuit" (Oct. 1, 1940), Folio on S.1793, 77th Cong., 1st Sess., RG No. 46, Stack Area 8E2, Box 43 for SEN. 77A-E1, National Archives, Washington, D.C. (hereinafter Veron Pamphlet).

30. Veron Pamphlet, at 2.

31. *Bank of Am. v. Commissioner*, 90 F.2d 981, 983 (9th Cir. 1937). *Lang v. Commissioner*, 304 U.S. 264, 267 (1938, holding that *Bank of America* was "not accurate and conflicts with [Supreme Court precedent]").

32. *Lang's Estate v. Commissioner*, 97 F.2d 867, 870 n.2 (9th Cir. 1938).

33. *See*, e.g., 1990 Hearings, at 12, stating that "we have found" the Ninth Circuit's size to cause the problems of "too many judges spending too much time traveling and too little time hearing cases" and "a growing backlog of cases so large it threatens to bury each judge" (statement of Senator Slade Gorton). Veron Pamphlet, at *2.

34. Act of Mar. 3, 1911, ch. 231, § 266, 36 Stat. 1087, 1162–63. *See generally* C. Wright, *Law of Federal Courts* § 50 (4th ed. 1983). Act of Mar. 4, 1913, ch. 160, 37 Stat. 1013. Act of Feb. 13, 1925, ch. 229, sec. 1, § 129, 43 Stat. 936, 937. Act of Aug. 24, 1937, ch. 754, § 3, 50 Stat. 751, 752–53.

35. Act of Aug. 12, 1976, Pub. L. 94-381, 90 Stat. 1119. Veron Pamphlet, at 3.

36. Veron Pamphlet, at *5; *see also* 4–7.

37. The amount of travel was the complaint about the existing system that was expressed most often (*see Portland Oregonian*, July 30, 1941, at 10, col. 2; *Seattle Post-Intelligencer*, July 29, 1941, at 1, col. 4). *Seattle Post-Intelligencer*, July 30, 1941, at *8, col. 1. The editorial continued: "Litigants can hardly enjoy being billed for the extra time and expense involved in the appearances of their lawyers at San Francisco, nor does a busy lawyer relish the interruption of his office schedule involved under the present arrangement." Report of the Resolutions Committee, Proceedings of the Oregon State Bar Association, 20 Or. L. Rev. Supp. *65 (1940). 2 Or. St. B. Bull. 5 (1941). Denman, "What the Seven Circuit Judges of the Circuit Court of Appeals for the Ninth Circuit Have Created for the Service of Their Litigants," at 4 (Aug. 20, 1941), Denman Papers, Bancroft Library (hereinafter Denman Pamphlet).

38. *Proceedings of the Fourteenth Annual Meeting*, 1941 St. B. Cal. *216 (address of William Denman, quoting 28 U.S.C. § 449, now codified at 28 U.S.C. § 333).

39. S.1793, 77th Cong., 1st Sess., §§ 1, 3, 6, 87 Cong. Rec. 6330 (1941); Folio on S.1793, 77th Cong., 1st Sess., RG 46, SEN 77A-E1, National Archives, Washington, D.C. H.R. 5489, 77th Cong., 1st. Sess., 87 Cong. Rec. 6734 (1941); Folio on H.R. 5489, 77th Cong., 1st Sess., RG 233, HR 77A-D20, National Archives, Washington, D.C.

40. *See San Francisco Recorder*, Aug. 7, 1941, at 1, col. 5, and at 8, col. 5. The *Recorder* also noted that district judges participated in appeals and rare emergencies and wrote 2 of the Ninth Circuit's 214 annual opinions.

41. Bert Emory Haney to Alan B. Aldwell, Sept. 5, 1941, *reprinted in Proceedings of the Fourteenth Annual Meeting, supra* note 38, at *210. For the report of the internal operating rule change, *see San Francisco Recorder*, Aug. 13, 1941, at 1, col. 6, and at 8, col. 4. As he wrote to Wilbur, "Inasmuch as the substance of the order has been in all of the California papers, I think my signature is not very important in the matter. Under all the circumstances, I think I will not sign the order, and I am returning it herewith to you" (Haney to Wilbur, Aug. 20, 1941, Bert Emory Haney File, Wilbur Papers).

42. Denman Pamphlet, at 1.

43. Denman Pamphlet, at *3–4.

44. 1936 Att'y Gen. Ann. Rep. 161; 1939 Att'y Gen. Ann. Rep. 199. Denman Pamphlet, at 4.

45. The *Seattle Post-Intelligencer*, however, did hint at prejudice, editorializing that "California has a splendid opportunity to show the friendly spirit that should characterize the Pacific Coast states in their relationships" (July 30, 1941, at 8, col. 1). *Haney to Wilbur, July 29, 1941, Haney File, Wilbur Papers.

46. Denman Pamphlet, at *8, *10. These adjoining states were Connecticut and Rhode Island. *See* 1937 Court Statement, at 3. As of 1991, these states are still in the Second Circuit.

47. *See* Denman Pamphlet, at 13. Unfortunately, this Minute Book is missing from the court's records and it is thus impossible to verify Denman's claim.

48. Veron Pamphlet, at 6–7. Denman Pamphlet, at 16, *17.

49. Denman Pamphlet, at 18.

50. The second administrative difficulty identified by Veron—panel assignments—struck Denman as completely illusory. He was unaware of any judge ever having objected to a calendar assignment by the senior judge (Denman Pamphlet, at 19–20).

51. *Textile Mills Sec. Corp. v. Commissioner*, 314 U.S. 326 (1941). In this case, the Supreme Court employed the unusual canon of analyzing the statute, not for Congress's intent to permit *en banc* courts, but, rather, for whether Congress had foreclosed this result (*see generally* Note, "The Power of a Circuit Court of Appeals to Sit En Banc," 55 Harv. L. Rev. 663 [1942]). *Evaporated Milk Ass'n v. Roche*, 130 F.2d 843 (9th Cir. 1942); *see also San Francisco Chronicle*, June 13, 1942, at 12, col. 3. *See* 1990 Hearings, at 468 (testimony of former Chief Justice Warren E. Burger).

52. *San Francisco Chronicle*, Aug. 29, 1941, at *12, col. 6. *San Francisco Chronicle*, Aug. 31, 1941, at *7, col. 1.

53. *San Francisco Chronicle*, Sept. 4, 1941, at *13, col. 2. *Portland Oregonian*, Sept. 4, 1941, at *12, col. 5. *Seattle Post-Intelligencer*, Sept. 4, 1941, at *3, col. 1.

54. *See Proceedings of the Fourteenth Annual Meeting, supra* note 38, at *209, 211. Other minor criticisms of Judge Denman's analysis included his using data from 1930, which had not been used by Judge Haney; the fact that in 1939 Judge Haney had been told by Clerk Paul P. O'Brien that 100 cases had been docketed, whereas Judge Denman listed 99; and, finally, that Judge Denman had included docketings for the fiscal year ending June 30, 1941, when Judge Haney's pamphlet had been written more than ten months prior to this date (*see id.*).

55. *Id.* at *212, *214.
56. *Id.* at 209.

CONCLUSION

1. Stone, "Report of the Judicial Conference, September Session, 1941," at 18 (1941), Judicial Conference 1941 File, Wilbur Papers. *See* Commission on Revision of the Federal Court Appellate System, *The Geographical Boundaries of the Several Judicial Circuits: Recommendations for Change,* 62 F.R.D. 223, 228 (1973). D. Barrow and T. Walker, *A Court Divided* 236 (1988). Baker, "On Redrawing Circuit Boundaries—Why the Proposal to Divide the United States Court of Appeals for the Ninth Circuit Is Not Such a Good Idea," 22 Ariz. St. L.J. 917, *933 (1990). See also Chapter Ten note 1.
2. Confidential interview.
3. Confidential interview.

Index

Compositor:	Braun-Brumfield, Inc.
Text:	10/13 Sabon
Display:	Sabon
Printer:	Braun-Brumfield, Inc.
Binder:	Braun-Brumfield, Inc.